FAVELA

FAVELA

FOUR DECADES OF LIVING ON THE EDGE IN RIO DE JANEIRO

Janice Perlman

OXFORD
UNIVERSITY PRESS

2010

OXFORD
UNIVERSITY PRESS

Oxford University Press, Inc., publishes works that further
Oxford University's objective of excellence
in research, scholarship, and education.

Oxford   New York
Auckland   Cape Town   Dar es Salaam   Hong Kong   Karachi
Kuala Lumpur   Madrid   Melbourne   Mexico City   Nairobi
New Delhi   Shanghai   Taipei   Toronto

With offices in
Argentina   Austria   Brazil   Chile   Czech Republic   France   Greece
Guatemala   Hungary   Italy   Japan   Poland   Portugal   Singapore
South Korea   Switzerland   Thailand   Turkey   Ukraine   Vietnam

Published by Oxford University Press, Inc.
198 Madison Avenue, New York, New York 10016

www.oup.com

Oxford is a registered trademark of Oxford University Press.

Library of Congress Cataloging-in-Publication Data
Perlman, Janice E.
Favela : four decades of living on the edge in Rio de Janeiro / Janice Perlman.
p.   cm.
Includes bibliographical references and index.
ISBN 978-0-19-536836-9
1. Slums—Brazil—Rio de Janeiro.   2. Poor—Brazil—Rio de Janeiro.   3. Violent crimes—
Social aspects—Brazil—Rio de Janeiro.   4. Drugs—Brazil—Rio de Janeiro.   I. Title.
HV4075.R53 P47 2009
307.3'364098153—dc22   2009007840

Portions of this book appeared in a different form in the following publications:
"Re-democratization in Brazil, A View From Below: The Case of Rio de Janeiro's Favelas, 1969–2003," in
Democratic Brazil Revisited, edited by Peter Kingstone and Timothy J. Power (Pittsburgh University Press, 2008);
"Elusive Pathways Out of Poverty: Intra- and Intergenerational Mobility in the Favelas of Rio de Janeiro," in
Moving Out of Poverty: Cross-Disciplinary Perspectives, edited by D. Narayan and P. Petesch (Washington, DC:
World Bank; and Basingstoke, UK: Palgrave Macmillan, 2007); "The Myth of Marginality Revisited: The Case
of Favelas in Rio de Janeiro, 1969–2003," in *Becoming Global and the New Poverty of Cities,* edited by Lisa Hanley,
Blair Ruble, and Joseph Tulchin (Washington, DC: Woodrow Wilson International Center for Scholars, 2005);
"Marginality: From Myth to Reality in the Favelas of Rio de Janeiro 1969–2002," in *Urban Informality in an Era
of Liberalization: A Transnational Perspective,* edited by Ananya Roy and Nezar AlSayyad (Lexington Books, 2004);
"Chronic Poverty in Rio de Janeiro: What Has Changed in 30 Years," in *Managing Urban Futures: Sustainability
and Urban Growth in Developing Countries,* edited by Marco Keiner, Martina Koll-Schretzenmayrm, and Willy
Schmid (Burlington, VT: Ashgate Publishing, 2005); "Globalization and the Urban Poor," UNU-Wider Research
Paper No. 2007/76, November 2007.

1 3 5 7 9 8 6 4 2

Printed in the United States of America
on acid-free paper

For the billion people around the world who live in favelas and for my mother and father who taught me to care and to persist.

contents

foreword

"Paradise is here, hell is here, madness is here, passion is here." So the lyrics of Francis Hime's *Sinfonía do Rio de Janeiro de São Sabastião*, lyrics by Geraldo Carneiro and Paulo Cesar Pinheiro, describe the city of Rio de Janeiro. But Hime's antipodes only begin a description of Rio's squatter settlements—our favelas.

In *Favela: Four Decades of Living on the Edge in Rio de Janeiro*, Janice Perlman shares with us her experiences, insights, and the results of her research into the madness, passion, paradise, and hell experienced by Rio's favela dwellers.

This is a keenly insightful and eminently readable book that continues the research Perlman chronicled in her acclaimed book, *The Myth of Marginality*. In *Favela*, we have a study of four generations over forty years. The narrative traces the lives and fortunes of hundreds of the favela residents met in *The Myth of Marginality*, comparing them with the lives of their parents (mostly rural), their children, and their grandchildren.

Perlman's study is both rich in detail and rewarding in its analyses. She faithfully describes her subjects' daily struggles and strategies to affirm their individual and collective rights and dignity from within an increasingly hostile and violent environment. She uses the survey data she collected in over 2000 interviews and her ethnographic insights to test facile generalizations about the wonders or horrors of favela life and to explore the improvements as well as the setbacks. Her analysis and observations on social mobility and inequality are particularly compelling as she looks at the issue from the individual and family level and the community and city level simultaneously.

In doing this, Perlman has produced a portrait of a multifaceted society in turmoil—a society in which life force and ingenuity coexist with desperation and destruction.

Thirty years ago, the fear of those living in the favelas was a fear of displace-ment—to be uprooted and carted off from their homes to a distant, unwelcom-ing government housing project far from work and community. Today, they fear for their lives—never knowing when they may be caught in the crossfire of drug gang violence or shot indiscriminately during a police raid.

Fatal violence in the favelas has reached an intolerable level as powerful drug gangs battle each other over territory, militias use weapons to enforce extortion, and the police enter with brutality. The youth and teens are the most vulnerable—both in terms of death rates and in terms of being drawn into the traffic themselves.

In 1976, at the time of the publication of Perlman's seminal work about Rio's poor communities, Brazil was living under the weight of authoritarian rule—a military dictatorship that continued from 1964 through 1985. It is now more than 20 years since the restoration of democracy to Brazil, but its promise has yet to be fulfilled. Corruption and impunity undermine the rule of law. These failings rest at the very heart of the distrust of the people toward government, politics, and politicians—in fact the entire political milieu.

A democracy is not only a government of rules and institutions; it is an honest assurance of the safeguard of human rights and equality of opportunity. Democracies provide the opportunity for everyone to participate in and influ-ence the decisions that affect the present and the future of their community.

Either a democracy is guided toward ensuring that its citizens' lives may be lived in dignity, or apathy, cynicism, and disaffection toward the political sys-tem will prepare the way for a resurgence of an authoritarian populism that we thought had become a thing of the past. An informed and empowered citizen-ship is the most effective antidote to this danger.

This brings me to one of the real strengths of Perlman's narrative. She views the poor and their communities as bearers of skills and capacities. The common view, fed by the media portrayal of the favelas and their residents, is based on a long list of shortcomings: violence, poverty, unemployment, drug addiction, corruption, early pregnancy, disrupted families, and inadequate public services.

This view seems compelling and yet it is deeply flawed. Needs and deficien-cies are real but are not the whole reality. The people in the favelas have prob-lems but they are not "the problem."

Perlman's research is oriented by a different vision. She looks beyond appar-ent shortcomings to grasp the impalpable assets of individuals and commu-nities. Each individual possesses skills and capacities. Every community has resources of trust, solidarity, and reciprocity.

This change in perspective drastically recasts public policies. The focus on liabilities leads to assistance and enhances dependency. Investment in peo-ples' assets sets into motion a sustainable process of individual and collective empowerment.

There is much more in Perlman's book: insight into the formation and development of Brazilian civil society, and the danger to civil society inherent in violence and criminality. These are issues that go beyond Rio and Brazil and give the book its reach and its broad appeal.

A vivid lesson in history, a collection of colorful human and social experience, *Favela* is essential reading for scholars, civic leaders, policymakers, and all those who are interested in grasping the pressing challenges of urban development and politics.

Fernando Henrique Cardoso
Former President of Brazil

preface

This book is not about places. In a sense it is not really about favelas. It is a book about the people who have shaped the places and spaces that are called favelas—squatter settlements, shantytowns, or "popular communities." It is about four generations of people who have lived in favelas or whose families lived in favelas—about people balancing on the narrow precipice between surviving and thriving. It is about their struggles, sufferings, and successes in their efforts to rise above a hostile environment. This is a chronicle of poor people's attempts to claim their rights to personhood—their fight to be perceived as *gente*—to be treated with respect and granted human dignity.

The stories told here are those of people I have known over 40 years, and of their parents, children, and grandchildren. Some of them are like family to me; many are close friends; and some I barely know. This book bears witness to the trials and accomplishments of their lives. Between 1968 and 2008 I interviewed almost 2,500 people for this book. Their stories reflect the experience of some 3 million people (or more) living in the informal sector (squatter settlements or clandestine subdivisions) in Rio de Janeiro and a billion urban poor throughout Latin America, Asia, and Africa.

The life histories on which this book is based cover the entire twentieth century and into the twenty-first. The oldest people I interviewed were born in 1903, which made them 65 the year I started the study—the upper limit for inclusion. The youngest were 16 when the study began—the lower limit for inclusion. I did not limit my inquiry or my curiosity to heads of households. I was interested in all varieties of favela experience.

My relationship with Brazil came about serendipitously. I had no prior relationship (no family ties or cultural roots) to Brazil, to Rio de Janeiro, or to the favelas where migrants from the countryside built their homes and their communities.

In retrospect, I imagine that the (mostly untold) story of my grandparents, fleeing Russia, Poland, and Romania as teenagers and building new lives for themselves in New York City in the beginning of the twentieth century, imbued me with empathy and admiration for migrants who have the courage to start anew in an unfamiliar place.

When I was 15 years old I participated in a summer program in Oaxaca, Mexico, in which I was immersed in the language, archeology, and cultural traditions of the region.[1] Later, many of us who were touched by this experience went on to study anthropology. I attended Cornell to work with Alan Holmberg, who was challenging convention with his radical work in Vicos, Peru.[2] My first semester as a freshman there coincided with student auditions for a Latin American theatrical tour—a revue of the musical comedy from the *The Black Crook* (1866, considered the first musical) through *Oklahoma* (1943) and *West Side Story* (1957) to *Fiorello!* (1959). The tour was sponsored by the American National Theater Association as part of the Kennedy administration's outreach to Latin America during the Cold War. The idea was to use students as cultural ambassadors as a way to build closer ties with the region and counter the (perceived) threat of communism. I was the only one in our group of 18 students who was interested in learning about Latin America per se—the others were theater arts graduate students who had applied in order to gain professional experience. Brazil was considered the highest political priority, so we spent six weeks of our 12-week tour there, performing at universities all over the country. I fell in love with Brazil. Every night after the show was over, the rest of the cast went to get their beauty rest, and I stayed up all night speaking with the students.

The summer of 1962 was a time of great political ferment in Brazil. The compelling issue was how to create a system that would overcome the failures of both capitalism and communism. The country was thrust into this challenge when the president, Jânio Quadros resigned suddenly, on August 25, 1961, and sailed off to Europe in a dramatic gesture, hoping to incite a popular uprising demanding his return with expanded powers over Congress. Instead, the bereaved citizens poured out onto the streets in dismay that their beloved father figure had abandoned them. A constitutional crisis arose when the political elites proposed a national vote to move from a presidential system (in place since 1946) to a parliamentary system in order to prevent the leftist vice president, João Goulart from becoming president of Brazil.

Everywhere our student group traveled in Brazil, there were heated discussions of *reformas de base* (structural reforms) such as land and tax reforms. A man named Francisco Julião was successfully organizing peasant leagues to demand rights to land from landowners in the Northeast. The governor of the state of Pernambuco, Miguel Arraes, had just mandated payment of the minimum wage to agricultural workers in his state. The archbishop of Recife and

Olinda, Dom Helder Camera, was preaching liberation theology; Paulo Freire's *Pedogogy of the Oppressed*—a method to teach adult literacy through conscious-ness-raising about the fundamental rights of human dignity—was becoming a movement of "each-one-teach-one," and Leonel Brizola was mobilizing labor unions in the industrial South. Students around the country had mounted a coordinated strike to demand one-third representation in the governance of the federal universities.

It was a heady time to be in Brazil. Each individual was being called on to contribute his or her energies, ideas, and skills to the project of creating an inclusive and just country on behalf of "o povo" (the people, particularly in reference to the rural poor). The feeling that everyone could make a difference intrigued me and made me curious to know more about the "povo"—who were they, what were their lives like, and what changes did they want?

I had a chance to find out the following summer while living in Arembepe, a small fishing village in the interior of the state of Bahia.[3] Today the trip from Salvador, the state capital, to Arembepe takes less than two hours by car, but at that time it entailed a day-long journey. The only way to get there was to take the bus north along the coast to the end of the line, where you found a small boy and an old man waiting with a donkey, which took you on dirt roads and then footpaths to a lagoon, where still other young boys or old men ferried you across. From there it was a short walk to Arembepe.[4]

The village consisted of several dozen wattle-and-daub houses with thatched roofs of palm fronds, loosely arrayed along a protected cove of coral reefs, making it a choice site for fishing. There was no electricity, no running water, no mail service, and little contact with the outside world. The priest came once a year to conduct all of the weddings, baptisms, confirmations and funerals; an occasional traveling salesman came through who traded fabric, kerosene lanterns, matches, salt, and other essentials for fish. A handful of local boys who had served in the Marines came back with stories of their adventures.

Unlike what the urban university students I had met the year before had imagined, the villagers were neither suffering nor frustrated. They had not heard anything about the struggle for reforms. They were living pretty much as their forebears had since the end of slavery in 1888 and had no connection with the discourse of the outside world in which they figured so prominently. In fact, they did not know who the president was, or even what year it was. The only year they could identify was 1500, the year that Pedro Alvares Cabral discov-ered Brazil. It was the one thing everyone had memorized in school.

Arembepe was so isolated that the people living there had never heard of other languages. They said, "Janice, you speak just like a parrot" or asked me if I were retarded (um débil mental) saying such things as "My son is only four years old and speaks better than you do!" My attempts to explain that where

I came from everyone spoke a different language were met with incredulity: "What do you mean? Dogs go 'Bowwow,' cats 'go 'Meow,' and humans speak— just as we are speaking right now."

The villagers were loosely organized in a kind of primitive communism, with no political leader and with everyone sharing equally when the *saveiros* and *jangadas* (fishing boats) returned with the catch of the day. The only functioning institution was a chaotic one-room schoolhouse. Children of every age played, chatted, did their lessons at their desks, or wandered around. The teacher in whose house I lived was barely literate herself. She sat at her desk attending to them one at a time while breastfeeding her baby. I am fairly certain that no one learned to read in that school. The pedagogy of the day was syllable based. The students were taught to sound out the letters one by one, and then sound out each syllable—but they never made the leap to putting the entire word together and recognizing it as something with which they were familiar.[5]

I went to Arembepe to do research on how young people form their worldviews, values, and aspirations. According to the development literature of the time, these mental maps and motivations played a decisive role in the intergenerational transmission of poverty. In keeping with "modernization theory," these attitudes were supposed to hold the key to explaining why some countries and people stayed poor while others thrived and became wealthy.

The year I arrived was the very year that everything changed. Just like the miraculous arrival of ice in the fictitious village of Macondo described by Gabriel García Márquez in *One Hundred Years of Solitude,* the transistor radio had appeared. It was the first time that most of the people heard directly about life beyond the parameters of their village. The technology that enabled music and messages, word images and information to be carried on airwaves into otherwise inaccessible places changed life options from that moment on. The opening of new horizons—for better or worse— beckoned people to the "bright lights, big city."

Young people were no longer content to spend their lives fishing, hoping to die in the arms of Yemanjá, the seductive goddess of the waters or to work the land with the hoe, as their families had always done. They were attracted to the excitement of the unknown—they wanted to go where the ("movimento") action was. I could feel the magnetic pull that the city exerted on the youngsters and wondered what would happen to the newly arrived hopefuls if they got there, given their illiteracy and inexperience. It dawned on me that this was the beginning of an enormous sea change, one that would coincide with my own lifetime. As people became aware of broader horizons, there would be a massive migration from the countryside to the city—not only in Brazil but all over Asia, Africa, and Latin America.

Years later, for my doctoral research, I followed the migratory flow from Bahia and elsewhere in the Brazilian countryside to the big city of Rio de Janeiro.[6] To find out where people went when they arrived in the city, I met the trucks bringing newcomers from the Northeast. These were open-backed flatbed trucks whose brightly painted and decorated sides were covered with mud and dust. They were called parrot's perches because of the way people sat jammed together on wooden slats laid around their perimeters and across the width of the truck bed. Some of the newcomers were met by relatives or people from their hometown who had arrived before. The rest were taken to a shelter

FIGURE P.1   Fishermen are out on their small *saveiros* and *jangadas*. Arembepe, February 1967—taken on a return visit four years after I had lived there.

FIGURE P.2   Roof tiles and stucco facades had replaced the thatched palm roofs and packed mud walls of these houses in the center of the settlement.

until they could find someplace to stay. Most had sold all they owned to pay for the ticket to Rio and had no money at all for housing. The solution to their problem of finding shelter was to build shacks and eventually settlements on vacant lands, typically on steep hillsides, or *morros,* or in flood-prone swamps. Thus the favelas grew from tiny settlements into larger communities with distinctive personalities.

My initial research topic, "the impact of urban experience" on the new migrants, turned out to be a nonissue. The people adapted rapidly and astutely to the city and developed creative coping mechanisms to deal with the challenges they faced. The problem was that the city did not adapt to them. Rio had been the seat of the Portuguese empire during the Napoleonic wars, and it became the national capital when Brazil became a republic, in 1989. It was a citadel of the elite, the place where Brazil's large landowners, and later large industrialists, enjoyed their urban amenities. The streets were laid out following Haussmann's Paris, and the buildings were elegant. The favelas, as they grew, were seen as blight on the urban landscape, a menace to public health, and a threat to urbane civility. The incoming migrants, and even those born in favelas, were seen as dangerous intruders.

From the beginning, I found the favelas visually more interesting and humanly more welcoming than the upper-middle-class neighborhoods. They could be seen as the precursors to the "new urbanism" with their high-density, low-rise architecture, featuring facades variously angled to catch a breeze or a view, and shade trees and shutters to keep them cool. The building materials were construction-site discards and scraps that would now be called "recycled materials." They were owner-designed, owner-built, and owner-occupied. And they followed the organic curves of the hillsides rather then a rigid grid pattern.

The city's refusal to provide running water and electricity to these communities indeed created a danger to public health, but electrical connections were hooked into the power lines, and people took great pride in the cleanliness of their homes and persons. They were immaculate, despite the fact that all water for cleaning, cooking, and washing had to be carried from a slow-dripping communal standpipe along the road below. Women and children waited for hours and then hauled their water up the hillside in square five-gallon oil cans, sometimes set on a circular rolled-up cloth on their heads, sometimes hanging from both sides of a pole across the shoulders.

The migrants, rather than being the "dregs of the barrel"—the most impoverished among the rural people, were more often the "cream of the crop"—the most farsighted, capable, and courageous members of their communities. They were the ones with the motivation and willingness to work in the least desirable jobs for the longest hours at the lowest pay in order to provide their children with opportunities they had never had. While in the eyes of others they were

FIGURE P.3   The favela of Catacumba in 1968, showing the texture of low-rise/high-density urban settlements that is favored today by the "new urbanism."

uprooted masses ready to rise up in revolt when confronted with the riches all around them, in their own eyes, they were proud of doing so much better than those who had stayed behind.

Doing research and living in the favelas in 1968–69 was one of the happiest periods of my life. I have never felt as safe or as welcomed in any community before or since. My presence was met with warm acceptance. People took care of me as they did of each other. To use Jane Jacob's phrase there were always many "eyes on the street,"[7] and I admired the residents' *jeito* (knack) for inventing solutions and using humor as a survival skill.[8]

People loved being interviewed. It was the first time anyone had given value to their life stories, had actually written down their words. I bore witness to their struggles and triumphs and validated their opinions and ideas.[9] Many who were not selected in the random sample kept asking me, "Janice, when are you coming to my house? You were at my neighbors' last week for the entire afternoon, and my son-in-law said you were at the Juventude AC (for Atlético Clube, the Youth Athletic Club) on Saturday—when is it going to be my turn?" I eventually had to make up a short pseudo-questionnaire just for that purpose.

If my low status as young, female, and foreign engendered a certain degree of dismissal in official policy and research circles, the very fact of not being taken seriously allowed me to obtain government documents and aerial photographs I needed for the study. Similarly, being an outsider made the interview process a lot more natural. Asking questions as a foreign student eager to understand and learn was much easier than it would have been for a Brazilian student, who might easily have sounded condescending, impolite, or suspicious.

I collected these interviews during the most repressive years of Brazil's military dictatorship. On the absurd side, social science courses were banned; books with red covers in the University of Brasília library were pulled off the shelves and burned. On the horrific side, those accused of opposition were imprisoned, tortured, and murdered or exiled. While I was doing fieldwork, a law was passed forbidding foreign researchers to take their data out of the country.

In late 1969, I learned through one of our field interviewers who had contacts within the military that I had been declared an "international agent of subversion." The military police could not imagine any other motive for someone choosing to live in a favela, nonetheless a foreigner. Fortunately, all the interviews had been completed by that time and the questionaires and life history matrices had been verified, coded, and independently cross-checked by a second person. We rushed the coded questionaires to the IBM office in downtown Rio where they were digitized and saved on a small circular tape in a metal container that could pass for a makeup compact. The medical doctor at the U.S. consulate who had become a friend of mine agreed to send the original questionnaires and punch cards back to my MIT office via the official mail pouch (which did not go through Brazilian security). I left on the first available flight out. Shortly thereafter, the shack I had been living in was ransacked, the floor boards torn up, and the furniture destroyed as the military police searched for evidence of subversive materials.

When I tried to return to Rio in 1973, I was advised to get a new passport with a new number and to be sure someone of importance was at the airport to meet me in case I was detained upon entering. I did get into the country, but I was not allowed to enter the favelas without written permission from Rubens Vaz da Costa, the director of the BNH—Banco Nacional de Habitação (Brazilian National Housing Bank). It was due to him that I had the chance to find out what was going on in Rio and to observe favela policies in the other eight metropolitan regions. By this point, one of the three favelas in which I had lived had been forcibly removed by a state-sponsored favela eradication program and the residents had been relocated into distant public housing blocks called conjuntos.

The results of that research became the basis for my 1976 book, *The Myth of Marginality: Urban Poverty and Politics in Rio de Janeiro*.[10] In its time, the book provoked a paradigm shift away from perceiving the urban poor as "marginal" or irrelevant to the system to seeing them as tightly integrated into the system, albeit in a perversely asymmetrical fashion. The favela residents contributed their labor, allegiance, and cultural wealth to the city—they built their communities, they built most of the rest of the city, and they voted as they were permitted, and in return they were excluded, exploited, and denigrated.

I stayed in touch with many of the families, particularly those with whom I had lived. We had developed close ties and were mutually interested in what was happening in each other's lives. I would have liked to update the study every decade, but during the 1980s and 1990s the development community turned away from issues of poverty and inequality to focus on macroeconomic issues. The neoliberal wisdom that prevailed during that time among policy-makers and many funding sources was that only through a series of rigorous austerity measures, collectively known as "structural adjustment," could market forces produce sufficient economic growth to trickle down to the poor. The donor community was focused on macroeconomic reforms and "getting the prices right." Once it became clear that urban poverty and human suffering was growing rather than shrinking under these reforms and that the high levels of inequality were limiting economic growth as well as the growth and the development of intellectual capital of the country, funders became interested in understanding the dynamics of urban poverty and the way it was transmitted—or not—across generations. Only then was I was successful in attaining support for this longitudinal study.[11]

In 1999, I received a grant from the World Bank research division for a preliminary study to determine the feasibility of locating the original study participants after a 30-year hiatus.[12] I did this with the help of two Brazilian colleagues at the Instituto de Pesquisa e Planejamento Urbano e Regional (Research Institute for Planning and Urban Research, known as IPPUR) at the Federal University of Rio de Janeiro.[13]

This exploratory phase was surprisingly fruitful, due to the close ties that people in the favela communities had maintained with each other. It opened the way for further support. Funding was provided by The Tinker Foundation, two consecutive Fulbright Research Fellowships, the World Bank, the British Department for International Development (DFID), the Dutch Trust Fund, and the Mayor's Office of Rio de Janeiro. During the writing phase, I received support from the Ford Foundation and won a Guggenheim Fellowship Award

When I lived in the favelas in 1968–69, I felt safe and protected, while everyone from elites to taxi drivers to leftist students foolishly perceived these settlements as dangerous. The community was poor, but people mobilized to demand improved urban services, worked hard, had fun, and had hope. They watched out for each other, and daily life had a calm convivial rhythm. When I returned in 1999, the physical infrastructure and household amenities were greatly improved. But where there had been hope, now there were fear and uncertainty. People were afraid of getting killed in the cross fire during a drug war between competing gangs, afraid that their children would not return alive after school, or that a stray bullet would kill their toddlers playing on their verandas. They felt more marginalized than ever—further from gaining the respect others assume (or are granted) as a birthright.

Just as with my original study in Rio's favelas, I found reality did not conform to the conceptual framework or the painstakingly crafted set of hypotheses I had developed to guide my inquiry. My intent for the restudy was to explore the connections between the ups and downs in the lives of the urban poor and the changing context in which they lived. I hoped to find corollaries between the macro political, economic, and spatial changes of the period and the vicissitudes of daily life of the individuals I had interviewed. To do this, I would examine the year-by-year changes in the residential, occupational, educational, and family histories of everyone I had interviewed.

The idea was to search for patterns of connections that would reveal the interdependence of the personal and the political, possibly differentiated by age cohort, phase in the life cycle, or historic moment at each point in time. I commissioned detailed chronologies from Brazilian experts, asking each to map benchmark changes in their area of specialization over the twentieth and early twenty-first centuries with an eye toward overlaying the life changes of the interviewees on these historic processes. The hope was that this new knowledge would in turn inform policy and practice.

However, no matter how I looked at the data, I could not find convincing linkages between macro-level changes—such as the transformation from dictatorship to democracy, the progression from economic boom to inflation, stagflation, and relative stabilization; or the changeover from punitive to pro-poor public policies—and the ups and downs in the lives of the favelados. What I found was a much more complex situation, with contradictory implications that did not lead to simple conclusions or solutions.

This book explores the shifting landscapes and messy realities of the urban poor and questions whether the constantly produced and reproduced inequalities that characterize Brazil will weaken or strengthen as the country assumes its role as a prosperous, rapidly growing world economy. If the tenacity and optimism of the people I met are any indication, there is a chance for change; if precedent is any guide, there is cause for concern. It is my profound hope that what is written here, by giving voice to the disenfranchised, may lead to a rethinking—and perhaps a transforming—of policy and practice, and that others will pick up where I have left off.

WHY I LOVE FAVELAS

In response to renewed threats of favela evictions, on July 7, 2004, IBASE, a well-respected NGO, organized a symposium titled Favela é Cidade: Não a Remoção (The favela is the city: No to removal). I was asked to address the new plans for favela demolition. I had thought that this issue was long dead and buried, but evidently, it is resurrected from time to time as policy-makers see the potential use of the favela territory for land speculation and capital accumulation (often under the pretext of environmental protection). The speakers and the audience were a mixture of favela residents and leaders from all parts of Rio, city, state, and federal government representatives involved with housing and urban development, academics, the media, and foundations linked with big banks and microfinance.

I had prepared a talk about the differences in conditions between the late 1960s and the current moment, and had created a PowerPoint presentation showing the contrast, along with scenes of the demolition of Praia do Pinto that I had witnessed in 1969. But as I began to talk, other words came out. I spoke of how I had felt in the favelas when I lived there earlier, and how fearful I was in entering the same places today. Yet once inside the homes of the people, it all came back.

Someone recorded what I said after that and asked me later if they could quote me. I would never have been able to remember my exact words, but here they are:

> Favela is life, favela is love.
> Favela is freedom, friendship and feijoada.
> Favela is people persevering.
> It is laughter and tears, life and death—only a hair's-breadth apart.
> It is a place where the unexpected is expected and spontaneity is the norm.
> It is not all pain, poverty, and passivity.
> It is people living their lives amid a civil war.
> People who would prefer to work and to study.
> People trying to be recognized as people by other people
> For whom they are invisible and inconsequential.

Still today, despite all, the favelas provide a free space, tolerant of diversity and deviance. They welcome nonconformity, small seeds of oppositional behavior bubbling up to the surface and sustaining hope. Favelas are not the shadow side of the city; rather, the city is the shadow side of the favelas. With all the hardship and grief within them, there is still a life force there that is absent in the most costly condominiums in the rest of Rio. In many ways, the rich have imprisoned themselves, walling themselves off from urban conviviality in the process of protecting themselves from those whom they would not include in their city. Outsiders, whether drawn to eliminate or emulate the favelas, do not see that they represent a way of life, a state of mind. They possess deep roots, spiky thorns, and fragrant flowers.

acknowledgments

As my work on this book has spanned forty years and taken me from the favelas on Rio's hillsides to their counterpart communities in the megacities of Latin America, Asia, and Africa, it is impossible to name all of the people who have generously given their time and shared their knowledge with me along the way. For those I have failed to mention, please accept my appreciation. You know who you are.

My foremost debt of gratitude is to my friends in the communities: Zé Cabo, Djanira, Marga, Jacob, Nilton, Hélio Grande, Tio Souza, Dona Rita, Sr. Levi; to their children and grandchildren; and to the thousands of others who opened up their homes and hearts to me. They have been my teachers.

Meeting again the people whose lives are portrayed in this book has been a moving experience for them and for me. In reconnecting with these individuals and families—more of them than I thought I would ever see again—there has been poignancy, a reminder of how precious friendships are, and how precarious life can be. The gains they have struggled to achieve remain tenuous, and their lives may change from manageable to miserable in a moment.

Their trust and courage amid this condition of vulnerability have made this study possible. I hope that the results provide a deeper understanding of how poverty and inequality are perpetuated and what it takes to turn that logic on its head.

Ruth Cardoso was an inspiration from the beginning of this work. Her camaraderie, humor, and conviction that research and civic action could make a difference never changed as she went from an anthropologist working with at-risk youth to the First Lady of Brazil. Her personal warmth and profound insights permeate this work. I miss her.

The godfather of this book is Tim Campbell, whose engagement and belief in this project go back to our first meeting at the University of California, Berkeley, in 1973 and whose major contributions inside and outside of the World Bank made it all possible.

The local team I assembled in Rio did an outstanding job in challenging, often dangerous, circumstances. The core team evolved over time to include Graziella Moraes, Lia de Mattos Rocha, Sônia Kalil, Edmeire Exaltação, Christina Vital, Emanuelle Araujo, Gisele dos Santos, Beatriz Taunay, Ana Beatriz da Silva, and Rosana Ribeiro. Professor Ignácio Cano provided valuable methodological guidance and managed the final phase of the fieldwork and Professor Valéria Pero added her own favela research and her lovely spirit to our collaboration.

My buddies Lourival, Adjilson, and João and the staff of *Ipanema Tower Residencia,* gave generously of their time to explain many mysteries to me, even though they had so much else to do and were often under surveillance.

Collecting survey and interview data in the favela communities and analyzing the findings is a daunting task, but making sense of the findings and putting them in the context of a larger body of work on the topic is equally formidable, particularly for a nonnative. In 1968 when I did my first study there were only a handful of scholars writing about Rio's favelas, among them my friends Licia Valladares, Luis Antonio Machado, and Carlos Nelson, who died too young but whose influence lives on.

By contrast, in Rio today there are many renowned scholars working on favelas, social mobility, informality, and marginality. I sought out many such experts who gave selflessly of their time, often welcoming me into their homes. I thank Professors Paulo Knauss, Sonia Rocha, Lena Lavinas, Dulce Pandolfi, Celi Scalon, Marcelo Baumann Burgos, Carlos Lessa, Alba Zaluar, Manual Sanchez, Herminia Maricato, and Raquel Rolnik, many of whom played key roles in policy as well as academia. Professors Teresa Caldeira, James Holston, Mariana Cavalcanti, Ananya Roy, and Elliott Sclar also helped me in various ways along this journey.

I admit to being a bit surprised to find an extraordinary willingness on the part of policy-makers to share their wisdom and experience with me. Many of these discussions have continued for years. In the late 1960s I would never have imagined that the world-renowned sociologist who spent hours talking with me about dependency theory and the urban question, would become the president of Brazil—Fernando Henrique Cardoso—nor that as president he would still engage with me in that dialogue. My dear friend Wanda Engel Aduan, likewise was always there for me even as she went from professor of education to the founding director of a nonprofit to municipal secretary to national minister to the Inter-American Development Bank and currently to director of the Unibanco Foundation. The same holds true for André Urani as he moved from Rio's first secretary of labor to founding and directing the

Institute for the Study of Work and Society, all the while continuing to teach and conduct research.

It is easy for academics to criticize city government, and without doubt, holding public officials accountable is vital for good governance. Yet I was struck by the knowledge and commitment of many public figures. Rio city government has been in the forefront of upgrading squatter settlements since the mid 1980s. Mayor César Maia provided office space in the Palácio da Cidade (when we ran out of funds for our Santa Teresa office), met with me numerous times, and invited me to discuss my research findings at his monthly meeting of department heads and top staff.

Lu Petersen has championed the rights of favelas through all the changes in Rio municipal administrations, and I am grateful to her for sharing her deep repository of knowledge and for the hundreds of hours she spent with me over the years of this study—some in her office, some visiting favelas where innovative projects were underway, and some on the beach at Arpoador. Other friends and colleagues who guided me along the way include: Alfredo Sirkis; Sérgio Besserman, Sérgio Magalhães, Ana Petrik, Marcelino Germano, and Tania Castro. At the invitation from Arlindo Daibert, I had the opportunity to offer an intensive course on favelas at the newly created School of Public Policies (*Escola de Políticas de Estado*) in September 2008, which provided priceless feedback from the participants, experts in their own right.

The first mayor to support favela upgrading was Israel Klabin, whom I have known too long to mention and who, along with Lea, Tania, Michel, and their children have treated me as family. Clara and Jacob Steinberg are my other adoptive family in Rio and have helped me in this research in more ways than I can count. And my thanks go to Hélio Jaguaribe, my graduate school professor whose own work and that of his daughters Anna Maria and Beatriz have been a constant delight.

The role of civil society (nongovernmental and nonprofit) organizations in Rio has been decisive in the fight for the rights of favelas and favela residents. Among the many dedicated professionals whose work I admire, my special thanks go to Itamar Silva, Moema Miranda, Jailson Souza, Claudius Ceccon, Heloisa Coelho, and the late Herbert de Souza (Betinho), my coconspirators.

Without the personal support of my Carioca friends, Rosana Lanzelotte, Thereza Lobo, Nadia Rebouças, Gilda and Luis Blanc, Renaud Leenhardt, Francoise Schein, Cynthia Zanotto, the much-missed Rose van Lengen, Orlando and Ilara Cano, and many others, this task would have been considerably more difficult.

I am grateful to Mila Freire who hosted me in the Urban Projects Division during my time as Visiting Scholar at the World Bank in 2004–05. The Advisory Committee included Frannie Lautier, Francoise Bourgenhon, Greg Ingram, Francisco Ferreira, Michael Woolcott, Guy Pfefferman, and Sérgio

Margolis from the World Bank; Jose Brakarz from the Inter-American Development Bank; Nancy Birdsall and Carol Graham from the Center for Global Development and Brookings Institutions respectively; and Jorge Fiori from the Development Planning Unit at University College London. This book benefited greatly from the help of Sarah Anthony who started on the project as a student intern at the School of Advanced International Studies at John's Hopkins and then became my research assistant at the World Bank, in Rio de Janeiro and in New York.

The guardian angels whose willingness to answer urgent questions (ranging from the ridiculous to the sublime) at the last minute carried this work on their wings to its conclusion include Paulo Knauss, Antonio Carlos Vidigal, Mario Sergio Brum, Mauro Amoroso, Jim Shyne, Laura Scheiber, and Alison Coffey. I am indebted to Fernando Cavallieri, Vânia Amorim, and Gustavo Peres Lopes at the Instituto Pereira Passos, who were kind enough to interrupt their own schedules to generate updated maps and charts for this volume at the last minute. Unless otherwise indicated, all translations and photos are mine.

My wonderful agent, Regina Ryan, and Oxford University Press editor, David McBride, were the two who brought this work from a manuscript into a signed book contract, and Laura Ross's edits moved it along. It was Oxford editor Angela Chnapko, perfect pitch, sound judgment, and good natured enthusiasm for sticking with this project above and beyond any call of duty that brought this work to fruition.

There is no gift quite as valuable as the candid feedback of a brilliant reader. For this I thank John Friedmann, Bryan McCann, Leandro Benmergui, Laura Randall, and above all, Janet Abu-Lughod and Lisa Peattie, who, as dear friends and colleagues, offered to read this in proofs, at a stage when I could no longer see the words on the page.

I want to thank the Mega-Cities Project Board, especially John C. Whitehead, James Hyman, Peggy Dulany, Jacques d'Amboise, and George Bugliarello for their unqualified support and encouragement as I took time off from my duties as director to work on this book. I learned much from them and from our Global Advisory Board Members including Manuel Castells, Sir Peter Hall, Jorge Wilheim, Jaime Lerner, Ignacy Sachs, Yves Cabannes, Shabbir Cheema, David Ramage, Ira Michael Heymen, Alan Altshuler, Larry Susskind, Ingrid Munro, and Tadashi Yamamoto, and from our city coordinators including Enrique Ortiz, Marlene Fernandes, Cecilia Martinez, Pablo Gutman, Pedro Jacobi, Remy Prud'homme, Herbert Girardet, Susanne MacGregor, Mounir Neamatulla, Om Prakesh Mathur, Dinesh Mehta, Pratibha Mehta, Arif Hasan, Darrundono, Me'An Ignacio, Akin Mabogunje, and Elwood Hopkins.

Without funders who believed in the importance of this project and were willing to take a risk that such an unprecedented endeavor might be possible, there would be no book. My deepest gratitude goes to the Tinker Foundation, the Fulbright Fellowship Program, the Ford Foundation, the World Bank, the British Department for International Development (DFID), the Dutch Trust Fund, and the Mayor's Office of Rio de Janeiro. A Guggenheim Memorial Foundation Fellowship came just in time for the writing phase and was most appreciated.

Working on a book over such a long time period has had its share of agonies as well as ecstasies. My family and friends kept me on track when I was wandering and cheered me on when I was flying. I am deeply grateful to my soul sisters Peggy Dulany, Jane Pratt, Meg Power, Noreen Clark, Leonie Sandercock, Naomi Carmon, Nadine Castro, Judith Rose, and Rebecca Goldstein, and to my soulmate Rick Spreyer who kept it all together through his persistence of vision.

FAVELA

INTRODUCTION

Sodium vapor lamps give an eerie, yellow glow to the evening streets along the scallop-shaped curves of Copacabana, Ipanema, and Leblon beaches. This is the "Gold Coast" of South America's famous destination for "fun and sun"—Rio de Janeiro. The distinctive black-and-white patterned tiles that form the broad sidewalk separating the car traffic from the sand of Copacabana beach mimic the waves of the Atlantic and melt into the fantasy that is the *cidade maravil-hosa,* the "marvelous city" of Rio.

The Copacabana Palace (see figure 1.1) presides in graceful splendor over the Avenida Atlantica, across from the sea at Copacabana beach. Its white exterior takes on a warm caramel hue from the street lights. The light emphasizes the activity of cabs, uniformed hotel doormen and bellhops, tourists, Cariocas (as the residents of Rio are called), *moleques* (street urchins), and VIPs—all drawn to the regal presence of the hotel.

On the balmy evening of September 30, 2008, I was on my way to join Patricia, whom I had never met, for a late dinner at the sidewalk café Santa Satisfa-ção, around the corner from the Copacabana Palace, on Rua Santa Clara.

Patricia lives in the neighborhood and is a regular customer there. By coincidence, I too know the place well as it is just around the corner from a yoga

FIGURE 1.1 The majestic Copacabana Palace Hotel, designed by French architect Joseph Gire, was opened in 1923. It was built at the request of President Epitácio Pessoa for the centennial of Brazil's Independence. (Photo courtesy of Copacabana Palace)

studio where I go on Tuesday and Thursday evenings when I am in Rio. She is waiting for me, and we recognize each other immediately.

Patricia is the granddaughter of my friend José Manoel da Silva (known as Zé Cabo), whom I have known since I began this study in 1968. I lived with him and his wife, Adelina, in the favela of Nova Brasília, and we have kept in close touch ever since. He was one of the earliest settlers and among the most highly respected community leaders in Nova Brasília. He had built his house in a prime location, close to Avenida Itaoca, the main thoroughfare. He had invested a lot in the house—it was three stories high, with an open rooftop for laundry and leisure.

PATRICIA'S STORY: FROM NOVA BRASÍLIA TO COPACABANA

As Patricia and I were enjoying getting to know each other over dinner, the twinkling lights from the favelas on the hillsides of Copacabana began to appear. Once she learned that I had not called her with any bad news of her grandfather's health, she told me that she had not been to her grandfather's house since the death of her grandmother 14 years earlier. She told me, "I never see him, but he still remembers my birthday. He is the only one who sends me a card every year. He never forgets. He's so organized about those things....I live in Copacabana now—it's another world entirely. I will probably never go to Nova Brasília again. It's very dangerous."

Patricia, who uses the name "Paty," is a well-dressed professional woman who radiates competence and self-confidence. She was born in 1977, nine years after I had lived with her grandparents. She told me that she had begun working as an intern in a bank when she was 15 and never stopped. "I like to work. I studied at night and got my degree in business administration and communications technology. I just started a new job with *Oi,* the largest cell phone company in Brazil. I have a staff of five people and am the director of invoicing information systems. I think there will be more room for advancement than in my former job at the bank."

She and her brother, Mario, who is a professor of computer sciences in the nearby coastal town of Angra dos Reis, are the most successful of all of Zé Cabo's grandchildren. Their father, Wanderley, Zé's eldest son, left them and their mother when they were children. Wanderley had a steady job as a *motorista* (driver) for the Brazilian National Housing Bank (BNH). He earned a good salary and had excellent civil service benefits, but he never contributed

FIGURE I.2   Patricia sitting across the table from me at the Copacabana sidewalk café the night we met, September 30, 2008.

very much to the children's support, and he rarely visited them. Their mother and grandmother raised them and, with great sacrifice, managed to get both of them through private school, the gateway to university and professional jobs.

Their mother is a housewife who never finished elementary school. She baked birthday cakes to bring in money. They lived in Madureira, a low income suburb, but not in a favela. When Paty's parents married, her mother refused to move to Nova Brasília, so Wanderley moved in with his wife's family. Once they had children, they moved to a larger house in Paciencia (see figure I.6) where Paty's mother still lives.

Paty's uncle Waney, Zé's second son, was like a father to her and Mario. He died in 2007 of heart problems—a death which could have been avoided if he had had better medical care.

Paty lives with her boyfriend, who has a good job in human resources and earns a decent salary. She said:

> We are renting now, but we are in the process of buying an apartment just a little way from here—up the street from where we live now. We are not going to have children. It took a lot to get where we are today, and we want to be able to enjoy life and not work until we are dead.
>
> My grandfather sold his house in the best area of Nova Brasília so that he could divide the money among his children while he was still alive. With what remained, he started all over again, building a new house in a less accessible and more dangerous area of Nova Brasília; then he was harassed into leaving by the drug dealers and the ceaseless violence on his street and in front of his house.... All he ever thought about was improving the community and taking care of his children. It didn't get him anywhere. Now he has nothing for himself. I worry about his health. I told him to call me if he ever needs anything. But I don't think he will. He does not like to ask for help... he is a very independent person.

Paty insisted on paying for our dinner and then took a taxi with me back to my apartment, paying for that as well. She was taking care that I not get into trouble. As it was almost midnight when we finished talking, she considered it too dangerous for me to return home alone. This concern encapsulates at once her generosity to me as a visitor—and friend of her grandfather's—and internalization of the fear of violence, which had widened the gap between her current life and her grandfather's life. The fact that she has not invited Zé Cabo to visit her Copacabana apartment or meet her fiancée may indicate that somewhere in her mind, she is still not a safe distance away from living on the edge.

On January 5, 2009, Patricia sent me an e-mail telling me she had just begun a new job doing internal systems auditing at the Universidade Estácio de Sá, a private university run like a large corporation. She is thrilled, as this was the topic of her senior thesis when she was a student. She plans to buy her apartment by the end of 2009, if she can afford it.

Today, Nova Brasília is only a 45-minute drive from Copacabana, but it took three generations for Patricia to get there. Not every grandchild of the people I met in my original 1969 study has moved across that divide as Patricia has done. In fact, her achievements are the exception rather than the rule. More than half the grandchildren are currently without any work at all and just over a third of them are still living in favelas (half if you count those living in the conjuntos habitacionais).

SABRINA'S STORY: FROM CATACUMBA TO CONJUNTO TO LIMBO

Sabrina, whose grandparents migrated to Rio as Zé Cabo did, has not been as lucky, despite many advantages not shared by others whose parents were born in favelas. Her father Nilton was born in 1943 in the favela of Catacumba, which is situated on a hillside overlooking the Lagoa Rodrigo Freitas, in walking distance from Copacabana. It was obvious from an early age that he was extremely intelligent, and his parents managed to send him to a private Jesuit school. When I met Ntilton and explained what I was doing there, he immediately understood the value of the research and offered to help. He was unemployed so he had time to work with me, and he was always one step ahead of me. He was a close friend of Margarida's, with whom I was living, and the two of them helped me understand what I was observing and included me in community parties and weekend trips to the Island of Paquetá.

Nilton met his wife Neusa just prior to the demolition of Catacumba in 1970. As with the other Catacumba residents, they were assigned to a small apartment in one of the housing projects Quitungo and Guaporé, which were separated by a hillside. The projects were composed of dozens of identical five-story walkups in undesirable areas of the city where land values were at a minimum. Nilton and Neusa went to Guaporé. When they arrived, the walls of the building were unfinished, the apartments lacked doors—even bathroom doors—the floors were bare concrete and the same key opened all of the apartments.

As soon as he left the favela, Nilton got a job in the Polícia Militar (military police), after having been turned down several times before. Neusa worked in a sewing factory during the week and at home as a seamstress on weekends and evenings. Eight years later they were ready to start a family. Sabrina was born in 1978, and her younger sister, Samela, was born five years later. The one-bedroom apartment became too small, and Nilton sold it and used the money to build a house on the vacant property between the apartment buildings and the river that ran alongside them. He built a spacious, two-story house with a flat open roof deck, and, in short order, several of his relatives built houses next to him. Eventually, they constructed a secure family compound with a three-car garage and locked iron gates. Nilton and Neusa decided to limit their family to only two children in order to give them every possible advantage. I recall visiting them in 1993, when Sabrina turned 15. They had given her a desktop computer for her birthday. We all went upstairs to her bedroom where it sat on her pink dresser, covered in hand-woven lace, and they showed it to me with a mixture of pride and wonderment. I remember thinking how the future and the past clashed in that bedroom as Nilton explained that he had forbidden any internet connection because he did not want Sabrina to exchange messages with boys. These were the very reasons that parents in Arembepe and Abrantes had given for not wanting their children to learn to read and write. I last spoke with Sabrina in 2008. She was 30 years old, married without children and without work. She was actively looking for work and going to interviews, but she felt trapped. Six years earlier she had begun her studies at Universidade Estácio de Sá, one of the three largest private universities of Brazil. Coincidentally this is where Paty is the internal systems auditor.

Sabrina wanted to become a lawyer. She was doing well in school but, during her second year, while running to catch a bus home after class, she tripped and fractured her ankle. She did not have medical insurance, so she went to the public hospital. She spent two months with her leg in a cast and several more months on crutches but the fracture did not heal correctly, and when her parents sent her to a private doctor, he told them that the operation had been botched and there might be continuing complications. She was unable to get up and down into the bus and had no other way to get to the university, so she had to "trancar a matricula" (take a leave of absence).

The cost of treatment with the private doctor nearly depleted the family's savings. To help out, Sabrina began working for a telemarketing company. They did not hire her as a regular employee, so she was paid less than the minimum wage and received none of the benefits or protections guaranteed by labor law. She worked 10–12 hours a day, six days a week, and when she and the others demanded their rights they were told that if they did not like being paid "under the table," they could leave.

After three years, Sabrina became deaf in one ear from the constant use of earphones. She was let go, even though she had won sales awards for two of the three years she worked there.

Sabrina's boyfriend, who she met during night classes at the university, was working at Unibanco, one of Brazil's major banks. He helped her get temporary work at the Caixa Electronica (electronic banking section) of Unibanco. In order to avoid paying the costs of full-time wages and benefits, the bank kept her for just under a year and then hired someone else.

Her boyfriend pressured her to marry him, and they had a wedding in 2004. They could not afford to buy an apartment, so they rented a small one in one of the apartment buildings near Guaporé. To make extra money, Sabrina's husband took a second job as a walking sandwich board advertisement.

"I never see my husband," Sabrina told me, "because he has to work both jobs to keep us going. I am afraid to be alone in our apartment. It is not a safe area, so I stay at my parents' house when he's not home. My mother is also afraid to be at home alone, so that's good for her, too. My father had retired and was working as a private night guard, but he needed to make more money so he is now a traveling salesman and is away a lot."

Sabrina's promising start to a career in law has proven as fragile as her ankle bone and as easily fractured. Her family has moved out of the favela and out of public housing, and she now lives in a legally rented apartment in the legitimate city. But her dream of becoming a lawyer was shattered by nothing more than a chance accident.

These narratives introduce many of the central themes I will explore in the pages that follow. Both start with families who came from the interior of Brazil to Rio de Janeiro, a trend that has tipped the balance from a predominantly rural world to a predominantly urban world during the period of this study. Both show the clear improvements that each successive generation has made in educational levels and living standards and the critical role played by jobs in attainment of these things. And both highlight the ongoing multigenerational struggle to "become *gente*"—literally to become a person, to move from invisible to visible or from a nonentity to a respected human being. Sabrina, despite her university studies, which put her in the top 8 percent among all the children in this study,[1] is not considered gente, and those few, like Patricia, who seem to have made it are ever-vigilant about their precarious toehold on that status.

These two vignettes also highlight a disastrous development for the people and places I studied over the past 40 years—the rise in violence and in lethal violence in particular. The entrance of drug and arms traffic into the favelas, beginning in the mid-1980s, and the concomitant high levels of homicide have permeated the favelas and the city at large with an atmosphere of fear. Competing drug gangs with sophisticated weaponry far exceeding that of the police use the favelas to conduct and protect their business. This is illustrated in Zé's story of being driven out of Nova Brasília by the violence around his home and on his street; by Patricia's insistence on accompanying me in a taxi back to my hotel after our dinner; by Nilton's building having a locked metal gate to protect his family in Guaporé; and by Sabrina's fear of staying home alone in her apartment. The threat of violence has slipped down the favela hillsides and permeated daily life even in the classy neighborhoods of Copacabana and Ipanema. Not only do people feel uneasy walking on the streets at night, but drivers are at such high risk of being mugged when stopped at traffic lights that it has become legal to go through red lights between 10 P.M. and 6 A.M.

Talking with the children and grandchildren of the original study participants crystallized several other points as well: the political cynicism of the
best-educated young people; the way global standards of consumption have
conditioned people's "needs," desires, and expectations of everyday life; and the
critical importance of jobs as a key to their futures.

This book is based on 40 years of study that have paralleled the largest population shift in the history of humankind—the shift to an urban world. One hundred years ago, only 10 percent of the world's population lived in cities; now it is
over half; and by 2050 it is projected to be 75 percent. Virtually all of this urban
growth will be in cities of the global South (Asia, Africa, Latin America), and
the majority of it will be concentrated in "informal settlements," shantytowns
and squatter settlements like Zé Cabo's Nova Brasília and Nilton's Catacumba.

These communities, which are generally built incrementally by the residents
on unused or undesirable lands, do not conform to the norms, standards, and
zoning regulations of the "formal city" (any more than the mansions of the elite
do), but they are an integral part of the urban economy, society, and polity. In
many cases and for many reasons, including a bogged-down bureaucracy and
antiquated permit process, they are becoming the norm rather than the exception in many cities.

Despite decades of policy interventions by local, state, and national governments, international aid agencies, and nonprofit organizations and community-
based groups, the growth of informal settlements continues to outpace that of
the cities at large. New communities spring up faster than existing ones are
upgraded or linked into urban service networks.[2]

The exclusion of a billion urban poor people from full citizenship rights in
the cities where they live deprives these cities of these people's valuable intellectual capital and problem-solving capacities, as well as a formidable number
of producers, consumers, and citizens of the polis. And marginalizing four of
every ten urbanites in the global South has negative repercussions for personal
security and environmental sustainability that reach well beyond the confines
of any single city or metropolitan region. High levels of inequality are associated with the epidemic of violence that is constraining the conviviality and trust
needed to keep the social contract intact.

Relegating the urban poor to the fringes of habitability, in swamps, in garbage dumps, in cemeteries, on rocky hillsides, or in abandoned factories and
office buildings has exacerbated the damage to the already-strained urban eco-
system. Where no provision is made to incorporate the burgeoning low-income
population or prepare for the thousands still to come, settlements creep into
areas of critical environmental importance—along riverbeds, into watersheds,

into forest preserves, and along bayside tidal pools. When such large numbers of people lack suitable areas in which to build their homes and lack access to urban water and sanitation, the contamination of rivers, watersheds, and bays by human habitation is inevitable.

In the desperate race to become "global cities" with all the lifestyle and technological amenities required to compete for investments, business locations, and inclusion in the information society, poverty itself has been criminalized, and inequality has become invisible. The future of these cities depends, however, as much on how they deal with their vulnerable underbellies as on how broad their broadbands are. The lack of a well-educated labor pool, safe drinking water, reliable electric power, or open space may deter investment, but the fear of getting killed on the way to work or having one's child mugged on the way home from school is a much larger concern.

The mirror image of these problems of the cities of the South may be found in the cities of the global North. As the collage (figure I.3) implies, every "first-world" city has within it a "third-world" city of high infant mortality, malnutrition, unemployment, homelessness, and contagious diseases; and every third-world city has within it a first-world city of high finance, high technology, high fashion, and high culture. The urban question is how these two worlds might interface with each other to create a diverse, vibrant, convivial city that works for everyone.

In addressing the question of the exclusion of Rio's poor, it helps to better understand the dynamics of urban poverty, as well as the dynamics of urban prosperity. Much research has been done toward this end, and many excellent books have been written, yet the mystery of how an inclusive city "with liberty and justice for all" might come into being remains unsolved.

This book is the result of 4 decades of research following hundreds of people who, drawn by the magnetism of Rio de Janeiro, made their homes in the interstitial spaces left vacant by the urban elite. By tracing the life histories of these men and women whom I originally interviewed in 1968 in Rio's favelas I have tried to go beyond a one-time, snapshot view and see the connecting threads of changes across time and space. By interviewing children and grandchildren of the original respondents, I have sought to address questions regarding intergenerational transmission of poverty. And by looking anew at the current population composition of the three communities studied, I have endeavored to see how these places themselves have changed and whether the gap between them and the rest of the city has narrowed or widened.

THE ORIGINAL STUDY

The three favelas I selected for my original research in 1968–69 were located in the three areas of Rio de Janeiro in which poor people could then live: (1) Catacumba,

FIGURE 1.3   Every third-world city contains a first-world city, and every first-world city contains a third-world city. (Collage created for the Mega-Cities Project by Stephan Hawranick, 1990)

a favela on a steep hill in the wealthy South Zone; (2) Nova Brasília, a favela on a series of rolling hillsides in the industrial North Zone; and (3) Duque de Caxias, a separate municipality, mostly flat, on the northern border of the city of Rio in a swampy region known as the Baixada Fluminense (the Lowlands of the State of Rio), where I studied three favelas and five unserviced subdivisions called "loteamentos." (See figure 1.6 for the locations of the three areas and the relative locations of the zones.)

The origins of each settlement followed the pattern of Rio's expansion outward from the center: Catacumba was settled mostly in the 1940s (although some houses had been there since the 1930s); Nova Brasília in the 1950s; and the favelas of Caxias in the 1960s. Their density was inversely proportionate to their age and proximity to the center. At the time of the study, Catacumba had a density of 110,000 inhabitants per square kilometer (the entire favela was only 1 square kilometer); Nova Brasília had 34,000 inhabitants per square kilometer, and Caxias had 1,400 inhabitants per square kilometer, though its density dropped radically from the center outward. In the entire municipality of Caxias, covering 442 square kilometers, there were only 600,000 people.

To put these figures in perspective, the density in Rio city today is considered high at 4.7 inhabitants per square kilometer, whereas the density in Rio's favelas is almost 10 times higher, at 31.7 inhabitants per square kilometer—just about what Nova Brasília was in 1968.[3]

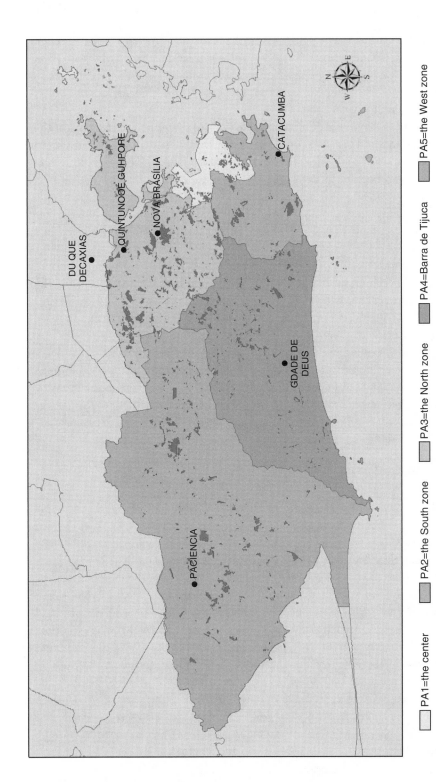

□ PA1=the center   □ PA2=the South zone   ■ PA3=the North zone   ■ PA4=Barra de Tijuca   ■ PA5=the West zone

FIGURE 1.6   Rio de Janeiro zones (planning areas) with study sites. (Courtesy of Instituto Perreira Passos, 2008)

I spent six months living in each of the three areas. In Catacumba I lived in one of the wooden shacks (barracos) with Margarida, a maid who worked in Copacabana, her brother and her two children (figure I.4). When I returned in 1973, they had been moved to an apartment in the government housing project named Quitungo (see figure I.5).

I hired and trained a field team selected from among the students in the research methods courses I offered at the Brazilian Institute of Municipal Administration and the Getulio Vargas Foundation. Together we interviewed 750 people. In each area, I drew a random sample of 200 people, men and women 16–65 years of age, and a leadership sample of 50 people selected according to their position as directors of community-based organizations or their reputation as an opinion leader to whom others turned for advice.[4]

Throughout this book I refer to these two groups as the random and leadership samples. My intent was to compare the life trajectories of the ordinary residents with those of the "favela elite," who tended to be predominantly male, older, have lighter skin, be better educated and have higher incomes.[5]

For both samples we used a detailed survey instrument, which included a year-by-year life history matrix tracing changes in residential, occupational, educational and family history from the birth of each person to the moment of the interview.[6] I integrated the results with dozens of open-ended interviews, contextual interviews reconstructing the histories of the communities and existing census data, maps, documents, and publications.[7]

THE MYTH OF MARGINALITY

What I discovered from that research became the core of *The Myth of Marginality: Urban Poverty and Politics in Rio de Janeiro* (1976).[8] This book was part of a critique of the prevailing view of the urban poor and the irregular settlements in which they lived.[9] In the development literature, migrants from the countryside were seen as maladapted to modern city life and therefore responsible for their own poverty and failure to be absorbed into formal job and housing markets. Squatter settlements were seen as syphilitic sores on the beautiful body of the city, dens of crime, and breeding grounds of violence, prostitution, family breakdown, and social disorganization. It was the fear of the Right and the hope of the Left that the disparity between their conditions and the surrounding opulence would turn the squatters into angry revolutionaries.[10] The population at large viewed the squatters as *other*, rather than as part of the urban community, and this view was legitimized by social scientists and used to justify public policies of favela removal. *Marginality* thus moved beyond the simply descriptive to become a material and ideological force.

FIGURE I.4   Close-up of the favela of Catacumba, 1968, showing the barraco (shack) where I lived with Margarida, her two children, and her brother.

FIGURE 1.5   My reunion with Margarida and her husband in 1973 in the Conjunto de
Quitungo—where they were relocated three years earlier when Catacumba was eradicated.
She is holding a Polaroid photo I have just taken of her family.

Beginning in the mid-1960s, several seminal writers, including José Nun,
Anibal Quijano, Manuel Castells, Florestan Fernandes, and Fernando Henrique Cardoso, challenged this conventional "wisdom." Empirical studies of
Latin American cities including Rio de Janeiro, Salvador, São Paulo, Santiago,
Buenos Aires, Lima, Bogotá, Mexico City, and Monterrey served to discredit
the propositions of marginality and the erroneous stereotypes surrounding the
urban poor. William Mangin and Robert Morse each published review articles
on the subject in the mid-1960s and early 1970s. These pieces, along with my
own work, showed how the concept of marginality was being used in academic
and public policy discourse to blame the victim. We demonstrated that there
was a logic and rationality to the attitudes and behaviors of the people living
in the "slums," and that there were strengths and assets in the squatter settlements of Latin America that belied the stereotypical deficits, deficiencies, and
pathologies.

My study revealed that residents of favelas are not "marginal" to society but
tightly integrated into it, albeit in an asymmetrical manner. They give a lot and
receive very little. They are not on the margins of urban life or irrelevant to its
functioning, but actively excluded, exploited, and "marginalized" by a closed
social system. In demonstrating that the negative stereotypes used as a justi-

fication for the favela eradication policies were false, I hoped that the favelas might be granted land tenure so they could grow into thriving working class communities integrated into the rest of the city.

As it happened, people did not get land titles (though massive removal did stop by the end of the 1970s); favelas and their populations continued to grow faster than the rest of the city, and the stigma against them (and fear of proximity to them) increased sharply after the rise in drug traffic and violence that began in the mid-1980s.

Meanwhile, the results of a variety of well-intentioned poverty alleviation policies and programs were disappointing, leaving city, state, and national governments and multilateral agencies wondering what to do. Even as "slums" were upgraded, new ones were growing, and there was a sense of futility at being behind the curve.

It was exciting to think about how a restudy of the same individuals[11] after 30 years could provide a time-lapse view of what had happened to them and why. Poverty is not a static state, and very little is known about the dynamics of urban poverty across generations. Few longitudinal studies exist on urban shantytowns, and those that do tend to study the same communities but not the same individuals—failing to address the change process.[12] The Brazilian census bureau—the Brazilian Institute of Geography and Statistics—conducts a census every 10 years and a yearly household survey called the National Research by Household Sample (Pesquisa Nacional por Amostra de Domicílios). Although this is very useful for many purposes, it is based on a newly drawn random sample each year, making it impossible to follow the same people over time, much less explore what happens to their descendants.[13]

Only a panel study of the same people, their children, and their children's children can begin to reveal how patterns of context, attitudes, behavior, and luck play out in the struggle to overcome the exclusion and dehumanization of poverty.

RETURNING 30 YEARS LATER: THE RESTUDY

In 1999, I went to Rio to test the feasability of finding the original study participants after 30 years. Finding positive results, in 2000, I mounted a research team in Rio and initiated a full-fledged effort to locate as many of the 750 original study participants as possible.

Catacumba, where land values were the highest, had been eradicated in 1970 and its inhabitants relocated into *conjuntos* (government housing blocks). Nova Brasília became part of the Complexo de Alemão, an enormous merging of 11 favelas, which became infamous for its high degree of drug-related violence and the lack of government social programs, infrastructure investment, or protection of personal safety. The favelas of Caxias remained the poorest of all the study sites. The people who had bought or rented a lot in the un-serviced subdivisions (loteamentos) ended up doing best of all the original interviewees. The second best were those who were brought up in Catacumba and had the lifelong advantage of the contacts and networks they had developed while living there.

Finding the people was a daunting process. It would be hard enough to locate anybody after 30 years, but the fact that favelas do not have street addresses and that I had omitted people's last names to protect their anonymity at the time of the original study) made it all the more so. And we had serious concerns about the safety of entering the favelas due to the violence that had arisen with the rise of the drug traffic in the mid-1980s. There were many days when we planned to be working in the communities and were told it was too dangerous to come as there was a "war" going on that day between drug factions or between the police and the dealers.

We used many different approaches and kept following up on leads for the next two years. After securing permission to enter the communities, we began by putting up large colorful posters saying that we were eager to meet people who had participated in the 1968 study. The poster featured a photo of me (the way people interviewed would have remembered me) from that time and the cover of the Brazilian paperback edition of my book, which I had given to many of the study participants.

Fortunately, due to a newspaper story about my return to Rio to follow up on my favela study, I was invited to be interviewed on the popular Brazilian television show *Fantástico*. That gave me the opportunity to reach a huge audience and appeal to viewers to call in if they or someone they knew had been part of the original study. Likewise, I spoke on popular radio stations and community radio, and we posted ads in the most widely read newspapers in the communities. Then, for one Sunday afternoon in each place our team rented a van with a loudspeaker—the type used in electoral campaigns—and drove around each of the communities announcing a barbecue that afternoon and asking for help in our search for original study participants.

Simultaneously with those unconventional outreach efforts, I began to contact the families with whom I had lived in each favela and the friends with whom I had maintained contact over the years. Some of them or their friends, neighbors, or children were interested in helping with the search, so I trained and hired them.

In the process of searching for an individual, the first step was to look for the location of the home. This was complicated by the fact that many of the dwellings had no numbers or street name at all, and even when we had a partial address, the streets and numbering had long ago changed or been reconfigured, often several times over. Once the house was located, we had a fifty-fifty chance of finding the same family still there. If not, we asked if

FIGURE I.7 The poster, titled "LET'S MEET AGAIN!" reads "If you participated in this study or know anyone who did, help us recuperate the history of your community by contacting [name of specific person in each community].

anyone knew where the family had gone or how to contact any relative or friend. We went to the local hangouts, the corner stores, bars, community organizations, evangelical churches, *terreiros* (centers for Afro-Brazilian religious ceremonies such as condomblé or macumba), and soccer games.

We ran into the problem of finding "false positives": people with the same first name and general location who had not actually participated in the study but did not remember whether they had participated or not. To avoid this, we went back to the original handwritten questionnaires from 1968 and composed short profiles of each of the 750 people interviewed. Each profile gave the person's name, household location, and birthplace and names of all his or her family members at that time. The scouting team took these lists with them when they went to the communities.

We managed to find 41 percent of the 750 study participants—an extraordinary feat, given that after 30 years, and under the difficult conditions we were working, it would be considered a success if we found more than 5 percent of them. About half of those we found were still living in the same home they had been living in 30 years before—in Nova Brasília, Caxias, or, in the case of Catacumba, the same apartment in the conjunto to which they had had been assigned in 1970 when their favela community was eradicated.

The most difficult place to find people was in the subdivisions of Caxias, where people tended to be more individualistic and isolated—having never needed to mobilize to remain in place or to get urban services. Although Catacumba was the one favela to have been uprooted, it was the one that had the strongest community ties, so the success rate there was the highest.

My search for original study participants took me across the entire state of Rio and to João Pessoa (Paraíba), Natal (Rio Grande de Norte) Brasília, Belo Horizonte (Minas Gerais), Porto Alegre (Rio Grande doSul), and São Paulo. They had left for jobs elsewhere or to escape the violence, often returning to their place of origin or that of their spouse. With two exceptions, these were the poorest families in the entire study.

IN DEFENSE OF INTERGENERATIONAL INVESTIGATION

When we had reinterviewed all of the original study participants and compared their attitudes, behaviors, knowledge, and level of living in 1969 and in 2001, we faced a conundrum. Since everyone was 32 years older it was difficult to ascertain whether the changes we found were the result of their being at a different stage in the life cycle (many were living on pensions and no longer in the job market); the result of changing conditions in the social, political or economic context; or the result of a different logic of integration of favela residents into the larger urban fabric. We were able to begin addressing these questions only by looking at their children who were approximately the same age at the time of the restudy (mean age of 40) as their parents had been during the initial study (mean age of 36).

The results of the interviews with the next generation were disappointing. The children's lives were better than their parents had been in some ways but worse in many others, and certainly did not live up to the expectations for which so many sacrifices had been made. Reluctant to write a depressing saga with a hopeless ending, I considered the possibility that due to the high degree of inequality in Rio and in Brazil and the multiple stigmas of being migrants, being poor, living in a favela, and perhaps having dark skin color, it might take two generations for upward social mobility to appear. With that in mind I went ahead with the idea to interview the grandchildren of the original sample. Their mean age in 2001 was 24, and I thought that they might be the ones to fulfill the hopes of their grandparents. In chapter 9 I present what we found from looking at all three generations together.

All the interviews with the three generations were conducted in 2001–02. However, I was still left with doubts as to whether the changes in the lives of this group of families might be misleading due to the fact that I had found less than half of the participants from the original study (41 percent). It was possible that my findings would all be biased toward the most successful or least successful. For example, perhaps the best had all moved up, out, and away and those I had been able to find were the ones who had the worst lives and been left behind. Or, on the contrary, perhaps the poorest had been forced out and were living on the streets, under bridges, or in shop doorways (as is frequently seen in Rio after dark) and those I had been able to find were the success stories.

By looking at what had changed in the entire population of the three study communities, I hoped to address this uncertainty. That way, rather than tracing the ups and downs only in those families we happened to find, I would be able to compare the overall composition of the same places in 1969 and in 2003. With the help of a sociology professor from the State University of Rio de Janeiro whose specialty is research methods, we drew new random samples in each of the original study communities. For Catacumba, which was no longer in existence, we used the conjuntos of Quitungo and Guaporé, where the majority of Catacumba's residents had been placed. Nova Brasília had expanded upward and outward but was still in the same location. The three favelas and five subdivisions in Caxias were also in the same locations, although the favelas had also grown beyond their original boundaries. To account for the growth in size of all of these settlements, we doubled the size of the random sample in each site from 200 to 400 and, due to the decreased number of community-based organizations, we reduced the leadership sample by half—from 50 to 25. We then followed the same procedures I had used in 1968–69—sampling from men and women 16–65 years old.

When the findings of this place-based research confirmed the multi-generational findings, I finally felt confident that the study results corresponded as closely as possible to reality and were not an artifact of the viewer's eye.[14]

In 2004–05, as a visiting scholar at the World Bank, I was able to analyze my data and give periodic talks to various groups of experts, benefiting from their feedback. Even with the analysis of the communities and the families, I remained puzzled about why and how some people managed to become more successful than others. Using the aggregate data and statistical analytical tools provided some clues—such as the importance of the parents' educational level—but could not provide the nuanced insights needed to understand the issue in its full complexity.

To figure out why some did better than others, we decided to conduct in-depth open-ended interviews with the most successful and least successful individuals from the original interviewees. I did this during 2005, with a young Carioca anthropologist. We taped and transcribed the interviews and used them to look for patterns that might not have been evident from the survey questionnaires. We found that location, networks, family values and individual differences, along with just plain luck, had a lot to do with upward or downward mobility.

The final part of the research was conducted in 2007–08, after I had already begun writing this book. During the analysis of the ethnographic and statistical data and the writing of various chapters, I returned to Rio several times to follow the key protagonists of this book and to interview policy-makers and NGO leaders about their ideas and community interventions. I was interested in seeing what current and future directions might hold promise in helping to overcome the barriers perpetuating poverty and exclusion. I also conferred with my Brazilian academic colleagues doing research in this field to learn how they interpreted the changing realities of life for the urban poor.

At the end of September 2008, when the book was nearly completed, I was invited to give a course at the newly created School of Public Policy of the Rio municipality for experts in the area of favelas and favela policy. The course was free, and the participants were selected by the course sponsors to represent a mixture of policy-makers, program administrators, planners, activists, and academics. During this week-long intensive course, the ideas for this book were tested and honed. It was a wonderful two-way learning process. Before returning to New York, I spent another week meeting with the grandchildren of the families I knew best and making sure we could stay in touch by e-mail once I was back home.

The chapters that follow are loosely organized into four parts. The first two chapters provide the setting for the book. In chapter 1, I relate the history of favelas, the early attempts to demolish them, and the variations of urban informality, raising the question of which citizens have a "right to the city." In chapter 2, I look at the urbanization of the global population. The chapter is structured like a funnel, starting with the rapid urbanization of the global South, then situating Latin America within the trends in Asia and Africa; situating Brazil within Latin America; and finally situating Rio de Janeiro within Brazil. While each city—and each squatter settlement—has its own individual historical, cultural, and political/economic specificity, the challenges confronted are sufficiently similar for the findings presented here to provoke a rethinking of informal settlements everywhere.

The second part of the book consists of the stories of the three communities and introduces one of the early founders of each, who act as our guides into this uncharted territory of untold histories. Chapter 3 tells of the initial settlement of Catacumba, a hillside favela in one of the most desirable locations in the city—and of how it developed, how its residents mobilized to demand urban services, and how all 10,000 of them were forcibly removed in 1970 and "resettled" in distant conjuntos. Chapter 4 is the contrasting story of Nova Brasília, a favela in the northern industrial zone of the city that has become part of an enormous complex of contiguous communities now infamous for its high degree of lethal violence. Chapter 5 is about Duque de Caxias, a municipality in the Baixada Fluminense, just north of the city of Rio, whose economy and population have grown exponentially since the first study. I found divergent histories between the three favelas and the five low-cost loteamentos that I studied there: the favelas have become trapped between drug gangs, extortionist militias, and corrupt police, and the loteamentos have become integrated into the surrounding working-class neighborhoods. Together, these three chapters illustrate the critical importance of place—of differences in locality and legitimacy—in structuring opportunities and constraints for individuals.

The third part of the book is organized around key themes that emerged as early as the pre-test of this study. Chapter 6 is about the transformation of marginality from myth to reality. In it I trace the metamorphosis of "marginality" as a concept and show how the conflation of its meaning with criminality has come full circle with the rise of drug gangs in the favelas. In chapter 7, I address the most devastating change that has occurred over four decades—the rise of the drug and arms traffic in the favelas and the takeover of community control by organized narco-traffic or self-appointed militias or both. The loss of trust, community unity, and freedom of movement—and the erosion of social capital—are among the consequences of this new (dis)order and of the inability or unwillingness of the state to provide personal safety and public security in the space of the favelas. Chapter 8 addresses the thorny questions of geographical and socioeconomic mobility. I explore what aspects of life have gotten better or worse for the people in this study and contrast their own perceptions with various measures of success. In chapter 9, I talk about the disappointment with democracy among the urban poor. I show how favela residents remain pseudo-citizens who have yet to reap the benefits of Brazil's 1985 return to democracy. I identify a disconnect between beliefs and behavior regarding political participation (especially in the youngest, best-educated genera-tion), a cynicism bred of the unhidden corruption and injustice witnessed on a daily basis.

The final part of the book places the discussions of the earlier chapters in the context of globalization and teases out the theoretical and policy impli-cations of those findings. In chapter 10, I explore the relationship between poverty, inequality, and globalization, looking particularly at how the people in this study think about the relevance of globalization—and its positive and negative consequences—for their lives. Chapter 11 provides an overview of favela policies from removal to upgrading, tracing the learning curve and the pragmatic as well as ideological changes that led to this reversal. I argue that while moving to housing projects was devastating in the short run, it turned out to be a stepping-stone to legitimacy and upward mobility in the long run, and that Favela-Bairro, a large-scale upgrading project, would have had better results if the investment had been made in people rather than engineering and architectural infrastructure. I address the question "What is to be done?" challenging the assumption that all problems can be addressed through well-informed public policy. In chapter 12, I confront the fundamental issue of how poverty has been construed to deny person-hood and how the urban poor struggle to become gente, to attain the status of a human being worthy of respect and dignity.

No matter how many obstacles they face, the people I interviewed for this book are full of hope for the future. Their optimism in contagious—while few think that life in Brazil or Rio will become better in the next five years, a majority think that their communities will be better and almost everyone thinks that their own lives will be better. Figure 1.8 shows the community leader in the favela of Vidigal, beaming with pride in what he and his community have already achieved and looking forward to greater achievements yet to come.

FIGURE I.8 Welcome to the Cidade Maravalhosa—the Marvellous City! A favela leader proudly shows me the new developments over the past decades, inadvertently mirroring the outstretched arms of the Corcovado on the mountaintop behind him (2005).

one

DEEP ROOTS IN SHALLOW SOIL

On a hill called Canudos in the northeast region of Brazil, a bush with spiked leaves and oil-yielding nuts survives in stony soil. It is a favela bush, and it provides food for flocks of small, green-feathered Illinger's macaws. This hardy bush is very likely the source of the Brazilian name for the squatter settlements that grow along the hillsides and in the lowlands of Rio de Janeiro, São Paulo, and other Brazilian cities. Like their namesake, the favela communities thrive on little and provide sustenance to many. To tell their story, a bit of history is in order.

On May 13, 1888, the Brazilian monarchy signed the Golden Law, abolishing slavery after more than 300 years. This act left thousands of former slaves wandering around the interior backlands of the Northeast with neither occupations nor resources. During the late 1870s, and again during the late 1880s, droughts brought death to a half million people in the interior. Landowners made money meting out water for drought relief and otherwise exploited those lacking money or influence.

In 1889, a bloodless military coup overthrew the Brazilian emperor Don Pedro II and established a republic backed by the landowning elites. Into this mix strode Antonio Vincente Mendes Maciel, later known as Antonio Conselheiro (the Counselor). The son of a Bahian cattle rancher, Antonio Conselheiro became a peripatetic preacher, wandering the Brazilian backlands and preaching the pre-eminence of God, the predominance of sin, and the promise of penance.

After years of this nomadic existence, the Counselor settled in Canudos, below Monte Favela, and there he created a millenarian outpost. The soil of Canudos was fertile—fed by underground artesian wells and by the Vasa Barris River. Thousands followed him—landless farmers, freed slaves, disgruntled workers and indigenous peoples. The Canudos community was run without money, without alcohol, and with a minimum of sin—and it prospered. Naturally, there were those who were envious of the community's successes.

The *fazendeiros* (large landowners) were jealous because they were experiencing labor shortages, while many of their former workers were now living off the land in Canudos. The republican government was jealous because Antonio Conselheiro preached loyalty to the monarchy. The Catholic Church was jealous because Conselheiro called the priests sinful and decried their indifference to the plight of the poor. It was just a matter of time before the situation erupted into violence.

In the fall of 1897, after several unsuccessful attempts to forcibly break up the community, the republican federal government sent thousands of troops to Canudos, where they killed 15,000 residents, mostly male. The troops ran off the rest of the men, raped the women, and sent many of them to brothels in Salvador, the capital of the state of Bahia. Antonio the Counselor died of dysentery during the siege. He was later disinterred, and his decapitated head was sent to Salvador, where it was displayed on a pole.

The decommissioned soldiers returning from the Canudos war disembarked in Rio and, waiting in vain for land grants promised by the army, pitched their tents on a hillside alongside the former slaves and street vendors already camping there. This hillside later became known as the Morro da Providência, and the people there gradually built shacks to replace their tents. In the same year, a rotting, overcrowded tenement (Cabeca do Porco, Pig's Head), was razed, and 1,000 displaced persons came to join the veterans on the Morro da Providência. The landlord of the Cabeca de Porco owned a vacant plot of land there and gave the displaced residents permission to construct shacks with wood provided by the government—but not to use any permanent building materials.[1]

Some say that the Canudos veterans named the hillside after Monte Favela; others believe that there were bushes there reminiscent of the favela bushes in Canudos—in either case they called their settlement "favela."

Figure 1.1 shows the Lagoa Rodrigo Freitas, the former site of Catacumba favela, which long clung to the hillside, withstanding floods, droughts, and winds, only to be torn down by dictate of government policy in 1970.

FIGURE I.I   View of Lagoa Rogrigo Freitas (2008) 38 years after the removal of the favela of Catacumba.

UNWANTED FROM INCEPTION

Throughout their history, favelas have been rejected by the "formal" city and have continually been threatened with destruction. The moment people began building their own homes and communities outside the control of the state or the market, they were seen as a menace to the city of privilege. When the Morro da Providência was first occupied, an edict was promulgated giving the residents 10 days to evacuate. Since the late 1800s, in the ongoing effort to rid the city of these "leprous sores," laws have been passed, building codes established, eviction notices posted, civil and military police deployed, and fires set in the dark of night.

During the period 1890–1906, Rio experienced a severe shortage of low-income housing. The abolition of slavery in 1888 led to a large-scale migration of former plantation workers to Rio, which had become the national capital with the 1889 creation of the republic. Pereira Passos, the mayor of the federal district of Rio in the early years of the twentieth century, imagined Rio as a "tropical Paris." He was inspired by Hausmann's grand-scale planning of the French capital, with majestic boulevards, monuments, and gardens. To achieve that, he had to destroy the "unsightly" favelas, *cortiços* (tenements), *casas de comodos* (rooming houses), and *albergues* (shelters) where the city's poor were living. His early urban renewal project destroyed untold numbers of favelas, 1,691 *cortiços*, and thousands of other buildings.[2] But 100 *barracos* (shacks) remained on the Morro da Favela. In 1907, Osvaldo Cruz, the federal director of public health, launched his own campaign to sanitize the Morro da Favela, giving residents 10 days to evacuate the land it occupied. His orders appear to have been in vain. History shows that by the early 1920s, the number of shack dwellings had increased more than eightfold (to about 839), and by 1933, the number had grown to 1,500—housing a population close to 10,000.

Only in the 1920s did "favela" become the generic term for squatter settlements, shantytowns, and all types of irregular settlements, or "subnormal agglomerations" as they were referred to in census and planning documents. In keeping with the earlier view, favelas were seen by the government and public opinion as a grave threat to the well-being of the then two million people of the city. The first legal recognition of favelas was in the late 1930s, when the government categorized them as "an aberration." The 1937 Codigo de Obras (Building Code) prohibited them, expressly forbidding the building of new favelas and banning the expansion of existing ones, or the use of permanent building materials in favela construction. So from early on, the squatters were caught in a bind: city planners found their self-built barracos abominable but prohibited any efforts to make them into decent homes; they wanted them destroyed but failed to provide any alternative.[3]

The infamous Building Code notwithstanding, in the post–World War II period, cityward migration to Rio increased dramatically, swelling the populations of existing favelas and creating new ones anywhere vacant land could be found. The first favelas developed at the bottom of hillsides and the edges of the bay, but as those prime locations (as it were) began to fill up, the newcomers went further up into the hillsides, further out into the water, and further away from the city's core. After the military coup of April 1, 1964, established a dictatorship, Rio and Brazil's other metropolitan areas lost the right to elect their own mayors. These positions, considered critically important for "national security," were made appointed positions accountable only to the national government in Brasília.

During those years, the mayor's office and the City Council of Rio were beset by favela commissions and committees requesting/demanding water, electricity, paving, steps, street lighting, and assurances that they could stay where they were. To handle these multiple requests—often made by entire busloads of men, women, and children—the city government required each favela to create a Residents' Association. In order to have a single entity representing the community. Residents elected a leader and a slate of other officers, and the Residents' Associations took on many essential functions. Together they organized coalitions, first a Federation of the Favela Associations of Guanabara (FAFEG), and then—after the fusion of the city and state in 1975—the Federation of Residents' Associations of the State of Rio de Janeiro (FAMERJ).

These federations enjoyed considerable autonomy and had a fair degree of bargaining power over candidates for positions on City Council (*vereadores*) until the mid-1980s, when the drug lords began to take them over.

Despite all efforts to discourage the growth of new favelas and contain the growth of existing ones, Rio's favelas have grown considerably faster than the rest of the city, in every decade from 1950 to 2000. An addition to the formation of new favelas, the older ones have expanded vertically and horizontally as new migrants arrive, families grow and rental units are added on. The volcanic upward thrust of vertical expansion as seen in figure 1.2, reflects the high demand for space in the South Zone favelas especially, and the total freedom from zoning regulations or construction codes.

Favelas also expand horizontally, gradually growing up into the hillsides and out into forested areas. Aerial photographs taken yearly by the City Planning Department track their growth on superimposed images. The latest government attempt to prevent such expansion was begun in 2009 under Rio's Mayor Eduardo Paes who began the construction of reinforced concrete containing walls around the favelas, starting with Santa Marta, as shown in figure 1.3.

The walls are supposedly to protect the natural environment by limiting favela growth, and to "pacify" the favela territories by controlling the drug traffic, but the people I spoke with say they are being built to hide the favelas from view in anticipation of the 2014 World Cup and the 2016 Summer Olympics for which Rio is competing. The residents feel imprisoned and demeaned by the walls, which are agressively ugly and out-of-place in a colorful community

FIGURE 1.2   Vertiginous vertical growth in Rocinha, Rio's largest, best located, and most famous favela. (Photo courtesy Rio municipal government)

FIGURE 1.3   Santa Marta favela in Botafogo, on the left, walled off from the forested area on the right and from the formal city glistening down below. Sugar Loaf is visible in the background. (Photo courtesy of ISER, July 2009)

situated in the midst of greenery. Santa Marta is only the first of 80 favelas currently in line to be thus fenced in.

WHAT'S IN A NAME?

The word "favela" has taken on such negative connotations that most people now use *morro* (hill), *communidade popular* (popular community), or simply *communidade*. The word *favelado*, referring to a favela resident, is considered perjorative and insulting. Yet the definitions of favela and favela resident remain problematic. *Webster's Dictionary* defines "favela" as "a settlement of jerry-built shacks lying on the outskirts of a Brazilian city." This is wrong on two counts. First, many of the favelas in Brazilian cities have evolved over the years from "jerry-built shacks" of wood or wattle and daub to brick-and-mortar dwellings several stories high. Second, they are not necessarily on the outskirts of the city—many are built on hillsides, tidal marshes, garbage dumps, or other undesirable spots right in the midst of the city. These discrepancies are only the tip of the iceberg of ambiguity that confounds attempts at defining favelas or encapsulating the concept in the popular imagination. All of the conventional distinctions between the "formal" and "informal" city, even security of tenure, have begun to blur, as the favelas that have been around for decades have become physically consolidated within the urban fabric of Rio[4]—while continuing to be stigmatized as "territories of exclusion."[5]

The classic designators of *irregular* or *informal* settlements, as opposed to *regular* or *formal* settlements continue to erode. This is not to say that the city of the poor and the city of the rich are indistinguishable, but that the division of the urban space into formal and informal (as suggested by books such as Zuenir Ventura's *A Cidade Partida*—The Divided City[6] is no longer applicable, if it ever was. The often used descriptor of a "dual city" is neither accurate nor useful. In my view the two sides of the city have always been interdependent and intertwined. Nowadays, drawing the line is more subtle and perhaps even more pernicious.

Favelas can no longer be defined by their "illegality" (as the original invasions of open land on hillsides or in marshes were regarded), as their legal status is in limbo, with most now having a form of de facto tenure.[7] Nor may they any longer be defined by their lack of (or deficits in) urban services, since almost all of them have obtained access to water, sewerage, and electricity. Favelas may no longer be defined according to the precarious construction materials as explained above. Favelas can not even be defined as free places to live, as there is now a thriving internal real estate market for rental and purchase, with prices in the well-located favelas rivaling those of legitimate neighborhoods.[8]

The distinction of last resort is to define favelas as communities of misery or chronic poverty. But even that is misleading. Not all of the people living in favelas are poor, and not all the urban poor live in favelas.[9] Today, even more than in the 1960s and 1970s, there are significant differences in wealth and well-being within and among Rio's favelas.[10] Perhaps the single persistent distinction between favelas and the rest of the city is the deeply rooted stigma that adheres to them and to those who reside in them.

Even after the extensive 10-year Favela-Bairro upgrading program, which was carried out in 144 favelas and 24 loteamentos,[11] with the aim of integrating them into the surrounding neighborhoods—even after plazas were built at favela entrances, lookout points cleared along the pathways, main internal streets paved, muddy hillsides replaced by concrete stairways, polluted canals and streams dredged, and household connections to water, sewerage, and electricity established—there is little doubt as to where the *asfalto* (pavement) ends and the morro begins.[12] Where the words fail to define, shared cultural understandings prevail.[13] The visual markers of each are unmistakable, whether viewed from above or on street level. The formal city is *rectilinear*, the favela *curvilinear*. The contrast is visible in figure 1.4.

The older, consolidated, and well-located favelas can be easily spotted as existing off the grid. The infrastructure has been retrofitted to the existing settlement, built incrementally from the street upward or inward, following the contours of the land. Depending on the size of the favela, there are hundreds or thousands of individual structures in every stage of construction, made (to

FIGURE 1.4   The *morro* and the *asfalto*—the informal and formal city, one curvilinear, the other rectilinear. (From the Rio municipal archives)

varying degrees) of large hollow red bricks set at different angles as the topography permits, rising two to five stories, with flat cement *lages* (roofs) that have
satellite dishes and mysterious-looking tall metal poles sticking out of the top,
already beginning to rust. These are the reinforcing rods built in anticipation
of securing the next story. And there are usually several young boys flying kites
from the roofs, either as recreation or as a signal for the arrival of drugs into
the favela.

The newer favelas and irregular settlements in the West Zone of the city are
easily identifiable. Although there may be several brick structures in the parts
that were first settled, many people still live in barracos in their early stages of
construction, and many of the favelas and loteamentos have minimal access to
urban services. At high tide, the barracos are often partially inundated, and the
pathways turn into muddy streams overlaid with wooden planks for walking.

In the upscale South Zone, favelas creep up the lush green hillsides of the Tijuca forest, offering spectacular views of the ocean, the lagoon, the famous Pedra de Gavea and Dois Irmaos, and the Corcovado (statue of Christ) that rises with outstretched arms above it all. These favelas look down on the glass, steel, and marble high-rises of the formal city that the informal city residents construct in their day jobs. Only the richest of the rich and the poorest of the poor have stand-alone homes; the rest live in apartment buildings. In the North Zone, a working-class area with large factories and apartment buildings, the irregular shapes of the favela buildings and the banana and fruit trees stand out clearly among the homes further up the hillsides. The visual delineation is reinforced in both cases by the armed guards and gatekeepers who stand at the entrances to the favelas. These fig-ures represent the dominant drug faction of any given moment, and they exercise total control over who enters and leaves the community.

I find it ironic that two of the distinguishing characteristics of favelas are shared with the richest neighborhoods in Rio. First, only in favelas and the most elite areas of the city do people live in detached houses rather than apart-ment buildings. Second, only in favelas and the condominium developments of the rich are the communities gated and the entrances patrolled by armed guards. This came to me during a conversation with a young boy who defined favela for me as "a place where you need permission to enter." In a "city of walls," to borrow the title of Teresa Caldeira's book,[14] it is hard to tell who is keeping out whom and who are the ones trapped behind the guarded gates. It caused quite a scandal when the favela of Jacarezinho (Little Alligator) "dared" to become a "gated community," putting up walls with surveillance cameras around its perimeters.[15]

But not all informal settlements are gated or guarded like favelas. Lotea-mentos, one of the fastest-growing types of informal settlements in Rio in the current moment, are subdivisions carved out of vacant lands on the peripheries of the city and divided into small plots, generally lacking roads or any urban services or amenities. They are most frequently located in the West Zone, which is not densely settled and is the location of huge *fazendas* (landhold-ings) that are used for agriculture or grazing. These lands are not well patrolled, making them prime targets for small-scale *loteamentos irregulares* (irregular/ unauthorized subdivisions) or larger *loteamentos clandestinos* (clandestine sub-divisions). The latter are generally invaded and laid out by a profiteer developer, who sells the plots and then disappears, leaving the government to install ser-vices or abandon the people. The city either ignores their claims, or faces the dilemma of whether to remove and relocate the families or pay for the land and bring urban services out to them—a costly proposition. The people are caught in the middle, often having spent all their money to buy a phony title. Some loteamentos are perfectly legal because they were created by the gov-ernment or by legitimate landowners. These sell for low prices and generally lack services. Nonetheless, as in the case of the loteamentos we studied in Caxias, they sometimes serve as communities that are transitioning to becoming neighborhoods.

Loteamentos are visually quite distinct from favelas, in large part because the land is subdivided and streets laid out in advance of occupation rather than piecemeal. As shown in figure 1.5, there is a grid pattern to these subdivisions. They are called "irregular" or "clandestine" not because they are helter-skelter but because they are often hidden behind large buildings or in the midst of grazing lands and they occupy the land illegally. They are growing rapidly in size and number, mostly in the West Zone.

FIGURE 1.5   Aerial view of a loteamento in the West Zone, showing the characteristic settlement pattern and the extension of lots beyond the original boundaries of the subdivision. (Courtesy of Instituto Pereira Passos—Rio de Janeiro)

In common parlance and for statistical purposes, loteamentos are often conflated with favelas, making it difficult to track the different types of low-income settlement across the urban landscape. The same is true of the conjuntos—housing developments that the government has built for displaced favela residents.

Technically, conjuntos do not belong in the category of "informal" housing. They are official apartment complexes constructed by the government on land owned—or acquired—by the government. They exist in a state of semilegal limbo—neither *asfalto* nor *morro*. The financing system was designed on the basis of residents making monthly payments toward a full purchase at the end of 25 years. However, more than 35 years later, the apartments are predominantly occupied by informal arrangement rather than formal ownership or rental.

Because the conjuntos are not on the urban street grid, because they are occupied by fairly low-income residents, and because they are without police protection and subject to violent turf wars among competing drug gangs, in the eye of the public and compilation of city statistics they are called favelas and considered part of the informal housing sector. The now infamous City of God (Cidade de Deus) was one of the early conjuntos. Figures 1.6 and 1.7, taken in 1969, show its original layout, obviously the result of a planned housing project, but it is referred to as a favela in the movie that bears its name and by the general public. The other conjuntos, such as Cidade Alta where *City of God* was filmed, are likewise referred to as favelas.

Even the better conjuntos, built with some private financing for families with higher incomes, started out looking desolate, as shown in the 1973 photo of Padre Miguel (figure 1.8). But unlike Cidade de Deus, Cidade Alta, and most other conjuntos, it has been well maintained and today is not considered a favela. Tio Souza,[16] the girl's soccer coach who we will meet in chapter 3, moved there when Catacumba was torn down in 1970, and it is now considered a good place to live.

There are other forms of informal housing which have traditionally accommodated Rio's urban poor, but today they reach a relatively small part of the population. Among them are *corticos* (old single-family houses that have been subdivided to accommodate multiple families); *cabeças de porco* (tenements), and *vilas* (workers' housing consisting of attached, one-room apartments running back from the street along both sides of a narrow passageway).

As of 2008, the informal city in Rio accounted for about 37 percent of the population. The formal city, which accounts for the rest of the population, is composed of legitimate neighborhoods called *bairros*—which range from low-end to high-end. The difference between the upscale bairros of Lagoa, Leblon, Ipanema, and Jardim Botánico and the popular bairros such as Tijuca, Irajá, and São Goncalo show up on the Human Development Index as the same difference from Belgium and Burkina Faso. Glass and chrome modern high-rise apartment buildings are crammed side-by-side along the beachfront. They have generated demand for vast shopping malls and cultural centers as well as a large pool

FIGURE 1.6 AND 1.7   *Cidade de Deus* (City of God), 1973. Figure 1.6, an arial view of the conjunto, built for the refugees of demolished favelas, shows the range of housing types. Families with the lowest household income were assigned to the barracklike structures in the foreground—one family per room; those in the middle range went to the "core" or "embrio" houses that appear as little boxes; and the five-story walk-ups in the background and in figure 1.7 were for families in the highest income bracket.

FIGURE 1.8 One of the new conjuntos in 1973, Padre Miguel on the far northern fringe of the city, which those accustomed to favela vitality in the heart of the city saw as "o fim do mundo" ("the end of the world").

of cheap labor, in turn giving rise to the rapid growth of favelas and loteamentos irregulares in the region inland.

I was perplexed that many of my colleagues who work in Latin America or speak Spanish continually had difficulty with the term "bairro," simply meaning "neighborhood." Then I figured out that the problem was that the spelling and pronunciation of "bairro" is strikingly similar to the Spanish words *barrio* or *barriada*, terms that mean "squatter settlement" in different places in Latin America. I wonder whether the use of "barrio" and "barriada"—words that, like "bairro," simply mean "neighborhood"—to designate shantytowns stems from the same quest for dignity that has led favelas to be called "communities" or "popular communities." My friends in Lima said it made a significant difference when the city started calling invaded lands *pueblos jovenes* (young towns) instead of the pejorative terms previously used for them.

TOXIC TERMINOLOGY: A *FAVELA* IS NOT A *SLUM*

In line with the importance of language in conferring or denying status, the word "favelados" has become so derogatory that it is rarely used to refer to a resident of a favela, and the term "subnormal agglomerations" has been replaced by "areas of special interest" in official planning terminology. In this light, I find it objectionable to refer to favelas—or any other squatter settlements—as "slums."[17]

While favelas and "slums" are both territories of exclusion in cities that increasingly criminalize poverty, they exist in very different contexts and serve different functions. They are worlds apart.[18] The word "slum," which had rightly fallen into ignominious disrepute, was revived in the joint UN-World Bank program known as Cities Alliance—notably in its "Cities Without Slums" initiative[19]—and in the Millennium Development Goals (MDGs). Goal 7, target 11, of the MDGs reads: "Have achieved by 2020 a significant improvement in the lives of at least 100 million slum dwellers."[20] In this case, "slums" are defined by deficits—including "inadequate access to safe water, sanitation, and other infrastructure, poor housing quality, overcrowding, and insecure residential status."[21] Although there is no realistic expectation of ridding cities of poverty, the goal of improving the lives of 100 million "slum dwellers" by 2020 is a mockery, given that the UN itself has projected that an additional 1.4 million people will be living in squatter settlements by that date.

The use of the word "slum" for informal housing is an unfortunate throwback to an earlier period of class-based moralizing that gave rise to that term. Hoskins, the British historian, traces the origins of the word to the 1820s as deriving from "the old provincial word "slump," meaning "wet mire." The word "slam" in Low German, Danish and Swedish, also means "mire"; and that roughly described the dreadful state of the streets and courtyards on these undrained sites."[22]

The *Oxford English Dictionary* defines "slum" first as a squalid and overcrowded urban area inhabited by very poor people, and second as a house or building unfit for human habitation. The emotional valence of the word, however, is better captured in a recent *New York Times* article about the cholera epidemic in New York City in 1832. It was described by a prominent civic leader in letters to his daughter as "exclusively confined to the lower classes of intemperate dissolute & filthy people huddled together like swine in their polluted habitations...the very scum of the city."[23] Charles Dickens, having visited the area, described it as "a slum that had metastasized.... All that is loathsome, drooping and decayed is here."

This nineteenth-century association of the urban poor with animals (swine), garbage (filthy, scum, decayed), and immoral behavior (intemperate dissolute)—as well as the reference to the "slum" as a cancer—have precise parallels in references to favelas in the second half of the twentieth century. However, in the twenty-first-century city of the global North, huge low-income housing complexes or areas of deteriorated and/or abandoned housing are more likely to be considered slums. There the similarity ends. There are no vacancies in favelas. Every space is used, and most households rent out a room or use part of the home for day care, commerce, or manufacturing. Favelas in Rio tend to spread within the urban space rather than to be concentrated in one place, and favela residents have had more leverage to escape than those living in the slums—that is, they did before the entrance of the drug traffic.

It is overly simplistic to say that the "slums" of Europe and the United States are places of last resort for those left behind (slums of despair),[24] whereas favelas are pass-through places on the way up and out. As I discuss later, this process has been complicated by the violence found in these areas, but a third of all the people I first interviewed in Rio's favelas are no longer living in favelas. I doubt that the turnover is so high in racially or ethnically defined ghettos in the United States and Europe.

Favelas have served some of the same functions that U.S. ghettos do for the poor or newly arrived—a place to live that is sufficiently undesirable to be affordable and provide a toehold in the city, with the expectation that with hard work and time, the family will move out and up. The conflation of the huge low-income housing projects and deteriorated (even abandoned) neighborhoods in cities of the industrial countries (e.g., the ghettos of New York, the *banlieu* of Paris, or the housing estates of London) with the incrementally self-constructed and constantly improved homes of extended families in favelas does a disservice to both. The problems and possibilities faced by each and the context in which they exist are profoundly different, despite their shared poverty and exclusion. Ironically, one of the major barriers to meeting MDG target 11 is the stigma of living in a space that is defined as undesirable, which the label "slum" serves to reinforce.

In my discussions about this, some have defended the word "slum" as a word of defiance. The case often cited is that of an excellent grassroots network started in Mumbai in the early 1980s and has spread to many other cities around the world. It is called SDI—Slum/Shack Dwellers International. Some colleagues argue that their embrace of "slum" in their name signals that it is not a pejorative term, but that is hardly the case. As David Satterthwaite points out, these particular "slum dwellers were negotiating and winning particular rights.... [such as] getting their settlements formally recognized by the government as a 'notified slum' which implied provision of some basic infrastructure and services, as well as certain safeguards" such as the right to be rehoused by the government if their home is demolished)."[25]

In Brazil there is no advantage to being labeled a slum, and the term itself has neither the spirit of protest that the word "ghetto" can evoke nor the reverse pride of the word "favela" as used in rap, funk, and hip-hop music.

Jacarezinho, a consolidated favela in the North Zone and large enough to comprise a census area of its own, has a higher score on the Human Development Index than some of the poorest neighborhoods. Looking at figure 1.9, one can almost feel the life force jump out of the page. Construction, reconstruction, expansion, improvement, commerce, community projects, candom-

FIGURE 1.9   Jacarezinho, a consolidated favela in the North Zone is so large it comprises its own administrative district (2007).

blé alongside Catholicism, thriving real estate markets characterize daily life there. The city is investing heavily in its upgrading, and the Bauhaus School in Germany has taken an interest in opening up a central plaza for a community center. The main problem is not the lethargy or passivity of the residents but the complicity of drug gangs, militias, and police in constraining the freedom of the residents.

FASCINATION WITH FAVELAS

When I first came to live in Rio's favelas in 1968, few if any people outside Brazil knew what they were. Today, the word "favela" is part of the lingua franca the world over. As of April 4, 2008, there were more than 2.5 million entries for "favela" on the Internet, reflecting the various myths as well as the realities of these communities. There are many references to drugs, danger, and death but also to food, fashion, and funk. Movies, television programs, MTV songs, and newspaper articles fan the flames of the phenomenon known as "favela chic."

Today, among scholars and social scientists, favelas are the most studied of all low-income communities. In *Pensando as Favelas*,[26] a Brazilian author selected 668 critically important books on favelas, most of which were published between 1980 and 2000. Over the past 9 years the production has continued to climb.

The Google Scholar search engine lists over 12,000 scholarly articles; and there are a vast number of doctoral dissertations and master's theses on favelas. Commenting on this proliferation, one scholar writes: "Social scientists themselves have served as some of the foremost intermediaries between 'favela' and 'cidade,' between the extralegal conglomerations of the squatter settlements and the institutions of political power and cultural capital in the legal metropolis."[27]

I would guess that over 90 percent of this scholarly production is derived from studies of a tiny number of Rio's favelas—those located adjacent to the most expensive areas of the city, in the South Zone. The living standards there are good, the views are great, and the close proximity to beaches, restaurants, and cultural amenities including high-speed Internet access make this handful of favelas the destination of choice for students, scholars, and tourists alike.

Needless to say, the more picturesque favelas exert the most magnetism. It is difficult to imagine tourists visiting the so-called Gaza-strip favelas of the North Zone, epicenters of police and gang warfare; the steaming-hot, mosquito-ridden favelas in the reclaimed swamps of the Fluminense Lowlands; or the distant West Zone favelas run by armed militias. There are, however, a few studies of North Zone favelas, including Jacarezinho, Tuitutí, and Acarí and at least one of Rio das Pedras in the West Zone.[28]

In 1985, when the dictatorship ended, it became apparent that the drive to eradicate the favelas was dead, as no elected government could risk alienating over one-third of the electorate. Nevertheless, efforts to remove or "contain" them have continued and as of September 2009 several were being walled off. Since then, there have been proposals to remove them due to environmental risk and concerns about public safety. The favelas persist, just as the favela bush has persisted through droughts, floods, and fires.

two

THE WORLD GOES TO THE CITY

The growth of cities will be the single largest influence on development in the twenty-first century.... Over the next 30 years, the population of African and Asian cities will double, adding 1.7 billion people—more than the current populations of the U.S. and China combined.

UN STATE OF THE WORLD POPULATION REPORT
(JUNE 27, 2007)

Virtually all of the projected population growth on the planet in the coming decades will be urban growth, will be in the cities of the "global South" (Asia, Africa and Latin America), and will be concentrated in informal settlements—the shantytowns and squatter settlements that Brazilians call favelas.[1]

The anticipated shift from a predominantly rural world to a predominantly urban one (originally predicted to coincide with the turn of the millennium) is now a reality, forcing us to rethink our most basic paradigms, not only paradigms of the urban condition but of the human condition as well. What remains unclear is whether the policy-makers and donor agencies of the world will regard the economically disadvantaged with the same degree of concern as they cross over from being rural peasants to becoming urban squatters.

The world's population has more than doubled in the last half century (2.54 billion to 6.67 billion), and almost all of this growth has been in cities. At the beginning of the nineteenth century, only 5 percent of the population lived in urban areas; at the beginning of the twentieth, this percentage was still a relatively low 13 percent; today, it is 50 percent; by 2050 it is projected to be 75 percent.[2] Think about it this way: since 1950, the world's cities have absorbed the

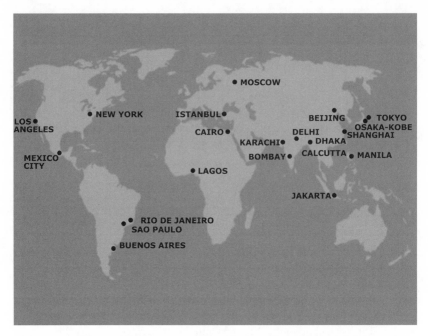

FIGURE 2.1   The world's megacities, each with ten million or more inhabitants.

equivalent population of an additional New York City every other month. This amounts to an additional 120,000 urban residents every day.

In the hundred-year span from 1950 to 2050, the population will have grown by over three and one-half times, while the urban population will have multiplied more than eight and one-half times—virtually all of it in the informal settlements of the global South.

THE FEAR AND THE FAILURE

This so-called urban explosion has been viewed as a threat to political, social, economic, and moral stability, and dire consequences have been predicted. Recently *Forbes* magazine published an article saying:

> Malthus, a British economist, famously predicted in 1798 that population growth eventually would outpace food production, resulting in mass starvation. Ever since his time, the phrase "Malthusian nightmare" has been applied to dystopian scenarios [of]...demographic doom and gloom. For the most part, these predictions...have turned out to be overly pessimistic.... Still, we are not yet free of this antiurban bias.... The spectacular growth of Third World megacities holds the depressing possibility that Malthus may turn out to be right after all.[3]

TABLE 2.1   *World Population and Urban Population in Billions*

Year	Population	Urban population	Change in urban population	Percent increase in urban population	Percent urban
1950	2.54	.74	–	–	29
1975	4.08	1.52	.78	105	37
2000	6.09	2.84	1.32	87	47
2025	8.01	4.58	2.01	71	57
2050	9.19	6.40	1.82	40	67

Almost every country has responded to urban growth by attempting to hold people on the land, redirect them to planned towns, or in some other way limit the growth of the large cities.[4] In the past 50 years, strategies to stem the flow of migrants to the megacities have included (1) rural development aimed at equalizing the standards of living in the countryside and the city; (2) diversion of the flow into new towns, new capitals, or smaller cities; (3) prohibition of new residential or commercial construction within city limits; (4) control of apartment allocation (as in Moscow); (5) the requirement of passports or identity cards for nonresidents entering the city (as in apartheid South Africa); (6) food rationing (such as rice in China); and (7) the limitation of free movement (as in Cuba).

Each of these efforts has failed, either totally or partially, and some have proven counterproductive. Rural development programs, based on the assumption that equalizing the quality of life between countryside and city would stop outmigration, had the opposite effect. The greater the investment in rural roads, electrification, industrialization, and education, the higher the rate of outmigration to cities became. This can be explained by the fact that the roads, education, work experience, and improved health made it easier to get out and harder to "keep 'em down on the farm." (This is not to imply that rural development is not useful for upgrading life in the countryside, but it is a failure as a strategy for limiting outmigration.) In the developing countries, it will take several decades before life in the countryside comes close to offering the same opportunities and amenities as life in the city. Consequently, it will be a long time before these developing nations experience the demographic shifts *away from* the big cities that are beginning to occur in Europe and the United States.

New towns or small cities designated as "growth poles" for targeted industrial and residential investments have been built with the intention of redirecting migrants away from the large cities. These "growth poles" have been successful in some highly industrial countries, but they have not taken hold in the global South. Like the resettlement schemes tried earlier in Indonesia, they have proven costly in infrastructure and are unable to compete with existing cities. The "growth pole" cities lack critical mass, economies of scale, and the dense networks of local suppliers and consumers that lower the cost of doing business in large cities.

New capitals such as Brasília have attracted migrants, but not in sufficient numbers to detract from or diminish the numbers of the migratory flow to the large, established cities. And most of the closed-city policies (such as those in India) have become embarrassments. If urban migrants could not build during the day, they built at night; if they could not live in legal housing, they invaded land; if they could not get an apartment permit, they doubled up with relatives (leading to massive underestimation of the population of Moscow for years); and if they could not obtain a rice ration, they shared with other families or became part of the vast "floating population" of Chinese cities.

Only command-and-control societies, in which policy is backed by lethal force, have even come close to keeping people out of cities, and that "success" has been of limited duration. In South Africa, the end of apartheid broke down this control. In Cuba, the revitalization of Old Havana—and the attendant infusion of tourist income—have dampened the antiurban ideology that kept potential rural migrants out of the city.

Throughout the global South, people have been voting with their feet. As Ignacy Sachs puts it, they have been taking their chances at the "urban lottery," and it seems a better bet than staying in the countryside. In fact, it is not the most destitute and helpless people from the countryside who come to the city but the best and brightest, those with the foresight and courage to change their lives. And they have done much better, even as squatters, than their counterparts who stayed back home. No matter how difficult life may be in the city, these migrants are betting that their children will have greater opportunities in the city than they would have in a fishing village or as indentured servants on someone else's land.

Some of these migrants are "pushed" off the land by starvation, subjugation, and suffering, just as others are "pulled" toward the city by the lure of opportunity. In either case, the argument that cutting off housing and social services for the poor will discourage migrants from coming to the city has proven spurious. Even as unemployment has risen, squatters have been forced to the peripheries, and violence has become the norm; people keep coming—and what they are leaving behind is worse. They are not seeking to be "freeloaders" but free agents, masters of their own destinies.

It is only in the past few years that major international development agencies have begun to accept the reality that city growth and megacities are here to stay. They will not self-destruct, and return migration at a significant scale is not in the cards. As a recent UN document concludes, "It's pointless trying to control urban growth by stopping migration. It just doesn't work."[5]

CITY GROWTH SHIFTS TO THE SOUTH

If the first major transformation marking this era is the one from a rural to an urban world, the second is the transformation from North to South: a total reversal in the locus of the world's major cities from the highly industrialized countries of the North to the developing countries of the South. In 1950, only three of the ten biggest cities in the world were in the global South—Shanghai, Buenos Aires, and Calcutta. By 1990, only three were in the North—Tokyo, New York, and Los Angeles. London, Paris, and Moscow were eclipsed in population size by Mexico City, São Paulo, and Mumbai, which, by 2000, were among the five largest cities in the world. Asian and African cities, for example Jakarta and Lagos, have been added to the ranks of the most populous.[6]

Today, three-quarters of the world's urban population resides in developing regions. Figure 2.2 shows the sizes of the 21 megacities—that is, those with 10 million or more inhabitants in the year 2000—in 1950, 1990, and 2000.

The developing regions continue to outpace the developed ones in urban growth, with an average urban growth rate of 2.7 percent (4.1 percent for the least developed regions), compared with the 0.6 percent rate of the developed regions. By midcentury, the urban population in the developing regions of the world will have doubled from 2 billion to 4 billion.

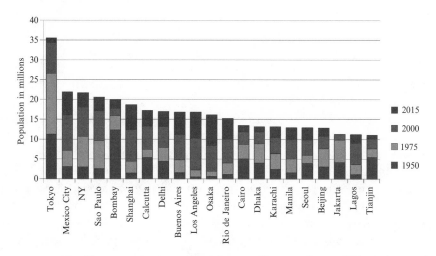

FIGURE 2.2   The 21 megacities in order of size as of 2008, indicating the population of each in 1950, 1975, and 2000—and population projections for 2025. *Source*: UN-Habitat, *State of the World's Cities* 2008/2009 and United Nations *World Urbanization Projects*, 2007 *Revision*.

THE URBANIZATION OF POVERTY

The third great transformation during this historical moment has been from the formal to the informal city.[7] Each day, the city of the elite continues to give way to the city of the masses. Yet despite this overwhelming trend the majority of all international assistance funding continues to be earmarked for rural areas. The future of the urban poor in developing cities, and perhaps of humanity itself, depends on a clearer understanding of the dynamics of poverty and new approaches to integrating the poor into the larger urban and global populations.

In the cities of the global South, informal settlements are growing much faster than the cities themselves. As of 2007, more than 30 percent of the world's urban population—1 billion people—resided in squatter settlements, and 90 percent of squatters lived in the developing world. The UN predicts that within 30 years, that figure will have doubled to 2 billion—a third of the world population. In the global South, more than one out of every four urbanites lives in an informal settlement—that is, more than one out of every seven people in the world—and four-fifths of them are in the most destitute regions of the world.[8]

Although slums have existed since the Industrial Revolution, until recently, poverty and human suffering have been most severe in rural settlements. Today, poverty is fast becoming an urban phenomenon, a trend that is unlikely to be reversed.

LATIN AMERICA IN CONTEXT

Latin America is the most highly urbanized region in the global South. With 78 percent of its population living in cities, its degree of urbanization is second in the world only to that of North America, which is 81 percent urban. The rate of urban growth in Latin America has exceeded those of North America and Europe. In 1950, less than 41 percent of Latin America's population was urban. It took just three decades to complete the urban transition that took six decades in North America.[9] The next wave of urbanization will be in Asia and Africa, which are currently 40 percent and 38 percent urban, respectively.[10] But Latin American cities will continue to grow for the foreseeable future, and the region is projected to reach 89 percent urban saturation by 2050. In other words, the rate of urban growth in Latin America will drop, but the cities themselves will continue to grow.[11]

Within Latin America, 32 percent of the population of the cities lives in squatter settlements, making it over five times more likely for a Latin American to be living informally than a person in a developed region. The problems faced by the 134 million people living in Latin America's shantytowns are similar to

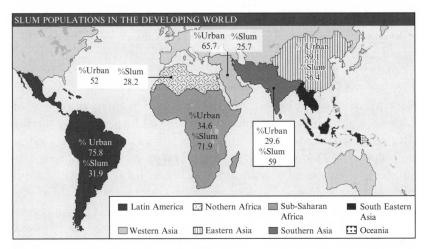

FIGURE 2.3   Map of the global south indicating the percent of the population living in cities (% urban) and the percent of the urban population living informally (% slum) for each region.

those faced by the 581 million squatters in Asia and the 199 million in Sub-Saharan Africa.[12] The map (figure 2.3) shows the percent urban by region in the developing world, along with the percent of the urban population living in shantytowns.

Although Latin America is relatively well-off when compared with absolute levels of poverty in the global South, its skewed distribution of wealth has earned it the dubious distinction of having the highest level of inequality of any region in the world.[13] In the world's high-income nations, the average income of the richest 20 percent (quintile) is about six times higher than the poorest quintile. In Latin America, the richest quintile earns 12 times more than the poorest.[14]

BRAZIL IN CONTEXT

Brazil, long-called "the sleeping giant," is now awake and positioned to become one of the world's superpowers.[15] Its 2009 population of 198.7 million inhabitants make it the fifth-largest country in the world, and it is one of the most highly urbanized. Over 85 percent of Brazilians are living in cities, a figure expected to rise to 90 percent over the next twenty years (surpassing the 86.8 percent projected for the United States at that time). With approximately one-third of the city population living in favelas and other types of informal settlements, it is clear that urban poverty will become one of the most salient social, economic, and political issues the country will face.

As the Brazilian social entrepreneur Ricardo Neves has written, "No other country of comparable size managed, in only two generations, to go from a rural country to an urban one."[16] In the four decades loosely corresponding to the period of my favela research (1960 and 2000) Brazilian cities absorbed 108 million new residents, most of them poor. Before the World War II, only 15 percent of Brazilians lived in cities; by 1975, it was 62 percent; and by the turn of the century, it was 81 percent. By the time I had completed the first favela study three out of five Brazilians living in the countryside had pulled up stakes and migrated to a city, most often a big city. These are people similar to the ones I followed over the past four decades, people who ended up in squatter settlements for lack of other options once they arrived in the cities.

Contrary to popular image, poverty in Brazil is not primarily rural poverty. Over three quarters (78 percent) of poor people live in cities, not in the countryside. This percentage of poor people in Brazil puts it on par with countries like Nepal and Bangladesh, which have only one-third of Brazil's per capita income. How can that be?

Brazil's economy is the tenth largest in the world. Its GDP (gross domestic product) in 2009 is US$1.99 trillion—and it has been growing and withstanding the global recession relatively well. In 2007, Brazil's economy grew by an average of 5.3 percent; in 2008, by an average of 6.3 percent. New offshore oil reserves found in 2009 in the waters off the state of Rio could make the country the seventh-largest oil producer in the world. In short, there is more than enough wealth to alleviate urban and rural poverty if that wealth were more equally distributed.

But Brazil has one of the highest inequality levels in the world, and is the most unequal among countries of its size. Several small countries in Latin America, such as Haiti and Paraguay, and in Africa, such as Sierra Leone, Namibia, and Botswana—have greater inequality, but they are not in the same league economically or politically as Brazil.[17] However, there are signs that this is beginning to improve. Over the past five or six years, the inequality index for Brazil has been declining. This is due in part to the effects of the wide-reaching Conditional Cash Transfer (CCT) Program, Bolsa Família, which provides stipends to poor families on the condition that they invest in the health and education of their children. I discuss this further in chapter 11.

Sonia Rocha, a Brazilian expert on poverty and inequality shows that the per capita income of the poorest half of the Brazilian population rose by 14 percent in 2004, an increase of four times the national average and has continued to improve. Her analysis reveals a change from the 1990s when the richest fifth (quintile) of the nation's population earned 30 times more than the poorest fifth, to 2007 when the ratio dropped to 20 times more—nothing to brag about, but an undeniable improvement. Still, half of the country's total income is in the hands of the top 10 percent and of that half, 85 percent is concentrated in the top 5 percent.[18]

The consequences of this high degree of inequality and of the coexistence of so much wealth and so much poverty are sharply illustrated in the landscape of Brazilian cities. Rio de Janeiro is an ideal laboratory in which to observe how these dynamics play out at the local level.

RIO DE JANEIRO IN CONTEXT

In January (*Janeiro*) of 1502, Portuguese navigators, mistaking the entrance of Guanabara Bay for the mouth of a river (*rio*), gave the city of Rio de Janeiro its name. Two hundred and sixty-one years later, in 1763, Rio de Janeiro became the capital of colonial Brazil supplanting Salvador da Bahia. After independence,

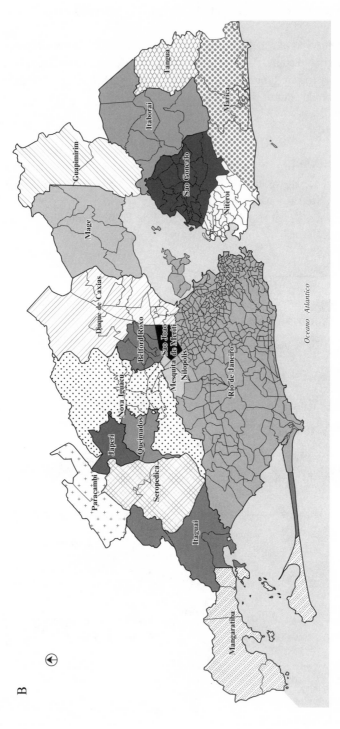

B

FIGURE 2.4   A and B. Maps showing the location of Rio de Janeiro state within Brazil and the city (municipality) of Rio de Janeiro within the state.

in 1822, and the declaration of the republic in 1889, Rio continued to serve as the national capital. In 1960, under the administration of Juscelino Kubitschek, the capital was moved to Brasília, the geographic center of the country, in an effort to develop the interior and redistribute the nation's population (95 percent of whom lived within five miles of the coast). The territory belonging to the former Federal District was converted into the state of Guanabara, with Rio as the state capital. Niteroi, on the other side of the bay, was the capital of the much larger, poorer, and more rural state of Rio de Janeiro. In March 1975, despite strong opposition that continues to this day, the two states—Guanabara and Rio—were fused to form the new state of Rio de Janeiro with the city of Rio as its capital.

Currently, the population of the state of Rio de Janeiro is 15.6 million. Rio's metropolitan region accounts for 75 percent of the state's population, of which 6 million live within the municipality. This earns Rio the rank of third largest of the four megacities of Latin America (smaller than Mexico City and São Paulo but larger than Buenos Aires) and fourteenth largest of the 19 megacities in the world.

Unlike most Latin American countries, which follow a primate city pattern (that is, the single largest city in the country has more than twice the population of the next largest), Brazil has nine large metropolitan regions.

Among the nine, Rio de Janeiro has consistently been the first to indicate a national trend. It led the rapid urban growth in the post–World War II period, with growth rates of 42 percent in the 1950s and 29 percent in the 1960s. It then led the gradual decline in growth rates through the 1970s to the present. As shown in table 2.2, Rio's population nearly quadrupled in the second half

TABLE 2.2   *Population of Brazil's Metropolitan Regions in 1950 and 2000 with Estimates for 2007 (regions ranked by size in 2000)*

	Population in 1950 (thousands)	Population in 2000 (thousands)	Rate of increase (1950-2000)	Population estimate for 2007 (thousands)	Estimated rate of increase (2000-2007)
Sao Paulo	2,334	17,099	7.33	19,226	1.12
Rio de Janeiro	2,950	10,803	3.66	11,381	1.05
Belo Horizonte	412	4,659	11.31	4,925	1.06
Porto Alegre	488	3,505	7.18	3,897	1.11
Recife	661	3,230	4.89	3,655	1.13
Salvador	403	2,968	7.36	3,599	1.21
Fortaleza	264	2,875	10.89	3,437	1.20
Brasília	36	2,746	76.28	3,508	1.28
Curitiba	158	2,494	15.78	3,125	1.25

on the twentieth century, from 2.95 million to 10.8 million—but that was the lowest overall growth rate of any metropolitan region in the country.

Rio has suffered severe job loss due to deindustrialization; the move of the national capital (and its related jobs) to Brasília; and the move of business, commercial, cultural, and intellectual centrality to São Paulo. It also suffered a decline in tourism due to fear of violence starting in the mid 1980s.

Unemployment increased for the urban poor in particular. The proliferation of take-out food, washing machines, dishwashers, and laundries, along with new labor laws guaranteeing a minimum wage to domestic employees (plus the full package of labor benefits), sharply reduced the demand for live-in or full-time maids. This means that women who worked for one family (and often stayed during the week, with their children, who went to school in that neighborhood) are now are working one day or two for that family and need to find three or four other jobs to make up the difference. Likewise, with the consolidation of the center and the North and South zones, the number of construction jobs has dropped.

Yet Rio has managed to remain one of Brazil's major economic centers, second only to São Paulo in per capita GDP. The degree of upward mobility of Rio's urban poor, however, is constrained by its legacy of inequality, its declining employment potential, and its lagging economic growth rates. According to calculations by Valéria Pero, Rio has the lowest rates of social mobility among all the metropolitan regions of Brazil.[19]

THE FAVELAS OF RIO

Rio de Janeiro has the largest favela population of any Brazilian city, accounting for one-fourth of the favela population in the entire country. Table 2.3 shows how Rio compares with the other major metropolitan areas.

TABLE 2.3   *Favelas in Brazil's Cities*

City	Favela pop.	Total pop.	%	Total dwellings
Rio de Janeiro	1,092,476	5,857,904	18.7	308,581
Sao Paulo	909,628	10,434,252	8.7	229,155
Belo Horizonte	268,847	2,238,526	12.0	67,441
Salvador	238,342	2,443,107	9.8	61,322
Curitiba	145,242	1,587,315	9.2	37,752
Porto Alegre	143,353	1,360,590	10.5	37,665
Recife	134,790	1,422,905	9.5	34,674
Fortaleza	353,925	2,141,402	16.5	83,203
Belém	448,723	1,280,614	35.0	100,069

Rio has over 1000 favelas and the largest favela population of all Brazilian cities.
Sources: IBGE 2000, IPP 2008–09

São Paulo, the only Brazilian city larger than Rio, has a smaller favela population and a lower percentage of its population living in favelas (9 percent as compared with 19 percent). [20] The only metropolitan area with a higher percent living in favelas is Belém de Para, at 35 percent. In the calculations for Rio, which include loteamentos and conjuntos as favelas, the portion rises to 37 percent.

Despite three decades of public policy efforts in Rio—first to eradicate favelas and then to upgrade and integrate them into their surrounding neighborhoods—both the number of favelas and the number of people living in favelas has continued to grow.

The four maps in figure 2.5 show the spread of favelas over the landscape of Rio in 1940, 1960, 1990, and 2008. These maps drawn from aerial photographs, show favela's growth from tiny dots into large blotches. They have merged with one another across adjacent hills into vast, contiguous agglomerations or *complexos*, each composed of multiple favela communities. Any one of these complexos is the size of a large Brazilian city. The four largest—Rocinha, Jacarezinho, the Complexo do Alemão, and the Complexo da Maré—have a combined population of over half a million residents.

The other major change visible in the time sequence of the four maps is the spread of favelas outward from the South Zone (1940s), to the North Zone (1960s) and the West Zone (1990)—following the growth of the city and the location of jobs.

The 2004 maps below show the enormous increase in favela growth since 1990, and the simultaneous proliferation of irregular or clandestine loteamentos. Both of these maps are topographical and illustrate the tendency for favelas to be located around hillsides and for loteamentos to be on flat terrain—particularly concentrated in the West Zone.

Growth rates of favelas have exceeded that of the general population of Rio de Janeiro for every decade except the 1970s, when more than 100,000 favela residents were evicted and 62 favelas were demolished in the three years from 1970–73. [21] As seen in table 2.4 below, the highest growth rates were immediately after World War II, when urban in-migration took off, and in the 1960s, when my initial study was conducted. During the period 1980–90, the city's overall growth rate of Rio dropped from 20 percent to below 8 percent, while the favela populations surged from 11 percent to over 40 percent. During the last decade of the twentieth century, the city's overall growth rate leveled off at just below 7 percent, while the favela population grew by 24 percent.

Looking at the second half of the twentieth century as a whole, the city of Rio grew by 2.5 percent, and the favelas of Rio grew by 6.5 percent. In other words, the favela growth rate was almost two and half times that of the city as a whole. Still, these comparisons are weakened by the fact that favela growth is part of the growth of the city as a whole. The full difference can only be

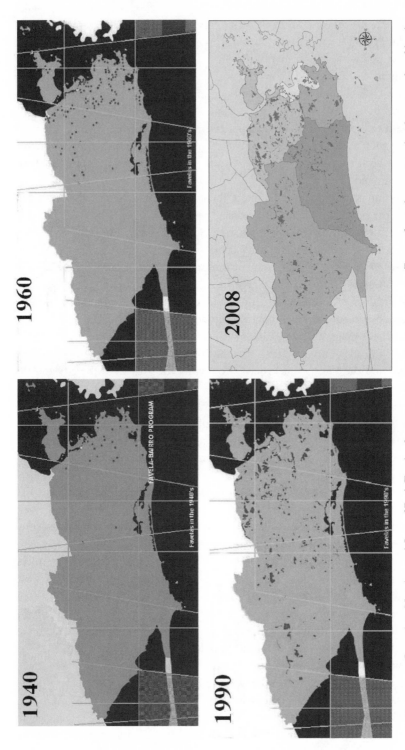

FIGURE 2.5 Growth in Number and Size of Rio's Favelas from 1940 to 1960 to 1990 to 2008. (Image from the municipal archives, produced by the planning and research department, Pro-Urb)

TABLE 2.4   *Favelas Grow Faster than City of Rio*

Year	Population of favelas (a)	Total population of Rio (b)	a/b (%)	Favela growth rate by decade (%)	Rio growth rate by decade (%)
1950	169,305	2,337,451	7.24	–	–
1950-60	337,412	3,307,163	10.20	99.3	41.5
1960-70	563,970	4,251,918	13.26	67.1	28.6
1970-80	628,170	5,093,232	12.33	11.4	19.8
1980-90	882,483	5,480,778	16.10	40.5	7.6
1990-2000	1,092,958	5,857,879	18.66	23.9	6.9

From 2000-2005 favelas grew six times more than nonfavelas.

Source: IBGE (Brazilian Institute of Geography and Statistics), 2000, IPP (2008–09)

appreciated when the comparison is between favelas and nonfavelas. For the last decade of the twentieth century, the favela growth rate was 2.4 percent while the nonfavela growth rate was merely 0.38 percent.

This divergence is visually depicted in figure 2.6, which compares the growth of the favela and nonfavela population of Rio over 50 years. Taking 1950 as a baseline, the graph shows the increasing divergence between the two groups, particularly in the last decade, when the rest of the city barely grew at all, while favela growth accelerated.

This growth rate of favelas did not occur evenly across the space of the city. Favela growth started where the city started and grew upward and outward as the city grew. As discussed in chapter 1, the first settlements, such as the Morro de Providência, were in the center; the next wave followed the city's residential expansion into the South Zone (the site of Catacumba), and not long thereafter, favelas followed the industrialization in the North Zone (the site of Nova Brasília) and in the Baixada Fluminense (the site of Vila Operária and the other Caxias favelas). Starting in the 1980s, Rio's newly wealthy expanded along the coast into the Barra de Tijuca (sometimes called "little Miami" for its style of architecture and land use). This move created a huge demand for labor in construction, maintenance, and domestic services in the West Zone. As seen in table 2.5, the result was a historic expansion of the favela population in the West Zone starting in the 1980s, and paralleled by the new clandestine and irregular loteamentos.

So many migrants were arriving from the Northeast that a business developed in nonstop buses from the state of Paraíba directly to the Cidade de Deus in Jacarepaguá, a convenient access point to the entire West Zone. The starting-from-scratch atmosphere in the West Zone favelas today is reminiscent of what it was like in the favelas I lived in at the end of the 1960s.

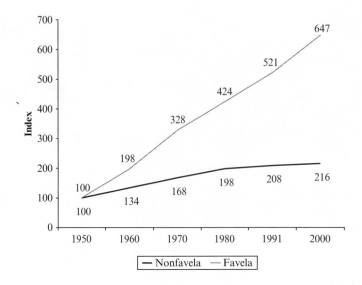

FIGURE 2.6   Favela and Nonfavela Growth in Rio de Janeiro, 1960–2000. Population
Index 1950 = 100
Source: Instituto Pereira Passos–Rio de Janeiro (2008–09)

TABLE 2.5

Zones	1950	1960	1970	1980	1991	2000
South + Center (old wealth)	58%	42%	34%	29%	24%	20%
North (working + low/middle class)	38%	54%	60%	58%	54%	50%
Southwest (new rich/ upper middle)			1%	4%	8%	13%
West /periphery (new poor)	4%	4%	5%	9%	13%	16%
Total	100%	100%	100%	100%	100%	100%

Source: Instituto Pereira Passos–Rio de Janeiro (2008–09)

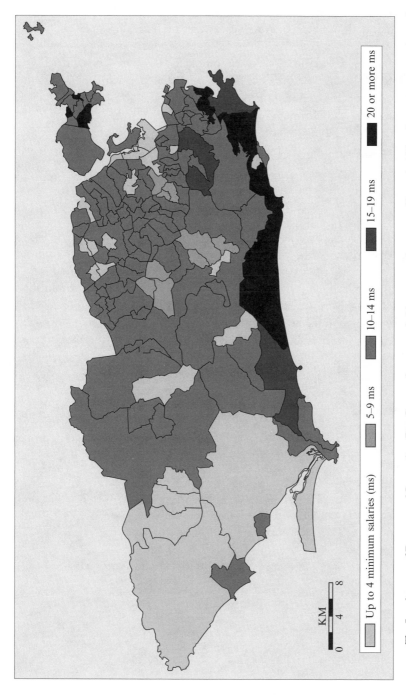

FIGURE 2.7   The Landscapes of Poverty and Inequality. Rio Census Areas—coded by average incomes of household heads in minimum salaries (ms).
Source: Instituto Pereira Passos—Rio de Janeiro

KM

Up to 4 minimum salaries (ms)   5–9 ms   10–14 ms   15–19 ms   20 or more ms

During the same 12-year period from 1980–1992, for example, when 109 new favelas arose in the West Zone, only a single new favela arose in the South Zone and only three in the North Zone. The 21 percent and 14 percent favela population growth rates in the South and North zones, respectively, were due to consolidation (verticalization, densification, and commodification of the existing favelas)—just the opposite of the sprawl of the new settlements in the West Zone.[22] The density in Rio city is high, at 4.7 inhabitants per square kilometer, but density in the favelas is several orders of magnitude higher, at 31.7 per square kilometer, and in the South Zone the favela density is higher still, going up to 100,000 per square kilometer (the density of Catacumba in its heyday).

THE GEOGRAPHY OF POVERTY

The landscape of inequality is shown on the municipal map in figure 2.7, showing the average income of the heads of household in each census region. Appreciating the inequality between the monthly earnings of favela and nonfavela residents is fundamental to understanding the position of favelas within the larger city. The size of the earnings gap depends on the zone. The differential ranges from a high in the South Zone, where average monthly earnings outside of favelas is 5.6 times that in favelas, to a low in the West Zone, the poorest area of the city, where the average nonfavela earnings are one and a half times the average earnings in neighboring favelas (as shown in table 2.5).

These differences reinforce the choice of our three study communities as three distinct areas for comparison.

DEFINITIONS AND DATA: A DISCLAIMER

Despite the official-sounding sources of the facts and figures I have presented above and the truth of the trends they reflect, the actual figures are somewhat suspect. Population numbers in this part of the world are reported variously—

TABLE 2.5   *Comparison of Monthly Earnings (in reais) for Favelas and Nonfavelas, by Zone*

Area of residence	Favela	Nonfavela	Total average	Diff.(%)
South Zone	437	2,476	2,173	566.6
North Zone	361	1,284	1,179	355.7
Near suburb	382	880	694	230.4
Distant suburb	363	728	655	200.6
Jacarepaguá	391	896	806	229.2
West Zone	368	564	542	153.3

Complied by Valéria Pero from the 2000 Census.

sometimes widely so. As an example of the magnitude of difference, in 2005, various sources report Rio's favela population at anywhere from just over a million to 4 million. How can the discrepancies be so great?

The first answer is that the definition of what constitutes a favela is not consistent across agencies or studies. The Brazilian Institute of Geography and Statistics, the Brazilian census bureau, for example, states: "A favela is a settlement of 50 housing units or more located on public or private property and characterized by disordered occupation without the benefit of essential public services."[23]

Definitions of this type are problematic for many reasons. (1) There are many "settlements of 50 or more shacks" that have gone unnoticed by the authorities, either because they are adjacent to another favela, between two conjuntos (e.g., the favela Piquirí between Guaporé and Quitungo, which was already huge and thriving before it was detected), or in a particularly remote area. (2) "Located on public or private property" is meaningless, since all housing is on public or private property, and this definition doesn't specify whether the land is being occupied legally or illegally. (3) "Characterized by disordered occupation" only applies to some favelas, while others such as Favela Central, one of our study sites in Caxias, comprise extremely orderly vilas—classic workers' housing on both sides of a narrow passageway with utilities and drainage running down the center of it. (4) As for "without the benefit of public services," anyone who has seen Rio's favelas knows that most older favelas are fully serviced, whether as a result of the Favela-Bairro urban upgrading program or the hard work of their residents.

The second reason for the unreliability of population figures is that there are several categories of informal housing that are not considered part of the asfalto, but are also not morros, or favelas. One example is the loteamentos clandestinos (illegal or quasi-legal subdivisions), which have become increasingly prevalent as the lands occupying the hillsides have become fully occupied and inroads have been made into periurban grazing and agricultural lands—typically by the fraudulent "developers" who sell off worthless parcels without services to poor families, leaving them stranded with no recourse. There are no reliable records of how many such loteamentos there are at present, where they are, or how many households or people are living in each.

Conjuntos (conjuntos habitacionais, called "popular housing" or "social housing") are another example. They are dense, dreary, undifferentiated five-story walk-ups, poorly constructed due to the pocketing of funds, and poorly maintained due to the government's lack of interest. They are legal but full of poor people; in limbo neither asfalto nor morro, fall into a void between the formal and the informal city. The incidents of fatal violence there are as high as in the favelas, and government census takers like the police, think twice before entering.

Some apartments in the conjuntos are occupied by large families or multiple families who sleep in rotating shifts. Others are rented out. Some have been sold and resold many times with no official registry, and some have been abandoned when the occupants could neither sell nor rent and could no longer remain. There are high turnover rates in some of the *blocos* (apartment buildings) and a kind of "floating population" that includes individuals who are constantly appearing and disappearing—hiding from the law or from the rival drug gang—making it extremely difficult to obtain reliable population figures.

Beyond those definitional difficulties, there are other challenges to obtaining accurate figures on favela populations and numbers of households. These include:

- *Boundaries*—where does any given favela begin and end? How many separate favelas are in each complexo? What constitutes a new favela as opposed to an expansion of an existing one?
- *Households*—how does one properly count extended family compounds with a shared entrance leading to separate units above, behind, or beside the main house, or to cottages in the back, or rental units?
- *Street names and house numbers*—these generally do not exist, and attempts to institute them have been consistently disrupted by the traffickers, who want to make it as difficult as possible for the police to find them.
- *Physical difficulty*—it is tricky to reach the highest, most remote areas, which also tend to be the most dangerous. Census takers tend to avoid them.

Those problems have always existed. What has complicated the process in the past 20 years is the fear factor on both sides:

- Census takers are seen as government agents and treated with suspicion and noncooperation.
- To be able to enter the community, they need authorization from the controlling drug faction, and usually the head of the residents' association as well.
- Cooperation and communication are imperfect, so the order of protection may not be honored by all or may not reach all the drug traffic soldiers.
- Interviewers are fearful of getting caught in crossfire or coming by accident upon a *boca* (drug sales point).
- Many favela residents prefer to remain "below the radar"—whether they are hiding out, conducting "business," keeping a mistress, or supporting a second family.

With these myriad challenges, it is a clear that all figures must be taken with a certain degree of skepticism. Probably the most reliable data come from communities such as the Complexo do Maré, where the Observatorio das Favelas is located and where a complete household census is self-conducted by local residents as a planning and program development tool.[24]

The statistics most often used are those of UN-Habitat, which are based on 2000 census data gathered by the Brazilian Institute of Geography and Statistics; these show 19 percent of Rio's population living in favelas, 12 percent in conjuntos, and 6 percent in loteamentos—adding up to 37 percent of the city's total population living informally. We can take this as a broad estimate but for all the reasons I have discussed, I would not count on it.

What I endeavor to do in the chapters that follow is to go behind and beyond dry statistics and explore/uncover the living complexity of people, places, and processes that get lost in the broad generalizations.

three

CATACUMBA

THE FAVELA THAT WAS

This chapter and the two that follow tell the stories of the three communities included in this study. While no three favelas could ever represent all of Rio's diverse communities, the three I chose were as different as possible—in terms of location, settlement pattern, and history—as could be found at the time of the original study. These communities provide the context in which their inhabitants took action for improvements, were subject to abuse from government policies, and creatively reinvented their lives and livelihoods on a daily basis.

Among the three communities I studied, Catacumba was the hardest to revisit. The dynamic beehive of 10,000 people, the vibrant street-side commerce, the dozens of associations and organizations that were Catacumba, were no longer there (see figures 3.1 and 3.2). The 2,200 dwellings had been demolished in 1970 and their residents relocated variously around the city. Even those families who had lived there before it was a favela were not spared.

Eighty percent of Catacumba's residents had been relocated to the conjuntos of Guaporé and Quitungo. I had kept in touch with Margarida, the woman in whose home I had lived, so I had a place to start. She and her family were living in a one-bedroom apartment in Quitungo. Margarida was wary of meeting me. The situation was very tense. The drug traffickers who controlled Quitungo

FIGURE 3.1 Catacumba, 1968—a thriving community rising above the Lagoa Rodrigo Freitas.

FIGURE 3.2 Former site of Catacumba, 2008—a little-used park and million dollar condos.

were constantly on the lookout for nonresidents entering the area, fearing they were police agents or spies from the opposing faction. Margarida wanted to see me but was terrified to be seen seeing me, and she had health problems that made it difficult for her to leave her apartment and meet elsewhere.

Fortunately I had a backup. Several years before this, I had unexpectedly found my friend, Jacobi, a former Catacumba leader. Our paths had crossed one enchanted evening during a formal reception at the ornate Guanabara Palace, the former British Embassy. The occasion was the 1992 Earth Summit marking the twentieth anniversary of the founding of the UN Environmental Program. Heads of state, ministers, and mayors mingled with business leaders, celebrities, and activists from around the world, filling the reception rooms and spilling out onto the verandas. The band was playing bossa nova, samba, and classic old-time favorites; cocktails and finger foods were passed around on engraved silver platters by dark-skinned men in tuxedos who did not make eye contact with the guests, and photo ops were being captured by an unobtrusive photographer.

Toward the end of the evening, having just taken a picture of me between the arch enemies Governor Leonel Brizola and Mayor Marcelo Alencar, the photographer came up to me and asked if I was the same Janice who had lived in the favela of Catacumba. When I looked more closely, I recognized Jacobi, whom I had not seen in twenty years. He had been a freelance photojournalist at the time we met and was now the official photographer for the city of Rio. We kept in touch after that, and he was the next person I looked for when I came back in 1999 to start the follow-up research.

FIGURE 3.3 Washing linens and clothing on the banks of the Lagoa, in front of Catacumba, 1968.

FIGURE 3.4A Jacobi in the Rio municipal government office where he works, 2005.

FIGURE 3.4B Jacobi during an interview with me in the backyard of his house in Jacarepuguá, 2005.

THE ORIGINS OF CATACUMBA

The favela of Catacumba occupied a series of steep hillsides along the Avenida Epitácio Pessoa, which encircles the fresh-water lagoon, the Lagoa Rodrigo Freitas. It is a short walk from Copacabana, Ipanema, and Lagoa, and it is easily accessible from the city center and port area. It is on the main road that connects the South Zone to the North Zone and to the rest of the city via the Túnel Rebouças, which was opened in 1967. The convenient location, stunning views, and high land value put Catacumba high on the list for favela removal.

History tells us that in the late 1800s, the Baroness of the Lagoa Rodrigo Freitas leased the land, known as the "Chácara das Catacumbas," from a federal company and, upon her death, graciously bequeathed it to her servants. When the lease expired in 1925, the federal company reclaimed the land, expelled the residents, and started dividing it into lots for sale. Property owners of adjoining parcels immediately filed claims and began litigation to prevent this subdivision. The continuing tangle of competing title claims kept the hillside vacant and provided an ideal spot for newly arrived migrants seeking a place to settle. The issue of title was not resolved until the federal government gave the land rights to the state government in the early 1970s for the creation of a park.

In the early 1940s, as World War II was roaring through North Africa, Europe, and Asia, migrants from the countryside, particularly the neighboring state of Minas Gerais, came to Rio in search of work, food, and shelter. They built makeshift housing on those hills above the Lagoa Rodrigo Freitas and began creating the favela that would become known as Catacumba.

Tio Souza, an early settler in the area, told me that, to prevent land invasions, municipal guards patrolled the area every day so the migrants built their barracos at night.

Tio Souza had arrived in Catacumba in 1947 from the Vila de São Jose do Rio Preto, an agricultural area in Petropolis (in the state of Rio). Both of his parents were illiterate, and, among their six children, only Tio Souza and his elder brother learned to read and write. His father died when he was 10, and his mother died six years later. Orphaned at 16, he left the fazenda where he and his father had worked and jumped a train bound for Rio de Janeiro. Failing to locate his elder siblings, who had been killed working on a construction site, he found himself a place in Catacumba. As he remembers it, the favela had been growing rapidly, but there was still plenty of free land on which to build new shacks.

He vividly recalls that the guards found *namoradas* (girlfriends) in the community and "more than one ended up helping with the construction of the homes." Once a minimal structure was in place, the family occupied it immediately. The law stated that removal of families had to be accompanied by an *oferta de moradia nova para a familia* (the offer of a new residence for the family). This helps explain why migrants were frequently met by city authorities at bus and train stations and given return tickets before they could get a toehold on the city's hillsides. It also explains why the settlers were not so easily evicted.

In 1952, a second migratory wave came to settle in Catacumba, this time mostly people fleeing the droughts in the Northeast. The construction of the Bahia-to-Rio road made it possible for many to make this journey who would otherwise been unable to do so. There was no running water and no electricity in Catacumba, but jobs were plentiful. Catacumba's location provided opportunities for domestic employment, construction and a plethora of odd jobs.

In 1954, the city public works department installed several water spigots and collective wash basins in Catacumba. This was part of the *bico d'agua* (water-spout) approach that has come to symbolize the palliative and paternalistic gestures of that period. But for the women in the favelas, it made life much easier. I remember the long lines of women each morning and evening at the water standpipes waiting to fill up their five-gallon square tin cans and the frustratingly slow trickle of water that came out of the spigot when it was not cut off completely. Sometimes the young girls would fill two buckets and carry each of them on the ends of a pole across their shoulders as they wound their ways up the narrow alleys under and around the houses to reach the shacks higher on the hillside. Figure 3.3 shows a Catacuma resident earning income by washing (and drying) linens and clothes for the wealthy families living nearby, while keeping an eye on her young children.

THE STORY OF JACOBI

Jacobi was born in Catacumba on April 2, 1933. He was a middle child, born between two older and two younger sisters. His father, Elias, had immigrated to Brazil from Damascus in the late 1920s. Elias was a *barateiro* (merchant) who sold clothing, shoes, and sewing materials; and loaned money. Early on, when the South Zone was still deserted and residential and commercial activities were concentrated in the old city center and port area, Elias purchased land in Copacabana and Ipanema.

Instead of building his house "on the sand" along the beach front, he wanted to build it high up on the Morro de Catacumba. He loved the view of the ocean and the lagoon, the refreshing sea breeze, and the expansive space. So, he sold his land in Ipanema (which, today, has one of the highest costs per square meter in the world) and bought a large parcel in Catacumba.

At that time, in the early 1930s, Catacumba was not a favela. Elias was one of four landowners there. He grew vegetables, which he traded for goats, turkeys, and chickens, and took his son with him on foot or horseback as he traveled to the emerging commercial areas of Copacabana, Ipanema, and Humaitá.

Rio was the capital of the republic, so there was plenty of work to be had and services to be performed. As Jacobi put it, "rural areas had nothing, so people started coming to the city....Only the old people stayed behind." The early settlers of Catacumba built their homes starting at the top and moving downward over the hillside toward the main road, the exact opposite of how settlement proceeded later on.

Jacobi's mother, Raimunda, was from Valencia, a town in Minas Gerais that shares a border with the state of Rio. When a tuberculosis epidemic erupted in Catacumba during the early 1940s, those infected were required to go to the clinic in Copacabana every six hours for shots and had to lie down and rest in between inoculations. There was no place for them to rest in Copacabana, so they had to return and climb back up the hill to Catacumba each time. Raimunda saw how the exertion of going and coming exhausted her sick neighbors, so she learned to administer the injections herself, which she did free of charge for all who needed it.

Jacobi's father lost all of his assets during World War II. In 1939, he was taken from his home and put in a jail in the city center because the government considered him a Jew.[1] According to Jacobi, Olga the wife of Luis Carlos Prestes (the famous communist leader of Brazil who was known as the Knight of Hope similarly "disappeared"—probably to a concentration camp or to her death.[2] In 1942, when President Getútio Vargas joined the United States and the Allied powers, Jacobi's father was set free. By then he had lost everything he had amassed over his twenty years of hard work—including his store in Ipanema. His house remained, thanks to the canny politicians who were already promising to protect the community from removal in return for votes.

Jacobi's mother went to work washing clothes, and she taught Jacobi how to give the tuberculosis injections. He loved to read and wanted to stay in school, but the family needed money so he left school at 14 and started working repairing radios. As Jacobi relates it, he was always picking up newspapers and magazines from the trash at work and reading whatever he could find. He became particularly enthralled with photography publications.

Determined to buy a camera, he made money by persuading people to allow him to borrow photos they had in their homes. He would take these photos to an artist in Praça Tiradentes, who would use them to create tinted drawings that made the subject appear well dressed, prosperous, and happy. Jacobi then returned the borrowed photos and sold the painted portraits to the subjects, eventually making enough money to buy a camera. He set up a dark room in his house and tried to sell his own photos. He said "it was difficult, though, and there wasn't much profit in it."

About that time, a man from the magazine *Rádio Nacional* admired Jacobi's work and hired him to take photos for the publication, some of which ended up on the cover. People liked his photos because they were candid and spontaneous rather than posed. He was charming, talented, and intelligent. The music stars he met through his work became his friends and occasionally came to the favela to perform for free.

CATACUMBA BEGINS TO THRIVE

By the early 1960s Catacumba was densely settled from the roadside up to the steep rock outcropping above. Newcomers built all around Jacobi's father's land, but they respected his boundaries. What looked like an undifferentiated maze to the outsider was highly organized and divided into about eight distinct areas, with names like Marinhão and Café Globo, each with its own personality and identity.

At that time, water was only available at the spigots along the main road, and electricity was filched from the electric lines. The city refused to collect garbage, as favelas were not considered part of the city.

The original settlement pattern had been reversed from the earlier period and the new social stratification was based on vertical stratification. The houses at the bottom, along the Avenida Epitacio Pessoa, were the best—they were made of permanent building materials and had access to urban services which did not reach the top of the hill. The houses highest up the hillside had been using kerosene lamps (causing many fires in the dry wooden shacks), and further down, people had been illegally tapping into the electrical wires on their own, causing more than a few accidents.

Some of the leaders formed a "Comisão de Luz" (Light Commission) which siphoned off electricity from the main lines running along the street into a *cabine* (cabin), from which it was distributed to individual houses. The residents were charged a flat monthly fee for each outlet, which meant that they were paying more than their rich neighbors, whose use was metered. Years later, the private electric company, named "Light," realized what a promising market the favelas represented and increased their profits by 30 percent by adding favela residents as clients for their services.

Physical deprivations were offset by a rich community life of social organizations, community activities, and friendship networks. There were soccer leagues, such as the Aliança Futebol Clube, and an active youth athletic club, the Juventude AC, which organized dances and other social activities. Two friends, Hélio Grande and Tio Souza, ran the Juventude AC and—as of 2008—they continue to be active in their respective communities organizing youth soccer leagues for girls as well as boys.

There was a samba school in Praia do Pinto, the favela directly across the lagoon, in which many Catacumba residents participated—creating songs, dances, and costumes each year for Carnival. People also recall special occasions such as the Day of the Kings parade on January 6 and picnic expeditions to the

FIGURE 3.5   Tio Souza on my left and Hélio Grande on my right—at the 2002 celebration and raffle for all the study participants.

island of Paquetá on weekends. Many people from outside the favela joined the Afro-Brazilian religious ceremonies of candomblé, umbanda, and macumba. For evangelicals, there were meeting houses all over the community. The most prominent building in the community was the Assemblia de Deus (Assembly of God) freshly painted in powder blue with white trim.

CATACUMBA BECOMES FAMOUS

In 1961, *Life* sent the photojournalist Gordon Parks to shoot a photo essay on Catacumba as part of a series called "Crisis in Latin America." The editor's idea was for Parks to shoot similar communities in several countries, but Parks argued for a more in-depth approach, proposing an essay strictly on one favela in Rio. At that time, there were 205 favelas in Rio, housing a population of at least 700,000 people who had nowhere else they could afford to live.

Parks wrote to his editor arguing his case:

> During a trip to Rio several years ago, I had seen poverty at its worst in the infa-
> mous favelas. I had never forgotten those ugly slums festering like sores on the
> otherwise lovely city of Rio. I wanted to investigate this tragedy taking place just
> south of our prosperous land.

The underlying motive for the *Life* series was anxiety over the communist threat in Latin America. During the previous four decades, the population of Latin America had doubled, and the cities were seen as a breeding ground for discontent and revolt. This was the era during which President John F. Kennedy launched the Alliance for Progress, funded through the U.S. Agency for International Development. Its first project in Rio was the construction of three low-income housing projects, aptly named Vila Kennedy, Vila Aliança (Alliance), and Vila Esperança (Hope) to accommodate refugees from the removed favelas—the supposed hotbeds of communism.

Parks went to Catacumba to explore the story potential and was fascinated by a bright, energetic boy named Flavio, who seemed to know everyone and everything that was going on. He was suffering from asthma and close to starvation, working long hours to help his family. Parks later wrote a book entitled *Flavio* in which he recounts the entire story. He epitomizes one of his first moments this way:

> Fog hung over the favela....From our vantage point, [on the far] side of the lagoon...a cloud broke over the mountain of Corcovado...with sun bursting through. Then suddenly the giant concrete figure of Christ loomed up into the radiant opening, its great arms expanded over the valleys below, its massive back turned on the slopes of Catacumba. As if he had read my thoughts, [Flavio] said, "Papa says Cristo has turned his back on us here in the favela."[3]

Life ran Flavio's story on June 16, 1961, and the piece had such a strong impact that readers started sending money to the magazine to help Flavio, his family, and Catacumba. To deal with this outpouring of unsolicited contributions, *Life* set up a fund in Flavio's name.[4] According to Jacobi, there was enough money to completely urbanize Catacumba but Oca, the president of the Residents' Association and Galo, his assistant, only build cement stairs. The rest of the donated money simply disappeared.

The Brazilian press, ashamed of not having taken the lead, praised Parks for his important work. *A Manchete* (the Brazilian equivalent of *Life*), launched a photo essay series on Catacumba, contracting Jacobi to photograph the favela. This had a particular irony since Jacobi had earlier been dismissed as a freelance photographer from the *Revista do Radio* when it was discovered that he lived in a favela.

In this case, Jacobi won a prize for his work. It provided him with funds sufficient to move elsewhere, but he said, "I couldn't leave my mother, my roots, my base." The prestigious *Jornal do Brasil*, one of Rio's largest papers, hired him shortly thereafter.

A glowing letter from the Rio coordinator of the Flavio project to *Life* magazine gushed:

I wish you could come to Rio and see, hear and feel the enthusiasm and happiness in all those men, women and children who work on the project...Already the favela has 12 main alleys and several smaller ones paved with *concrete stairways that could last forever* [italics mine].The favelados themselves have been contributing all the labor by sacrificing their Sundays and holidays. The money sent by *Life*'s readers bought [all of the materials] and tools needed....We have built a community center and founded a self-help society of 400 people which holds meetings twice a week....Sargent Shriver, [director] of the Peace Corps [came to] visit Catacumba.[5]

I did not know of this story about Catacumba when I selected it in 1968, even though these events had taken place only seven years earlier. During all the time I lived there and among all of the hundreds of people I spoke with and interviewed, no one ever mentioned it. I did not learn about it until Jacobi told me about it in 2005 during one of our conversations. Parks died the next year at the age of 93, and the story came to light. The two men had a lot in common.

WHY CATACUMBA?

I was in Catacumba during the last year of its existence. I had selected it by chance among the many favelas in the South Zone. I needed an entrée and a place to live, so I had to make a connection with a resident. The small furnished apartment I had sublet on Rua Gomes Carneiro (in Arpoador, between Copacabana and Ipanema) came with a live-in maid, Margarida (known as Marga), and her two young children, Beti and Gilberto. They lived in the apartment during the week and went home on weekends to the favela of Catacumba, where Marga lived with her two children and her brother. Her husband had gone down to the local pharmacy for an aspirin one evening a few years earlier and never come back. We were the same age, and she was my teacher in many things. I was delighted when she invited me to her home one Saturday afternoon for a *feijoada* (the traditional Brazilian dish of black beans with various cuts of pork and *carne seca,* or sun dried beef).

In Catacumba, Marga introduced me to her family and friends and explained that I was a student from the United States who had spent some time in the interior of Bahia and was interested in learning what happened to people from the interior when they came to live in Rio. Everyone could relate to that, so it was decided: I became a part of the community of Catacumba and went to live in the shack where she lived (see figure 3.6).

In 1968, when I was drawing the random sample for the interviews, there were about 2,000 barracos in Catacumba, housing close to 10,000 people. It was difficult to get an exact count because so many dwellings were underneath

FIGURE 3.6   Catacumba, 1968. The unpainted wood shack with the single window almost at the top of the hillside (to left of center) is Margarida's home.

or behind others. An aerial photo was of no use, due to the steep incline; the only way to number the houses was by taking a series of photos from a boat in the middle of the lagoon and piecing them together in order to identify each house. Then the two architects who worked with us, walked up each alleyway with the map taken from those photos and added any hidden houses so we had a complete list.[6]

FIGURE 3.7   Local commerce in Catacumba along Avenida Epitacio Pessoa, 1968.

PRAIA DO PINTO: REMOVAL FORETOLD

One morning in 1969, while I was living in Catacumba, I woke up and smelled smoke. I looked out the only window of my room to see black smoke billowing across the lagoon. I could not imagine what could be burning so intensely. I dressed, put my camera into the ratty bag I used to conceal it, ran around the lagoon—and came to an inferno. The first favela ever settled in the South Zone, Praia do Pinto, was burning to the ground. No fire engines were there; children were crying for their mothers; old people were leaning on each other for support as they tried to escape the flames; and men were running back into the smoke to retrieve their families' valued possessions. (I remember seeing three men trying to haul out a refrigerator that a neighborhood woman had just completed buying after 10 years of payments.)

Military police in full battle garb, wearing helmets and carrying revolvers and night sticks, were herding dazed people, carrying whatever they had salvaged, into garbage trucks. People were screaming and crying, and the neighbors from down the street had all come out of their houses and were watching the spectacle. One woman told me she had called the fire department and was told they had orders not to respond. The two things left standing amid the rubble were an ancient, twisted tree with its leaves singed off and, just beneath it on the roadside, a bright red stop sign.

Praia do Pinto was in Leblon, the heart of the South Zone, standing on extremely desirable flat land on the Lagoa. It was surrounded by lovely, tree-lined streets of two-story homes. The city wanted the land, real estate speculators wanted the land, and no one wanted poor people living in their midst.

But the residents had resisted—they had organized. On the day originally scheduled for removal—when the military police battalions and trucks arrived—they found thousands of residents standing at the entrance to the favela: children in the front, women with babies next, all the other women and elderly behind them, and the men in back. The soldiers were not prepared for this—they barked orders over loudspeakers and told everyone they had 30 minutes to evacuate their homes and get their possessions into the trucks. No one moved. Silence. The residents held their ground. The standoff lasted for several hours in the scorching heat, until finally the police left.

It was a Pyrrhic victory. As locals tell it, the following night the police returned and set fire to the favela, burning the residents out like roaches.

As one person recalls it:

> In 1969, when they burned Praia do Pinto, they dispersed us to various places around the city. Some of us were thrown into a Parque Proletaria in Nova Holanda. We didn't belong there....We lived in much worse conditions there than we ever had in Praia do Pinto.

FIGURE 3.8   Praia do Pinto, 1969, the morning after the fire. The military police, in blue helmets, are moving people into garbage trucks with whatever possessions they have salvaged.

FIGURE 3.9   A young girl carrying her brother after their parents were killed in the fire in Praia do Pinto, 1969.

Soon, dense blocks of towering apartment buildings rose on the site: subsidized housing for the military that became known as the Selva de Pedra (Stone Jungle). The buildings stuck out hideously in an area where the tallest homes were three stories high and each had a flower garden in front. It wasn't until

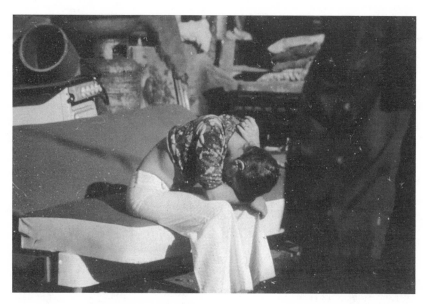

FIGURE 3.10   Total despair—all was lost.

years later, when I was teaching in the City and Regional Planning Department at the University of California, Berkeley, that I heard of a term to describe this: "aggressive architecture."

This aggression was the precursor to what happened to Catacumba a year later. Along with every building in Catacumba, those "concrete stairways built to last forever" were bulldozed to the ground less than a year after my departure.

FROM RESISTENCE TO NEGOTIATION TO COOPTATION

The residents of Catacumba lived under the constant threat of removal. In 1969, Waldevino, the president of the Catacumba Residents' Association, called SOMAC, launched a campaign against removal with a counter-proposal for urbanizing the favela. Waldevino's plan showed a series of high rise buildings on the site. They would be constructed by the residents who were skilled builders, electricians, and plumbers. His idea was to house the Catacumba residents in some of these and to rent out the rest on the open market to generate income. He went so far as to get the newspaper, *O Globo,* to publish a drawing of his plan, but no one took it seriously.

The famous architect Sergio Bernardes offered to create his own design for accommodating all of the Catacumba families on the site, with separate houses, full urban services, and small patios constructed with round cement platforms supported by large, hollow pillars. Each family was to build its own home on top of the platforms and the pillars would encase the electric, water, and sewerage connections. Avoiding the need to retrofit urban service lines to the existing settlement pattern would lower the cost of upgrading. The pillars, by holding the platforms above the ground like mushroom caps on their stems, would provide protection from flooding. Needless to say, nothing came of it.

In fact the community had no power against the removal policy, which was coordinated by a federal agency (CHISAM) created expressly to eliminate all favelas by 1976. Those located in upscale areas, such as Catacumba, were targeted first. The state government created a "Committee of Vigilance" within Catacumba to manage a household census and prevent anyone from moving in (so as to prevent them from becoming eligible for one of the conjunto apartments).

When it became clear that resistance was useless, people tried to negotiate where they would be sent, preferring areas closer to their original homes. This had little effect—they were assigned according to their reported family income, number of members in the household, and the political decision to separate the community leaders from the other residents.

As Tio Souza explained it, "community resistance to removal was no longer an option. SOMAC was too weak to fight the state. We had no choice. We could be expelled and disappeared before the removal, or accept the role of managing the process in the best possible manner for the community." Once the battle had been lost, he joined Waldevino and the other leaders in helping to facilitate the move.

Isabella, a 76-year-old woman resident, put it this way at the time of removal: "I am sure I will go crazy if I have to leave Catacumba. If we try to defend ourselves they will say we are communists. I'm not sure what that means, but I know it is very bad [*muito ruim*], and they will kill me and my children if we don't cooperate."[7]

CATACUMBA'S DEMISE

Early in the morning of October 10, 1970, in the midst of a cold rain, the military police and several large garbage trucks (note symbolism) arrived in front of Catacumba and proceeded to remove everyone and everything—and there was nothing the people could do to stop them. In the end, resistance had proven futile.

According to Jacobi, the military coup was the coup de grâce for Catacumba. The strong arm of the dictatorship accomplished what neither floods nor fires had achieved—the total destruction of his community. By pulling together and not giving up, the residents of Catacumba had rebuilt their homes after a fire in 1958; after a severe flood in 1968; and after yet another devastating fire in early 1968. This time there was no rebuilding.

Many Catacumba residents recall the day of removal as the worst day of their lives. Margarida, who was born and raised in Catacumba and was raising her children there at the time told me,

> We were given 24 hours' notice to collect all of our belongings and get them down to the curbside....No one was told where we would be going. I was trying my best to keep Beti and Gilberto dry and protect our things, but the rain soaked right through our mattress. I had been paying for that mattress for over a year in monthly installments and it was ruined.

She continued:

> It was dark when we started lining up before dawn and then everyone waited, shivering in the rain, until the "beggar collectors" [a sardonic play on the trucks which were garbage collectors] arrived to haul us and our sopping-wet belongings away.

Silvia, a single mother of four, said, "I was humiliated in front of my children. All we asked was the basic right to be treated as human beings [*ser tratado como gente*]." Some family members were separated from one another by as much as three to four hours by bus. Some were sent to the far North, others to the desolate West.

Jacobi was right. The forced removal of over 10,000 people in Catacumba and more than 102,000 in 61 other favelas between 1970–73 would have been impossible without an authoritarian state willing to back its housing policies with lethal force. Since the mayors and governors of all cities considered of national importance were appointed by the central government, the media strictly censored and opposition prohibited, decisions could be made without accountability. The 1964 creation of the BNH (Banco Nacional de Habitação—National Housing Bank) and the COHABS, the state public housing agencies, provided an institutional framework for implementing the long-desired favela eradication, with the goal of "cleaning the South Zone of human garbage."

In its 1973 report *Favelas Removidas e Respectivos Conjuntos* (Removed Favelas and Their Respective Conjuntos), CHISAM, the national agency invented to coordinate the favela removal in Rio, reported the removal of 2,207 dwellings, of which 1,420 families were sent to the adjacent conjuntos of Guaporé and Quitungo, 350 to Cidade de Deus, 87 to Vila Kennedy, and 350, too poor for apartments, were sent off to triage units in a remote area called Paciencia (see map in the Introduction). The dozens of families sent to Nova Holanda, Bras de Pina, and elsewhere were evidently not counted in CHISAM's report.

The families sent to conjuntos arrived to find unfinished apartments. The floors were raw concrete; the water did not flow, there were no internal doors, and the outside doors all opened with the same key. The families sent to the triage units found row upon row of attached one-room wooden houses in the middle of nowhere. There was no access to jobs, schools, clinics, or work. It is only fitting that the name of the place where they were left to rot was Paciencia (Patience).

In late 2001, I assembled a series of meetings in each of the communities to collectively reconstruct their history. I used a process called a DRP (Rapid Participatory Diagnosis), which gave people the chance to listen to each other and recall details they might have forgotten. Various people spoke at this meeting about what the removal had been like for them. One person recalled:

> We were in shock. We lost everything we had. The conjuntos were much worse than the favela of Catacumba. We were crowded into tiny spaces, far from jobs and everything we knew, our shopkeepers were not given anyplace to reestablish their stores, and many of us could not afford the bus fare to the city. Everything was sad and bleak and ugly.

Since Jacobi's family owned their land and home, theirs should have been a different story. As it turned out, Jacobi was working for the *Jornal do Brasil* at the time and was traveling for the three months prior to the removal, "making propaganda about the *maravilhas do Brasil*" (marvels of Brazil). He returned just as his family was being removed to Quitungo. His father had all his documents in order and showed the authorities the ownership documents for the property, but they simply ignored them. They paid no indemnity, stuck the family in the garbage truck with everyone else, and dumped them in Quitungo. Jacobi says:

> It was terrible. The government should have taken the group as a whole from Catacumba and moved us together. What they called remanejamento (remanagement) meant separating people by income, regardless of whether they were family, friends, neighbors or sweethearts. The government took people that could pay their bills and put them in the new projects—mostly Guaporé or Quitungo; those that couldn't pay were put into older projects like Cidade de Deus and favelas in Nova Holanda. People had underreported their income hoping to avoid high monthy payments, since rent for their unit was based on a percentage of their income, so they were squeezed. Some families with six or eight children were thrown into one-bedroom apartments. The leaders were separated from the others in order to prevent any community mobilization or protest.

When I returned to Rio in 1973, for the first time after the study was done, I went to Paciencia by bus—a trip of over three and a half hours—to see what it was like. I passed hundreds of acres of uncultivated lands and saw neither dwellings nor signs of commerce. What I found when we arrived was a variation on a debtors' prison, a dead end without exit. I will never forget speaking with a woman in her front door, who turned to me and asked, "Where does the end of the world end?...Where will they throw us, finally?" ("Onde é que o fim do mundo termina? Onde é que nos vão jogar por fim?").

Indeed, it did seem like *o fim do mundo*.

FIGURE 3.11 Conjunto de Quitungo Housing Project, 1973. Only three years after its construction, the housing blocks fell into ruin and the supposed green space became a muddy garbage dump.

FIGURE 3.12   Triage housing in Paciencia, 1973. One room per family in the middle of nowhere.

FIGURE 3.13   New triage units, Paciencia, 1973. Hundreds of ovenlike structures were added to accommodate all the families unable to make their monthly payments on the conjunto apartments.

The ranks of those sent to the triage housing from all of the removed fave-las were further swelled by those sent there for defaulting on their monthly payments in the conjuntos. Hundreds of additional triage units were under construction when I was there in 1973—red brick boxes with corrugated metal roofs all lined up in the dry dirt, baking in the sun.

AFTERMATH OF THE REMOVAL

Immediately after the demolition of Catacumba, every trace of human exis-tence there was razed, and the area was closed off with a high chain-link fence, on which a series of enormous billboards appeared advertising American prod-ucts hawked by blonde, blue-eyed models. Behind the ad-covered fence, weeds, grasses, and vines grew up over the hillside where the community had been. People asked me why they had been forced to leave a place that was still unused. They told me of rumors that one of the residents had gone crazy and refused to leave, hiding on the hillside and living in the woods for several years, until he disappeared.

Some say there are still a few families hiding out there.

Negrao de Lima, the governor responsible for the removal, was planning to turn the area into a monument to his achievements: the Parque de Catacumba, an outdoor sculpture garden with a trail leading up to the stunning view from the top of the hillside. On the portion of the hillside closer to the Reboucas Tunnel, several luxury high-rise condominiums with multimillion-dollar apart-ments were built.

It was during my 1973 visit that I formulated the negative picture of the conjuntos in my 1976 book. Residents said that moving there deprived them not only of the homes and the community they had built with their own hands, but of their very identities. As Margarida put it:

> We cried day after day. We didn't even know where our families and friends were. Many got sick. Some became alcoholics. Several older people died—they say it was stress or high blood pressure, but I think they died of broken hearts....We were not kept together as a community; no, it was a mixture of people from other favelas—we didn't know each other—we didn't trust each other....We lost our identity. We lost who we were within our communities. We were nobodies.

What a difference three decades make. My interviews from 2001 through 2009 reveal a more mixed view of the removal. Had I ended my study three years after the removal, rather than 30 years, I would have missed the long-term outcomes, which tell a different story.

In 2001, our research team convened former Catacumba residents to partici-pate in a collective process to reconstruct the history of the community. Over 85 people participated throughout the day. People continually challenged and embellished one another's recollections, and together they reconstructed the series of events before and after the removal of the favela. We discussed many other topics of interest as well: urban services and infrastructure, the start and development of the violence and drug traffic, leisure activities, schools and day care centers, and what people wanted to see for their communities in the future.

The similarities between what people said they most needed in 2001 and what they had reported needing in Catacumba 40 years earlier was eye-opening. As reported by Gordon Parks in his *Life* piece on Flavio:

> What the Catacumba residents said they most needed in 1961 included: a community center where they could meet and conduct civic activities; a crèche (day care center); a school for their children; medical and maternal clinics; literacy classes; job training; and a police station to "control the dope peddlers and criminals."[8]

More than thirty years later, at the meeting of the surviving Catacumba residents and their descendants, the list was as follows: a cultural center; an autonomous residents' association; a crèche; a better school for children and adolescents; full day schooling and social programs; preparatory courses (*prevestibular*) for the university entrance exams; a health clinic; a place for sports, leisure, and culture; work cooperatives for the manufacture and sale of products; courses on information technology and other professional skills; and help for *terceira idade* (senior citizens).

The similarities tell an interesting if somewhat sad story. The only differences seem to be that in 1961, the elderly were not an issue, since few in the favelas lived long enough to become senior citizens. In addition, finishing elementary school was rare and getting into university was unthinkable. Perhaps the most striking change was the reversal in attitudes toward the police—by 2001, the police were regarded as a source of aggression rather than a source of protection.[9]

THE DISPLACED OF CATACUMBA: GRIEF OR GRATITUDE?

Nothing is black or white in Rio, and not all of the changes since the removals have been for the worse. Personal descriptions of the impact of removals vary wildly, from residents who say they have never recovered from the loss to those who consider it the best thing that ever happened to them and, in retrospect, wish they'd left the favela earlier.

Grieving for a Lost Home

On the negative side, the removal meant that people in the South Zone were suddenly transported miles away from their places of work. In Quitungo and

Guaporé, residents had to cram into public transport to get to places they used to walk to. Their buying habits, leisure activities, and social networks were abruptly altered, and some people never managed to reconstruct these.

The authoritarian nature of the intervention, the fact that it was a move that none of them had chosen, deepened the feeling of loss people suffered. On a more practical level, they suddenly found themselves having to pay local taxes and utility charges. Their mortgage payments were new as well, and, though they were low, the former favela residents needed to expand their budgets to accommodate them. Those who had had the best houses in Catacumba rightly felt their circumstances had worsened.

Simone is the daughter of Laura Lana, one of the original interviewees from the random sample who was relocated to Guaporé. Her mother died in 1998, having lived in Guaporé for almost 30 years. Simone emphasized the rupture that the move caused in the life of her mother, who thought she would live in Catacumba for "her entire life." The removal was an uncontrollable and incomprehensible act that destroyed her sense of security and tranquility. The surprise and trauma of it were almost like a death (*assemelhados à morte*) for Laura Lana. In her memory, she idealized Catacumba as a place where poverty was offset by numerous and wonderful opportunities for family and social life.

Dona Antonia, the wife of an original interviewee named Claudionor, was similarly traumatized by the move to Quitungo. She and her family owned their house in Catacumba, and it was a nice one—a one-story brick home with a tile floor, water, electricity. "We liked our neighbors," she said. "Our house was close to everything: commerce, leisure, hospitals, public transportation, and marvelous schools. In the Lagoa schools there were theater, sewing, and cooking classes. And we had women's cooperatives working to make things and sell them. In Quitungo there is none of this."

Dona Antonia summed up the negatives by using a word I had never heard. She said that in the conjuntos (Quitungo and Guaporé), people live in a state of *desmazelo*—which the dictionary defines as "negligence, carelessness, and disarray."

Grateful for a New Start

Jair, one of my friends from Catacumba, is happy to live in Guaporé. "Some people didn't want to move there because they didn't want to pay *condominio* (monthly maintenance fees) or electricity" he said, but he appreciates the amenities. "People complain that there is nothing to do out here in the *suburbios* (suburbs, meaning the periphery, specifically low income), but there are ample opportunities for leisure," he says: "live music, bars and restaurants in Vila da Penha, and shopping in Madureira and Caxias. The only advantage of the South

Zone is the beach, but there are more *jovens* (youth) in the suburbio and more *velhos* (elderly) in the South Zone.

> The suburbio is much more tranquil, with easy access to the rest of the city, and it is easier for me to educate my children here because there are more affordable schools....As for the violence and drug trafficking, there's not much difference between the South Zone and the suburbio.

Jorge, another Guaporé resident, points out that some buildings in the conjuntos are better or worse than others, but the basic atmosphere is an improvement over the favela. "Better infrastructure confers greater dignity on us residents." According to Jorge, the main improvements were electricity and paved roads, but he added that the bakery, pharmacy, and schools were also important and that they now have doctors, churches, local commerce, and even land line telephones.

One huge improvement is having an address. Lately people have been giving street names and numbers to the roads and blocos (buildings), rather than the numbers and letters by which they have been historically identified. The residents like the feeling of being responsible. They are proud to have documents and receipts. They feel more like full-fledged citizens when they pay their housing, water, and electric bills—which they often pull out to show me during an interview or visit. Some are simply philosophical, saying they could be happy anywhere and "life is what we make of it."

Conceicao said that she didn't lose the strong ties she had in Catacumba because all of her neighbors were relocated to the same conjunto. Her kids all married ex-Catacumbans, maintaining their "community" and all that it meant to them.

The big advantage that the conjuntos have conferred is that they are one step closer to legitimacy than favelas, and it has proven easier to move from a conjunto into the asfalto than from a favela. In the conjuntos residents have full access to standard urban services (sewage, electricity, water, garbage collection, etc.) but more than that they have hope of escaping, at least to some degree, the stigma of living in a favela.

Over time people adapted to their new environment. They found jobs closer to their new homes, made new friends, and began to create social organizations. The football club Aliança Futebol Clube was refounded in the conjuntos in 1972. Attempts were even made, with varying degrees of success, to create residents' associations in the housing projects—though these were never as active as they had been in Catacumba.

Looking at this from a distance, the forced move has become a question of trade-offs. In some ways, the loss of community unity in the favela helped integrate the residents more fully into the rest of the city—made them less insular and ghettoized. But the residents continue to be stigmatized for living in the projects. As I mentioned earlier, conjuntos are often referred to as favelas, which lumps all those not in the formal city into a category of lesser worth.

One universal source of pride among all of the former Catacumba residents is worth telling because it reveals so much. During the time when they all lived in Catacumba, there were occasions when large numbers of fish died in the Lagoa and the Catacumba residents were blamed for it by those in the outer areas. It was considered a consequence of their filth—garbage and raw sewage runoff. This lent fuel to the environmental arguments favoring removal. Forty years after they were displaced, they have been vindicated—the fish in the Lagoa continue to die periodically in the same numbers.

SOME THINGS CHANGE, SOME STAY THE SAME

Like the favelas, the conjuntos have also improved with time—even in the absence of government attention. Several major transportation projects have helped link the conjuntos to a wider job market and shortened the working day by reducing commuting time. The opening of the Rio-Niteroi Bridge on March 4, 1974, the Linha Vermelha (Red Line) in 1992, the Linha Amarela (Yellow Line) in 1997, and the Metro in 1979 have improved mobility for workers across the city.[10]

In 1984, the administration of Governor Brizola carried out a modest urban reform in the conjuntos, and in 2001 the administration of Governor Garotinho, in anticipation of elections, repainted several of the buildings.

In 1992, a forested hillside beside the conjuntos was invaded, new shacks were built, and soon the community of Vila Piquiri was created. Paulo Cerqueira, a former resident of Catacumba currently living in Quitungo, claims to have played an important role in organizing this occupation. So there was a new favela. Some people sold their apartments and squatted there—with more space for their entire families and more freedom, without having to pay anything for rent.

THE STORY OF MARGA

From the time of Catacumba's removal until 2002, Marga lived in the same one-bedroom apartment. She made a comfortable home there with her husband Geraldo (nicknamed "Pingo"); their three daughters Eliana, Elisângela, and Viviani; and their son Wagner (see figure 3.17).

In 2002, after 32 years there, she was abruptly forced to leave after Wagner (who was 18 at the time) received death threats from one of the local gang leaders for supposedly looking at his girlfriend. This put the entire family in jeopardy. A common tactic for revenge used by the traffic is attacking family members. Marga and her family found a vacant apartment in Irajá, a working-class neighborhood in Penha, in the North Zone. One of Marga's daughters spotted it in the rental ads section of the newspaper, and they moved within two days of the threats, leaving clandestinely in the dark before dawn.

It is fortunate that I began this second round of research in 1999, while Marga and her family were still living in the same place they had been for the 30 years since the removal of Catacumba. If I had started three years later, I might never have found her. She was very isolated and unhappy in the new apartment for the first year. She only left her apartment to go to the evangelical church nearby and missed her friends and neighbors terribly—especially Regina from next door, who was a registered nurse and a wonderful friend.

Marga had high blood pressure, was having trouble walking, and had dark circles under her eyes, but she still managed to raise her grandson and cook for the entire family. She had met and married Pingo the year they left Catacumba. He had what was considered a very good job as a supervisor at a supermarket, and he needed to be there every day to open up at 6 A.M. and to close at 9 P.M. His commute was an hour each way by bus. He received one day off every two weeks. Often, when he got home, he was too tired to eat; he just took a shower and went to bed. If this is a success story, it is a brutal one.

Marga's daughter Beti, who was four when we first met, had been working as a caretaker for an elderly woman in Ipanema for many years, but the woman had recently died, and Beti was having trouble finding other work. She had completed high school and is an experienced seamstress, but was willing to do any kind of work at all—yet could not find anything. I could not help her. She is now 43 and has a 21-year-old son who dropped out of school and is also unemployed. They are still living in an apartment in Quitungo, not far from where Marga used to live. Marga's son, Gilberto, two years younger than Beti, was having trouble finding work since the furniture factory where he had been working had closed down. His wife had walked out, leaving him with their son, and has not been heard from since. He is still trying to get odd jobs repairing appliances, but it is not enough to support him and his son, Elbert, who lives with Marga.

The apartment in Irajá has two bedrooms and is very expensive (compared with the conjunto apartment, which was already paid off and which no one has bought or rented due to the violence). The expense is a source of constant stress. All three daughters live there and help out; the eldest two bring in income, and the youngest helps in the house. But the security and safety the family was seeking in its move remains elusive. The drug traffic is expanding into Irajá as rival gangs seek out new territory to control. If I had done this study in 1980, everything would have looked fine for these families. But poverty fluctuates so much at the lower rungs of the ladder and the smallest fluctuations up or down

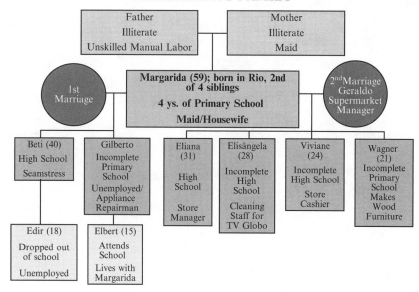

FIGURE 3.14   Margarida's family tree, 2003.

make such a large difference in daily life that it is hard to know whether what you observe at one moment will be the same the next.

Marga's family tree shown in figure 3.14 gives an idea of the achievements and setbacks of her family over four generations.

CATACUMBA LIVES ON

In 2001, when I returned to Negrão de Lima's Parque de Catacumba with Jacobi and several other displaced residents, it struck me that the name Catacumba (literally "catacombs") had become a perverse joke. Among the foliage that had grown up over the hillside were the skeletal remains of people's homes, people I had known; homes I had been welcome in and in which I had been fed wonderful meals (figure 3.15). Jacobi pointed out the tree that had once stood in his front yard. It was a mango tree, and it had fed the entire community in season. All that remained of his house and the others were a few of the grey cinder blocks of the foundations, partially buried by weeds.

As we proceeded up the *trilho*, the trail that had been created so that visitors could admire the view from the top, we saw it had been made into an ecological walk. A series of large plaques placed along the path show the geological history of the area and identify the local animals, birds, trees, and plants. There was nothing at all about the community of Catacumba or of people who had lived

FIGURE 3.15 Parque de Catacumba, 2001. The overgrown foundation of a home in the midst of the neglected sculpture garden is the only physical remains of the lives that were lived there.

FIGURE 3.16 This plaque about the favela of Catacumba, on its former site, is composed of text and photo and cover from the Brazilian edition of *Myth of Marginality*.

FIGURE 3.17   Quitungo, 1973. Margarida with her children Beti and Gilberto on the couch, Beti's son is in the foreground.

there for 50 years. To our astonishment, as we climbed to the top, the very last plaque was a huge blow-up of the Brazilian cover of *The Myth of Marginality*, with my photo of the Youth Athletic Club and several paragraphs of my text.

The works of art in the sculpture garden that had been erected on that picturesque hillside looked like tombstones. Where 10,000 people had raised families, earning a living and building a community that had more solidarity than any other part of the city, there were now lonely white marble statues that no one seemed to care about. In my many trips back there, I never once saw anyone in that garden, other than the guard.

There are both some positives and many negatives in the story of Catacumba. But as Jacobi had learned from photography and from Catacumba, with some effort and vision, negatives may be transformed into positive images for future.

POSTSCRIPT

At the time of my last visit to the conjuntos, in October 2008, Quitungo and Guaporé housed approximately 46,000 people; and two new favelas had grown around them—Piquiri, which I mentioned earlier, and Mangueirinha, running along the river.

In Quitungo, composed of 43 apartment blocks, with 40 apartments in each, at least another 250 households had been created by subdividing spaces, building additional stories on the tops of the buildings, and—most common of all—

creating *pushadinhos* (extensions) that expanded outward in all directions from
the apartments.

According to the current president of the Residents' Association of Quitungo, who goes by his childhood nickname "Nenem" (Baby), when the apartments were built and assigned to the ex-Catacumbans in 1970, their value was
3,500 cruzados (the Brazilian currency at the time) if paid in full on occupancy.
No one from Catacumba or any other favela could even dream of such sums
of money. For them, the payments were set at 46 cruzados per month for 25
years. The original Catacumba residents who are still there are all owners by
now, and many rent out their apartments at the going rate of about US$150/
month. To buy an apartment today costs an average of US$13,500. The Resi-
dents' Association is operating in an abandoned bread factory. The bread company went broke in 2004 and the building has been systematically vandalized
since then. The elderly owner from Portugal agreed to give the building shell to
the Residents' Association so it could be converted into a "community space."
After four years, Nenem finally got the legal permit to turn it into a tax-exempt
"public utility," and the state governor, Cabral, has provided 20 computers and
6 teachers through a program called the Foundation for Support of Technical
Education. The soccer field has been renovated, the gangs have been kicked out
for the moment, and the militias have not come in, so it has become a relatively
desirable location.

four

NOVA BRASÍLIA

FROM FAVELA TO COMPLEXO

SEARCHING FOR ZÉ

In July 1999, just hours after I landed in Rio from New York, I was on the bus to Nova Brasília, hoping to reunite with Zé Cabo. I had returned to Rio with the express purpose of testing the feasibility of finding the people who had participated in my first study 30 years before. I started by looking for Zé Cabo because I knew him well and he was well known in the favela. I hoped that he was still living there and that I would find him in the house in which I had stayed with his family.

I got off the bus on Avenida Itaoca, just across the street from the main entrance to the favela and walked up the principal internal street—Rua Nova Brasília—to Zé's house. I admired the widened, paved road and the modern commercial storefronts that had sprung up along the street since my last visit.

Avenida Itaoca is a major thoroughfare connecting various neighborhoods in the North Zone. It is lined on both sides with factories—many of them vacant—warehouses, car repair shops, deteriorating public housing, old office buildings, and high concrete walls with locked solid metal gates behind which are enterprises, many of which are illicit or illegal. Some of the abandoned

FIGURE 4.1   Rua Nova Brasília, 1973.

FIGURE 4.2   Rua Nova Brasília, 2003.

factories have been stripped down to bare bones, leaving no trace of electrical wiring, plumbing, windows or doors; others have walls but no roofs; some have been reduced to rubble.[1]

In the empty shells of some of these former factories, families have taken up residence—dividing the floor space into separate living quarters using cardboard, cloth, or makeshift wooden partitions. There is no electricity or running water, so the squatters bring water from across the street and use kerosene lamps for light. They keep a low profile. They are there because they find these buildings safer to live in than their houses in the favelas nearby. In midday, in the mid-week, when drug traffic is at a low point, they return to their homes and go take care of things needing to be done.

Nova Brasília is situated on the border between the neighborhoods of Ramos and Bonsucesso. There is a bustle of commercial activity around the entrance to the favela. You can easily see this when you are approaching Rua Nova Brasília. Vendors and stalls are set up in front of the cement wall, and the commercial activity spills into the street, covering every inch of sidewalk and forcing pedestrians to compete with buses, trucks, taxis, cars, and motorcycles for space on the road. Crammed together, in the shade of wide swaths of cloth strung between bamboo poles, are fresh produce; cotton candy; traditional sweets made from coconut, *goiaba* (guava), mango, banana, and lime; squares of cake; deep-fried empanadas filled with meat, chicken, or vegetables; stacks of coconuts; long poles of sugar cane being made into sweet juice; and a smattering of toys and electronic gadgets.

At the most dense part of this noisy, busy hub of activity, the stalls sweep shoppers from both sides of the street into the funnel-shaped entrance to Rua Nova Brasília, where more established shops line both sides of the cobblestone street all the way up the hill to the flat open area called the Praça do Terco. All along the way merchandise spills out onto the street. The stores have glass windows and shiny counters, and the families that own them live above them. There are several pharmacies, two bakeries, the poultry shop, a furniture store, and various other shops selling shoes, clothing, music, electronics, and sundries. On the right near the top is Dona Rita's clothing store—with dresses, skirts, and blouses, from children's to adult sizes. Dona Rita is another of my long-time Nova Brasília friends and teachers. She buys the clothes in São Paulo and brings them back in her truck. Then she adds her own design touches by hand or sewing machine. The shops and their owners are widely known, and people come from the entire region to shop in Nova Brasília, at least when commerce is not shut down due to a drug war.

I thought I would remember the location of Zé's house—it was not far from the entrance to Nova Brasília on the right-hand side, past the Residents' Association and before the powder blue Pentecostal church with the yellow and white trim. It had a tan-colored ceramic tile façade with a dark brown pattern, and the doorway had an ornately crafted wrought iron gate in front of it. But it was no longer there. In its place was a shop selling live chickens and eggs. I asked the shopkeeper about Zé. My voice was barely audible above the squawking, and the shop owner motioned that I should go upstairs. What had been the upstairs bedrooms of the house had been converted into a restaurant, with six or eight tables covered in floral print oilcloth. I sat down and ordered a *cafézinho* (strong, sweet Brazilian espresso) and a *mixto quente* (grilled ham and cheese)—always a safe bet. I asked where Zé Cabo and his family had gone. The proprietors either did not know or were not telling. The place had changed owners more than once since he'd sold it.

Feeling a bit disheartened, I continued up the cobblestone street toward the Praça do Terço. Along the way, I asked shopkeepers if anyone knew where Zé Cabo was. One of them nodded, ran up the hill, and came down dragging a friend by the hand. "He knows where Zé lives!" Word of my return traveled fast. Soon Dona Rita came out of her clothing store and—as if we'd seen each other just a few days before—she said, "Janice, you're back! Come on in, how are you? It's been so long. How is your mother? Look at these cute baby clothes I am making now. Do you want water or coffee? Yes, Zé Cabo is fine, I saw him go by here just the other day!"

I found it strange that no one offered to take me to Zé's house. I asked if we could go there to see him. Dona Rita and several others who had come over to see what was going on seemed to know where he lived but tried to discourage me from going. "It is too far…much too dangerous to walk there. You wouldn't want to go there." When we came out on the street in front of Rita's shop, one of Zé's former neighbors was just leaving the pharmacy next door. "Vem cá" (come over here), Rita called to him. "He lives nearby—He'll go back and tell Zé you are here, and then Zé will come to get you." I wanted to go directly, but that seemed out of the question.

Years earlier, there had been incessant talk of danger in favelas, but much of it could be chalked up to the stereotypes that equated poor people with criminals and gangsters. Now the danger was very real. When, to my great relief, Zé arrived, he was *emocionada* (moved) that I had come to see him but reluctant to take me back to his house. "Why don't we go someplace else to talk?" he suggested. In the end, he gave in and took me home, only because it was still early in the day and early in the week, when the dealers were still sleeping and the next drug shipment was not due until Friday.

Instead of going the most direct way, along the paths and through the alleyways of the community, we went down to Avenida Itaoca and along the street for about a half mile before turning left onto a steep, paved road leading up to his new house. Two uniformed men from the electric company were replacing the bulbs in the streetlights along the road to his house—something that would have been unheard-of in a favela years ago. When I asked him about this, he looked sad and tired rather than proud. The light bulbs had been shot out the previous night to darken the street for "operations," he told me. This had become a nightly occurrence.

Otherwise, the street looked normal. It was full of people: guys stopping in for a beer at one of the *biroscas* (cafés); children in their school uniforms of white short-sleeved shirts and blue pleated skirts or pants; the *vigias* (janitor/watchmen) sweeping the front of the Assembla de Deus (Assembly of God) church; and women carrying groceries up the street alongside men carrying sacks of cement. Women were sitting on stoops getting their hair or nails done, taking in the passing scene. Aside from Zé's move, which I did not yet understand, things seemed pretty much the same to me as they had been when I last visited.

I saw how wrong I was when we approached Zé's home. Instead of the lovely doorway that had characterized Zé and his wife Adelina's original house, I saw a bullet-pocked metal garage door blocking the main entrance. On the pavement, several belligerent-looking young men with bare torsos, wearing baggy shorts and multiple tatoos, were leaning or sitting against his garage door sniffing glue and smoking marijuana. They barely moved aside to let us enter and were clearly irritated at being disturbed. Once we were inside, Zé took me to a room behind the garage where he kept a file cabinet with all the records of the Residents' Association. After closing the door, he showed me the bullet marks on the walls opposite the windows and the patches on the water tank visible on the roof. He admonished me not to return to the community again until getting permission from the current president of the Residents' Association, who had apparently been placed in that position by the dominant drug faction (although Zé never said a word about that). He apologized for not being able to help me with this and warned that obtaining permission for my work might be difficult.

THE WAY IT WAS

At the time I first stayed in Nova Brasília, violence was not an issue. The issues were establishing a place to live, avoiding eviction and pressuring the local government to install basic urban services. Shacks were first constructed using a lattice-work of sticks packed with the mud-and-clay mixture the locals call *estuque* (wattle and daub). When conditions improved, the residents rebuilt their dwellings with wood. Later, they used alvenaría (cinder blocks or bricks), which they plastered and painted. Nova Brasília was among the best organized communities in Rio. There was thriving commerce, close to full employment, and a strong community spirit. Due to its peripheral location and the relatively low value of its lots, its occupants were under no immediate threat of eviction, so they felt free to invest in their homes—although I discovered years later that Nova Brasília appeared on at least two government lists of favelas to be demolished. It was one of the favelas in which the anthropologist Anthony Leeds and his students (or Peace Corps volunteers) worked in the early 1960s, which is how I happened upon it while looking for a North Zone favela for the original study.

At that time the population was 12,000–14,000, and the settled area covered 400,000 square meters—over four times the area of Catacumba, but with only 2–4,000 more people. The lower density allowed room for shade trees and flowering bushes, mango trees, banana plants, and all manner of fruit-bearing plants. Many families raised chickens, a goat or two, and sometimes a pig and her litter.

The use of space can be seen in figure 4.3, showing the unpaved pathway that wound up the hill from the Praça do Terco, the diversity of building materials, and the surrounding industrial area in 1969.

In order to draw a random sample of interview subjects for my original 1969 study, my research group used aerial photographs to map out each passage-way and dwelling and divided them into three areas: from the most developed to the least, as shown in figure 4.4.

Each house was numbered, and we used a random numbers table to select them. Then we used a periodic sample to select the person or persons within the household who would be interviewed.[2] The houses shown in black were the

FIGURE 4.3   View of Nova Brasília from the hillside above the Praça do Terco, 1969.

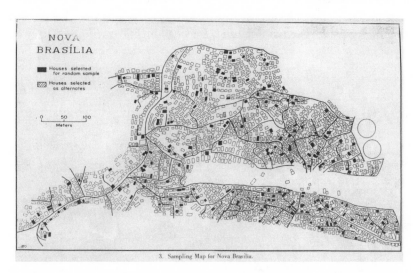

FIGURE 4.4   Sampling map of Nova Brasília, 1968, drawn from an aerial photograph in black are the ones selected through the random numbers table; those in gray are the alternates.

original 200 dwellings selected and those in grey were backups in case a substitution was necessary. The white area belonged to the Tuffy Factory and was not occupied. The two water storage tanks in the upper-right are not far from Zé's current house.

The Praça do Terco was the only flat open space in Nova Brasília, so it is the natural gathering place for the community. At the time of my first study it was an unpaved area serving as a soccer field, site for community dances and parties such as the traditional São João celebration, and place to buy cool drinks and homemade cakes or sweets on the way to or from work, school, or shopping. Nearly everyone passed through on their way to and from the main road.

Sr. Levi, one of the founders of the original Residents' Association (along with Zé Cabo) lived on the Praça just to the left of where Rua Nova Brasília ended. He kept songbirds under the eaves of his veranda amid flowering plants and bushes. Their song filled the air around the Praça. Sr. Levi had suffered an industrial accident several years earlier and was on disability pension, so he dedicated his time to the community. His wife ran a day care program for the children in the surrounding area so their mothers were able to go to work without worrying about their little ones.

By 1973, in a misguided or punitive public works measure, the Praça was paved and the left side covered with corrugated metal roofing and turned into a garbage collection center with four enormous dumpsters. Figure 4.5 shows the Praça do Terco as it was in 1969. The girl on the extreme right is Zé Cabo's daughter, Wandelina, nicknamed "Live Wire." (Figure 4.6 shows her with her father in 2004.) On the left, you can see a small mobile cart for selling sweets

FIGURE 4.5   Praça do Terco, 1969. Zé's daughter, Wandelina is on the right.

and cakes made at home. You can also see that the Praça was unpaved and many of the homes were made of precarious building materials, but they did have electricity. Later, this area became the most dangerous spot in the community.

A HISTORY RECONSTRUCTED

In attempting to reconstruct the history of Nova Brasília upon my return in 1999, I used three complementary approaches. One was to contract an urban historian, who did an archival and newspaper search on the area. A second was to interview the people who were the living memory of the locale spending hours talking about the community's past. Finally, I used a collective process called the Rapid Participatory Diagnosis, which was conducted at half-day meetings in each community in December 2001.

According to Zé, the land on which Nova Brasília is located once belonged to the family of a Portuguese merchant named Manuel da Veiga. He sold it in 1942, with the largest portion going to the Instituto de Aposentadorías e Pensões dos Comerciários (Retirement and Pension Fund for employees in commerce) and a smaller lot to a Portuguese man named Fernando Teixeira. At the time, the land was vacant except for a few scattered shacks. During the 1950s, it was used as a burning site for the waste products from the furniture industry and became known as Buraco do Sapo (Toad's Hole). The Instituto used it as a grazing pasture for cattle they owned.

The first people to live in Nova Brasília were Instituto employees, who were gradually joined by workers from nearby factories, including the furniture factory. Zé Cabo arrived there in 1956, a year after the establishment of the settlement, which the people called Itaoca.

The first water standpipe was installed in 1956. This was a memorable turning point. It freed up time and lightened the workload of the women more than any other service. When James Wolfensohn was president of the World Bank, I once accompanied him on a favela visit. We stopped to chat with a middle-aged woman who was sweeping the area in front of her house. When our host from the municipality introduced Wolfensohn as a person responsible for bringing running water to the homes of many people like her, she burst out crying in gratitude. She said it had changed her life from one day to the next, and that she would never forget the thrill of turning on the faucet and having water run out—right there inside her own home. She thanked him over and over again.

In 1957, large numbers of people, mostly from the Northeast, settled in Itaoca, swelling the population to over 2,000. There was still ample room to cultivate sugar cane and other crops, according to what people remember. Two years later, the community voted to change its name from Itaoca to Nova Brasília, in homage to the new federal capital being constructed in the center of the country. It was around that time that the Instituto, which owned the land, started a legal action to try to repossess the land from the squatters who were living there. Local leaders, headed by Zé Cabo, succeeded in mobilizing the community, getting favorable press coverage and generating enough resistance to block the action. In 1961, in response to a more serious attempt at removal, local leaders rented buses and drove residents from the community to demonstrate in front of the government palace, thus forcing the Instituto to negotiate. It was agreed that residents would have five years to regularize their situation or be expelled.

Five years passed; the agreement was ignored, and no other action was taken to remove the community. During the dictatorship, in 1973, and again in 1976, Nova Brasília was on the official list of the favelas intended for removal by CHISAM (the national-level institution created for the sole purpose of eradicating the favelas of Rio de Janeiro), but not high on the priority list. The fact that Nova Brasília was located in the North Zone, in the middle of an industrial area with low land values, helped save it, despite the lack of official property title.[3]

The mobilization to oppose removal stimulated the creation of an official Residents' Association in July 1961. The association, headed by Zé Cabo, was active in demanding urban services for the community, and they succeeded in getting help from some local politicians. Those who remember the time say they were grateful for the help, but did not like the condescending way they were treated. One woman said, "It was as if being poor meant we were like dim-witted children and they were the kind and wise adults."

The growth of the community was so rapid that in 1967, a census carried out by the Residents' Association counted a total of 8,899 inhabitants in the community. The association installed a system of loudspeakers to transmit information and music. In the late sixties, the community was further aided by a program called Bem-Doc, organized by the state with funding from the United States, aimed at the amelioration of living conditions in poor communities. Residents were expected to provide "sweat equity"—that is, to contribute their labor to the redevelopment work.

Living conditions in the community also improved. In 1961, the Light Commission, a locally run community organization, managed to supply electricity to the 400 houses closest to the main road, where they tapped into the electric power lines. In 1962 the state water company began to service the homes along the Avenida Nova Brasília. Two years later, the enormous water tanks were built on top of the hillside in an area known as Alvorada (Dawn). The construction of water tanks and their improvement over time was one of the key issues dealt with by the Residents' Association. By the end of the sixties, water, electricity, and sewage drains had reached in parts of the favela, and in the early eighties, under Governor Leonel Brizola, water and sewage networks were installed. Even today, though, coverage is far from universal, and the many houses along the small alleyways in the higher parts of the favela still lack services.

It was only in 1982 that some service providers began to recognize the favela residents as valuable consumers rather than derelict scofflaws. This shift in perception was led by Light, the Canadian/Brazilian electric company for Rio de Janeiro. Offering electrical service to favela homes on the same fee-for-service basis used for the rest of the city had the multiple advantages of lowering the prices for favela residents, adding over a million paying customers to the company's subscribers, and ending the Commissões de Luz that had controlled the internal distribution of illegally tapped electricity charging exorbitant rates as they had a monopoly.[4]

During the seventies, the areas of Alvorada and Inferno Verde (Green Hell) experienced intense urbanization. Inferno Verde was a large dumping site, considered the poorest section of the community. Nova Brasília expanded its boundaries to incorporate Alvorada, Inferno Verde, and Fazendinha (Little Plantation), and their residents began to upgrade and improve their respective areas. As is typically the case, people living in each area insisted that their part was fine—very *sossegado* (calm, quiet) and *tranquilo* (peaceful)—in contrast with "over there," which was "really dangerous."

As the city grew northward, land pressure and prices rose, driving out the least competitive among local industries as early as the 1980s. Environmental regulations demanded substantial investments from companies to remain in their original locations. Nova America Tecidos, the largest textile factory in Latin America, struggled to stay in business and finally left the area in the late eighties. There is a shopping mall on the site today. One by one, the factories began to shut their doors. The beer factory is now an empty shell. All the furniture factories, all the paper factories, and the plastics factory eventually went out of business or were relocated.

The last to go was the Coca-Cola bottling company, which was able to hang on until 1997, because it was part of a larger enterprise. Since all of these companies had employed local labor, unemployment has skyrocketed. There were no replacement jobs for the people who worked in those factories, drove trucks for them, cleaned the buildings, guarded the premises, or made lunch for the workers. It was not only the skilled male workers and their households who were affected by these closings but all those who provided goods and services to the companies and their workers.[5]

The beginning of drug trafficking in the area paralleled the beginning of deindustrialization. Both started on a small scale in the mid-1980s and got worse. Nova Brasília did not grow very much from 1997–2007. It is now a consolidated favela, with little room for newcomers. Although there have been no major upgrading projects there, at the time of my 1999 restudy, basic utilities (water, sewerage, and electricity) were nearly universal. Garbage collection is provided through a community organization and home postal delivery is available in exchange for a small fee to the Residents' Association—still a far cry from having a street name and house number recognized by the city postal service, but nonetheless much better than having no mail delivery at all. (Previously all mail was left at the Residents' Association).

Commercial life in the community is intense. There are hundreds of bars and several supermarkets, restaurants, drugstores, bakeries, opticians, newspaper stands, beauty parlors, and other small shops of various sorts. The nearby North Zone shopping mall does more business than the one in the upscale Barra de Tijuca.

Leisure and recreational activities, on the other hand, are few and far between. Aside from two makeshift soccer fields and intermittent *bailes funk* (funk balls), there is little else. Most people report having no leisure or recreational activities at all—in contrast to earlier, safer times. For many women, going to church is their only community activity. There are four Catholic churches, a number of Protestant churches, many dozens and types of Pentecostal and Evangelical churches, and a few remaining terreiros. The evangelical churches have the greatest presence in the community—from the tiny ones on nearly every street to the large temples that rise above the houses. They hold weekly or daily prayer sessions, and singing can be heard as you walk by. They have gotten a lot of press, and many stories have been told of how they saved young men from the drug traffic, but the truth is that their growth in membership is about the same as the growth of nonbelievers—people saying they have no religion. The big decline in the numbers of Catholics is what makes the evangelicals appear to be growing so rapidly. Few have paid attention to the fact that this growth in evangelicalism is offset by those giving up on religion entirely—which has equal if not greater implications.

Education, the great hope for social mobility, is a disappointment in Nova Brasília. The quality of schools is worse there than it was in the 1960s, though the number of schools in and near the favela has grown. The teachers are afraid to come to class and typically show up only a few times a week. According to a new regulation, students cannot be held back, so they are passed on to the next grade without necessarily having learned what they need to know to handle new material. It is no wonder that they get discouraged and drop out. There are a handful of kindergartens, a state-run primary and secondary school that was built in 2000, and a place offering the *prevestibular,* the prep course for university entrance exams. A popular saying captures the cynicism of the educational enterprise for the poor: "The students pretend to learn, the teachers pretend to teach, and the government pretends to pay them."

THE COMPLEXO DE ALEMÃO

Nova Brasília is one of a dozen favelas that have grown from their base along the main road to cover the top of the hillside, where they have merged with other favelas that have similarly expanded. Now they form one continuous complex called the Complexo de Alemão.[6] Its 300,000 people live in a space of three square kilometers that is referred to as the *faixa de Gaza carioca* (the Gaza strip of Rio de Janeiro). In 2007, a third of this population made less than the minimum salary, the equivalent of US$200/month.

The Complexo de Alemão was named for one of its 12 favelas: the Morro de Alemão. There are competing narratives as to how that favela came to earn its name. One story is that in the years after World War I, the area was purchased by Leonard Kaczmarkiewicz, a Pole who the people assumed was German, and so they called it the Hill of the German. The other explanation is that it came to be called the Morro de Alemão after World War II, when "German" became a synonym for "enemy" or traitor. Some say that the area was considered undesirable as early as the 1920s, so the name Morro de Alemão stuck in the postwar period.

Initially, the area was given to agriculture and pasture, where bananas and mangoes grew and goats and chickens wandered about. The advance of the twentieth century brought increased mechanization, and the area became increasingly industrial, beginning with a leather tannery. Migrants from the countryside came to work at the tannery and built homes nearby. In the early 1950s, the owner of the land divided it into lots and sold them. During the years of the dictatorship, new favelas began to grow on other parts of the hill-side, and their populations grew steadily until the mid-1980s, when they began to level off.

Today the Complexo de Alemão is so large that it comprises its own *regiao administrativo* (administrative region), as do three other immense favelas: Rocinha, Jacarezinho, and the Complexo do Maré. Nova Brasília is the largest of the favelas within the Complexo da Alemão and is home to a quarter of its inhabitants.

The Complexo de Alemão is one of the most violent areas of the city of Rio and one of the most neglected. Some attribute this lack of government assistance to bad feelings caused over 10 years ago, when the mayor was booed while giving a speech there; others think it is because the complexo is the head-quarters of the major drug gang Commando Vermelho (Red Command). The Commando Vermelho is generally better organized, better funded, and better armed than the government. It uses its machine guns, grenades, and antiaircraft weapons to both combat and corrupt the forces of the state.

On June 27, 2007, the Complexo do Alemão was besieged by an army of 1,350 civil and military police and the national security forces in one of the biggest combat operations against drug traffickers in the state's history.[7] Just before the onslaught, the military police gathered in a parking lot, where they joked and smoked and divided into teams. Among their vehicles was the *caveirão*, a black armored military vehicle bearing an insignia of a skull pierced by a sword. It is the sign of the Batalhao de Operacões Policias Especiais BOPE, (Police Battalion of Special Operations). Helicopters were also mobilized for use against the community, should they try to aid or abet the traffic.

The BOPE and the Polícia Militar had just completed Operacao Cerco Amplo (Operation Wide Net)—a coordinated effort to catch the leaders of the drug gangs—and, having been unsuccessful, were taking a more aggressive approach to "clean up the city" in advance of the Pan American Games and related events such as an upcoming Live Aid concert on the beach in Copacabana.

By the end of that day, at least 22 people had been killed and 11 wounded in the Complexo de Alemão; in the 60 days following the initial police occupation of the favelas, 46 people were killed and 84 wounded. Residents said that only nine of the people killed had been involved in crime and became incensed when the government issued a statement that there were no innocents among the victims. When the civil police failed to find criminal records for a single one of those killed, it confirmed people's worst fears. Many of the dead were young teenage girls and boys whose friends and families said had had nothing to do with the traffic.

As collateral damage to the community, the police action forced the closure of all commerce, places of worship, community centers, and eight schools in the region—keeping 4,600 children out of their classrooms. A UNICEF report said that the children who tried to go to school were left there without any teachers or transferred to another school, where they attended one of four daily shifts of two hours each.[8]

The people in the community do not trust the police. A BBC reporter said people were shooting off fireworks to warn the traffickers that the police were coming—a system the young kids in the traffic use to alert the community when a drug delivery is made, or a police raid is imminent.

Jurany Custódio, a 79-year-old woman, has lived for 50 of her years in the same barraco in Nova Brasília. She was very active in community life in earlier times and raised a large family as well. Now she lives on the *sobrado* (top floor) of her house and rents out the rest. Jurany said that it was the fault of Governor Brizola that the separate favelas had turned into violent complexos.[9] According to her:

> Brizola told us it would help us get water and other urban services more effectively if we merged into a unified complexo. What happened? We never got more services. Instead we got more deaths. Since not all of the favelas were controlled by the same *commando* (gang), the turf wars became very violent. Since then, we in Nova Brasília have been ignored by the government while favelas all around us have benefited from upgrading investments and programs.

NARCO TRAFFIC AND ITS CONSEQUENCES

Once basic services had been attained and the struggle against eviction was won, the role and relevance of the Residents' Associations declined in most of the favelas. But the coup de grâce was the pressure from the local drug dealers, who were determined to take over as the official leaders of the community. Betinho, the last independently elected president of the Residents' Association, took office in the early 1980s after serving informally as a local leader during the 1970s. When he ran for reelection, the drug lords told him that if he won, he would have to submit to their orders, and if he lost, he would have to leave the community. Despite his popularity, Betinho lost the election (which people say was rigged). But he and his family wanted to remain in the community. They had built up their home and family there over many decades.

Betinho was executed gangland style, to set an example and let people know who ruled the community. According to interviewees, this set off a new round of violence. Periodic killings involving rival criminal groups had not been uncommon, but this new phase was characterized by an increased level of disrespect for local leaders and for the community in general—to a point where independent community organizations were no longer viable.

It was in the Complexo de Alemão—in the favela called Grota[10]—that the admired investigative journalist, Tim Lopes, was tortured, quartered, and murdered. This one death got more media attention than the deaths of hundreds of favela residents caught in the *tiroteio* (crossfire).

I barely escaped the "Tim Lopes treatment" on the day of our community meeting to reconstruct the history of Nova Brasília using the DRP (Rapid Participatory Diagnosis). It was a Sunday morning in December 2001 with an unusually clear blue sky and bright sun setting off the vivid colors of the storefronts, houses, and churches. The street looked familiar and benign. The meeting had been set for 10:30 at the Residents' Association. We had chosen the day and time because most people would be at home, not at work, and because it was considered a safe time, when the dealers are sleeping off their Saturday night adventures.

In true Carioca fashion, no one had arrived by 11 A.M., so while the lunch was being prepared and the room arranged, I took the opportunity to go out into the street. I wanted to take photographs from the same vantage points as the ones I had taken decades earlier. I walked up the Avenida Nova Brasília toward the Praça do Terco, snapping shots of the shiny new commercial establishments and the colorful houses along the way. I took several shots in the Praça, trying to get one exactly like the one shown in figure 4.5.

Some men were having beers at an open bar looking out over the Praça, and I took their pictures as well. They smiled and seemed not to mind.

On my way back down the hill, rushing a bit so as to arrive before any of the invited participants, I suddenly found myself surrounded by a group of menacing young men wearing no shirts, baggy knee-length shorts, and guns, who blocked my way, asking me what I was doing. I told them I had lived on this street many decades ago and was taking pictures to compare with those I had taken then to include in a book I was writing. That did not convince them that I was not a journalist about to publish my photos in a newspaper expose, and they got increasingly aggressive. Fortunately for me, some of the old-timers were by then descending the street on their way to the meeting, and others had come up from the Residents' Association to look for me, so they managed to convince the group to go with us to see the president of the Residents' Association, who would be there to open the meeting.

Fortunately, I did not have a digital camera and was using film, so instead of giving my camera to them, the president got them to agree that I could take out the roll of film and give it to them instead. They couldn't believe anyone was still using film cameras and remained skeptical that I might have some digital backup inside the camera. But, in the favela, the word of the Residents' Association president is law, so they took the film and left—and the meeting began.

I had no idea that I had taken pictures of some of the main bocas. Evidently, the man I took a picture of drinking at the birosca on the praça was the *gerente* (manager) of the local traffic. Little did I realize that this naïve act could easily have gotten me killed—or worse.

As the research team and I were leaving, after an all-day meeting and dinner, we spotted some of the gang members sitting on a stoop opposite the Residents' Association. Evidently, they had disagreed with the others about letting me go free and were waiting for the end of the meeting to make their move. My friend shoved me into the nearest taxi, jumped in behind me, and told the driver to take off as fast as he could.

Figure 4.5 shows the Praça do Terco as it looked in 1969. The one *not* shown next to it is how the Praça looks today—that film has long been destroyed, and I never had the courage to try again. Even with the association president at my side it was too risky.

The next time I went to the area was with the president of the Residents' Association, who showed me the apartment where he kept several young girls as mistresses; the place where Tim Lopes was tortured and killed; and the location of the state-run primary/secondary school. While we were driving around in his car, a woman came up to him, crying hysterically. I did not understand a single word of their whispered conversation, but later my Brazilian research assistant, who was with me, told me what had transpired. Evidently, the woman was the wife of a man who had been badly beaten by the henchmen of the association president. They had, "worked him over, breaking nearly all of the bones in his body." At that very moment, he was writhing in agony where they had dumped him, in front of his house. In response to the wife's plea the association president said, "It was only 40 dollars—I didn't tell them to kill him, just to rough him up a bit and scare him into paying." He told her that he would have a car sent to take the beaten man to the hospital.

This was emblematic of the dilemma in which the population finds itself. The traffic is not a "parallel power" as often said. It is not a substate or a substitute for the state. There is a vacuum where the state should be, and the traffic has stepped into that vacuum unopposed by any governmental authority and accountable to no one except itself.

In late 2007 the price of cocaine began to drop, and the traffic has had to seek other ways of making a profit, imposing small fees on residents for "services" and security, in classic "mafia" style. Yet from my conversations with the association president it is clear that he sees himself as the savior of the community. He blames the community's problems on the failure of the government and the state's neglect of Nova Brasília. He has elaborate, unrealistic plans for employment and income generation in the community.

He tried to persuade me to help him develop favela tourism in Nova Brasília (in the mode of Rocinha and other South Zone favelas close to tourist hotels) and join the board of his proposed samba school, which needed sponsorship and large-scale funding. I did not dare to laugh or to disabuse him of those fantasies—I had seen that he holds the power to kill with a nod of his head. But it says a lot about his isolation from reality that he believed that tourists would be willing to travel over an hour to see a favela in a war zone, or come to dance at a samba school where their chances of getting killed in the crossfire were not negligible.

At the end of my interview, when I asked him to write down his name and contact information so that I could get back to him about his requests for my help, I saw that, much to his embarrassment, he could barely write. Most recently (in 2009) he had been arrested, but what a sad state of affairs for him and for the community.

ZÉ CABO'S JOURNEY

Zé Cabo was one of the most respected and established leaders in Nova Brasília when I first met him in 1968. He was 40 years old then and president of the Residents' Association. He had moved to Rio de Janeiro from a small city in the interior of Rio Grande do Norte when he was 16 years old. Neither of his parents had attended school. He was the fifth of 19 children. At the age of 29, after working as a marine, he moved to Nova Brasília. He finished elementary school, but also got educated mostly by traveling throughout Brazil, by being exposed to many ideas and people. This is why he was much more politically savvy than most others in the community. It was he who led the collective struggles throughout the 1960s and 1970s for water, electricity, drainage, sewer connections, and street paving. It was he who fought for a land title and who negotiated with candidates

FIGURE 4.6   Zé Cabo with Wandelina, Waney, and Waney's car in front of the house he was renovating in Irajá. Waney's newly constructed apartment is in the back (2004).

and government officials on behalf of the community. He also played a critical role in acquiring the land for constructing the Residents' Association on the corner of Avenida Itaoca and Rua Nova Brasília.

At the time of the original study, he and his wife, Adelina, had three boys and a girl. He was working for the military police, which is where he acquired the nickname, Zé Cabo (Corporal José). He and Adelina had incrementally improved their house to a three-story brick (alvenaria) home, which was filled with large dark wood furniture sets, embroidered doilies on almost every surface, and plastic flowers—prestige items of that time and place. It was cool and dark inside even on the brightest, hottest days, and the curtains were kept discreetly drawn. There was always something good cooking on the stove, and it was a place to which others came for help and advice.

I stayed in touch with Zé and his family over all these years. In the early 1990s, Adelina died of a heart attack, and he incurred huge medical bills for heart problems of his own. Because of his debts, the transformation of Rua Nova Brasília into a commercial street and a dangerous thoroughfare for drug traffic—and in order to leave something for his children—he sold his home. As described earlier he moved to a more remote area of the favela, where he bought a small rundown shack and rebuilt it. With the rest of the sale proceeds, he built a house for his grandson Wagner in a gated community on the outskirts of Niteroi and bought a house for his daughter in a development in Campo Grande, the extreme west of the municipality. None of his children from his first marriage stayed in Nova Brasília.

Zé loved it there and stayed as long as he could, living with his second wife, Maria, their two adult daughters, and two grandchildren—plus an ever-changing number of relatives whom he supported.

In the ten-year period during which I was doing my restudy (1999–2009) Zé Cabo's life became increasingly difficult. He developed heart problems and used up a good deal of his savings to pay medical bills. Because he had been in the navy, he was able to get the surgery he needed. He was finally driven out of his home in Nova Brasília in 2004 by increasingly specific threats from the traffic. He left his house to Maria and their two daughters.

It had long been Zé Cabo's dream to move out of the favela someday—but not to Sao Gonçalo in Niteroi or Campo Grande and certainly not to the northeastern state of Natal, where his brother and sister-in-law live. He wanted to live in an apartment in Gloria, close to the center of downtown Rio. When he was finally forced out of the favela in 2005, he could only afford to buy a small property with a ruin of a house on a highway service road alongside a raised viaduct in Irajá—still stuck in the North Zone.

He first built a separate house for his son Waney at the back of the property (shown in white in figure 4.6), then started to rebuild the old house for himself. He spent weekends with his daughter in Campo Grande when he felt like getting some fresh air.

As of 2008, at age 79, Zé was still supporting several family members. When I was there in October, he told me Waney had died the past year from heart problems, a death which might have been prevented with better medical care. His aunt, who had been staying in his room while he slept on the sofa in the living room, had passed away around the same time. Maria had come to stay with him in Irajá, after his heart operation, but he was the one doing all the shopping and cooking, working on the house and supporting his grandson, who had moved into Waney's little apartment after his mother kicked him out.

For all this, I found Zé fit and trim looking, with the same memory for detail, the same generosity, wry sense of humor, and life force as ever. He was undefeated. When he was walking me back to the metro station, he went so fast I could hardly keep up with him. Figures 4.8–4.11 show Zé at various points in his life.

Once when I had asked Zé what he was most proud of, he told me, "My greatest achievement in life is that none of my kids are on drugs, in the traffic, in jail, or murdered." From this, I understood that they were barely making it in life—but that turned out to be wrong. The family tree shows the educational and occupational profile of each of his children and grandchildren and reveals how far they have come from where he started in life.

Wanderley, the eldest of Zé's children, is a retired public functionary for the Caixa Economica Federal (Brazilian National Bank)—one of the largest government owned financial institutions in Latin America. He lives in Japeri, a municipality outside the metropolitan area of Rio de Janeiro, two hours from downtown. His son and two daughters have advanced degrees in information technology. The eldest daughter, Patricia (Paty), is the one I met in Copacabana as described in the introduction.

Waney, Zé's second son died in 2007 at the age of 54. He lived on his pension from years of work in the Civil Police. He would have received a higher retirement payment if he had stayed for his full term, but he left before full retirement age because he had been offered a full-time job as a delivery man for a South Zone company. The owner, a woman, took on two male associates and incorporated her company when the business started to take off. As Waney explained it to me, "She was assassinated by one of them, and they took all her money and closed the business." Waney was out of work from then on. He divorced, and he sold his apartment in Guadalupe. Until his death, he was living with Zé Cabo in Irajá. He was the uncle so beloved by Patricia, Zé's granddaughter.

Waney's eldest child, Wagner, lives in the interior of Niteroi, in a gated community. He purchased the land with the money from Zé's house sale. Waney and Wagner designed and built a simple, attractive wood-frame house. Wagner earns a livelihood as a mechanic specializing in fixing car air conditioners. His wife works in a boutique in an upscale shopping mall nearby. His younger sister, Mariana, is known as the "smart one" in the family. She attended law school for one year at the Estacio de Sá, but has not completed her degree. She instead dropped out to go to Candido Mendes University in Niteroi to study fashion design. When she finished, she started a clothing line using her own money. She took her clothing designs around to various stores and took orders. She bought the materials, cut the pieces, and contracted out the sewing. She did so well that she was able to open her own store in the same shopping mall where her sister-in-law (Wagner's wife) works. Her mother and grandmother help out in the store, and her stepfather takes care of the accounts and investments. The business seems to be thriving, and there were several women in the store when I went to visit, picking out party dresses for various special occasions. Waney's youngest daughter, Leticia, is 21 years old and is a university student.

José's daughter, Wandelina, knicknamed "live wire" when she was younger, was the trouble-maker of the family. She dropped out of school after five years, despite her mother's struggle to get her to finish high school. As a preteen, it was her dream to become a hairdresser. She is in her 50s now and lives in Santa Cruz in a subdivision for government employees, which she says is "rather boring and isolated but very safe." It is almost two hours by car from the center of Rio, and much longer by bus. She retired from working in the elementary

ZÉ CABO'S FAMILY

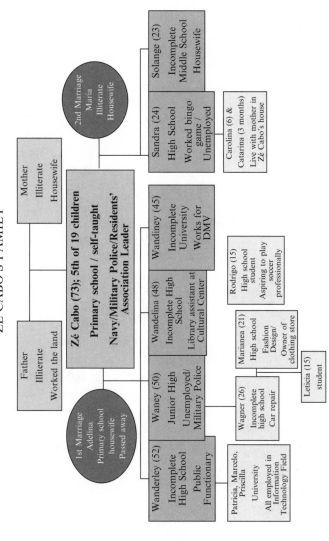

FIGURE 4.7   Zé Cabo's family tree, 2003.

school cafeteria and worked until 2006 in the small library of a newly renovated cultural center, which used to be the summer palace of the Brazilian emperor Dom Pedro.

As a single mother, Wandelina struggled to keep her teenage son out of trouble. She told me that for a long time she had no idea that he was missing classes, because the school never communicated with her. Then she started doing homework with him every night and making sure he attended classes. He was a star soccer player at his school, which provided a strong incentive not to drop out. He has a scholarship from a soccer school run by a well-known local player and has already traveled to Switzerland with his team to participate in an international competition. Wandelina proudly displayed his soccer photos with various famous people, including former U.S. president Jimmy Carter. However, when I went to see her in 2008, she said things had gotten so far out of hand that she could no longer have him living at home. He had dropped out of school and was not working—"just looking for trouble." They fought constantly. After his uncle Waney died, he went to live at his grandfather's house in Irajá. As soon as he is 18 he can go into military service, which will be a relief for him and the entire family.

Zé's youngest son, Wandiney, attended a university for a few years but never finished. He lives in Santa Cruz (West Zone) and works for the state motor vehicle bureau. He is the only one who, like his father, became involved in local politics. He has never married or had children, but he has been with the same girlfriend for two years. The family is hoping that he will get married.

Both of Zé Cabo's daughters from his union with Maria are still living in Nova Brasília in Zé's house, which he put in their mother's name so they could inherit it. Sandra, the first daughter, finished high school and took a computer course at the Service Nacional de Aprendizagem Industrial (National Technical School) but is still unemployed. She is a single mother and is raising two daughters, Caroline and Catarina. Solange, Maria's younger daughter, never finished junior high school. She worked at the bingo game until it was closed and then traveled to other bingo games until each, in turn, closed as well. She has had three children in the past three years, and the father, a salesman, stays with her and the children on a part-time basis. Zé continues to help both of them with expenses.

NOVA BRASÍLIA TODAY

During a conversation in 2008, I asked Zé whether he keeps up with what is happening in Nova Brasília. He does, of course. He told me that there is now a permanent police station up in the Alvorado area, headed by the commandante (commander) of the Third Battalion. But this has not provided any protection for the residents, since the police are afraid to come out of the police station.

The enormous water storage facility that Zé had hoped to turn into a new Residents' Association with a day care center, schools (elementary, professional, and technical), a clinic, and an outdoor youth sports facility has now become an evangelical church surrounded by a huge parking lot.

I asked him what he thought of the new president of the Residents' Association, who had been so polite to me when I requested permission to take photos of the area. According to Zé, the new president is an associate of one of the most powerful drug lords in the country—who rules from jail. If anyone he has placed in leadership positions fails to carry out orders, they are executed as an example for others.

Zé also told me that the Forca Nacional de Seguranca (National Security Force) occupied Nova Brasília for almost three years. They built a sandbag barricade at the entrance to Nova Brasília and took up positions behind it with rifles loaded and pointed into and out of the favela. According to Zé, that did not stop the drug traffic higher on the hillside, but quieted it down at the entrance area.

In early October 2008, the biggest conflict in the favela was about the highly contested mayoral election coming up on Sunday, October 5. During political campaigns, the drug gangs make deals to deliver votes to certain candidates and will go to any lengths to do so. It is illegal to put up posters or placards for political candidates without having a person there at all times, but the community was covered with such postings. Police kept coming in to tear them down, and before they had finished more would go up in their place. To "maintain peace and order" in this charged political climate, the National Security Forces were sent to Rio to occupy the favelas considered most prone to violence.

The day I went to see Dona Rita, as I was coming up the Avenida Nova Brasília toward her shop—without my camera—there stood the troops en masse. Dressed in tan-and-green camouflage uniforms with matching berets, high boots, and rifles, the young men appeared slightly embarrassed as they marched up and down the cobblestone street of Avenida Nova Brasília in formation, five or six abreast. The residents, going about their daily chores, ignored them. Some residents said they appreciated the little space of peace created by the soldiers' very visible presence—which would continue until election day and through any runoffs.

Part of the program of this occupation was to create goodwill in the community by offering various free services to community members. The innocent young men with their close-shaven heads were doing this as best they could. They had set up folding tables and chairs in the Praça do Terco, where they were offering free blood pressure and diabetes tests for residents, helping them fill out forms to get legal documents, and providing various other services. They were there from 9 A.M. to 4 P.M. every day. While one group

FIGURE 4.8   Zé Cabo as a young man serving in the Marinha (the Navy) in the 1950s.

served residents, the others continued marching up and down on the left side of the main street.

Dona Rita gave me the name of the current president of the Residents' Association, and I stopped there to try to see him on my way out. I called and knocked on the bolted door, and someone appeared on a second-floor balcony asking what I wanted. I was let in. When I spoke with the president, he was

FIGURE 4.9   Zé Cabo as president of the Residents' Association of Nova Brasília in
the 1960s.

quite interested in my project; he asked for photos of the community from
the early days—before he was born. He told me the public works department
was in the process of installing larger sewer pipes along the Avenida Nova
Brasília, as part of the nationwide Programa de Aceleração do Crescimento
(PAC; Program of Accelerated Growth) that President Lula launched in 2007.

FIGURE 4.10   Zé Cabo talking with me on roof of his house in Nova Brasília, 1999. (Photo Michel Filho/Ag O Globo)

He offered to accompany me or a colleague while taking photos but he never came through.

I was amazed and encouraged to see examples of positive government initiatives—the first that I had seen in my 40 years there. It was an eye-opening glimpse of what it could be like in Nova Brasília and elsewhere if the government made a sustained commitment to peace and human services in the favelas.

Zé Cabo was more cynical when I asked him about what I had seen and about the work of the new PAC. In response to my question about whether he thought that any government program or politician would do something positive for Nova Brasília, he replied, "I distrust all of them from the top to the bottom, from the police to the evangelicals to the national security forces....When they treat me well, I become suspicious—either they want my vote or want to rob me, or both..."

Now that he is too old to do all of the construction himself and Waney has died, he has to pay to contract labor to work on his house, so it is in a state of disarray. He gave the best room to the aunt who came to stay with him before she died, and he has kept it as it was when she was still alive rather than going back to sleeping there. After taking care of his community and his family for all of these years, he is now having a hard time taking care of himself.

FIGURE 4.11   Zé Cabo talking with me at his dining room table in Irajá, 2008.

His children think their father was a fool not to leave the favela earlier. They can't understand why he invested so much time and effort in the favela rather than in himself. It is hard for them to understand what life was like in those early, heady years, when the humble folk (*gente humilde*) took on the system—and won! It is even harder for his successful granddaughter Patricia to grasp what that meant.

FIGURE 4.12   A family from Nova Brasília that went back to the countryside to escape the violence and are having trouble surviving there due to lack of work.

ARE THINGS BETTER OUTSIDE OF RIO?

A handful of families from Nova Brasília left everything behind, fleeing from the violence. Many who returned to their hometowns have ended up back in Nova Brasília, as they found that there was even less work in the countryside than in the city and that food was similarly scarce.

Figure 4.12 shows one family who moved out of Nova Brasília a few years ago and bought a small house on the urban fringe of João Pessoa, the capital of the state of Paraiba, in the Northeast. There is no work for them and life is pretty dismal. Being accustomed to a big city has made it even more depressing to be isolated and jobless. Maria, the original study participate is in poor health and they have neither access to a clinic nor funds for medication.

Zé's brother and his wife moved to Natal, the capital of Rio Grande do Norte. They bought land on the outskirts of the city and built a lovely two-story house with a tropical garden and tiled veranda. They received me with great hospitality. They are able to live well there on savings from their work in Rio and their retirement pensions. They even built a room with a separate bathroom for Zé Cabo—and have asked him repeatedly to move there. He enjoys visiting for a month each year but cannot imagine living there. He insists he would die of boredom. He says he needs the "movimento," the rhythms and the energy of the big city.

five

DUQUE DE CAXIAS

FAVELAS AND LOTEAMENTOS

Just as space and meaning are defined and redefined by use, the physical aspects of a community reflect how life is lived within it. Both the text and subtext of a poignant human story are revealed in the following photographs—and the way one obscures and then reveals the other is the key to understanding life in Vila Operária, one of the Caxias in our favelas study.

What I noticed immediately on my return to Vila Operária after 30 years were the solid brick houses, ceramic tile roofs, electric and telephone wires, and improved plaza and sports facility. As I looked up the hillside, I saw how dense the community had become, how the homes had been improved, and how the majority of them had added second and third stories with water tanks and satellite dishes on the top—and an occasional boy flying a kite (figure 5.4). The new church caught my eye, as did the way the central plaza had been renovated, paved, and painted (figure 5.5).

What wasn't noticeable at first glance was the nearly total absence of people, even in the middle of the day, on normally highly populated streets. A close look at these photographs in this chapter reveals that there is no one going up the steps to the houses on the hill behind the plaza; not a single person is playing sports or going in or out of the community center. The few people on

FIGURE 5.1   Djanira (left) with schoolteacher, 1968, in front of the Municipal School of Vila Operária, 1968.

the street in front of the center are not relating to each other. Where did the conviviality go?

Thirty years ago, the streets were bustling with activity and the plaza crowded with people stopping to chat on their way to and from work, school, sports, shopping, or running errands. There was an amusement park there (figure 5.3). Now there is only absence, a sense of artificiality. What would have been abnormal has become normal. This favela is in a state of siege. Everyone is behind closed doors, locked gates, and grilled windows. If you could look more closely, you would see bullet holes piercing the side of the community center and bloodstains on the sidewalk in front of it. These photos reveal what it is like to live with violence. In that way, the story of Caxias is not unlike the stories of Catacumba or Nova Brasília.

The photos of Djanira (figures 5.1 and 5.2), a spirited community activist I met in 1969, are revealing. In the first photo, she stands strong and proud in front of the school she successfully fought for. In the second, taken with me in 2005 in front of her house, she is hard to recognize as the same woman. Her facial expression and body language communicate defeat and despair. It is not just that she has grown older. In her posture, there is a sense of grim resignation. She has decided that she can no longer live in the home she built and shared with several of her 25 siblings, in which she raised her 10 children, which she expanded to make apartments for two of her daughters and their families, and

FIGURE 5.2   Djanira with me in front of her house in Vila Operária, 2005.

where she has cared for her infirm aunt and disabled son. She wants to move away if she can. It is too dangerous.

After many years of litigation, Djanira was able to prove through DNA testing that José Barbosa, her late companion and fellow activist, was the father of four of her children. As his common-law widow, she is entitled to receive his state pension for his three terms of service on the City Council. His children

FIGURE 5.3   Vila Operária Amusement Park was used to raise funds for a professional schoolteacher. A member of our research team (left) and our kombi driver (right) are in the foreground; scattered shacks on the hillside are in the background, 1968.

FIGURE 5.4   Vila Operária, 2001. The same houses are now multi-story brick dwellings densely packed with electricity and phone lines visible.

FIGURE 5.5 The community health center and enclosed soccer field, built in 2000 on the plaza where the amusement park once stood, are locked and empty due to the drug-related violence.

will also be eligible for a portion of his assets. He had stock in Petrobras, Bank of Brasil, Light, Correios, and Telemar. The Justice Department refused to believe that someone with assets like those could be the partner of a woman in Vila Operária, a woman who has resorted to crocheting covers for tissue boxes and decorating baskets to make ends meet. They disputed the validity of the land title she showed them. And they were incredulous that she and her neighbors had been paying IPTU (land taxes) since 1980. This kind of behavior did not fit their image of favela residents.

    With the money she gets from the settlement of Barbosa's estate, she will be able to move to a safer location, which will be better for her physical and mental health.

But, even after the DNA proof, the process was still dragging on as of October 2008. In order to expedite matters, Djanira and Barbosa's children from his first wife had agreed on the division of his assets and had contracted the same lawyer to represent all of them in settling the matter. Still, no resolution is forthcoming.

FINDING DJANIRA

When I returned to Rio in 1999, I knew it would be difficult to find Djanira. The community in which she had lived was an "intentional settlement," an organized squatter community that the people called Vila Idéal (Ideal Vila) or Vila Operária (Workers' Vila).[1] I did not know whether she was still alive, still there, or even whether the favela had the same name. I couldn't remember exactly how to find her house, as I had been back only a few times since 1973.

Unlike the other sites in this study, Duque de Caxias, referred to simply as Caxias, is not a favela but an entire municipality, one of 16 that now comprise the Baixada Fluminense (the state of Rio Lowlands, called the Baixada). Caxias is further from the center of Rio than the other study sites and the most confusing to navigate. At the time of my original study, it was in a different state—the state of Rio de Janeiro—whereas Catacumba and Nova Brasília were in the state of Guanabara, which served as the federal district when the city of Rio was the national capital.[2]

I was interested in what difference home ownership made in the lives of the urban poor, and selecting the municipality of Caxias gave me an opportunity to explore that question. The municipality was relatively new and largely unsettled, and land values were very low in the undeveloped areas. These peripheral neighborhoods, which had no running water, electricity, paved roads, or other urban services, were subdivided into small plots of land which were called *loteamentos não-urbanizados* (unserviced lots). I set up a quasi-experimental design by dividing the sample between such loteamentos and favelas. I used municipal maps to determine the five poorest subdivisions and compared them with the three favelas in the municipality at the time. Figure 5.6 shows these selected neighborhoods and favelas.

Unlike the favelas, the loteamentos provided an opportunity for migrants to invest what little they had in owning land or in renting from another owner on a legal basis. The downside was that this left them with less money to use for building their homes, buying food and medicine, or paying school costs. The favela option meant better food and shelter in the short run, but more insecurity in the long run. I was curious to know which would prove to be the better strategy in the long run.

Djanira did not have a phone, and there was no one I knew in Rio who knew her, so my only recourse was to search for her house and hope she was still there. I brought old photos of her standing in front of her house with her

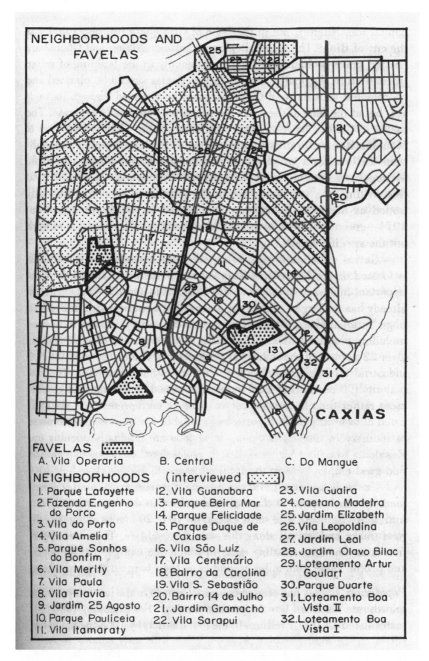

NEIGHBORHOODS AND
FAVELAS

CAXIAS

FAVELAS

A. Vila Operaria   B. Central   C. Do Mangue

NEIGHBORHOODS   (interviewed)

1. Parque Lafayette
2. Fazenda Engenho
   do Porco
3. Vila do Porto
4. Vila Amelia
5. Parque Sonhos
   do Bonfim
6. Vila Merity
7. Vila Paula
8. Vila Flavia
9. Jardim 25 Agosto
10. Parque Paulíceia
11. Vila Itamaraty

12. Vila Guanabara
13. Parque Beira Mar
14. Parque Felicidade
15. Parque Duque de
    Caxias
16. Vila São Luiz
17. Vila Centenário
18. Bairro da Carolina
19. Vila S. Sebastião
20. Bairro 14 de Julho
21. Jardim Gramacho
22. Vila Sarapui

23. Vila Guaira
24. Caetano Madeira
25. Jardim Elizabeth
26. Vila Leopoldina
27. Jardim Leal
28. Jardim Olavo Bilac
29. Loteamento Artur
    Goulart
30. Parque Duarte
31. Loteamento Boa
    Vista II
32. Loteamento Boa
    Vista I

FIGURE 5.6   Map of Caxias (1968) indicating the names and locations of the neighborhoods and favelas.

children and in front of the school next door. I also brought the photo of the amusement park that the Residents' Association had set up to raise money for teachers at their school.

Since I'd last visited the area, Zumba, a local leader well known for his progressive positions, had been elected to the City Council. He was the only Labor Party candidate to make it—the only nonwhite and nonelite among all 21 vereadores. I went directly to the Sede Municipal (municipal seat) to look for him. The building had been transformed from a greenish boxy structure to a shiny silver one with a slightly modernist facade and a more imposing entrance (see figures 5.7 and 5.8).

The receptionist, straightening out her uniform and sitting up a bit taller, informed me that without an appointment it would be impossible to see Zumba. I explained that I had come very far and asked her whether just this once, it might be possible for me to speak with someone from his staff so that I might request an appointment.

After insisting that this was not usually done, she called back to Zumba's office, and he came right out to see for himself what in the world an American woman might be doing in this provincial town hall, in the sweltering heat of the Baixada summer. I was prepared to explain myself, but as soon as I mentioned my name, he said,

FIGURE 5.7   Caxias City Hall, the curved building on the right with a garden in front, 1968.

FIGURE 5.8   Caxias City Hall, 2004, with security barriers and pavement replacing the garden. The front of the building reads "Câmera Municipal de Duque de Caxias" and the side lists a theater, a public reading room, and a historic archive.

Yes, I know who you are…You were here a long time ago and our librarian still talks about you—she still works here—I'll call her. I was very young at that time, but I remember your research—I have your book in my office. How many people do you think even knew about Caxias back then?! We learned something about our own reality from you. It took an outsider to put us on the map. Before that all anyone ever heard about us here was Tenorio Cavalcanti [the first elected state deputy from the Baixada] and the *esquadrãos da morte* [death squads].

In a matter of minutes, we were sharing stories over cafézinho in the dimly lit, air-conditioned conference room, and Zumba was bringing in his young assistants to meet me and pulling out old photographs. One of the students, Flavia, lived in Vila Operária, just up the street from Djanira, and offered to take me to her house. Once I had met everyone and promised to return for a longer discussion, I followed Flavia to Vila Operária.

It felt as though I were in a time-lapse movie. The last time I had been in Caxias, it had the air of a small provincial town. The entire municipality had only one *bairro nobre* (classy neighborhood), the *25 de Augusto*. Now, on our way to Vila Operária, we passed through 25 de Augusto, and there we encountered signs of dramatic growth: we crossed a major thoroughfare filled with traffic and outfitted with state-of-the-art pedestrian pathways, signals, signage, and lighting, and entered the small neighborhood park, which had been transformed from a hard dirt area with a few benches and a few trees into an oddly clean and shiny public space. The children's playground area had bright red-and-yellow structures for climbing and sliding, and on the right of the diagonal pathway dividing the space were several brightly painted hexagonal tables where adults could congregate under the shade of indestructible metal umbrellas. The trees were gone—I suppose they weren't part of the design plan.

After walking for another 10 or 15 minutes, we entered one of the poorest areas of the city. The pavement gave way to a gravelly road surface, and the smell of fear was palpable as soon as we turned the corner into Vila Operária. Women came out of shops clutching their groceries and their purses, looking in every direction at once. A few young men slouched menacingly in front of the birosca on the corner.

Yet even here, the physical improvements since my last visit were impressive. Where there had been an open field was a bright yellow-and-blue community center, with an asphalt soccer field in front of it and a clinic sign over one of the side doors. All of this was encircled by a barbed-wire fence with a locked gate. I soon found out that the center had remained locked since it was renovated in 2000, due to "security concerns." The precarious shacks on the hillside behind the sports center had been replaced by solid brick homes with glass windows covered by iron grates. The whole story of Vila Operária existed in that vista: more amenities, less security.

To our left was the entrance to the street where Djanira lived. On my own, I would have missed her house entirely. Where there had been an open garden with fruit trees, flowering vines, and songbirds, there was a high, grey metal wall with a locked and bolted gate. We pressed the buzzer and banged on the door. It took quite awhile before anyone appeared. Evidently, one of the young children of the house had been dispatched to the second-floor terrace to see who was there before daring to open the gate. A new fear, not present when I had lived there, permeated every aspect and had crept into every gesture of daily life.

Djanira burst out crying and laughing when she recognized me! In minutes, we were hugging and chatting and swapping clothing as though it had been only yesterday that I had been there. She did not look well. Her life had been particularly difficult over the years when she had been trying fruitlessly to claim the assets José had left for her and their children. She was worried about the health of her 32-year-old daughter, Janisse (my namesake), who was trying unsuccessfully to collect disability for the lung condition she had developed after years of public employment spraying DDT from a canister she carried on her back.

Vila Operária, where Djanira still lives, is one of the three favelas and five subdivisions included in my original study in Duque de Caxias. One hundred of the 200-person random sample had been chosen proportionally from the favelas and the other hundred from the loteamentos. These eight locations represented the poorest areas in the entire municipality. As shown in figure 5.6, the three favelas (labeled A, B, and C) were Favela Central, Favela do Mangue (also called Beira-Mar), and Vila Operária. The five least developed subdivisions were Olavo Bilac, São Sebastião, Sarapuí, Vila Leopoldina, and Centenário. In 2001, we selected one site for the DRP, as it was not feasible to conduct such an elaborate event in more than one of the 8 communities. Because of Djanira's archives, memory for detail, wide connections in the community, and willingness to give her time to this endeavor, we picked Vila Operária for the historical reconstruction and qualitative aspects of the Caxias restudy.

Duque de Caxias is one of the most rapidly growing municipalities in the state of Rio de Janeiro. Until its independence in 1943, it was part of the adjacent municipality, Nova Iguaçu. At the time of the first study, there were only a handful of municipalities in the Baixada Fluminense. At last count there are 16.

Until the first half of the twentieth century, the Baixada was an area of thinly populated swamps, some of them located below sea level. During colonial times, sugar cane plantations were expanded around the bay, but lowland areas could not be exploited until the early nineteenth century, with the introduction of new drainage techniques. As the importance of sugar cane plantations decreased, slave labor became scarce, and more fertile lands elsewhere were explored—the entire Baixada became impoverished. When the rivers became obstructed, the whole area turned into a big swamp. Malaria spread everywhere, and many of the residents were forced to leave. It was not until the 1930s that the government took measures to improve sanitation and provide fresh water through the city system. Shortly thereafter, the extension of the railway line of Leopoldina and the construction of the Rio-Petrópolis road gave new life to the area, and its population started to increase.

Starting in the mid-1950s, the Baixada gradually became an expansion area for the city of Rio. Intensive use of the land for residential and industrial purposes brought about a dramatic rise in population density. Immigrants who arrived in the city with very little money and no contacts often ended up settling in the Baixada, where work opportunities were expanding and costs were minimal. Growth rose rapidly in the 1960s and 1970s and has continued to rise. The population has increased from 430,000 in 1970 to 668,000 in 1991 to 776,000 in 2000.

At the same time, Caxias was becoming a major industrial center. By the turn of the century it accounted for over 20 percent of industrial production of Rio State. The national oil company, Petrobrás, inaugurated an oil refinery in Caxias in 1969 (still active today) that was the largest one in the country at that time. Petrobrás in turn attracted other industries, including a synthetic rubber plant, a National Motor Company factory, and producers of pharmaceuticals, chemicals, metallurgy, and electric motors. Ninety percent of this local industry was owned by the national government. This transformed Caxias from a bedroom community for commuters who worked in Rio into an industrial hub of its own, and then into a commercial center as well.

During the military dictatorship, as part of the Fifth Institutional Act, Caxias was declared an "area of national security," due to the critical importance of the oil refinery and other industries there, and most likely as a way to prevent any political or labor organizing against the regime. Thus, like the metropolitan capital cities of the country, the mayor was appointed by the military.

THE STORY OF VILA OPERÁRIA

Vila Operária is not a typical favela. In a way, it is not a favela at all, despite being classified and treated as such. In 1962 the owner ceded the land to the 150 families who had occupied it, and improved it, fought for the right to remain there. In 1980, the municipality officially granted the residents land title. They pay municipal taxes on their property—and take pride in showing their title papers and tax receipts. Nonetheless, the community began as a land invasion, the title papers are not always honored, and it is considered a favela by the government.

The large plot of land that became Vila Operária was originally owned by Genach Chadrycki, a rich miner from Poland who purchased it but never lived there. In 1959, a group of 10 men, led by José Barbosa, organized the 150 families to occupy a piece of it, selecting an overgrown, inaccessible tract that was not highly desirable. They got bricks donated from a brick factory in Olaría and wood donated from Petrobrás, and distributed these building materials to each family. Djanira said Barbosa insisted that only brick be used in the construction of the houses so that they would be permanent homes, distinct from barracos in favelas and thus less likely to be demolished.

Djanira described the creation of Vila Operária as follows:

> The area where we are living now was a fetid swamp. There were large numbers of poor people living on the streets, pregnant women, young children, and so on....Barbosa said he could not bear to see such suffering. He mobilized the men

and got machines to clear the land and lay out the main streets. Half of the streets were created by machinery and half by *mutirão* (collective self-help or mutual aid). The men and boys did most of the heavy labor, and we women cooked up immense quantities of food and brought it to the site along with cold drinks—it's so hot here, as you know.

We got the support of the most powerful political figure in the area—Tenorio Cavalcanti, you know, the state deputy. By 1960, the streets were open, and about 150 families were living here. We called it Vila Operária because everyone living here was a worker. We did not permit anyone with a police record or a reputation for drinking or starting fights to settle here.

Tenório Cavalcanti (1906–1987) was a figure of mythic proportions—admired by some, detested by others, and feared by all. He arrived in Caxias as a teen-ager from the *sertão* (drought-stricken backlands of the Northeast) at the end of the 1920s, when the entire area was a mosquito-infested swamp with a few packed-earth roads crossing it. He rose to become state deputy—the first from the Baixada—and because of his help to the thousands of migrants who followed, had sufficient electoral clout to be elected federal deputy.

He always wore a black cape, was always armed, and always had his body-guards with him. He was an old-style populist leader, able to buy votes by giving out food or cash, transporting people to the polls, and helping families and indi-viduals in times of emergency. His admirers called him "O Rei da Baixada"—the King of the Baixada; his detractors called him "O Deputado Pistoleiro"—the Pistol-shooting Deputy." (It is said that he thought nothing of shooting his ene-mies.) In 1960, in the last open elections before the coup, he ran for governor of the state of Rio and lost to Carlos Lacerda.

He lived on an enormous estate surrounded by a moat—complete with a drawbridge. When he gave me the tour of his property, the things he was most proud of were his zoological and botanical gardens and the variety of exotic birds he kept. His life inspired the film *O Homem da Capa Preta* (The man in the black cape), which came out in 1986, the year before he died.

Five years after the initial occupation of Vila Operária, in 1962, Chadry-cki, the land owner, returned. He met with Barbosa. In Djanira's words, "They formed a good relationship, and Chadrycki agreed to cede his land to the peo-ple living there. He obtained official government authorization to do so. Each family who had supported Barbosa got legal title papers to their land."

In that way, Vila Operária was officially founded on April 19, 1962, and its Residents' Association was inaugurated the same day. It was agreed that elections would be held every four years. Steps would be taken to acquire an ambulance, water, electricity, postal box, and school. In a concerted effort to prevent the community from becoming a favela, the leaders drew up a set of statutes for the community that every family agreed to sign. They specified that no one with a police record would be allowed to settle there and no unlawful acts would be tolerated. Property was to be registered in the name of the female head of household, so that in the event of a divorce, the man would be the one who would have to leave. A family council was created to mediate marriage conflicts and disputes, and every attempt was made to create an ideal community for working-class families. To this day many people refer to the community as Vila Idéal.

Just one year later, in 1963, Brazil's National Housing Bank tried to evict the settlers from the land. Their battle to stay there lasted for seven years. The bank had a strong interest in removing them, because of Vila Operária's proximity to the aforementioned wealthy neighborhood of 25 de Augusto. My friends tell of one occasion when the National Housing Bank sent armed agents to try to remove the residents, or persuade them to leave, and the men, women, and children together fought back with wood, stones, and bricks.

Some of the things Djanira recounted in our interviews were stranger than fiction:

> Barbosa ran for vereador and was elected three times. People really wanted an insider representing them politically. In 1970, when the dictatorship was in power, he was thrown in jail with a pig (literally). The politicos wanted him isolated. They accused him of being a communist even though he was a devout Catholic. When they took him to jail, I went with him. I was expecting and my baby was about due.
>
> Many community members came to the jail to support him. The police treated us very rudely: we were not allowed to drink the water or use the bathrooms. While we were waiting to see what they would do with him, my water broke, and I nearly gave birth right there. It was Barbosa's baby, and his wife came to help me and took me to the hospital.
>
> The baby was born healthy, which was wonderful, but that was a bad year for us. We were threatened with removal by a candidate for vereador named Armando Melo de França, and all the residents came down to fight against his candidacy. His supporters were there, too—I will never forget it. One yelled at me and said I was *uma mulher tomada pelo diabo* [a woman possessed by the devil].

Land title was a constant issue. The community members showed me the titles to their homes. The titling process, supposedly settled for the first 150 families in 1962, was taken up anew and contested for eleven years—1974 to 1985. Each family "officially" owns one lot. Djanira's is number 9. Nowadays, because of the drugs and violence, the land in Vila Operária isn't worth what it was earlier.

"Since the invasion of these bandidos, we have no freedom," she says. "No one can get a job if they live here, no matter what." To make ends meet, Djanira was trying to sell mail-order clothing by telephone, for which she would earn 10 percent of sales. But after paying her phone bill, she was left with almost nothing. Her son, who was disabled in a bus accident, used to sell hard candies in front of her house, but it became too dangerous for him to go out there.

VIOLENCE CHANGED THE LANDSCAPE

The violence associated with the Baixada has always included political violence, that is, violence in the dispute for power. Death squads composed of former policemen and organized by tradesmen and local leaders have acted freely for decades, killing petty criminals or rival leaders. There was a popular revolt in 1962, against hoarders and speculators of basic commodities, in which salesmen were attacked. This is generally considered the starting point of the militias and vigilante groups. Homicide rates in the area were among the highest in the country, in Latin America, and in the world. Killings are so common that, as a local resident and graduate student told us, "In the Baixada you have to kill six or seven at once to get into the newspaper."[3]

In December 2001, our research team held a day-long DRP in Vila Operária. The residents who participated told us that starting in the early 1980s, the independence of the Residents' Association was threatened by the drug dealers. Ten years later, there was no independent leadership left in the community, and in 2001 the Residents' Association was closed down altogether by the traffic. It happened when the person designated as president by the Commando Vermelho was challenged by a member of the rival gang (Terceiro Commando). Since then, there has been no organization representing community interests or attending to the needs of the residents. The health clinic has remained closed, as the earlier one had functioned within the Residents' Association building. For a place born out of a solidarity movement and the struggle for the right to exist, it is a sad time indeed.

During the DRP, Nilo and Fernando, adult children of one of the early residents named Alaide, told us of their humiliation when they were applying for work. They had to give a false address or be seen as bandidos (literally bandits, but colloquially used to mean drug traffickers). Isabella, a mother of six and grandmother of fourteen who is still working as a cook, related that when she bought a new refrigerator, the store refused to deliver it once she gave her address. They cannot pay anyone enough, they said, to get them to venture into their community.

When I asked about the police station I had seen on the higher part of the hill, Fernando told me that the police are afraid to confront the dealers, who have more sophisticated weapons and more people. The police stay inside the station and keep a low profile. When they emerge, it is to support an organized "blitz," during which battalions of Special Forces in armored cars come into the community on the pretext of capturing a dealer, but—nervous and drugged —they end up shooting at random. As one woman put it, "a police station is a waste since the bandidos just finish them off." There was an imposing-looking new church near the police station, but when I wanted to go up to see it, everyone said it was much too dangerous to go up that way.

As in all of the communities I studied, each sub-area thinks that the other areas are more dangerous. They all say "aqui e tudo tranquilo—lá e muito perigroso" ("here it is very peaceful—over there it is very dangerous"). That seems to be just one of many coping mechanisms for getting through each day. Also as in the other communities, life is relatively normal while one drug faction is indisputably in control, but when the turf is contested by a rival gang, or if the police arrest a gang leader, an all-out war ensues. The prisoners in these wars are the local inhabitants. The schools are often closed, the stores are closed and boarded up—and everyone stays in their homes, afraid to go out into the street. This state of siege can last for days.

During the period 1984–90, directly following the end of the dictatorship, Vila Operária was highly organized and active, as were other communities in Caxias, some of which brought Paulo Freire's literacy methods and the teaching of liberation theology with them from the Northeast. At that time, people in the favelas and the NGOs that worked with them were mobilizing for social justice and rights. They still had hope that they would become real citizens in a real democracy with real accountability.

At the end of the 2001 DRP meeting, the residents summed up the changes as follows:

> The entrance of *tóxicos* (drugs), narco-trafficking, and violence was the end of our freedom; the end of our happiness.
>
> The traffickers took over our Residents' Association, closed down our community radio, and even forced the church to close—the one where we used to hold our meetings. They threatened us with death if we did not comply.
>
> War between the Commando Vermelho and the Terceiro Commando—the Red Command and the Third Command—robbed us of our safety. Innocent people and children are always being killed by *balas perdidas* (stray bullets) or caught in the *tiroteo* (crossfire). The police are even worse—they just come in and shoot at any thing in their sight
>
> The little ones imitate the older ones and start taking drugs and enter the traffic; even the girls. They get pregnant at 12 or 13; they abandon their children to become the girlfriend of the gang leader.
>
> Due to the association of violence and drugs with Vila Operária, a "madame"— the "lady of the house"—doesn't trust anyone who lives here to work in her home. So many of us women have lost our jobs at the same time the men lost theirs due to all the factory closings.

The last part of the DRP, just before we served lunch for the participants, was to define priorities for the community. The participants easily agreed that the most pressing needs were "jobs, education, health, security, and a candidate whom we could trust to defend our interests in public office."

Work was the primary concern, and the stigma of living in Vila Operária has been a major obstacle to getting hired. People need jobs to replace the ones lost with the factory closures. They are willing to be trained for those jobs but do not know if or where such help would be available to them. For their children to have good jobs in the future, they wanted school hours expanded to a full day. But they insisted that even full-time in school would be of no use unless they could attract better teachers—which would require better pay and greater safety.

Health care was a pressing need. Since the Residents' Association had been closed by the traffic, there was no place for them to go—they desperately needed a clinic or health post in the community. They said they did not have an answer to the problem of violence and that things had only gotten worse since the militia had begun extorting residents for everyday activities such as the delivery of the gas canisters used for cooking or using the minivans that went up into the favela hills. One man summed it up by saying, "regaining our sense of personal safety would help us regain our freedom to live."

THE STORY OF DJANIRA

The story of Djanira and her children is emblematic of the difficulties faced and not always overcome by families like hers.

Because Djanira's income falls below the poverty line, she is entitled to a monthly *cesta básica* (basic food basket), but she doesn't get it. There is an unofficial cesta básica handed out at her church, containing items donated by church members, but since everyone's poor, there are hardly any donors, and there are many in need. The ones who go to church most are the ones who get it. When she cannot afford to pay her water bill, she gets water from the well, though she knows it is contaminated. She does some embroidering and handicrafts to make a bit of money, but what she earns barely covers the costs of the materials. She is currently living with one of her daughters, her son who was in the accident, his wife, and four grandchildren. They are struggling.

This is a sorry state of affairs for someone who has come so far in her life. Djanira was born in 1939, one of 26 children. Her mother, a washerwoman, died when Djanira was seven, and her father, a traveling salesman, died two years later. Like most people in the countryside in their generation, they were both illiterate. Djanira made her way to Rio and to Vila Operária. She was active in the creation of the community and the building of the school next door to her house and earned her living cooking *merendas* (lunches) for the school children and teachers. She has 10 children and 13 grandchildren.

Djanira had only three years of schooling, and that always bothered her. So in 1972, four years after our first meeting, she went back to school. She was 33 years old and already had seven children—one an infant and another a year old—and there was no adult education at that time, so she went into the classroom with youngsters. She says she was not ashamed but proud to be back in school. After completing her secondary school degree, she became a social worker and was employed by the municipal government.

Life in Vila Operária was improving, and her life improved during the many years when she and Barbosa were together. Although they never officially married they shared a life, and he was like a father to all of her children, four of whom were his.

To see change over time as reflected in this one family as a microcosm of favela life one need look no further than the educational and occupational levels of Djanira's children and their children.[4]

Her eldest, Marco Antonio, who never completed high school, works in the municipal health office. He has three children, two of whom finished high school and the third won a scholarship for the prevestibular preparatory course and is now studying at the Federal University of Rio de Janeiro, one of the best universities in the city. Jane Marcia only studied for three years and is a housewife who never had children. She and her husband live nearby, and he earns enough to get them through. Marta Janete the next got a degree in *pedagogia* (education) and now, after teaching for 15 years, is working in the Caxias Housing Department. She has two children, a daughter, now attending high school and raising her baby, and a son who has finished his studies through high school and cannot find work.

Jorge Luis is the most successful of Djanira's children. He is a lawyer and has a successful practice in Japarepagua. He has a child with his live-in girlfriend, whom he supports. He visits from time to time but has not helped with his mother's inheritance case and does not appear to contribute to her household expenses. Celia Regina never completed high school and works as a clerk at the local hospital—she has two boys. Almir was hit by a bus when he was young, and never went beyond third grade. He is married and has one daughter, Diana, who is about to finish school and wants to be a biologist. Raldo left school after junior high, is a transportation inspector, and has three children, all in school. Janisse, my namesake, is shown in figure 5.9 with her mother. She had only five years of schooling, worked at the municipal mosquito prevention program (SUCAN) until it affected her lungs, never married, and adopted a little girl. She lives in a legalized, almost rural loteamento about 45 minutes north of Caxias, on the road to Petropolis. Roberto did not complete high school and also worked for SUCAN as a sanitation worker and in pest control. The

FIGURE 5.9   Djanira and her daughter, Janisse, 2004.

youngest, Raquel, is a housewife who never went beyond junior high. Among Djanira's five boys and five girls, all but two (Raquel and Almir) have formal jobs with a *carteira assinada* (a signed work card guaranteeing the full range of workers' benefits)—an exceptional accomplishment.

As seen in the family tree (figure 5.10), Djanira's 10 children have produced 13 grandchildren. Six of her children have no children or just one; three of her children have just two children; and one, her eldest, has three children.[5]

This sharp drop in family size is characteristic of urbanizing populations. In the city, where medical care and medical knowledge are more accessible, the rates of infant and child mortality drop. Women who get more education are more likely to enter the labor force and tend to postpone childbirth and to limit the number of children they have. Large families are not a survival asset as they may have been when living off the land. Once women have access to birth control and have high aspirations for their children to go beyond their own limits in life, they reduce the size of their families.

The difference in the number of siblings and children that Margarida, Zé Cabo, and Djanira had reflects this difference between the countryside and city. Margarida, whose parents were already in Rio, was one of four siblings and had six children. Djanira and Zé, both born *na roça* (in the countryside), were one of 19 and 25 siblings, respectively; and they had 6 and 10 children, respectively. But none of their children has more than three children, and the trend among their grandchildren is to have only one or two. Many, like Patricia, Zé's granddaughter, have decided not to have any. This pattern emerged dramatically

DJANIRA'S FAMILY

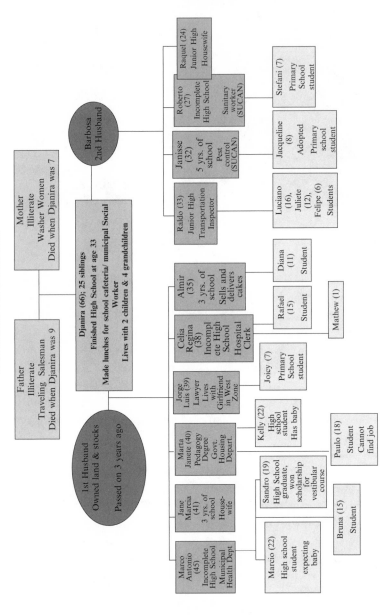

FIGURE 5.10 Djanira's family tree, 2003.

in all of the family histories, and it matches the demographic profile of urbanization worldwide. I found this particularly encouraging since the data analysis revealed small family size is strongly related to upward mobility.

Yet it is disheartening to see how little schooling Djanira's children managed to get and how many are still struggling to make ends meet, despite having a brilliant, determined mother who valued education enough to return to school at the age of 33, and (at least four of them) having had a sophisticated, well-to-do father. Individual differences in motivation and ability account for some of the variation, and luck certainly played a part, but birth order, which is considered one predictor of achievement, appears to have had no effect. The only two of the 10 siblings who got advanced degrees were Marta Janete and Jorge Luis, numbers three and four.

The occupational profile of Djanira's family is atypical, in that so many of them work for the Caxias municipal government. Djanira's position there undoubtedly opened the door for them, and they are all hard workers. In other Caxias favela families, there are more unemployed factory workers who went from one job to another as deindustrialization led to a chain of closures.

Family solidarity is not universal among the urban poor. A family I interviewed in 1969 because the father was a leader in Nova Brasília, had moved to one of the newer loteamentos on the Caxias periphery and was struggling to make ends meet. They were elderly and had to decide each month between food or diabetes medicine for the wife. Their daughter, who lived in a house they built for her behind their own, was helping out with household expenses by working as a *baba* (nanny), but after she got pregnant and had her own baby, she resented having to care for someone else's, so she quit.

One of the bedroom doors in their home was always closed, and a car and motorcycle were parked on the gravel driveway. I asked about that, and they proudly said that these were their son's things that he kept at home while he was away in the service. His room was a palace of consumption, with a large plasma TV, a speed bike, an air conditioner, and every luxury imaginable. It even had a new paint job and fancy curtains. They kept it for him with great respect and never entered it. I could see no evidence that he helped them out or that they expected his help or resented his lack of help.

UPDATE, 2008

The last time I was in Rio, in October 2008, I became worried about Djanira, because no one was answering her home phone. I tried every day of the week and all hours of the day and night, to no avail. I did not know any other way to contact her. Having learned my lesson in Nova Brasília, I was not inclined to venture into favelas on my own—but after a week of no answers, I could think of no other way but to go out to her house and see what was going on.

When I got to Vila Operária, I stood on the street in front of the metal gate that leads into her front garden and called out to her. Fortunately, her son Almir and his wife and daughter heard me. They live in a separate apartment upstairs, built on the rooftop of Djanira's house. They looked down over the balcony and when they recognized me, came down to let me in.

It turned out that Djanira had pneumonia and had gone to stay with her daughter Janisse. I had been there many times with Djanira. It is on the subdivided land of an old *fazenda* (estate). The place has the feel of the early favelas in Rio, although each plot of land has been legally purchased. It is a flat area with unpaved roads, and incomplete urban services. When Janisse first moved there, wells were the only source of water and there was limited access to electricity, but now they have running water and metered electricity. The streets are laid out on a grid, and the houses are still one-story wooden dwellings, many of them with low, decorative fences around them. Janisse has made herself a lovely flower garden around her house, and it has a breezy veranda in front. The community has its own Residents' Association, located in the abandoned manor house of the estate owner. It is surrounded by old shade trees, green grass, and an open field leads down to a small river. On my 2005 visit I was impressed with the ideas and actions of their elected president, who is independent of any drug faction. It is one of the few examples I have seen of an attractive, affordable community which is inaccessible enough that the drug traffic is not interested—at least for now.

When I called Djanira at Janisse's house, she said she was feeling better, the air was less polluted there, and she was being well taken care of. She told me that if I ever needed to reach her, I should e-mail her granddaughter, Diana, who would give her my message.

Diana, named after Princess Diana of England, is the only child of Djanira's son Almir and his wife Laudicea. I had watched her grow up, a shy girl who observed everything with great interest. She had blossomed into a self-confident and enthusiastic young woman, a tall, slender 17-year-old who loved studying and had a passion for natural sciences. She said she had known this was her calling since she was five years old. She has never missed a single day of school—ever. She is in her last year of middle school at the Colégio Miguel Corta in Caxias, and she has taken extra courses in English, Spanish, and information technology (the latter at the Foundation for Development of Technology).

Figure 5.11 shows Diana and her father on Djanira's rooftop terrace with Vila Operária visible in the background. Diana's mother Laudicia from Sahia is on the extreme right of the frame, laughing and trying to stay out of the picture, insisting that she in not photogenic. The air conditioner in the window of their bedroom is visible on the left. Their front door opens into a small room with the stove and kitchen sink against one wall, the refrigerator opposite it and the

FIGURE 5.11   Djanira's son, Almir, and his daughter, Diana, on the rooftop of her house where they live, 2008.

dining table against the back wall. The bathroom is to the left and Diana's bedroom is off to the right, separated from her parents' bedroom by a curtain hung from the doorway. The terrace was piled high with sand and bags of cement as Almir is about to build an additional room so that Diana can have privacy and her own place to study.

FIGURE 5.12   Diana's graduating class from high school, showing preponderance of females and lack of visual distinction from their peers in the South Zone.

Currently, Diana is trying to get an internship in biology or zoology. She wants to learn more by working with a teacher or researcher in the field. She showed me the nature films she had collected, the papers she was writing, and the way she used the Internet for research. At the same time that she is connected to cyberspace on a daily basis, she is living in one of the most dangerous favelas in Caxias, and she has never been to the city of Rio, only an hour away. The group that is graduating with her is shown in figure 5.12. If given half a chance, any of them could become gente.

Almir was nearly killed when he was only a boy. I remember him standing outside the front gate of their house selling hard candy to people as they passed by on their way up and down the street. He suffered a severe concussion and several broken bones; but he has recovered almost completely and now works with his wife, Laudicia, in a catering business they run out of their apartment. Laudicia, who has the Bahian touch, makes magic in their small kitchen. She cooks all the lunches for the school next door and makes hot lunches for workers to bring to their jobs and sweets for general sale. Almir makes the deliveries on his motor scooter and sells Laudicia's sweets and cakes in the central plaza of Caxias. It has become too dangerous to sell them on the streets of Vila Operária.

The entire family is waiting for Djanira's legal case to be settled. It has been nearly 10 years since Barbosa died, leaving sizable assets—land, savings, stocks. But his first wife claimed it all, and the case has been held up in the court system indefinitely, while Djanira's family has struggled to survive. Four years ago, a DNA test, which Djanira had to pay for, proved conclusively that Barbosa fathered these four children, but still they have not been allowed to receive anything from his bequest to them. The family thinks the lawyers are just playing games so as to continue being paid.

After Barbosa's first wife passed away, all of his children (hers and Djanira's) agreed on a settlement, and, fed up with the never-ending legal procedures, they decided to all use the same lawyer in order to expedite the process. Still the matter remains unresolved. They need someone to push this through but Djanira's lawyer son Jorge Luis says he doesn't want to get involved.

We were standing on the veranda, and I was about to take a photo of the multistory houses, when they told me not to even raise my camera. There is a boca (drug sales point) above on the hillside, where they have a powerful telescope that enables them to see everything even at great distances. The previous month, a family friend had been over and was shooting a video of the family on the veranda when a trafficante from the CV (Commando Vermelho) knocked loudly on their door demanding to know who was filming what and why. Vila Operária is in the worst situation possible—instead of being controlled, as are most favelas, by either the drug traffic or the militia, the residents of Vila Operária are subject to the abuses of both. Their every move is monitored by the CV; they risk getting killed in the crossfire of the turf wars, and they pay protection fees to the militia for everything from the delivery of their mail and their cooking gas canisters to their cable TV and Internet access.

WHAT A DIFFERENCE A PLACE MAKES

Place turned out to be a critical factor in the opportunity for moving up and out of all of the favelas I studied. When I compared the research results by the state of origin of the original migrants to Rio, there were no significant differences. But the location and type of community within Rio had a strong impact on the chances for upward mobility—not only for the original interviewees who were raised there (if not born there) but for their children and grandchildren as well.

Being raised in one of the favelas in Caxias put the residents at a relative disadvantage, while being raised in one of the loteamentos in Caxias conferred a distinct advantage. Being raised in Catacumba conferred long-term advantages, particularly for those who completed elementary school.[6] The educational and job opportunities were much better in the South Zone, and the daily contact with higher status social groups opened possibilities that would be unthinkable on the periphery.

Of all the study areas, those from the loteamentos in Caxias ended up with the highest level of integration into the formal sector. Although they were poor at first, they did not suffer the stigma of living in a favela, and many of them ended up owning their land, even if they had started as renters. Unlike the favelas, when the loteamentos got urban services, they became regular neighborhoods, often indistinguishable from others in the municipality. If in 1968 the loteamento residents had comparable incomes than those in favelas, having legal status enabled them to increase their advantage over time. Formality helped them climb out of poverty.

On all indicators of well-being, including an index of socioeconomic status—as measured by education, consumption of household appliances, and crowding (people per room)—the residents of Caxias loteamentos scored highest, followed by those from Catacumba, with Nova Brasília in the middle and the Caxias favelas scoring the lowest. Being peripheral and informal was a double condemnation.

It is fashionable to say that due to the Brazilian legacy of slavery and its deep inequalities, the poor are trapped and condemned to reproduce their poverty in each generation. That makes sense in theory, but in reality, the system is more permeable. The interpretation depends on the reference group. If you compare Djanira's illiterate parents with her computer-literate granddaughter, you see the family has come a long way. But how does the progress of Diana compare with that of her contemporaries from the South Zone? Is the gap closing or widening? How can the promising young people like her become competitive in the job market while living in the midst of the drug gangs and the militia as they do?

six

MARGINALITY FROM MYTH TO REALITY

EU SOU FAVELA

Sim, mas a favela nunca foi reduto de marginal, eu falei
So tem gente humilde, marginalizada
E essa verdade não sai no jornal
A favela é um problema social
É mais eu sou favela
Minha gente é trabalhadeira
E nunca teve assistência social
Sim mas só vive lá
Porque para o pobre não tem outro jeito
Apenas só tem o direito a um saláiro de fome
E uma vida normal
A favela é uma problema social.

I AM FAVELA

Yes, but the favela was never the refuge of the marginal, I said
There are only humble people, marginalized
And this truth does not appear in the newspaper

(Refrain) The favela is a social problem

And what's more, I am the favela
My people are workers
And never had social assistance
But can live only there

Because for the poor there is no other way
We only have the right to a salary of hunger
That's our normal life

(Refrain) The favela is a social problem.

NOCA DA PORTELA AND SERGIO MOSCA, 1994

This popular samba "Eu Sou Favela" says a great deal about the concept of "marginality" as it relates to poverty and pride in Rio's favelas.[1] The favelas in Rio de Janeiro house millions of inhabitants, people who would otherwise be homeless.

The songwriters embrace the favelas as themselves, declaring that they do not accept "handouts" or social assistance, affirming that they are honest workers who are marginalized by society, undermined by the press, and underpaid. Their lyrics are supported by this research. Of the more than 2000 people interviewed (which includes all three generations in 2001 and the new random sample in 2003), 80 percent had a monthly income of 170 reais (approximately US$68 at that time) or less, but only 18 percent thought this was "sufficient for a decent life." Sixty-seven percent stated that they would need almost twice as much, 300 reais per month (about $US120), to lead a "decent life." Only 19 percent of respondants earned that much or more.

The songwriters use the sarcastic refrain of the song, "The favela is a social problem,"[2] to mock the way favelas are seen by the rest of society, turning the patronizing phrase inside out and claiming it as their own. This is reminiscent of the song from *West Side Story*, in which gang members of East Harlem say to Officer Krupke, that they are down on their knees "'cause no one wants a fella with a social disease."

The view of the favelas as "a social problem" is produced and reproduced on a daily basis as those who live there are treated as a threat to the social system that created the favelas in the first place. If other housing options were available for the poor, perhaps favelas would not exist.

Taken together, the negative stereotypes about those living in favelas have formed an ideology of marginality powerful enough to blot out all evidence to the contrary. Insofar as the favela residents are seen as "social problems" the idea of getting rid of them will never be off the policy table. As a case in point, Eduardo Paes, the current mayor of Rio, was quoted in April 2009, saying that with regard to favelas, no options would be considered off the table.

The Myth of Marginality provoked a gradual shift in the perception of the urban poor. I made the case that the very people who had been dismissed as "marginal," or outside the system, were actually playing a vital role in the workings of the city—and were tightly integrated into that system, but in a perversely asymmetrical manner.

Continuing my research 30 years later, I once again found that the concept of marginality with its multiple and shifting connotations provides a window into the thinking of the general public and some policy-makers, flamed by the near hysteria in the mass media. In picking up the threads of my earlier study, I was eager to find out how the concept of marginality had evolved in relation to favela residents and to what extent such changes were reflected in policy and practice.

DEBUNKING THE MYTHS OF MARGINALITY

The concept of marginality has been debunked, deconstructed, dismissed, and, in turn, rediscovered and reconstructed over the past decades. I researched and wrote *The Myth of Marginality* during a specific historical moment, in the context of widespread antagonism toward the "masses" of migrants arriving from the countryside and invading the "citadel" of the civilized city. The following quotation, written in 1968 by the agency officially responsible for oversight of the favelas in Rio de Janeiro, sums up both official and popular views of the era.

> Families arrive from the interior pure and united…in stable unions. The dis-integration begins in the favela as a consequence of the promiscuity, the bad examples and the financial difficulties there…young girls are seduced and abandoned; they get pregnant but don't feel any shame…liquor and drugs serve to dull the disappointments, humiliations and food deficiency….The nights belong to the criminals…one can hear the screams for help. But no one dares to interfere lest they will be next….Policeman rarely penetrate the favela and then only in groups.[3]

In my fieldwork, I found that, despite their widespread acceptance at all levels of society, these propositions had no basis in reality. My research showed the propositions to be "empirically false, analytically misleading, and insidious in their policy implications."[4] In fact, I found the favelas to be socially well organized and cohesive and their residents capable of making good use of the urban milieu and its institutions. Culturally, they contributed their slang, soccer, and samba to the "mainstream," and aspired to improve their lives, particularly through the education of their children. They willingly took on the worst jobs (often more than one) for the lowest pay, under the most arduous conditions and with the least security. They consumed their share of the products of others (often paying more for them, since local shops had a monopoly [and were willing to extend credit]), and they built their own houses as well as the urban infrastructure of their communities.

Favela residents at the time were aware of and keenly involved in those aspects of politics that affected their lives, both within and outside the favela. They cooperated with the clientelistic local politicians, bargaining astutely with candidates for city council, while appearing to remain submissive and apolitical in obedience to the rules of the authoritarian regime. Radical ideology and the intelligentsia's hoped-for propensity for revolutionary activism were completely absent. The frame of reference for favela residents was not the millionaires in the neighborhoods that surrounded them but the impoverished rural families they had left behind. The favelas provided a cost-free solution to the lack of affordable housing and proximity to jobs and services, and they offered tightly knit communities within which reciprocal favors mitigated the hardships of poverty.

My conclusion was that the favela residents are not marginal at all but inextricably bound into society, albeit in a manner detrimental to their own interests. They contribute their hard work, their high hopes, and their loyalties, but do not benefit from the goods and services of the system. Although they are neither economically nor politically marginal, they are exploited, manipulated, and repressed; although they are neither socially nor culturally marginal, they are stigmatized and excluded from a closed class system.[5] To my disappointment, but not my surprise, this continues to be the case today.

The power of the ideology of marginality was so great in Brazil in the 1970s that it became self-fulfilling, justifying favela removal and perversely creating precisely the disaffection and disconnection that was professed to be a danger to the stable social order in the first place.

The ideology of marginality, with its moralistic, victim-blaming narrative, has persisted in the face of blatantly contradictory evidence. There are multiple overlapping and mutually reinforcing reasons for this persistence. First, it justifies extreme inequality while obfuscating the inability of the system to provide even minimal living standards for a vast subset of its population; second, it protects claims of legitimacy and the supposed "fairness" of the rules of the game; third, it provides a scapegoat for a wide array of societal problems, allowing others to feel superior, while preserving dominant norms; fourth, it "purifies the self-image of the rest of society (what I call a "specular relationship") by considering the "marginals" the source of all social problems (deviance, perversity, and criminality, etc.); fifth, it shapes the self-image of those labeled as marginal, so perniciously that favela residents often blame themselves for their plight, internalizing the belief that it is their own ignorance, incompetence, and inability that keeps them from getting ahead; and finally, it divides poor people, preventing those who might make common cause from coalescing into a unified political force.[6]

TRANSFORMATIONS IN THE LANDSCAPE OF POVERTY

Looking at how the meaning and repercussions of marginality have changed over the past 30 years is especially interesting in light of the macro transformations in Brazil's political economy and in the city of Rio de Janeiro. My original study was conducted at the height of the Brazilian dictatorship brought about by a military coup on April 1, 1964. A gradual political *abertura* (opening) starting in 1974 led, through a series of steps, to the end of the dictatorship in 1984 and redemocratization in 1985. After a period of repressed civil liberties, the "right to have rights" movement finally prevailed and, with the new constitution of 1988, considerably expanded.

In the wake of this return to democracy, community groups, federations of community groups, and nonprofits working in favelas flourished. Some of these promoted the rights of citizenship and attempted to correct past social injustices. Others were organized around cultural activities such as theater, dance, and filmmaking; sports from capoeira to soccer, volleyball, wrestling, and rowing; or around reclaiming weak or even lost racial or ethnic practices, as with the Afro Reggae movement. Still other groups were organized around religion, from preserving Afro-Brazilian practices such as *candomblé* and *umbanda,* to rediscovering Catholic liberation theology, to building the evangelical movement. Some of these were homegrown while others were inspired by or connected with political parties (including the communist party), labor unions, or both. The Federation of the Residents' Associations of the State of Rio became so politically "connected" that its president, Jô Resende, became deputy mayor in the first open election for local government.

In economic terms, the country went from the economic "miracle" of the 1960s to the hyperinflation of the 1970s, the so-called lost decade of the 1980s, and the attempted stabilization of the 1990s. In 1993, finance minister Fernando Henrique Cardoso introduced the Real Plan, which pegged the value of the currency to the U.S. dollar. This reined in inflation and temporarily raised the purchasing power of the poor,[7] but did not solve the problem of economic growth, which remained stagnant during the 1990s. The next 15 years saw financial instability, growing unemployment, and persistent inequality. The political system and the discourse on poverty may have changed over this period, but the country remains one of the most economically polarized in the world. The top 10 percent of Brazilians earn 50 percent of the national income, and the poorest 20 percent earn 2.5 percent. Thirty-four percent of the population lives below the poverty line.[8]

The global economic shift from manufacturing to services, from resource-based to knowledge-based production, and from place-based to mobile capital accumulation has had negative repercussions, particularly for Rio de Janeiro and its largely unskilled favela population. Deindustrialization, specifically the decline in the steel and shipbuilding industries in Rio, has led to the loss of hundreds of thousands of jobs.[9] Privatization and reductions in the size of the public sector, social spending, real wages, subsidies for basic staples, worker protections, and formal job contracts have made matters worse,[10] and Rio has become increasingly reliant on the informal economy (both illicit and illegal)[11] and a relatively small (but growing) modern service sector.

The erosion of the social contract[12] has undermined long-standing worker protections and social guarantees that might have helped to mediate the negative effects of economic and institutional restructuring.[13] In fact, in 2001 when we asked our original interviewees "which politician has most helped people like yourself?," the most frequent answer was Getúlio Vargas. During his populist regime, known as the Estado Novo (1930–45), Vargas set up the rudimentary protections of the welfare state, including workers' rights and benefits as well as the pension system. This answer surprised me at first since I had anticipated mention of the mayor who had initiated the Favela-Bairro program, or some local city councilman who had done favors for the community. Upon reflection, however, it made sense given that 54 percent of the original sample was living on state retirement pensions instituted during the Vargas era, and that many of them were supporting their children and grandchildren on these pensions.

THE UNMAKING AND REMAKING OF MARGINALITY

The term *marginality* was not widely used in academic or activist circles after the critiques of the 1970s. Those scholars who did write about it after the publication of *The Myth of Marginality* and other key works of the period focused on decoupling the theories of marginality from the reality.

With the democratic opening in the mid-1980s, voices of opposition emerged, and the discourse on urban poverty turned toward the less toxic[14] concepts of social exclusion, inequality, injustice, and spatial segregation. Each dimension of marginality seems to have reappeared in a new, more benign guise within the new architecture of progressive analytical discourse. Social marginality became a discussion of "social exclusion"; cultural marginality a conversation about "otherness"; economic marginality turned into "capabilities deprivation," "vulnerabilities," and a rethinking of "livelihoods" and "assets"; and political marginality became a dialogue about "lack of voice," "citizenship claims," and "rights." These concepts, developed by activists and intellectuals sympathetic to the urban poor, placed the blame for intergenerational and persistent poverty on the underlying structures of the state and society rather than on the deficiencies and deficits of the poor. They also exposed how being poor can annul the fundamental dignity of being human.

The material, cultural, historical, social-psychological, and political dimensions of marginalization are intertwined and mutually reinforcing. Each facet of the dehumanization (or criminalization) of the poor and of the way they are rendered invisible has been developed into a body of literature with its own set of concepts and assumptions. In the three chapters that follow, I explore the aspects of marginality related to violence and drugs (chapter 7); the limitations of democracy and citizenship (chapter 8); and the barriers to residential and socioeconomic mobility (chapter 9). In this chapter I take a closer look at the way stigma, social exclusion, and the lack of opportunity to fulfill one's capabilities perpetuate poverty, thereby perpetuating the belief in the inferiority of the poor.

STIGMA AND DISCRIMINATION

In trying to track the changing terms used to distinguish between "us" (the worthy in-group) and "them" (the unworthy out-group), I not only listened carefully to innumerable anecdotes of injustices based on prejudice but attended to the way the media and the academic community discussed this issue. While much has been written about race and gender in Brazil, there is no work I have seen comparing racism or sexism with the other forms of exclusion based on place of residence; place of community (central or peripheral) and place of origin (Rio-born versus migrant). These combined factors, signalled by clothing, speech, body language, and cues about class are what create the overall impression–the "pinta" of the person. These elements in turn bear direct consequence for the way that those from the formal city judge a person's character and make decisions about whether or not a person from a favela is qualified for employment. In my informal discussions with people in the communities, I heard so much about these sources of discrimination that I made them a focus of my 2001 and 2003 research.

I began by asking the people I interviewed in my follow-up study two questions that I asked in 1969: "Do you think there is racial discrimination in Brazil?" and "Have you or your children experienced racial discrimination?," asking for examples of both. In 2001 and 2003 I added a new question: "Is there discrimination due to other factors?" asking each person to mention all factors that applied and to give examples.

The graph in figure 6.1 shows how the original interviewees responded in 2001. The most frequently mentioned basis of discrimination was not racism, but favela-ism (i.e., being from a favela). Being dark skinned was the second most frequently mentioned stigma, followed by *"a pinta da pessoa"* (local slang for a person's appearance or the way they come across), which was followed by being born outside Rio (particularly in the Northeast) and living in the Baixada Fluminense. Only after those did being female enter the picture, and after that came living in the North Zone and living in a conjunto.

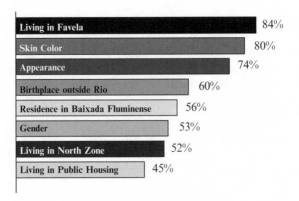

FIGURE 6.1   Perceived Stigma: Sources of Discrimination as Perceived by Original
Interviewees, 2001.

As this was not consistent with prevailing thought among scholars,
I wondered whether these other forms of exclusion were impediments only
for the older generation. Not so. When I compared their responses with those
of their children and their grandchildren, I found the younger generations'
responses very similar in order and magnitude to those of their parents. The
responses of the children were almost identical, but for them, living in a favela
and having a certain appearance were found to be even more detrimental (see
figure 6.2).

The grandchildren suffered from the same sources of discrimination but not
as much. This difference between generations was most dramatic for race—less
than half of the grandchildren even mentioned it. But, for them as for their
elders, living in a favela remains the worst source of discrimination (78 percent
cited it) and "pinta" is next (60 percent)—both greater barriers than race, gender, or place of origin. (Only the top four cited factors are shown in figure
6.2.) Living in a favela and not looking like a South Zone young person were
obviously impediments to getting work for the youngest generation, who
are the best educated and have the highest rate of unemployment—almost
50 percent.

Still I wondered why the grandchildren perceive less discrimination than
their elders. Thinking about Patricia (Zé Cabo's granddaughter), Sabrina
(Nilton's granddaughter), and Diana (Djanira's granddaughter) and others in
their cohort suggested to me that perhaps it was their higher educational level
and near-perfect adaptation of the South Zone style of speaking and dressing
that allowed more of them to "pass" and therefore experience relatively less
rejection.[15]

The next logical question for me regarding the bases of exclusion was whether
the answers found in the multigenerational study would be confirmed by the

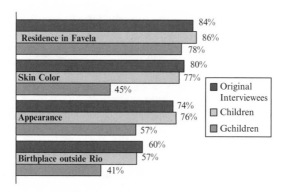

FIGURE 6.2 Sources of Discrimination as Perceived by Three Generations, 2001. Living in a favela remained the greatest basis of stigma and the only one that did not drop off by the grandchildren's generation.

new random sample study done 2 years later. I wanted to be sure that I was not picking up thought patterns transmitted within families before I could speak with certainty about sources of prejudice.

I found that the new random sample (16- to 65-year-old men and women) in the same communities perceived even greater discrimination than the original interviewees. The order of perceived bases of discrimination was similar, but more acute, with 92 percent mentioning favela residence and skin color and 88 percent mentioning appearance as bases for being negatively judged. They felt that prejudice against migrants (anyone not born in Rio) was worse, probably because more of them were migrants. But living in the Baixada was seen as less of a detriment, due to economic development and improved public transportation.

SOCIAL EXCLUSION

Attempts in the academic literature to differentiate the 1960s concept of marginality from the current concept of social exclusion often appear arbitrary and confusing to me rather than helpful in clarifying nuances of meaning.[16] The most interesting is the distinction Marcio Pochmann makes between the "old exclusion" in Brazil (1960–80), and the "new exclusion" (1980–2000).[17] In his view the old social exclusion, based on illiteracy (or low educational levels) and low income, focused on migrants from the countryside and was particularly concerned with women and blacks. The new social exclusion, as he sees it, includes people born in the city, such as most of the people in my restudy, who have higher levels of education, urban services, and household goods, but who are often unemployed, underemployed, or underpaid. The exclusion is a function of their precarious insertion into the job market. It makes sense that I found that the people I interviewed see jobs or work as their number one priority in life and that living in a favela is a source of social exclusion regardless of skin color or gender. Urban-born, light-skinned males who are unemployed and/or who live in a favela or conjunto are subject to more suspicion and discrimination in Rio today than black women who are employed. And so much the worse if the light-skinned male happens to be young, as this raises immediate suspicion of connection with the drug traffic. In sum, the age-old debates on whether the condition of marginalization is more class-based, race-based, or gender-based are not able to yield new insights into today's forms of exclusion.

CAPABILITY DEPRIVATION

Amartya Sen views poverty as not simply a lack of income or of low income, but as a denial of the ability to use a person's capability and capacity in pursuit of his or her own best interests.[18] Sen deems capability deprivations as "intrinsically significant," as opposed to low income, which may be a temporary condition or may be the result of a conscious decision to maximize another goal. Many of the people I interviewed have sacrificed income for education, raising a family, leisure, religion, the unwillingness to be humiliated, the freedom to work for themselves, or simply for peace of mind. The deprivation concept takes into consideration these and other circumstances, aside from low incomes that can result in living in a condition of poverty. A case in point is that residing in a designated "non-place" like a favela or conjunto confers low status and raises suspicion, regardless of a person's assets, education, skills, or intelligence—in turn, making it difficult to earn an income commensurate with that of a person living in a legitimate neighborhood. The person living in a bairro has a better chance of being hired and being treated with respect than a person with a higher income who has chosen to live in a favela. There are numerous individuals and families in favelas (over 10 percent in my sample) who have enough income to leave, but choose to stay.

Sen's well-taken point is that poverty may be considered independent from income. Crises, illnesses, or accidents can prevent continued earnings, eventually exhausting savings and assets as well. Sen argues that the relationship between low incomes and low capabilities vary among different groups, families, and individuals, and are often contingent on personal characteristics. This is borne out by the narratives and life stories of the most successful individuals from among all the original study participants, and by the conclusions I draw from those at the end of the mobility chapter.

"STREET TALK"

Returning to the theme of marginality, it is obvious that by any other name, it still depicts an equally condemning reality. Whether relabeled "social exclusion," "capabilities deprivation," or any other term in academic discourse, the bottom line is that over a third of Rio's inhabitants are rendered nonpersons.

While the term "marginality" may have been discredited within academic and nonprofit circles, it has never lost its cachet on the streets. It continues to have the dual connotation of the "poorest of the poor" and "outlaws and criminals." The conflation of these meanings in itself says a lot about the criminalization of poverty in Brazil. The following excerpts from focus groups conducted by Deepa Narayan's team in São Paulo favelas in 2000 illustrate both connotations and reinforce the sense of superiority by distinguishing "us" from "them."[19] The people in these focus groups all live in favelas but see *marginais* (marginals) as others. In one session, a woman described "marginais" as

> people who live under bridges or on the street, eat garbage, collect junk and cardboard, beg, depend on charity for food and clothes, and never send their children to school. They may use a piece of cardboard as a mattress and tin cans for cooking, and their shelter may be nothing more than a plastic bag. They do not want anything more from life. They are the ones most abused by the police.

In another community, "marginais" were portrayed as "having no scruples, being thieves, murderers and drug addicts, trying for the easy life by harming others." In a third group one man was recorded as saying:

> A few years ago, 50 percent of this community was made up of marginais, but nowadays it is zero [because people have either improved their circumstances or have been squeezed out]. Our reality is like this. We must not be passive. We must always strive for a better life. But at least we have our little shacks to sleep in, our TV sets to watch, and our daily meals. We are neither beggars nor marginais.

With this, the word "marginality," which was already used interchangeably with "bandidos," has come to refer to organized criminal gangs and drug traffickers. Before it was poverty that made the favela residents into marginais in the eyes of others, now it is the drug traffic—guilt by proximity.

Since much of the violent drug-related activity takes place within or at the entrance points to the favelas, there has been an erosion of the fragile acceptance of favelas by their surrounding neighborhoods. This erosion started to take hold during the period of abertura (opening) as the dictatorship was winding down. The unfortunate conflation of "marginal" with "poor" and "dangerous" easily reasserted itself, reinforcing former prejudices. As the press writes sensationalistic stories about the many innocent victims of the crossfire between police and gangs, the middle class once again fears proximity to the favelas.

This, in turn, is reflected in the job market, the real estate market, and the consumer market.

On recent visits I have heard a new twist of the term within the favelas: I am frequently warned to leave before dark or to avoid certain areas because they are controlled by "a marginalidade" (the marginality). With this new slang, marginality has made the transfiguration from a sociogeographical condition (on the margins, outside the mainstream) to a criminal position (member of a drug gang) to a collective noun for the gangsters themselves—the marginality.

More and more of my friends in favelas and conjuntos are considering moving after all these years due to their fear that their children might become involved in "the marginality." When used in rap and funk lyrics, the term is often used with defiant bravado: "We are not marginais, we are not the marginality—we are the marginalized." This is a call for an uprising or revolt.

ADVANCED MARGINALITY

Beginning in the late 1990s, the term *marginality* itself began to reappear in academic circles, in discussions of persistent poverty in First World cities. Terms such as the "new underclass," the "new poverty," the "new marginality," or "advanced marginality" were being used to describe the conditions of the chronic poor in the black ghettos of the United States and the migrant "slums" of Europe. The idea is that *advanced marginality* reflects the current stage of global capitalism, in which a large portion of the urban population is simply irrelevant and excluded from the rest of the city: warehoused in segregated ghettos.

Loïc Wacquant developed this concept most fully, starting with a 1996 article wherein he described the "contiguous configuration of color, class, and place" in the Chicago ghetto, the French *banlieue,* and the British and Dutch inner cities. He posits a distinctive postindustrial marginality characterized by new constraints, stigmas, territorial separation, dependency on the welfare state, and institutions within "territories of urban relegation."[20]

Four key "structural dynamics," Wacquant suggests, are reshaping urban poverty in advanced industrial societies: social inequality, an absolute surplus population; the retrenchment of the welfare state, and spatial concentration/stigmatization. Javier Auyero had already tried to apply these to Buenos Aires, and I wondered to what extent these four conditions would apply to the conditions I found in Rio de Janeiro and Brazil.

Social Inequality

The first of the structural dynamics of advanced marginality as postulated by Wacquant is that social inequality persists and deepens within a context of overall economic prosperity. This divergence is due to the simultaneous elimination of jobs for unskilled workers and proliferation of jobs for university-trained professionals. Brazil is one of the most economically polarized countries in the world (despite recent improvements), and Rio is a sharply stratified city. But despite the widespread perception of deepening of inequality, data show that levels have remained fairly constant over recent decades. And, Rio's economy is far from prosperous. Its economic growth is lower than most of Brazil's other metropolitan areas, and it has lost the prosperity of its golden years (pre-1960) due to the move of the capital to Brasília, the *de*-industrialization and decline of the port area, and the move of the business, cultural, and intellectual center to São Paulo. So, Rio does not fit the first proposition of advanced marginality.

Absolute Surplus Population

By "absolute surplus population" Wacquant means that a significant portion of the workforce is redundant—not needed—and that many of the unemployed will never work again. In addition there is widespread poverty among those who do have jobs because of low pay and the exploitation of temporary workers—as we saw in the case of Sabrina in her telemarketing job. Fewer employers are willing to provide worker protection and benefits since there are so many people who need work. Brazil's unemployment levels during 2001–03 were among the highest in its history, and Rio was among the metropolitan areas suffering most. Without doubt there has been a weakening of the labor unions and an erosion of conditions of formal employment. The difference in Rio may be that the proliferation of the informal economy masks what might be considered a surplus population. One-quarter of the households of our original favela sample reported having one or more unemployed household member of working age, but the majority of households included one or more people of working age currently active in the labor force. The big surprise was that the percentage of those working who had formal employment, with a carteira assinada (a signed work card) guaranteeing the full range of workers' benefits, had risen from 1969 to 2001, and rose with each generation studied. The other counterindication to a permanent underclass is the high degree of turnover. Within the space of a few months, there is a lot of movement into and out of the labor force, and into and out of formal labor contracts. There are some who remain inactive for one reason or another, but, in general, despite Rio's weak job market, I would not characterize the unemployed as a surplus population that will never work again.

Retrenchment of the Welfare State

Retrenchment of the welfare state in the United States and Western Europe is characterized by service cutbacks in social programs and—in some cases—turning such programs into instruments of surveillance and control. In examining to what extent this disinvestment and punitive focus applies to the case of Rio, it is critical to remember that Brazil never had a highly developed welfare state. There was no safety net beyond what had been instituted in the Vargas Era. As in other Latin American countries, Brazil has been under pressure to reform and rationalize state social expenditures as part of a fiscal austerity package demanded by international lending agencies under the term "structural adjustment."

Nonetheless, starting during the Fernando Henrique Cardoso presidency, the federal government initiated a series of grants or stipends to low-income families on the condition that they invest in their children's education or health. These "conditional cash transfers," often referred to as CCTs,[21] were consolidated into Bolsa Família (Family Stipend) in 2003 under President Luiz Inácio Lula da Silva (known as Lula).

I discuss this further in my chapter on policy (chapter 11). Suffice it to say here that this form of negative income tax or "citizen's wage," complemented by local city and state programs, has meant an enormous expansion of the welfare state rather than a retrenchment.

We also found a strong presence of the old welfare state in the form of retirement payments. Nearly 60 percent of the original interviewees said their retirement payments were their principal source of income, and for household heads it was 66 percent. Retirees receive about one "minimum salary" per month, (equivalent to about US$90.[22]) In many cases extended families, including unemployed children and young grandchildren, are living on that retirement check.

Spatial Concentration and Stigmatization

Wacquant posits that spatial concentration and stigmatization are "physically expressed in hard-core areas of outcasts, territorial stigma and prejudice, and in a diminishing sense of community life."[23] Although favelas may not be "hard-core areas of outcasts," they are punitively stigmatized spaces as demonstrated earlier in this chapter, and the community trust and unity that characterized them when I lived there years ago is being eroded.

I'll take the proposition piece by piece. First, in Rio, being poor does not mean being an outlaw any more than living in a favela means you are poor or an outlaw. Favelas are heterogeneous—racially, socially, culturally, and economically (some more so than others), and there is a high degree of variation among them. In contrast to the total racial segregation characterizing the new marginality, Rio's favelas have always been racially mixed. In the 1969 study, 21 percent of the randomly sampled favela residents were black, 30 percent mulatto, and 49 percent white; and these percentages were almost identical in the random sample in the same locations in 2003. That does not mean that the racial mix in favelas is proportional to that in the city as a whole (since blacks are disproportionately represented), but they are by no means racial ghettos.

Second, favelas in Rio are not concentrated in any one area of the city, but are intermixed geographically with more prosperous neighborhoods. If the meaning here is that the boundaries of the morro and asfalto are readily apparent, Rio fits the pattern well; but if spatial concentration means that all favelas can be located in one part of the urban landscape, Rio is just the opposite. As we saw on the map in chapter 2, Rio's favelas are scattered across the urban space rather than relegated to a specific area. Indeed, as Pedro Abramo has shown, some are so well located that rental and sale prices within them are higher than those in certain parts of Copacabana or Botafogo, two upper- and middle-income areas.[24]

Perhaps the most striking evidence against the premise of advanced marginality is that favela residents (even dark skinned) are not "forcibly relegated" to staying in their communities. As I discuss in more detail in chapter 9, only 37 percent of the original randomly selected study participants we found were still living in favelas—25 percent were in conjuntos and 34 percent were in neighborhoods, mostly located in the periphery of the city.

CONCLUSION

What I have been observing over these decades is the transformation from "the myth of marginality" to "the reality of marginality." In 1969, there was widespread hope that the sacrifices made by the cityward migrants would provide their children (if not themselves) with broader opportunities and a greater range of choice. This is one reason the expected radicalism of the squatters never materialized.[25] New migrants were not infuriated by the disparities between themselves and the upper classes surrounding them in Rio because their reference group was not the rich who lived in Rio but those who stayed behind in the countryside. Although their children and grandchildren have benefited in many ways from being born and raised in Rio, they face some challenges the older generation could not have foreseen, not the least of which is living with the constant fear of death.

I close this chapter with the lyrics of "Soldado do Morro" (Soldier of the Favela), written by the hip-hop icon of Rio de Janeiro, MV Bill.[26] He is from Cidade de Deus, where several Catacumba residents were sent after the demolition in 1970. Aside from using his music to denounce the marginalization of favela residents, MV Bill is an activist leader who runs a local teen center and is the founder of Central Única de Favelas, better known as CUFA (Central Association of Favelas), a network of nonprofit organizations dedicated to offering youth an alternative to the drug traffic. Along with hip-hop, break dancing, and graffiti, these groups teach young people computer and job skills and create a social identity and sense of belonging to counteract the appeal of drug gangs.[27]

The song beautifully reflects the major themes of marginality discussed in this chapter. First, that marginal status is the creation of society, not the fault of the poor. Second, that the poor are trapped between dealing drugs (which destroy their community and themselves) and trying to get a job—a humiliating and futile endeavour. Third, that even the lucky few who get a job for a minimum salary and work overtime still do not earn enough to support their families. Fourth, that policemen and politicians who are supposed to be protecting the poor are perpetrators of crime and violence themselves; and finally that the *soldado do morro* (favela soldier) is expendable and that if he dies, his death is just one more statistic in the daily news—no more than a small victory in the fight to rid the city of "bad elements."

In the song, the soldado do morro chose a path of early and violent death, and he protests the injustice of the system that fails to produce alternatives for him and others like him. This element of defiance and what he calls "disgust" is heard in many rap songs which are vehicles for exposing the way things are and calling for defiance.[28]

The lives of the poor have always been cheap, but in the milieu of drug and arms traffic, they been devalued even more. Death rates in the favelas are much greater than in the rest of the city—and for favela youth are higher still.[29] This new violence may be the ultimate manifestation of the marginalization of the poor, the reality of marginality.

SOLDADO DO MORRO

Várias vezes me senti menos homem
Desempregado meu moleque com fome
É muito fácil vir aqui me criticar
A sociedade me criou agora manda me matar
Me condenar e morrer na prisão
Virar notícia de televisão,
Já pedi esmola já me humilhei
Fui pisoteado só eu sei que eu passei
Tô ligado não vai justificar
Meu tempo é pequeno não sei o quanto vai durar
É prior do que pedir favor
Arruma um emprego tenho um filho pequeno seu doutor
Fila grande eu e mais trezentos
Depois de muito tempo sem vaga no momento
A mesma história todo dia é foda
Isso que gerou a minha revolta
Me deixou desnorteado mais um maluco armado
Tô ligado bolado quem é o culpado?
Que fabrica a guerra e nunca morre por ela
Distribui a droga que destrói a favela

Fazendo dinheiro com a nossa realidade
Me deixaram entre o crime e a necessidade
Feio e esperto com uma cara de mal
A sociedade me criou mas um marginal
Eu tenho uma nove e uma HK
Com ódio na veia pronto para atirar
Violência da favela começou a descer pro asfalto
Homicídio seqüestro assalto
Quem deveria dar a proteção
Invade a favela de fuzil na mão
Eu sei que o mundo que eu vivo é errado
Mas quando eu precisei ninguém tava do meu lado
Errado por errado quem nunca errou?
Aquele que pede voto também já matou
Vida do crime é suicídio lento
Na cadeia Bangú 1 2 3 meus amigos tenho lá dentro
Eu tô ligado qual é sei qual é o final
Um soldado negativo menos um marginal
Pra sociedade uma baixa na lista
E engordar uma triste estatística
Não sei se é pior virar bandido
Ou se matar por um salário mínimo.

SOLDIER OF THE HILLSIDE

Many is the time I've felt less than a man
Unemployed, with my child going hungry
It's easy to criticize me
Society created me and now demands my death
Condemning me to die in prison
Transformed into television news

I've been a beggar, already humiliated myself
Pleading for a job, "I have a small child, good sir"
Long waiting list, me and 300 others
After an eternity, "no openings at the moment"
The same story every day, all this generates revolt
I am hooked, who is to blame?
Those who are making this war, never die in it
I distributed the drugs that destroy the favela
Making money from our reality
I am caught between crime and necessity
Those who should be providing protection

Invade the favela with weapons in hand…
Those who come seeking our votes, they too have killed

The life of crime is slow suicide
Bangú, 1, 2, 3, my friends inside there
I am involved, I know the outcome
A negative balance, minus one marginal
For society to count, one fewer on the list
Adding weight to a sad statistic.…

I don't know which is worse, turning into a bandit
Or killing yourself for the minimum wage.…

seven

VIOLENCE, FEAR, AND LOSS

The most dramatic and devastating change for Rio's poor over the last three decades has been the growth of lethal violence. In 1969, the poor living in favelas feared that their homes and communities would be demolished. Today, they fear for their lives. They are afraid that they will be caught in the crossfire of the turf wars among rival drug gangs or that they will be in the wrong place during a police raid. They are terrified that their children will not return alive at the end of the school day or that their baby will be shot while playing on the front steps of their home.

Favelas are appealing locations for the drug gangs, with their narrow, winding alleys, abundant hiding places, and unemployed youth. They provide the ideal staging area for breaking down large shipments of drugs into smaller packages for sale to Rio's rich playboys (or "daddy's boys") and for shipping them to Europe via North Africa or to the United States via the Caribbean.

Violence follows poverty. The traficantes or bandidos, as the drug dealers are called, began entering the favelas in the mid-1980s, and their presence spread quickly to the conjuntos and loteamentos. Now the dealers are becoming a problem in the poor neighborhoods to which the favela residents have fled. It was heartbreaking to discover that those who managed to move their families out

FIGURE 7.1   The criminalization of poverty and the militarization of the police create constant fear and intimidation for anyone living in a favela. (Photo used with permission from *O Globo*)

of the favelas and rent or buy in the more affordable bairros on the urban fringe had only a short reprieve before the traffic and the violence followed them.

In some ways, the traffickers managed to do what no state authority had ever been able to do—drive people out of the favelas. Although only a small fraction of favela residents are involved in the arms or drug traffic, the drug trade and the police response have been responsible for the deaths of thousands of innocent people in the favelas, barrios, and conjuntos. The violence has made Rio's most vulnerable population fearful of going about their daily lives, reduced their chances of getting jobs, lowered the value of their homes, weakened the trust and solidarity that has held their communities together, and co-opted homegrown community organizations.

From the time I returned to Brazil in 1999 to undertake this follow-up study until 2009, when this account was written, increasing numbers of communities have been taken over by one of the three *facções* (drug gangs): the Commando Vermelho (CV), the Terceiro Commando (TC), or the Amigos dos Amigos (AMA)—(Friends of Friends).

THE POLICE

The police are the face of the state in the favelas. They are the most visible government presence in these communities, and they contribute to the problem by their unwarranted use of lethal force, technically referred to as extrajudicial violence. Community residents consider the police worse than the traffic because the police enter the favelas prepared to kill anything that moves and leave once they are finished. One woman from Nova Brasília told me that the police suspected a dealer was hiding in her house, so they broke down the door, rampaged through the living room and bedroom, and shot her husband as he was coming out of the shower, preparing to go to work. They told her to stay inside and not try to get him to a hospital until they had completed their morning's work there.

Security is a function of state government in Brazil. Cities do not have a regular police force. In 1990 a "Municipal Guard" was created under the office of the mayor. The guards are uniformed but unarmed. Their brief is neither to maintain order directly nor to conduct investigations. All they are authorized to do is give traffic tickets and intervene in public disturbances, a limited scope of action at best.

The police who appear in favelas are the Polícia Civil (Civil Police) and the Polícia Militar (Military Police). Both are part of the Segurança Publica (Public Security), which reports to the governor and is paid by the federal government. The Civil Police are responsible for investigative functions in criminal justice. The Military Police are part of Brazil's national defense apparatus. They are heavily armed and they apprehend suspects, whom they then turn over to the Civil Police for investigation and processing. In some ways, the Military Police are similar to the U.S. National Guard. They work for the state governors but are paid by the federal government. The entrances to wealthy neighborhoods in Rio have Military Police stations the size of telephone booths, in which officers are stationed to maintain order. Both the civil and military police have elite squads: the Batalhao de Operacoes Policias Especiais (BOPE) in the Military Police and the Corenadoria de Rescursos (CORE) Special Operations Group in the Civil Police.

In 1808, when the Portuguese royal court moved to Brazil, King Joao VI patterned his Royal Palace Guard after those whom he had commanded in Lisbon. When the monarchy returned to Portugal, the city of Rio de Janeiro became the federal district, and from 1889 until 1960 the federal police patrolled Rio. With the moving of the national capital to Brasília in 1960, Rio lost its federal district status.

The role of the police has never been clearly defined in Rio. Since the police evolved from the palace guard of the monarchy, they retain a sense of absolute authority more appropriate to a monarchy than to a democracy. During the 20 years of dictatorship (1964–85), the distinction between military and police functions continued to be blurred. The rigid hierarchy and strict adherence to order that are central to military training became part of the police culture. This mixture has resulted in a unique style of policing in Rio—indeed in all of Brazil. The low pay for the average policeman, around 400 reais per month (US$200) is an invitation to graft, corruption, and retribution. Most of the police violence in favelas is committed by the Military Police, but both special forces, BOPE and CORE, are specially trained for violent confrontations and known for their brutality.

Governors of Rio state have traditionally been reluctant to call on the federal forces for help, as these forces are generally under the control of an opposing political party, and, as the governors often have presidential aspirations, they do not wish to appear weak. In extreme situations, such as the one in the Complexo de Alemão in July 2007, the reluctant governor of Rio state called in the federal police, who marched eight abreast, down the main avenues. The result was neither an end to the violence nor help for its victims.

The current governor of the state of Rio, Sergio Cabral, was elected on the basis of his antiviolence and anticorruption campaign. At the end of December 2007, before his January inauguration, the drug kingpins staged massive city-wide actions protesting his taking the post. They paralyzed the city for several days, but Cabral did assume his post as governor and has endeavored to get the situation under control. As of December 2008, he had succeeded in cleaning up one of the oldest and best organized favelas of the South Zone, Santa Marta, which has a valiant history of independent community organizing going back several generations. It would be a great victory for the people and the state if they succeed in maintaining Santa Marta free from any drug faction and from any militia.

THE SCOPE AND STYLE OF THE NEW VIOLENCE

If the greatest change in Rio's favelas from the 1970s to 2000 was the entrance and takeover by drug gangs, the greatest change since 2005 was the rise of armed militias. These self-appointed, off-duty, or retired policemen take "law and order" into their own hands—sometimes in opposition to the traffic, sometimes in complicity with them. Between 2003 and 2009, I witnessed an increase in the number of favelas controlled by militias, now said to be well over 100. These vigilante groups purport to expel the drug gangs and offer "protection" to the community. Any "security" they provide the residents comes at a steep price.

The militias impose stiff fees on the residents for normal aspects of their daily lives, including entering and exiting the favela, traveling by taxi or motor-bike from the favela entrance up to their homes, and delivery of the propane gas canisters used for cooking. These are taxes the poor can ill afford to pay, yet they have no choice.

As Djanira explained to me, "They [the militias] control everything; they impose curfews; they make you pay for coming and going in your own community.... If you don't do what they say, they shoot you—not to wound but to kill. That's their way."

FIGURE 7.2   Helicopter surveillance serves to reinforce the attitude that favela residents are suspects. Women hanging out their wash to dry are confronted by a loaded assault weapon pointing right at them. (Photo used with permission from *O Globo*)

Once again, the favela residents have traded one fear for another. Where fear of removal was replaced by fear of the drug traffic, now fear of the drug traffic has been replaced by fear of the militias. Whatever freedom Rio's poor had is now brutally curtailed as they find themselves trapped between the police, the dealers, and the vigilantes.

On Friday, June 13, 2008, the *New York Times* ran a full-page piece under the headline "In Rio Slum, Armed Militia Replaces Drug Gang's Criminality with Its Own."[1] In the article, it was estimated that close to 100 militias (operating separately) have taken over favelas from the traffickers.

RACE AND POWER

It is not surprising that the police in Rio are violent and corrupt. They are underpaid and afraid. Many of them grew up in and still live in favelas themselves. For many, joining the police force was an attempt to gain respect. When police are not respected, they intimidate. At a mother's group discussion I attended, the women commented that the black policemen were the most arrogant and violent: more likely to have a drink and sandwich at a local bar and walk off without paying; more likely to use their guns and abuse their power.

The women explained this by saying that blacks got less respect from society than whites and that many grew up in violent homes.

The race question in Brazil and in Rio's favelas is a subject for another book. Although the favela population in the places I studied was—and continues to be—about one-third white, one-third mulatto, and one-third black, a much higher percent of Rio's total black population live in favelas than do whites. As Edgar Pieterse says, "the intertwined position of being social outcasts and being economically redundant dooms black youth to truncated futures as long as the criminal justice institutions of the state are not transformed to embrace a philosophy of inclusion."[2]

In Brazil, the question of racial categorization is tricky in itself. After generations of interbreeding, gradations and combinations of skin color, hair type, and facial features are infinite and, as Conrad Kottak showed decades ago, there is no consensus regarding what racial term to use for any combination of these attributes.[3] Brazil's mythical racial democracy, hiding behind class differences, has long since been exposed for what it was, but the notion of Black Pride, imported from the United States, has influenced the perception of color so greatly that many of our original interviewees who had classified themselves as white in 1969 changed their designation to moreno or mulatto in 2001. Many who had told us they were mulatto or Moreno back then now claimed to be black.

This is a complete reversal of the traditional pattern of "whitening" a person's racial designation according to wealth, education, or profession. A black doctor, for example, would be listed as mulatto, while a mulatto with a Ph.D. might be called *moreno claro* (light moreno) or white. I recall from my first visit that when women were pregnant—whether in the countryside or the city—family and friends always said, "I hope the baby comes out 'clara'—light skinned. Brazil, where nearly everyone has some black blood, does not use the same racial definitions we do in the United States. They use skin color not ancestry in defining race. Thus, a single family can have children of several racial categories.

In an interview with a couple—former Catacumba residents—now living in a densely packed housing complex known as Cruzada Sao Sebastião, I asked whether racial discrimination exists in Brazil and whether it had gotten better or worse in the past 30 years. The couple had nine children, some of whom were hanging around, sitting on the edge of the couch or watching the television. The father answered first, saying that in Brazil there was no racial discrimination. I was writing down his answer when his wife interrupted. "How many of our children have jobs?" she asked him. He counted up, thinking of each in turn and said, five. "Yes, five," she repeated, "and what is the difference between those with and without jobs?" He hesitated, and she turned to me and said, "In this racial democracy, all of our light-skinned children are employed, and all of our darker-skinned children are unemployed." She rested her case.

SOME STARTLING STATISTICS

A UN study of violence in 60 countries bestowed on Brazil the dubious distinction of having the highest rate of homicide in the world. Ninety percent of the homicides in Brazil are caused by firearms. The report stressed that "most of the lethal violence is concentrated in cities, with the rates higher in the favelas and other low income areas than in the population at large."[4]

Sadly, the "marvelous city" of Rio de Janeiro is one of the most violent cities in the world. Its homicide rate is among the highest of all Brazilian cities. In 2006, Rio's homicide rate was 37.7 per 100,000 (an absolute number of 2,273 people), with São Paulo second, at 23.7 per 100,000. The rates of violence were so bad in 2004 before the Pan American Games that the government proposed building a high, impenetrable wall around all the favelas—literally creating a walled fortress within the city, to "protect" the city. The death toll for one day (June 26, 2004) during this period was 22 people killed and 11 wounded in Nova Brasília and the 11 other favelas that comprise the Complexo de Alemão. An army of over 1,350 men backed by tanks and helicopters was mobilized in an effort to hunt down gang leaders and members there.[5]

It was even worse in 2002, according to one source who quoted a murder rate for that year of 62.8 cases per 100,000 residents. In both Rio and São Paulo, the homicide rate dropped between 2002 and 2006—but to give a sense of the death rate in Rio, imagine what it was like to lose almost 50,000 people (more than the total population of many Brazilian municipalities) to homicides between 1978 and 2000.[6]

Comparable figures exist for the city, the metropolitan region, and the state of Rio. As of 2007, the homicide rate of the metropolitan area was close to 80 victims per week, with the majority dying by assassination, assault, or stray bullets. In the same year, Rio state had 39 murders per 100,000—four times the rate in the São Paulo metropolitan area, the second most violent area.

The favelas and other poor communities have become the frontlines of Brazil's drug wars. If the victims had been from Ipanema, Leblon, Lagoa, or Gavea in the South Zone, their deaths would have created a scandal, and the response would have been immediate and decisive. The lives of the poor are seen as less valuable. As I mentioned earlier, my colleague from Caxias, José Claudio, said to me, "In the Baixada you have to kill six to seven at once to get into the newspaper."

Many years ago, when I was in Cartagena, Colombia, for a conference on the "informal sector," I was seated next to the city's mayor, who was a medical doctor, specializing in epidemiology. When I asked him what the worst epidemic in his city was, he said, "violence." It took me awhile to register what his answer meant, but I never forgot it. An epidemic of violence is precisely what I have seen in Rio. And like any epidemic, this one does not strike all segments of the population equally. Youth are the most frequent victims.

YOUTH AS VIOLENCE VICTIMS

Among 82 countries surveyed in a study by Liana Leite in 2008, Brazil ranks fourth in violent deaths of youth aged 15–24 years. The rate was 79.6 deaths per 100,000 in 2005. The mortality rates attributable to violence have dropped slightly since 2003, due to a series of youth-focused policies, including a disarmament campaign that offered amnesty and payment for weapons surrendered. However, the rates of mortality by violence remain among the highest in the world, and the figures are sobering. A 15- to 24-year-old in Brazil is 170 percent more likely to be a homicide victim than those younger or older.[7]

Rio's murder rates for youth are higher than the Brazilian rates. Rio has "the highest absolute number of youth killed by assassination" of all 86 cities in the Leite study. In 2006, 879 young people were killed in Rio, which translates into 83.6 violent deaths of youth for every 100,000 inhabitants. The report attributes the high number of homicides among youth in Rio to high levels of social exclusion. The analysts used a measure of income inequality in a multivariate statistical analysis and found that social exclusion levels accounted for 63.5 percent of the variation in youth murder rates among cities. But not all youth who live in Rio share the same probability of being murdered. Studies conducted by the Laboratório de Análise da Violência (Laboratory for Analysis of Violence) at the State University of Rio de Janeiro show that, holding the social exclusion levels constant, some youth are at greater risk than others. They found marked differences in the homicide rates for youth depending on age, race, gender, and poverty—and whether they live in a favela or in the formal city.[8]

Table 7.1, comparing homicide rates by gender and age, demonstrates the point. The number of male deaths is significantly higher than female deaths, and the age ranges show wide variations, with the highest number of deaths for those aged 20–24—at 303 per 100,000.

While favela residents do not have these figures at hand, they are well aware of the vulnerability of their sons. Zé Cabo told me that the one thing that he was most proud of in his life is that none of his children had joined the traffic. Adão, another parent in Nova Brasília (I tell his story in chapter 9), is unable to discipline his 20-year-old son because the boy threatens to join the traffic if he cannot do as he pleases.

The trend is for children to enter the traffic at increasingly younger ages. They are recruited to be spies (*olheiros*) and carriers (*aviões*), or jets because the laws protect minors from going to jail. As Nilton, my friend from Guaporé, explained, "In all the talk of rights of children,' we forgot about the other side—

TABLE 7.1   *Homicide Rates per 100,000 People by Gender and Age of the City of Rio de Janeiro*

Age Range	Gender		Total
	Male	*Female*	
0–9 years	1.98	1.06	1.79
10–14 years	13.26	6.29	9.80
15–19 years	232.58	14.33	122.57
20–24 years	303.49	11.63	155.08
25–29 years	235.63	12.55	120.64
30–39 years	130.72	9.69	66.72
40–49 years	78.65	6.62	39.37
50–59 years	48.40	5.36	24.51
60 years or older	28.97	6.90	15.52
Total	108.79	7.80	55.18

Source: Cano *et al.*, "O Impacto da Violencia," UERJ (2004)

the traffic recruits kids under 15 because they have impunity and cannot be prosecuted in criminal court." They have a short life expectancy.

INGREDIENTS OF THE VIOLENCE STEW—A *MISTURA FINA*

When I began this research work in 1968, none of the communities I selected was particularly violent. At that time, the fear outsiders had of entering favelas was not warranted by the facts. I think it had more to do with the "otherness"— an alienation that was related to the image of marginal masses invading the citadel of the elite.

Even then, however, there was more violence in the city than in the countryside. I recall that in the list of things that people reported they most liked and disliked about living in Rio; 16 percent said they disliked the violence. In the restudy, that response was 86 percent. I had no way of predicting that Nova Brasília and Caxias would become two of the most dangerous places in the city 30 years later.

Among the coping mechanisms for living under a state of siege is a certain physical displacement of danger. It took me awhile to register this, but I noticed that in all my conversations and interviews, every person I spoke with said (as I noted earlier) that his or her particular area of the community was safer, more *tranquilo* (peaceful) than "that part over there, which was really violent and dangerous." For example, the residents of the conjunto of Quitungo rarely dared to go to the conjunto of Guaporé, and vice versa—each thinking the other was too dangerous—and residents of both avoided passing through the favela of Piqueri, which lay between them, even though it was the shortest route. An exception was certain areas of Nova Brasília, near the Praça do Terço and up by Zé Cabo's house, where the violence was so persistent that everyone acknowledged it was hell to live nearby.

Still, during the time I was doing field research, I was not fully aware of the dire nature of the Rio situation in comparison to that in other large cities in Latin America or in the world. I saw the death tolls from drug wars and police raids in the papers and on television, but I did not realize that Rio had the highest homicide rates of any city in the world, or that the number of adolescent boys killed or the murder rate by police were several magnitudes higher than in cities of similar size.

How can I explain this? How did things get so violent, when Cariocas (Rio residents) seem more inclined to be affectionate, generous, and easygoing than the people in the other 20 megacities in which I have worked? In grappling with this question, I came to the conclusion that the answer lies in a *mistura fina*—the fine mixture of 10 ingredients that have simmered simultaneously over the past 20 years to create this stew of violence. Like the Brazilian feijoada, originally made by the slaves who added unwanted discarded pieces of meat to their rice and black beans, this fine-mix of violence could never have been planned. It is the brew of leftovers and leftouts.

I count ten essential ingredients for this feijoada: (1) stigmatized territories within the city that are excluded from state protection; (2) inequality levels among the highest in the world; (3) a high-priced illegal commodity with the alchemist's allure of turning poverty into wealth; (4) well-organized, well-connected drug gangs and networks; (5) easy access to sophisticated weaponry; (6) an underpaid, understaffed, unaccountable police force; (7) a weak government indifferent to "the rule of law"; (8) independent militias and vigilante groups who can kill at will (9) a powerless population of over 3 million people in poverty; and (10) a sensationalist mass media empire fomenting fear to sell advertising and justify police brutality.

INGREDIENT 1: STIGMATIZED TERRITORIES EXCLUDED
FROM STATE PROTECTION

Since their inception, favelas have been considered a no-man's-land. They are deemed to be outside the state's mandate to protect life and limb or to ensure the personal security of citizens. It took almost 100 years for favelas to appear on city maps—during which time the number of inhabitants grew to a third of the total city population.

The police harassment and mistreatment of favela residents goes back a long way. I learned about the vagrancy laws from my friend Hélio Grande, who said they were enacted to keep the people from the favelas from "loitering." He vividly remembered being arrested while walking home to Catacumba from a nearby party, one night in 1947, when he was 19. The policeman, assuming that any dark-skinned youth from a favela out alone at 3 A.M. was up to no good, grabbed him, took him into custody, and put him in the local precinct jailhouse overnight. It was only when the police chief arrived in the morning and recognized Hélio as the champion soccer player on his son's team near the Lagoa that Hélio was permitted to leave.

After the coup of 1964 established a military dictatorship, police saw the favelas as enemy territory harboring communists and criminals. There were many unheeded complaints of police brutality, but both the mayor and governor of Rio were appointed, not elected, during that time, and there was no recourse.

Leonel Brizola was elected state governor in 1982 when the military government was still in power but the political opening had began. In 1985 he forbade the police to enter the favelas. It is unclear whether he intended to protect the favela residents from police brutality that had been going on during the dictatorship or whether he cut a deal with the criminals to get their support in return for not allowing police to enter their territory. In any case, his decision deprived favelas of state protection. The absence of police in the favelas made them attractive locations for the illicit activities of the traffickers. The abnegation of police responsibility for safety and security in the favelas, which happened around 1985, coincided with the rise of the drug traffic. Within five years, the traffic had become sufficiently well organized and well armed to take control of many favelas and had begun to challenge the hegemony of the state in these areas. The level of violence and the extraordinary sums of money involved in the narco-traffic necessitated a reversal of the earlier order for police not to enter favelas. As I understand it, by 1990, the Military Police were entering the favelas en masse, not to protect the residents but to kill the local drug lords and to confiscate drugs and arms. Between 1985 and 1990, the favelas gradually became fair game for police surveillance and coordinated raids.

The topography of the favelas makes them ideal hiding places. The natural environment is often hilly and steep, with very narrow passages crawling up to the topmost parts of the settlement, and plenty of trees and rocks for hiding places. The built environment takes advantage of the topography by using every inch of space—houses are built on stilts, and in back of, on top of, alongside, under, and over other houses. It is easy to get lost in the maze, and that is a second factor making favelas ideal places to hide. The ultimate advantage from a strategic point of view is that most favelas are on hillsides, providing vantage points from which to look down on anyone coming up the entryways. This makes them easily defendable.

As Zé Cabo put it, "the urban territory of the *gente humilde* (humble folk)—no matter which way you look at it—is outside the control of the state."

INGREDIENT 2: EXTREME INEQUALITY, POVERTY,
AND LACK OF JOB OPPORTUNITIES

Inequality levels in Rio, like those of Brazil in general, are among the highest anywhere. Several years ago, the United Nations Development Programme developed a quality-of-life index called the Human Development Index (HDI), which includes education, life expectancy, and health care as well as per capita income. The index, rating each issue from a low of 0 to a high of 1, can be used to compare countries, cities, and neighborhoods of any size. The Complexo de Alemão, where Nova Brasília is located, scores lower than Gabon and much lower than Cape Verde, while South Zone neighborhoods such as Gavea and Lagoa have living standards comparable to Scandinavian countries.[9] But rather than being continents apart, residents of Nova Brasília and Gavea coexist within an hour's bus ride in the same city and pay the same prices for food, electricity, public transit, and other basics.

This makes the sense of relative deprivation much more acute for favela youth. Their aspirations are set by the consumption standards they constantly see on television and are reinforced every time they enter the wealthy South Zone.

One young man I met while on my way to an interview in the favelas had several cell phones, pagers, and beepers attached to his belt or in his pockets, as well as a portable media player in his hand. I asked him why he needed all that stuff; he assessed me, then smiled, and said, "Oh, nothing. They don't work. I find them in the trash and I like to wear them." He was accessorized in status symbols, and he gave me a hearty thumbs-up and "See you around" when he saw that I caught on. That was charming in its own way, but everyone knows of similar young people killed over a pair of brand-name sneakers.

Gang members often mention the freedom of having cash to spend as one of the payoffs for entering the traffic. They don't become rich overnight, but they might earn in a single week the equivalent of what they could earn over several months at a minimum wage job—and they do not incur the cost of transportation and bringing or buying lunch. Their role models have such prestige items as motorcycles, gold chains and rings, designer shirts and shoes, and unending supplies of gifts for the most desirable young women in the community.

There is no ready alternative to this level of earning outside the drug trade.[10] But there is a high price to pay. As one young man in Guaporé told me, on condition of anonymity, "Traffic pays well but you don't reach 30! We love the imported sneakers and brand-name clothing—sometimes we use up all our money on prestige items and clothing—sometimes we help support our families.... It is an escape from poverty but.... Did you ever wonder why you never see an aging dealer?"

In an interview about drugs, MV Bill, the rap star and youth activist, said:

It breaks my heart to say this, but crime nowadays has tragically become a great choice for those who are born with no prospects. I am not going to be hypocritical and say the opposite because this...is the truth....I have difficulty saying to someone "Get out of the drug traffic"—because I don't have anything better to offer. And it is not enough to offer charity assistance because television shows the good things in life, and this is what everybody is after."[11]

In 2004, while I was visiting the favela of Rocinha with my husband, he mentioned to a local community leader who was accompanying us that the boys who we saw flying kites from the roofs of the houses all around us were "flying their dreams." This was a poetic thought of which my husband was quickly disabused. "Not at all," he was told, "that is the way they signal to customers that a drug shipment has arrived in the favela."

INGREDIENT 3: A HIGH-PRICED ILLEGAL
COMMODITY—COCAINE

In the mid-1980s, coinciding with the end of the dictatorship and the rise in globalization, Rio de Janeiro became the main South American distribution center for cocaine and marijuana to Europe (via North Africa) and the United States (via Miami and New York).

The marijuana trade had been present in Brazil at least since I lived there in the 1960s, but it was only with the diversion of the cocaine trade through Rio, beginning in the mid-1980s, that the explosive mixture of cash and crime began to devastate life in the favelas.[12]

Brazil does not have the proper climate for the cultivation of coca, the raw material used to make cocaine. Coca grows ideally at high altitudes in cool climates. Brazil became involved as a repackaging and distribution hub when the United States' War on Drugs closed down Colombia's borders, creating the need for new distribution routes. It was a natural option due to the impossibility of controlling Brazil's vast perimeters and the possibility of entering the country by land or water. More recently, the jungles of Brazil at the borders with Paraguay, Bolivia, Colombia, and Peru have become sites for processing laboratories that manufacture cocaine from the raw coca that has been brought across the border into Brazil.

The increased volume of cargo traffic due to trade liberalization and globalization makes it even easier to hide material in air, land, or sea freight for import and export. Rio is an ideal port as well as an ideal distribution center. Cargo ships sailing from Rio are checked for drugs and found clean. They then pull out of the harbor, and small fishing vessels come out at night and load the precious freight. The same thing happens when boats arrive in Rio. The ships stop and offload the drugs onto islands just beyond the bay—again by fishing boats—and the ships come in for official inspection squeaky clean.

When the shipments enter the city, they come in bulk and need to be broken down, repackaged, and distributed from an out-of-the-way place. Rio's favelas are ideal for this. The rich "playboys" (the derogatory term those in the favela use for them) make up a significant segment of the market for these drugs, and they come to the bocas in the favelas to buy their supplies.

This is a classic example of the role of favelas in a high-stakes global game. (I return to this topic in chapter 12.) The value chain of production, refinement, manufacturing, warehousing, distribution, and consumption of cocaine locally, nationally, and internationally hinges on spaces of exclusion like favelas. With the collusion of the security forces, the drug gangs have almost total control of their territory, which is why so much is at stake in the turf wars. The favelas of Rio, for all they suffer as a consequence, are but a small cog in an enormous profit-generating wheel.[13]

INGREDIENT 4: WELL-ORGANIZED DRUG GANGS COMPETING FOR TERRITORIAL CONTROL

The first organized drug gang in Brazil was born in the prison on Ilha Grande, in Rio state, during the time I was first living in Rio's favelas in 1969. The military regime made the mistake of placing political prisoners together with common criminals who were typically poor and often came from favelas. The students and leftist intellectuals started teaching the others about exploitation and injustice, while the criminals taught the leftists how to function outside the law.

The government, realizing its error, then compounded it by separating the inmates from Ilha Grande and sending them to different prisons around the country—thereby enabling them to spread their new knowledge. When the dictatorship ended and many got out of prison, they organized a collective called the Red Phalanx, later called the Commando Vermelho (Red Command, known as the CV), Rio's first powerful drug gang. The initial capital for the drug trade was provided by the kingpins of the illegal gambling racket called the *jogo de bicho* (referred to in English as the number's game).[14] This happened just about the same time that the U.S. War on Drugs closed Colombian borders, redirecting the lucrative cocaine traffic through Brazil, particularly through the port of Rio.

Most favelas already had bocas for locally grown marijuana. These became the focal points for cocaine dealers who set up shop inside the favelas, recruiting locals to help work with them.[15] Within a few years, conflicts over the spoils within the Commando Vermelho led to the creation of two splinter groups that became bitter rivals—the Terceiro Commando (Third Command) and the Amigos dos Amigos (AMA-Friends of Friends). Then the wars began in earnest.

Things changed very quickly after that in all of the favelas. Gradually, the Residents' Associations were taken over by the traffic. A BBC news story of July 3, 2007, read: "Brazil launches slum reform drive: The Brazilian government has pledged [US]$1.7 [billion] ... to improve conditions in Rio de Janeiro's shanty-towns and counter the grip of the drugs gangs." But no perceptible difference has been seen since then.

Luke Dowdney, one of the experts in this field, explains the organizational structure of the Rio gangs as follows:

> The CV [Commando Vermelho] and other trafficking gangs in Rio do not oper-
> ate on the traditional model of an organized crime unit (like the Italian mafia),
> with a powerful don figure and overarching hierarchical structure. Instead, the
> individual gangs installed in various favelas which make up the CV and other
> gangs are linked through a network of "affiliated independent actors." ... Within
> an individual gang in a favela there is a rigid hierarchy, [but] across the indi-
> vidual gangs affiliated together through the network, the relationship is more
> one of cooperation in a "horizontal network of mutual protection" than a vertical
> hierarchy.[16]

The hierarchy from bottom to top starts with the aviões, generally young boys who pick up and deliver the product. The next level is the armed sol-dados, then the *gerente da boca* (boca manager), who organizes the sales and security, and above him, the *dono da boca* (boca owner), who is in charge and who arranges things with the suppliers (*atacadistas*, wholesalers). The suppliers cover several bocas, but are still limited to the local level. The top-level kingpins or drug lords, the *grandes chefões* (big chiefs), control the entire operation.[17] Fernandinho Beira-Mar, one of the most famous among these, is from the favela Beira-Mar (also known as Mangue, or "swamp"), which was one of the three Caxias favelas in this study. The residents are very proud of him as he con-tinues to run the drug traffic from the maximum-security federal penitentiary in Catanduva, Parana. He is their version of "home town boy makes good"!

According to the collective meetings I held to reconstruct the history of each community (the DRPs) it was not until the early 1990s that violence became a daily problem and the *bailes funk* (funk balls) became popular in the favelas. These ritualized weekend dance parties held in the favelas hold a powerful attraction for wealthy white youth from around the city. As many as 200,000 revelers may attend these events in the favelas on a weekend. To the loud, pounding bass rhythms of 1990s U.S. funk music, young people perform dances that mimic sexual activity. The lyrics are often sexually explicit and con-tain references to violent acts. They often refer to women in derogatory terms, for example *cachorras* (female dogs) and *popozudas* (large asses). The bands are funded by the drug gangs. The lyrics generally glorify the gangs and their lead-ers as heroic figures, the only ones with the guts to stand up and challenge the police and the government. These songs are known as *probidão* (extremely prohibited), as such lyrics are against the law in Brazil. Compact disc recordings of probidao songs are sold regularly "under the counter" in Rio. Some see the bailes funk as an integration of youth from the favelas and from the asfalto—and say they lead to a better understanding between classes. Others see them as orgies of sex, drugs, alcohol, and violence that take an extraordinary toll on the lives of favela residents.

INGREDIENT 5: SOPHISTICATED WEAPONRY
AND ACTIVE ARMS TRADE

If the drug gangs had only fists, knives, and broken beer bottles for fighting (as was the case with the troublemakers when I first lived in the favelas) the death toll would be a fraction of its present size. Today's drug gangs have access to highly sophisticated military-based automatic and semiautomatic weapons, including AK47, M-16, AR 15, IMBEL MD 2, FN FAL, and H&K G-3 military assault rifles, as well as bazookas, grenade launchers, and even antiaircraft missile launchers. As I have mentioned, as the drug dealers are better financed than the police, their weapons are more advanced than those of the Military Police. As shown in the documentary *Noticias de Um Guerra Particular*, every favela child who is old enough to talk can identify the exact models and types of a dozen weapons. They grow up with them as they do with soccer and samba.

The police are a critical element in the profit and power equation. After they confiscate the weapons in one favela, they keep some and sell the rest to a gang in another favela. Most of these weapons are manufactured in the United States, Russia, and Europe. Some are swapped at the border of Paraguay for drugs, so that no cash is required, or sold by rebel armies such as the Revolutionary Armed Forces of Colombia (FARC). Arms are a big business, akin to the drug traffic.

Jailson de Sousa e Silva, the founder and director of the Observatory of Favelas in the Complexo do Maré, says that it is not the drugs that are responsible for so many deaths among the favela youth, but the arms. He has said that if the United States really wanted to be a good neighbor and help the poor in Brazil, it would close down its weapons manufacturers or at least prohibit their export into Brazil, Mexico, and the other Latin American countries. The countries that manufacture and sell the arms are as much a part of the problem as the dealers, and they could become part of the solution.

As one of the Catacumba residents who had been relocated to Quitungo said at the DRP:

> Violence was greater in the conjuntos 'cause they were a mixture of people from different places and we didn't know who was who. Before the removal there was more respect among families; youth were not involved in violence, marijuana was

the only drug then—it was more about beer and *cachaça* [sugar cane rum]—and the bar fights were with fists, knives, or broken bottles. It's the guns that have made the difference.

INGREDIENT 6: AN UNDERPAID, UNDERSTAFFED, UNACCOUNTABLE POLICE FORCE

The police in Rio have a long history of corruption and of functioning without formal sanctions, accountability, and transparency. Most members of the police come from low-income families, many from favelas. For them, getting a job in the Military Police is a great leap upward and puts them under pressure to "perform well" so that they can continue to support their families. Yet their salaries are hardly sufficient for a decent life. On average, they earn about US$440–500 per month (US$5,250–6,000 a year).

And they are scared. In the film *Tropa de Elite* (*The Elite Squad*), which takes place in a favela when preparations are being made for a visit from the pope, the police are shown as jittery and anxious about carrying out a cleanup operation in a favela known for its violence. It is clear that they are out-armed by the traffic. They know they will be at a disadvantage entering turf familiar to the locals and full of ambush opportunities against them—and that the local residents do not want them there.

The majority of police recruits are young men who are experiencing power and demanding respect for the first time. Once they get the rush of power that wielding a lethal weapon gives them, they are sorely tempted to abuse that power. There are no sanctions or deterrents within the force. They can kill indiscriminately and use torture with impunity. And they make no distinction between favela residents and drug dealers—all are targets in their efforts to "restore law and order." Yet with all this leeway, Rio's police solve only 3 percent of the murders reported.[18] As a large number of murders of poor people remain unreported, even this paltry figure makes the police look better than they really are. It does not help that only 20 percent of the state police are deployed in the city of Rio, where 40 percent of the murders are committed.

The police can earn a lot more and have much more effective weapons when they act in complicity with the drug traffic. Many police officers meet up with the bandidos to divide the spoils when their workday is over. Even my friend Nilton, who was himself in the Military Police, is disgusted with this behavior. He said to me: "Things are quiet around here (Guaporé)—when one command is in control. But if the leader is killed or imprisoned, all hell breaks loose—there is a war over who will control the turf....Do you think the police help protect the innocent from dying?"

Margarida, with whom I had lived in Catacumba, invited me to visit her in Quitungo one afternoon. It was August 12, 1999, and I was just starting the restudy and trying to understand what had changed. She picked that time for me to come, saying: "Now it is better because the turf is divided. Before this it was impossible to have anyone come over or leave the house. Everyone was being killed, mostly by people from outside our community. We didn't recognize them. After the truce and division, order was restored, and then we succeeded in keeping the police out."

Margarida is the least politicized person I know, but still she sees the police as the worst enemy of the community rather than a source of protection. This view is widely shared. A survey published by Human Rights Watch in 1997 found that 76 percent of Rio's population thought police were involved in death squads, 65 percent thought they used torture to get confessions, and only 12 percent of those who had been robbed or assaulted said they had bothered reporting it to police. They had no faith in the willingness or ability of the police to enforce the law.[19]

INGREDIENT 7: GOVERNMENT INDIFFERENCE

Each of the ingredients I have mentioned so far is necessary but not—in itself—sufficient to explain the degree to which violence has gotten out of hand and taken over daily life in Rio. The inability of the state to maintain the rule of law is essential to the mix. The indifference of the government to what occurs in the favelas opens the space for the cat-and-mouse game that the traffic and the police are playing. It also means turning a blind eye to convenient payments of drug money to members of the judiciary, political candidates, and officeholders at every level.

As this book goes to press, twenty-five years have passed since the return to democracy in Brazil. That is three years longer than the duration of the military dictatorship. People who turned voting age in 1985 are now over 40, and many have children of voting age themselves. Yet, to use James Holston's dead-on phrase, Brazil remains an "incomplete democracy,"[20] with a weak government and a population divided between full citizens and pseudocitizens.

Regina, Margarida's neighbor in Quitungo, is a registered nurse who was 27 when she was removed from Catacumba. "The government does nothing to help us" she said. "In terms of the community, all I ask for is respect for our lives—but it's not good. The gun battles are out of control—we worry about our families all the time—this is no way to live! Where is the government?"

As the sociologist Loïc Wacquant sees it, government policy is implemented on a short-term basis in the favelas, strictly to put a stop to incidents of civil unrest and

> for its broader theatrical value in the eyes of middle- and upper-class audiences.
> To them the state offers thus a vivid public performance of "criminal policy as

the shedding of the blood" of the loathsome and despoiled poor, the rootless, useless, and faceless "individuals" who stand as the living antonyms to the proper Brazilian incarnation of the respectable and recognized "person" [gente]—much as the "underclass" has been depicted in the U.S.... as the collective condensation of all the moral defects and physical dangers with which the decaying inner city threatens the integrity of the United States as a nation essentially made of decent, law-abiding, suburban "working families."[21]

Waquant goes on to argue

that the promotion of the market as the optimal mechanism for organizing all human activities requires not only a minimalist "small government" on the social and economic front but also, and without contradiction, an enlarged and diligent state armed to intervene with force to maintain public order and draw out salient social and ethnic boundaries.[22]

INGREDIENT 8: MILITIAS AND EXTORTION

As the drug factions fought each other over the spoils of the trade and bargained with the police over their take, newly formed militias started taking law and order into their own hands. The militias are not part of a network like the dealers or part of the government like the police. They are autonomous, self-appointed vigilante groups composed of retired and "off-duty" policemen and firemen who take control of the communities through their brand of violence. They create drug-free favelas by shooting users or sellers, executing those known to be involved in the traffic, and demanding complete control over all aspects of life in return for "protection."

Without anything to sell, the militias supplement their salaries through extortion, charging the residents a series of fees for everyday necessities, as I mentioned earlier. In addition to charging fees for delivery of propane and communications services, they have a monopoly on all vehicles, vans, and motorbikes that go up into the favela and charge a "tax" for every trip.

Until 2004–05, only one favela—Rio das Pedras in the West Zone—was controlled by a militia. But by 2008, militias controlled over 100 communities—some, like Vila Operária in Caxias, in conjunction with the traffickers. A BBC news story of March 8, 2008, "Vigilantes Take Over Rio Shantytowns," quotes one woman as saying, "They control everything, they make demands, they kill. If you don't follow their way, do what they say, you go straight to the grave."[23]

No government action has been taken to stop the activities of the militias or to hold them accountable for unwarranted deaths. In fact, in some circles there is talk of supporting them, and perhaps eventually legalizing them. The rationale is that the state cannot occupy 800 favelas but the militias can.

The sums of money involved in militia activities are astronomical. According to one source, the black market businesses that the militias run (and drug dealers are increasingly involved in) bring in about US$200 million per year, according to estimates by trade unions and police intelligence. Tolls on van service bring in an estimated US$72.5 million; illegal tapping of cable TV (called "gato-net"), about US$59.5 million; broadband Internet access about US$60 million; and the markup on the sale of cooking gas canisters about US$8 million.[24] There are also profitable businesses in taxing the "motor-taxis" that bring people up and down within the favelas and in various forms of gambling, from the traditional jogo de bicho to bingo to electronic one-armed bandits.

These lucrative businesses—along with the drop in the street price for cocaine—have induced some to leave narco-traffic and go into the extortion racket instead. This puts them on a second collision course with the militia. As of this writing, the militias appear to control broadband Internet access, and the traffic is running the underground Internet service providers. The police estimate that at least 70 percent of the favela residents pay for pirated TV and monopolized Internet. In fact, many favelas use their community loudspeakers to remind the residents when their monthly gato-net bills are due.

With such vast profits at stake, the violence continues to escalate, and innocent people continue to be killed. In their use of extrajudicial lethal violence, both dealers and militias enjoy impunity from prosecution, and government gets its cut one way or another.

The Poor Pay More

In the perverse logic of power, money, and freedom, people with sufficient means to live in the formal city of Rio have the liberty to shop for the best price among a variety of providers of cable television, Internet access, propane, transportation, and a host of other services—while the poor pay more.[25] Favela and conjunto residents live in a controlled monopolistic territory and are obliged to purchase from a sole source at a premium rate.

I found precisely the same form of exploitation in the favelas 40 years ago and wrote about it in *The Myth of Marginality*. At that time, the community had to tap into the electric and water networks illegally. Those who lived along the main road were able to get a monopoly and then pass the service on at a steeper price than that paid in the rest of the city. Just as there is gato-net for cable TV, there was a similar setup for electricity: families paid by the outlet and number of appliances, as they did not have meters. The electric company would not provide service in the favelas. Even grocery and clothing items were more expensive inside the favelas, as the merchants who had monopolies there were often asked to extend interest-free credit to the favela residents. These merchants might also hold a small inventory, buy in small quantities, and divide up a loaf of bread or a pack of cigarettes to make their wares affordable for the local residents.

INGREDIENT 9: A POWERLESS POOR POPULATION

Simply put, the degree of lethal violence in Rio is only possible because a third of the population is disenfranchised and considered worthless. If they were well organized, the poor would have the numbers to constitute a potent voting bloc and mount a convincing consumer boycott. But the firearms are in the hands of the traffic, the militia, and the police. The poor, whether in favelas, conjuntos, loteamentos, or low-income neighborhoods, are pawns in a much larger game, unable to turn to "the authorities" for protection and intimidated into quiet compliance. The middle and upper classes have come to accept the lack of human rights in these poor neighborhoods, as they see it as the price for their own protection and peace and privilege. This harks back to the legacy of the "masters and the slaves," the "*casa grande* and *senzala*,"[26] which has engrained ideas of entitlement into even the most open-minded of the elite. And this is a situation similar to the fear of communism that the Brazilian dictatorship directed toward favela residents in the 1960s and 1970s. Now this fear is directed toward murderous drug addicts.

As Daniel Brinks puts it, "the public, including even relatives of victims of police killings, often make public statements in support of killing criminals. The public perception of increasing criminality (real or imagined) has motivated much of the population to (at least tacitly) accept the extralegal methods by which police act."[27]

INGREDIENT 10: SENSATIONALIST MASS MEDIA

In no small part, the public acceptance of unjustified (illegitimate) police violence within an otherwise civilized city is facilitated by a media-induced frenzy of fear. Not a day passes when Roberto Marinho's media empire, Rede Globo, does not add to the panic over safety and security, whipping up public sentiment against the "bandidos" who are often conflated with law-abiding, hardworking favela residents.

In this way, the coverage reinforces the stigma and criminalization of poverty and strengthens preexisting stereotypes of favela residents, which in turn makes it even more difficult for them to get jobs. No one wants to let favela residents into their home or shop or office—it's "just too dangerous." The cycle is self-reinforcing, since the fewer jobs there are, the stronger the temptation to enter the traffic.

On the other hand, all the "glory" of appearing on television and in newspapers turns the drug lords into larger-than-life antiheroes of favela youth, making them into role models. As Jacobi, my friend from Catacumba, said, "Kids now prefer to enter the traffic because they earn more money than if they stay in school and then go out looking for work. They can show off their brand-name clothing and shoes. That's why, today, those who orient the youth and become their role models are the trafficantes."

When the president of Xerox do Brasil came to talk to the youth in the favela of Mangueira, where the company had invested in education and sports for several years, he gave a pep talk about what wonderful opportunities awaited them if they continued to study hard and went to university. One boy asked how much he earned per year. When he answered, the children's faces fell in disbelief. "That's so little," they said, comparing his salary with that of their heroes Fernandinho Beira-Mar or Marcelinho VP. These children might go home to a lack of food and sleep head-to-toe with other family members in a single bed in a room without a window, but the lifestyle they imagine for themselves is based on that of the infamous trafficantes.

In short, aside from selling well, the constant images of violence perpetuated by the media fan public hysteria, increasing acceptance of militaristic solutions to public safety. They also turn drug lords into antiheroes for the youth, reduce tourism—one of the few remaining sources of revenue for the city of Rio—and legitimize the escalation of violence on all sides.

A VICIOUS CYCLE

These 10 ingredients reinforce each other and create a self-perpetuating vicious cycle. The profits from the drug traffic enable the competing factions to acquire ever more sophisticated weapons to use in their wars over the "contested space"[28] of the bocas. The police are known to confiscate these weapons for their own use.

The police justify this violence as necessary to get rid of the traffickers. Instead, it challenges them and provokes the gangs to make dramatic demonstrations of their control over the city and the government. For example, the gangs have shut down commerce for a day in the South Zone (under penalty of death for those who dared to open their enterprises for business); shot bullets into the municipal government building (without being seen); blocked traffic on the major access road between the two elite areas of the city (the South Zone and the Barra de Tijuca) one Easter (shooting a woman who got out of her car); set fire to buses; closed down the access road to the airport; and have otherwise spared little effort to make their point.[29]

If the state is absent in the favelas and impotent in the city at large, the question of the "right to the city" becomes even more pressing. Putting drug lords in prison in no way hinders their ability to command their vast operations. They easily bribe the (underpaid) prison guards for use of cell phones even in the "maximum security prisons," and they have total control over who lives and who dies.

In this way, the marginalized poor are trapped in a five-way vector of violence: they are caught between (1) the drug gangs, who are fighting for territorial control; (2) the police, who kill them with impunity; (3) the government, which is absent or complicitous; (4) the militias, who control them through extortion and death threats; and (5) the media, which sell their message by terrifying the audience and reinforcing the divide between "us" and "them."

This cycle is constantly recreated, completing the marginalization and victimization of the poor, the criminalization of poverty itself, and the militarization of the police.

THE CONSEQUENCES OF VIOLENCE FOR THE URBAN POOR

It is unconscionable that while millions of dollars from the Rio drug and arms traffic are enriching criminal networks extending beyond Brazilian borders and "greasing the skids" of all branches of the Brazilian government, thousands of people in the favelas are being killed as "collateral damage," and millions are being taxed because they live under the control of traffickers and militias who are more dictatorial toward them than the dictatorship was.

I have accompanied my favela families and friends through many times of difficulty and loss, but I have never seen anything as devastating as the effects of this reign of violence and terror. Unlike the ethnic and religious wars going on around the world today, the killings in the favelas amount to a war on the poor. This implies tremendous loss—at the individual and family level, at the community level and for both in terms of social capital and civil society.

LOSS FOR INDIVIDUALS AND FAMILIES

At stake for the people living in the "war zones" is the loss of peace, freedom, and personhood, and all too often loss of life. Among all those whom I interviewed in 2001, in all three generations, one in five had lost a family member to homicide. In the interviews, we asked each person "Have you or a family member ever been a victim of violent crime?" The results are shown in figure 7.3.

These results not only reflect life in favelas, but in conjuntos and low-income neighborhoods as well. The types and frequency of violence were virtually identical in the responses of the original interviewees, their children, and their grandchildren.

People have nowhere to turn for help. The notion that the traffic constitutes a "parallel power" or a "parallel state" that provides services to the community in lieu of government services is totally misguided.[30] It is true that it is a ruling faction that fills a vacuum created by the state's absence, but the traffic takes

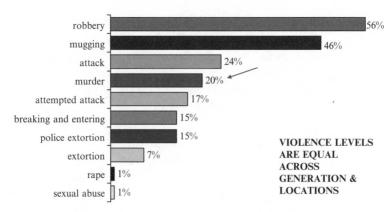

FIGURE 7.3   Violence and victimization: Types and percentages.

no responsibility for the general welfare of the population. The only benign aspect of their internal code of ethics is that the traffickers do not deprive the community of the potential benefits from the operation of any nonprofit or government program (or research project in my case) that wishes to work in the favelas. After all, they need some level of community acceptance (if not support) in order to operate there.

Early on, when the traffic called itself "the movement," there was a certain Robin Hood mystique to the community having its own force against the police. The term "parallel power" was sometimes used to glorify the image of the dealers as the protectors of the community, but more often it was used by the authorities to justify the extrajudicial use of lethal force that characterizes the war on the poor. I even found it in a United States Security Report which states (erroneously) that "the drug gangs control and serve as parallel government in many of the poor areas of the city, known as favelas."[31]

It is true that from time to time, the ruling gang will drive a woman in labor to the maternity hospital, arrange a private school fellowship for a student, get medicine for an elderly person, or distribute other favors—as whims. This is a far cry from providing the social services and benefits that are the responsibility of the state. On the other hand, the gangs feel no compunction about ordering someone's arms and legs broken if he or she is late in repaying a debt, or in ordering someone killed or tortured if they feel they have been betrayed. This hardly qualifies the traffic as a community service provider.

In fact, community residents feel trapped between the dealers and the police. In the eyes of the residents, neither the dealers nor the police help them very much, and both do more harm than good. In the 2001 interviews with the original study participants and their descendants, only 13 percent reported being helped by the traffic, while 37 percent said they were harmed. Most were afraid to give any answer at all. They judged the police about the same—more harmful than helpful. There is no place for them to turn for help.

When we asked, "Who commits more acts of violence against the community" in our 2003 interviews (with over 1,200 people randomly selected from Quitungo and Guaporé; Nova Brasília; Vila Ideal; and the other favelas and loteamentos in Caxias), the response was even more emphatic: 81 percent reported that the police, the traffic, or both commit violence harmful to the community, and another 7 percent said they did not know (which probably meant that they were afraid to answer the questions). Table 7.2 shows that almost half answered "both," and that among the respondents who picked only one, twice as many said the police were more violent. I suspect that the 19 percent who responded "none" or "don't know" are reflecting fear rather than ignorance or innocence.[32]

In March 2008, a BBC reporter in Rio summed up the situation: "Here the idea of the state has been replaced by the organization, hierarchy, and power of drug-trafficking networks."[33] The impunity of the police in the face of this excessive violence and their total complicity in the confiscating and reselling of arms and drugs from faction to faction and community to community have made matters much worse for the favela residents. The police are willing to use torture and extortion to deal with anyone they suspect of foul play or noncooperation, and no authority holds them accountable.

This generates the third consequence: the loss of peace of mind, of tranquility, of the privacy of one's home. In favelas and conjuntos, people are living under constant stress, unable to sleep through the night, listening to the sound of gunshots. This siege atmosphere takes its toll on both the mental and physical health of the residents. Stress-related diseases such as hypertension have become endemic. People age early; they lose their health. (You can see the toll taken in the photos of Margarida and Djanira.)

TABLE 7.2   *Who commits more acts of violence against the community?*

New Random Sample (2003)	
	Percent
Police	22
Traffickers	11
Both	48
None	12
Don't Know	7
Total	100.0

This constant stress from an ongoing state of war was what eventually drove Zé Cabo out of his home in Nova Brasília. When we spoke on July 30, 2003, he was still living there. He said:

> The day before yesterday from midnight to 4:00 A.M. there was a full-fledged war between the CV and TC [Commando Vermelho and Terceiro Commando]. No one could sleep. People are getting sick from their nerves always on edge. Every night the traffic shoots out the street lights. When they are replaced, they are shot out again.

Almost all the women I spoke with also expressed anxiety and dread at the loss of privacy—even within their own homes. They said that when the police barge into homes under the pretext of searching for bandidos, they pull everything apart, tear up the furniture, rip bedspreads off the beds, and break kitchenware. When they fail to find anything, they leave the wreckage behind and storm out disgruntled. The things they destroy have taken a lifetime of care and savings and—like the sense of security—cannot easily be put back together. The other side of the coin is that if a trafficker wants to hide in your home in a favela or conjunto, you will be shot if you do not allow it.

No one talks publicly about such matters. People are fearful of opening their mouths—they are intimidated. I was told repeatedly, "We have to be like the three monkeys—we don't see anything, don't hear anything, don't say anything." They tell me, "If you talk you die.... There is *pavor* [terror] everywhere, not only here, but *por todo canto* [in every corner]." Is this not a loss of the freedom of expression?

With the added stigma of conflating favela residents and bandidos has come the loss of work opportunities. Employers are reluctant to hire anyone who lives in a favela, whether as domestics who will have a set of keys to their homes or sales clerks with access to cash registers. In Djanira's words, "because of the association of violence and drugs with Vila Operária, a madame does not want to accept people who live here to work in her house."

During the DRP with the Catacumba community, a 43-year-old man living in Guaporé said, "Once they learn where we live, there are no jobs for us—we have to support our wives and children. What are we supposed to do? We need to earn money just like everyone else, but we are not given a chance. I cannot move my family—there is nowhere else that we can afford."[34]

Nenem, the president of the Quitungo Residents' Association, owns a warehouse where he sells cooking gas canisters, among many other household necessities. He wants to sell the canisters for the going rate outside the conjunto, but he is obliged to buy them from the local militia, who charge him a higher price plus a fee. If he tries to go around them, they will close down his store. He cannot take the risk even though he considers it "grossly unfair that the people who live here pay more than those who are not in conjuntos, like the people living in the buildings on the other side of the street."

But that is a small thing compared with the devastating loss in home values. People's homes are their single greatest assets and their greatest lifetime investments. Favelas and conjuntos have thriving real estate markets, despite being "informal" or—in the case of conjuntos—in limbo between formal and informal.[35] But as violence has increased, home values have dropped, often to the point where leaving means walking away with nothing. No one wants to move into a place like Nova Brasília or Vila Operária today.

Zé Cabo found himself caught in that exact situation. He had never wanted to leave his home or his community unless he could move to Gloria, his favorite neighborhood. But he was forced to move to a less central part of Nova Brasília in 1990 due to the traffic. He described the house he bought in Nova Brasília in a conversation on July 30, 2003:

> This house was worth US$15,000 when I bought it in 1990, and I invested another $5,000 adding on and improving it—now it's worth zero. I moved here because I had to get out of the way of the traffic—I was right in the middle of things there. When I came here to this remote corner, there were only a few houses—it was a long, steep uphill climb, not convenient to anything. Now it has grown, and the traffic has followed. Look at my garage door—full of bullet holes. I had to teach the grandchildren to duck under the bed when they hear gunfire—one night a bullet came right through the window.... Did you see those guys who hang out in front of my door sniffing glue, smoking *maconha* (pot), and snorting cocaine in broad daylight? I would leave right now if I could sell or rent it, but no one wants it.

By the time I came back a year later, Zé had given his home ownership papers to his common-law partner, Maria, to make sure she would have something in her name if things improved, and he had moved to his present ruin of a house on a tiny plot of land under the viaduct in Irajá.

The loss of liberty and freedom to move about at will is less tangible, but no less devastating. As a rule, the traffic has "soldiers" with loaded rifles stationed at the entrance to each favela, and anyone not recognized as a resident is stopped and asked what he or she wants. In order to keep police vehicles out and protect their turf, the traffickers construct road blocks that can be removed when they want to let someone pass. They also control who leaves after dark. If you are working in the favela in an approved activity, you generally blink the headlights to let them know that you are "OK" to go.

Ironically, drug traffic has turned favelas into places where you need permission to enter—just like the gated ghettos of the rich.

The residents' movements within the favelas are constrained as well. As Nilton told me in 1999,

> We live in a place where you do not have the liberty to act freely, to come and go, to leave your house whenever you want to, to live as any other person who is not

in jail. It is imprisoning to think, "Can I go out now or is it too dangerous?" Why do I have to call someone and say that they shouldn't come here today? It is awful, it is oppressive. No one should have to live like this.

In 2001, Djanira said, "The entrance of the narco-traffic and the violence ended our freedom, ended our happiness, and ruined everything."[36]

The families who had left Rio and gone back to their hometowns were driven out of the favelas by the violence and its consequences. I went to interview Zé Cabo's brother Manuel José on the outskirts of Natal, the capital of the state of Rio Grande do Norte, in early December 2001. He lives with his wife in a two-story house with a small tropical garden, which she tends. He said:

> I lived in Nova Brasília since I was a young man. I married there, raised a family. I left in 1990 because of the violence. My house was just behind Zé Cabo's house.... There were so many assaults. The last straw was when my wife and I were returning from visiting her relatives in Botafogo [a neighborhood on Guanabara Bay near the center of Rio]. We were assaulted coming home on the bus. The guys said to her "Não é nada, não, tire as jóias [this is no big deal, nothing—take off your jewelry]." There were five of them—we were near Jacarezinho [the biggest favela in the North Zone]. After that we said let's leave and go back to our *terra* [land]—we paid 750 reais (US$375) for a small plot of land here and spent three years building this house.

They were doing fine there but felt rather isolated. Zé Cabo had visited them several times. They have a room for him and are constantly urging him to move there, but he is not interested. He says it's a nice place to visit but he would die if he had to live there—too little going on for him. He would miss the *movimento* (action) of the city.

LOSS FOR THE COMMUNITY

In addition to the consequences for individuals and households mentioned earlier, the violence has dire repercussions for the community as a whole, for community life, for conviviality. The loss of public space—or, to be more precise, its expropriation and control by the traffic—means there is no place for sitting and watching the parade of life go by, for playing soccer, for recreation, for leisure. In the DRPs, one of the most striking findings across all of the communities was the absence of leisure activities.

Speaking of Vila Ideal in Caxias, Djanira said:

> We used to have *festas juninas* [São João festivals in June] *futebol* [soccer] *brincadeiras de alunos* [student games]—now we can't do anything. Since 2000, when they renovated the *praça*, it's never been used. It is the only open space we have here and—just take a look, it is always empty—the one place our kids could

play basketball and our elderly could sit under a shade tree, and it is deserted. Everyone is afraid. The Residents' Association even closed down our community radio broadcast from the church. The bandidos threatened us that they would destroy the building if we kept it going. They don't want any other voice heard but their own.

Juracy, a 61-year-old resident of Nova Brasília, said, "Starting as early as 1982, things became different here—that is when the factories started to close one after another and when the traffic started here.... It was better before, now *não tem o que fazer* [here there is no leisure, there is nothing to do]." She continued, "the Praça do Terco, where we used to play soccer and have parties, is now off limits. It is controlled by the boca." Binha, who is 37, added:

Things are worse now than before. When I was growing up in Brasília, we would go dancing here until dawn, we would go out at two or three in the morning. I worked late. I would arrive home alone at one in the morning. There was nothing to fear. Now it's not like that. I walk down the street keeping an eye out in case I see something or other—you know what I mean?

The loss of independent Residents' Associations has meant the loss of voice, the loss of the only institution that represented the interests of the favelas. Now most of the elected presidents have been assassinated or forced out of the communities. At the start of this restudy, in 1999–2000, about half of the favelas in Rio still had independent Residents' Associations with popularly elected presidents. One by one, as the years progressed, the elected presidents have been eliminated, and, by 2005, almost all of the Residents' Associations were controlled by the traffic. The one exception was Rio das Pedras, where the Residents' Association was controlled by militias.

As of 2009, Rio had over 1000 favelas but only a few were still independent. As I discuss in the next chapter, the small favors that the former associations were able to wrest from candidates for vereador (city council) no longer exist since political campaigns and negotiations are all controlled by the traffic according to their self-interest.

As Nilton described this loss,

We had two Residents' Associations—one for Quitungo and a separate one for Guaporé. Then marginals took over the Residents' Associations of both and formed a new one of their own. The mayor at the time, Luis Paulo Conde, and the governor, Garotinho, did nothing to stop this—nor have they done anything to prevent it in any of the other conjuntos or favelas."[37]

The fear of getting killed in the crossfire or hit by a stray bullet has kept much-needed urban services and programs out of the poor communities. This loss of service providers, teachers, nurses, social workers, day care workers, NGO programs, and even home deliveries and ordinary taxi service has deprived residents—especially youth—of what they most need to overcome the challenges they face just by living in favelas. It is hard to get qualified people to work in an "area of risk," and even when there is a police station right inside the community, no security is provided, as the police literally barricade themselves inside the station and do not emerge until they go home for the day. To my horror, I found that it can take children years to complete primary school because many teachers show up only two or three days a week. A recent decision was made to pass all children on to the next grade whether or not they passed the year—just one more indication that the lives of these youngsters are considered expendable and their prospects have been written off.

As the Nova Brasília Residents' Association president told me a few years ago, "Teachers don't want to come teach at our school because the state declared this an 'area of risk' and they were afraid.... Even taxi drivers are afraid to go up the hill, so we have our own Kombis."[38] On July 4, 2007, there was a massive police assault on Nova Brasília and the other favelas in the Complexo de Alemão that led to the closing of eight or ten schools in the communities. As one journalist reported it, "for several days, some 4,600 children were kept out of the classrooms. UNICEF issued an alert on the situation of children stopped from studying because they live in zones of conflict and compared the students in the Alemão complex with those in the Gaza Strip and Iraq."[39]

LOSS OF SOCIAL CAPITAL AND CIVIL SOCIETY

One dire consequence of what I have called *o mundo de medo* (the sphere of fear) is the erosion of social capital, one of the few resources that was available, abundant, and effective in poor communities. (In the analysis we measured social capital by level of memberships, friendships, social networks, and participation in community activities.)

The violence and its twin offshoots—fear and distrust—not only prevent the use of public space but also diminish socializing among friends and relatives, reduce membership in community organizations, weaken trust among neighbors, and erode community unity. The flow of information about jobs, programs, and all manner of opportunities that was spread through informal community networks has dried up, and the coping mechanisms based on *mutirao* (mutual aid) are barely intact.

Robert Putnam and others have shown that a strong civil society and high degree of social capital in a region or community are closely correlated with economic vitality and political stability. There are two types of social capital: bonding, which creates networks among people within a community, and bridging, which creates networks outside of the community and linkages with diverse people and institutions.

Bonding Social Capital

For the purposes of this study, I looked at changes along four dimensions of bonding social capital: membership, socializing, trust, and unity. Membership and participation in community-based organizations is one of the classic measures of social capital and civil society. Comparing the participation levels of the original interviewees in 1969 with that of their children in 2001 (at approximately the same age) showed a dramatic drop across the board.

Participation in every type of community organization and activity had dropped off—for some more dramatically than others. Membership in the Residents' Associations dropped from nearly 30 percent to a mere 3 percent. Participation in labor unions, sports groups, and samba schools—never high to begin with—dropped by half. The exception to the drastic decrease was in the percentage of respondents who attend religious meetings. This number decreased slightly but remained at a higher level than any other community-based activity. The follow-up questions showed that elderly women were the most likely to be part of a religious group. For many of them, going to their church meetings (particularly evangelical meetings, which are always close to home) had become their one chance to get out of the house and their only form of "leisure" activity.[40]

As for other forms of participation, there was a surge of community-based mobilization just after the return of democracy in 1984–85, but by the early 1990s all popular movements had gone downhill—from Residents' Associations to federations (of Residents' Associations) to unions to base communities to the incipient Movimento dos Sem Teto (Homeless Movement). The entrance of the traffic killed everything.

Socializing, as measured by how many of your closest friends and relatives live near you, how often you visit with friends and relatives in the community, and how often your friends or relatives visit you also diminished considerably. The same pattern applied to the degree of trust among neighbors. In 1969, over half said that they could "count on most or all of their neighbors"; by 2001, only a third felt that way—and there was no significant difference by generation.

As for community unity, or more accurately the perception of community unity, 85 percent of the original interviewees said that their communities were "united or very united," while in 2001, only half (51 percent) of the original interviewees, 45 percent of their children, and 42 percent of their grandchildren felt that way. Nonetheless, there was a decidedly greater sense of unity in the favelas than in the conjuntos, and the bairros had the least of all. But even in the favelas, there is a diminished sense of unity.

This erosion of social capital and internal solidarity represents a marked decline in community residents' quality of life. When I first went to live in the favelas, the community spirit and solidarity were among the great pleasures of favela life. In stark contrast to the well-to-do areas where no one knew their neighbors, in the favelas of Catacumba, Nova Brasília, Vila Operária, Beiramar, and Vila Central, most people knew each other by name and took care of each other in times of crisis. The mutual support networks were part of the survival mechanisms that the poor could count on to reduce the vulnerability of *living on the edge*.

To borrow a phrase from Mercedes de la Rocha, there has been a change "from the resources of poverty to the poverty of resources."[41] The fear of getting caught in the crossfire or on the wrong side of a friendship in a drug war has resulted in people going out less and keeping to themselves more. Every measure of community unity, trust, socializing, and participation has declined dramatically. This cannot be attributed solely to the drug, police, and militia violence in favelas, since the erosion of social capital over the past decades has been documented in many places.[42] Conversely, there is no doubt that favela life would be more convivial and social cohesion more robust had the drug traffic been located elsewhere.

Bridging Social Capital

If violence erodes the connective tissue within communities, does it strengthen the connections between the community and the rest of the city? Do the number and strength of ties and contacts external to the favela influence chances of upward mobility?

Our study showed a very strong relationship between external connections and socioeconomic status. It was clear that for each group studied in all time periods, the more ties a person had to others outside the favela, the higher his or her socioeconomic status (as measured by educational level, number of domestic appliances, and extent of crowding) Granovetter calls this "the strength of weak ties."[43] What was not clear was whether having more education and income enables people to make more connections outside the community or whether having more connections outside the community means more exposure to people who have stayed in school, have good jobs and earn well and can serve as role models for another type of life. Or, could it be that having external connections opens doors to better schools and jobs? Perhaps all are at play simultaneously. Either way, the increase in violence has weakened both types of social capital—bonding and bridging.

The one contradiction we found with Putnam's thesis is that for our samples, there was a negative relationship between bonding social capital and levels of socioeconomic status. If Putnam were correct, those with greater participation in community activities and more social networks should be the ones with the highest socioeconomic scores, but we found just the opposite. We tested this quite carefully, as it goes against the grain of a large body of literature.

What we found is that for newly arrived migrants, the bonding social capital did help integrate them into the community and the city and gain their bearings. There seems to be a threshold of community engagement above which internal socializing becomes a limiting factor in moving up the social ladder or out of the community, as I discuss further in chapter 9. One possible explanation for this is that those who are working during the day and studying at night are the ones most likely to get ahead, but have the least time to go to community meetings or socialize with friends and neighbors. Many menial jobs demand six days a week of service; some give a day off only every other week. On the other hand, those with the closest affective ties to the community and a strong sense of *raízes* (roots)—often expressed as "that's where my *umbigo* (umbilical cord) is buried"—are the ones least likely to move out, even when they have the financial resources to do so.

CONCLUSIONS: COMPARING THEN AND NOW

It would be misleading to give the impression that there were no drugs and no violence in the favelas in the 1960s and 1970s. The main "drugs" then were beer, cachaça, and marijuana. As I already mentioned, the instruments of violence were fists, knives, or broken beer bottles, and the cocaine and weapons that are now ubiquitous were not readily available then.

Jair, one of my old friends from Catacumba, said that in Catacumba there had been "mafiosos," but they didn't infringe on the community. They respected the residents and didn't break up the dances at the youth club. There were also drug dealers and drug users, but it was mostly marijuana, they were not armed, and they didn't infringe on the population.

Once Catacumba was torn down and residents were put in the conjuntos, he said, things got worse. There were a large number of assaults in Guaporé, where he and his family were put. "Now the traffickers don't really want a lot of violence and killing," he explained; "their business is selling drugs." ("O negocio deles é vender tóxico.") The particular traffickers who dominate Guaporé are the children of ex-Catacumbans, so Jair and his neighbors are left alone. In his view, traffickers don't want to disrupt residents' lives—"they just want to do their business and keep the peace . . . unless some other gang wants to take over their area."

Respect is a recurring theme in the narratives of the people I interviewed. The following quotations offer a small sample of the often-repeated comparisons the favela residents in all of the study communities make between the past and present in terms of the traffickers' relations with them and other residents.

For a long time, the bandidos were respectful of the leaders—everyone knew them and knew their parents.

The gang members and drug dealers were generally boys from the community—they grew up here, they knew who we are—they respected the old-timers, the workers. They did not threaten them; in fact they protected them.

It is better to have bandidos you know than bandidos from outside. Community bandidos are more trustworthy…I would rather ask the trafficantes for help than the police.

The precarious equilibrium between residents and trafficantes is breaking down…. The traffickers no longer respect anyone; they have started using drugs in the street.

In the last 10 or 12 years, drug dealing has become more and more like a big business. Nowadays, we don't know many of the bandidos—they come here from other places—they don't care if you are innocent or hardworking, or young or old, or if you sacrificed to build this community.

Parallel with the decline in respect and the increasing anonymity of the traffickers is the increasing leniency of the law. As Nilton explained it: "Today it is easier [than 30 years ago] for people to get away with criminal behavior—starting with impunity. The marginality has more leeway now—can control the community residents with fear and terror—do as they choose."

The other major change is a growing trend toward consumption of drugs inside the favelas. When the drugs first entered, repackaging and selling them for the *asfalto* was a way to earn money, and people in the community were in no financial position to consume cocaine themselves. But lately, many of the younger gang members are being paid in drugs instead of cash and are becoming addicted at an increasingly early age.

PROFITS AND PUNISHMENT

The most recent changes I observed in Rio in October 2008 and June 2009 relate to the drop in the street price of cocaine due to the increasing demand for such drugs as ecstasy and crystal methamphetamine, which are synthetically produced. Drug sales in Rio are becoming a two-way street—the "playboys" go to the favelas to buy cocaine, and the favela boys go to the South Zone to buy ecstasy. Those who work for the traffic are also getting paid less. Some only get one minimum salary, plus drugs and bonuses. But to put this in perspective, many police earn only one minimum salary themselves. The results are increased intensity of violent contestation over turf, lower pay for drug traffickers, and the rise of alternate sources of money—so that more money is wrung from the poor through extortion by the militias and the traffic.

The people whose *lives* are lost—and those whose *quality of life* is lost—in Rio's favelas are small players in a high-stakes global game. They are considered expendable and easily replaced. Those who enjoy the profits are safe in their luxury penthouses in Rio, Europe, and the United States. Poor people in poor neighborhoods fulfill specific functions in what Lopes de Souza calls an "extensive...value chain of production, refinement, manufacturing, warehousing, distribution and consumption [of drugs] in local, national and global markets."[44] The brutal violence in the favelas creates a convenient diversion so immediate that antidrug police and policies are focused on the "lower end of the drug economy value chain without touching the upper rungs of control and profiteering."[45]

As MV Bill said about crime and punishment: "What you have to understand about this society is that questions of violence and crime [are] not just about guns and drugs. In Brazil, the only people who go to prison are those who steal a little. Those who steal a lot go free."[46]

I give the last word of this chapter to Nilton, who took so much time and patience to explain his reality to me and who so powerfully goes to the core of the matter:

> Those most responsible for the existence of drug traffic are not the small dealers, no...they are the people with enough power and influence to promote the introduction of drugs on a vast scale and in enormous quantities. Taking advantage of political immunity, these individuals grab money, influence, and power...it's them and the politicians who are responsible for our problems with drugs here.

eight

DISILLUSION WITH DEMOCRACY

Democratic governance, inclusive citizenship, and rights—human, civil, and political rights—cannot be divorced from the issue of poverty. "Freedom from want" is the most basic of rights, although it is often not considered in that light.

During Brazil's military dictatorship, the fight for citizenship and for "the right to have rights" was seen as highly subversive. In a series of "Institutional Acts" decreed between 1965 and 1974, elections for mayor, governor, and president were suspended. Regime opponents were routinely arrested, tortured, and "disappeared." For the urban poor, however, citizenship was not a salient issue. Favela residents did not join protest demonstrations. Their time and energy were consumed with the day-to-day struggle for survival, and their pressing concern was to prevent their children from going to bed hungry.

What does Brazilian democracy in the first decade of the twenty-first century look like from the viewpoint of the urban poor? Have the favela residents—in their own view—been included as full citizens? Have their lives and communities improved since the end of the dictatorship? How have their political interests, knowledge, perceptions, and participation evolved?

For the underclass, it appears that the 20 years of political repression during the military government have been replaced by more than 20 years of growing belief in democratic principles coexisting with continuing exclusion from full citizenship. Democracy has made many things possible that would have been unthinkable before, but in terms of inclusion and equality under the law, the transition is still incomplete. The urban poor have yet to enjoy the benefits of full citizenship.

Brazil's experience with democracy was sporadic. From 1889 until the beginning of the republic in 1930 when the Getúlio Vargus dictatorship began, Brazil had a taste of democracy. It was restored in 1946, and lasted for 18 years, until 1964, when the military coup abolished all democratic rights. For 20 years—an entire generation—democracy was completely stifled. Since then, Brazil has been trying in fits and starts to pick up where it left off. The strains of this interrupted democracy are evident in my research findings.

At the time of my first study in 1968–69, there was a pervasive fear that squatters and newly arrived migrants would become radicalized in light of the wealth that surrounded them. On the contrary, the reference group of these urban poor was not the rich urbanites with whom they shared the city but the family and friends they'd left behind in the countryside. The squatters of Rio were happy with their move and looked expectantly toward the future.

I remember a discussion I had in 1968 with Gilberto, a young man who had come to Rio by himself from the Northeast in 1961 and settled in Catacumba because he knew some people there from his hometown. When I asked him how he felt about looking across the Lagoa Rodrigo Freitas every day at the luxurious houses of the rich and seeing all of the public services available to those in upscale communities, while Catacumba lacked even running water and electricity, he replied,

> It's not like that, not at all. We little people [*gente humilde*] have a lot of patience. We do not compare ourselves to them....Even as a *biscateiro* [odd jobber] I live much better than anyone in my family back home. We are not in a rush. After the government helps the rich and the less rich, then, later on, it will be our turn—our time will come.

POLITICAL TRANSFORMATIONS

Profound political changes occurred during the time span of my longitudinal study, culminating in the transition to democracy in 1985 and the new constitution in 1988. My follow-up research started during the first mandate of President Fernando Henrique Cardoso (1995–2003) and ended during the second mandate of President Luis Ignácio Lula da Silva, also known as Lula (2003–11). The political transformation of Brazil was the result of enormous struggle. Yet for favela residents, these vast sea changes made little difference in many aspects of daily life and appeared to make some things worse even as others improved.

The sense of disenfranchisement among those who lived through the dictatorship has grown since the return to democracy. As their children and grandchildren have become better educated and more politically savvy, they have become both more cynical and more hopeful. From the perspective of the thousands of people I interviewed for this study, Brazilian democracy has a long way to go in terms of equal treatment under the law, protection from harm and responsiveness to their concerns.

Clearly, a democratic state that ignores the needs of a third of its urban population does so at its peril. The only regular contact the people have with the state apparatus is the police, who enter the favelas with their weapons loaded and follow the motto "Shoot first, ask questions later."

FOUR THEMES EMERGE

The narratives, life histories, and survey responses in my studies reveal some promising trends but also a disenchantment with democracy as it has evolved since the end of the dictatorship. Four of the recurrent themes I will touch on here are:

1. *Disappointment with democracy*: The redemocratization after the end of the dictatorship did not empower the poor as hoped, or bring benefits to their communities as expected.
2. *Corruption, clientelism, and cronyism*: Traditional misuse of privilege and power, somewhat curtailed under military rule, resurfaced with the return of the multiparty system, and now appears to permeate the polity at every level.
3. *Citizenship, rights, and duties*: Since the end of the dictatorship and increasingly in each successive generation, more people recognize the difference between citizens' rights and duties, *feel entitled to* their rights, and believe that it is possible to influence government decisions through active participation.
4. *Belief-behavior disconnect*: Despite a strong *belief* in democracy as an ideal, political *participation* remains minimal—with the younger, better educated, most politically knowledgeable generation remaining the most cynical about government and the least participatory.

As I address each one of these points, I am drawing on the answers to a set of political questions we asked in our survey research in 1969, 2001, and 2003. I am reporting only on answers of the random sample—600 original interviewees in 1969, 126 of them in 2001, 295 of their children, and 158 of their grandchildren. In 2003, we added interviews with a new random sample among those in the three communities we had studied—400 in each and 24 extras—for a total of 1,224. This is the subgroup of the 2,182 interviews, which, in various combinations, provide the data for the sections that follow. To make sense of the comparison among the generations, it helps to know their ages—

the average age of the original random sample in 1969 was 36; their average age in 2001 was 64; the average age of their children in 2001 was 40; and of the grandchildren was 24.

Disappointment with Democracy

Tio Souza who we met in Catacumba and now, at the age of 74, lives in Padre Miguel explained disappointment with democracy to me as follows:

> Politics is like this: at election time the candidates always appear, afterwards, they disappear. This has never changed and never will. It was always like this. I vote because it's obligatory. They make many promises and never do anything. At election time, they come to our community, hang up a huge banner across one of the buildings; once the election is over, they disappear and never return.[1]

With the return to democracy, the hope was that once people could vote directly for their mayors, and for the president, the urban poor could use their numbers to hold officials accountable to their campaign promises, have a greater voice over decisions directly affecting their lives, and thereby gain stronger bargaining power to negotiate for community improvements.

However, the people we interviewed do not feel they have gained a voice in the political arena—only a *potential* voice. They do not perceive increased receptivity or fair play among government officials. What they see is the impunity of police and drug dealers, both of whom continue to terrorize their communities. While the redemocratization may have granted the urban poor *de jure* citizenship, they do not feel that they have *de facto* citizenship. They remain pseudocitizens. The majority of our sample—79 percent of original interviewees—said "*the end of the dictatorship had no significant impact* on their lives."[2] That is certainly a major difference between the underview (view from below) and the overview (view from above).

In a follow-up question for those who responded affirmatively, we asked what kind of change? Just under a third (32 percent) mentioned positive changes such as greater *liberdade* (liberty) and increased government transparency; while just under a quarter (23 percent) mentioned such negative changes as fewer jobs, less security/tranquility and—surprisingly—decreased bargaining power. Several went so far as to affirm that things had been better during the dictatorship. This came up in several of the in-depth and semi-structured interviews as well. It fits into the current discourse about the nostalgia for the law and order of the authoritarian regimes in Latin America. A recent UN survey of 19,000 Latin Americans in 18 countries reported that a majority would choose a dictator over an elected leader if that person provided economic benefits. The Latin obarómetro surveys show that this sentiment is less prevalent in Brazil than in the other Latin American countries, but it was mentioned by

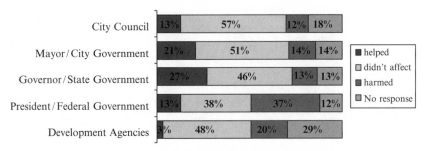

FIGURE 8.1   Perception of Various Levels of Government as Helpful or Harmful.

many, including Nilton, who was outraged that the government had lost control of the city to the bandidos.

To further explore this, we asked all of the respondents, "How would you compare your life during the military dictatorship with your life since the dictatorship ended? What got better, stayed the same, or got worse?" The most frequently mentioned improvements were public transportation (80 percent said it was better now); housing quality (76 percent); water and sanitation (76 percent); and access to (but not quality of) education (71 percent). Assessments of the economic situation were mixed: 44 percent said better; 32 percent said worse; and 14 percent said no change. Sixty-eight percent said that personal and family safety had gotten worse. We did not ask them to specify whether they thought these changes were linked to the return of democracy or simply the passage of time, because we found during the pretest of the questionnaire that almost everyone gave the sensible answer—"Do not know."

We did find a much greater awareness of citizens' rights than we found in the 1960s, but when it came to exercising those rights, 69 percent reported feeling more excluded than they had been during the dictatorship. Even faith in the good intentions of government had eroded since the height of the dictatorship. In 1969, 61 percent of our sample thought "government tries to understand and solve the problems of people like ourselves"; while in 2001 and 2003 only 38 percent thought so.

Theoretically, the closer the level of government to the people, the more responsive and helpful it should be. To see whether this held up, we asked: "In the past few years, have you and people like yourself been helped or harmed by: the city council, the mayor/city agencies, the governor/state agencies, the president/federal agencies and international development agencies (such as the World Bank, the Inter-American Development Bank, etc.)?" The most frequent response from all three generations, as well as from the new random sample, was that "government does not affect our lives at all"—regardless of the level of proximity. And, among those who gave an answer, more felt "harmed" than "helped." Figure 8.1 shows the comparison of perception of the original interviewees about each government level.

Generally, people felt the most helped and the least harmed by city or state government, but the majority said that government made no difference in their lives. The children of the original interviewees were slightly less negative in their assessments, but even among them, more rated the federal government and international institutions as harmful rather than helpful. They gave the city government the highest approval rating (35 percent), followed by the state (29 percent)—not exactly a resounding endorsement.

The most prevalent answer in all generations was that government did not affect them either way—a profound problem for the democratic project.

As I mentioned above, among the older generation there were frequent expressions of nostalgia for the law and order of the dictatorship. The people I interviewed have seen so much corruption, been betrayed by so many candidates and been subjected to so much violence that they sometimes yearned for the past when their lives were more secure and it was easier to earn a living. Evidently, this feeling is not uncommon in Brazil or in other Latin American countries that were under authoritarian regimes and are now democracies.

Corruption, Clientelism, and Cronyism

Starting in 1979 the government party, Aliança Renovadora Nacional (ARENA), was forced to compete for electoral support against a recently formed opposition party—the Movimento Democratico Brasileiro (MDB). The resumption of party politics opened the way for a return to the pre-1964 system of patronage politics—often called clientelism or cronyism—which entails an exchange of votes for favors, contracts, or government appointments. This swelling of the public payroll became out of control under President José Sarney, who became president due to the untimely death of Tancredo Neves. Neves had the strength of character, intelligence, and dedication to the public welfare that made him a popular choice although he was chosen by the congress because the military regime was unwilling to risk an open election. He died before assuming office. Many say that if he had lived, Brazilian democracy would have evolved differently.

As it happened, patronage politics became the norm and continued to be the norm through the 1990s even as other reforms were successfully introduced. The poor remained politically powerless. Scott Mainwaring captures it precisely: "although the poor may receive a portion of politicians' patronage, this can hardly be qualified as a process of integrating the poor into the system; it is a mechanism to reinforce dependency, not to empower." I tend to agree with him that the contemporary form of clientelism is worse than the traditional buying of votes because "it limits the legitimacy of the still-fragile democratic system, favors the elite minority over the poor majority, cripples the government's ability to work professionally, and weakens social programs through poor performance and by diverted resources."[3]

Still, the old patronage system—even at the height of the dictatorship—allowed some benefits to flow into favelas in exchange for votes, which were negotiated through the Residents' Associations. This channel of favors to the poor has been increasingly closed off since the mid-1980s, when drug lords began dominating the Residents' Associations. As Desmond Arias has shown in his recent work on criminal and community networks, the drug dealers who have taken over the Residents' Associations negotiate directly with the candidates and "deliver" the votes of the community, taking the spoils for themselves.[4]

Putting police stations within the favelas does not protect the right to vote for the inhabitants. As I mentioned, the police are afraid to come out into the community. They stay behind their barred windows—in a sense becoming the prisoners. Teresa Caldeira discusses this paradox eloquently in her book *City of Walls*.[5] Since the drug dealers took over the Residents' Associations, they have been able to pressure people into voting for the candidate of their choice (as I detail in the following box) without interference from the police, the judiciary, or any level of government. The magnitude of the drug money—and the willingness of the gangs to use deadly force—buy the complicity of officials all the way to the top. That is a setback to the faith in democracy for all.

HOW THE DRUG LORDS CONTROL THE VOTE

When I was in Rio for the two weeks prior to the mayoral and city council elections in October 2008, I learned just how little choice the favela electorate may have in the voting booth. Posing one of the worst threats to electoral democracy that I had ever seen are the arrangements between the drug gang leaders and the candidates.

Favela residents explained to me that one of the worst threats to independent voting inside the favelas was that the drug dealers made deals with politicians, and then, in order to deliver the votes, the dealers demanded that every person take a photo of his or her ballot before pulling the lever, to verify his or her vote. People were taking these photos with the cameras on their cell phones—and for those without cell phones, the dealers would graciously lend theirs for the purpose. A person could be beaten or even killed for failing to vote for the candidate specified by the drug faction in command of the community.

Due to historically high illiteracy levels, each candidate is given a number, and when the voter selects that number, the candidate's face is shown along with the name of the political party. It is this image that the people are obliged to photograph. Once you pull the lever, the image disappears, and the system is ready for the next voter.[6]

Citizenship, Rights, and Duties

In terms of rights and freedoms, however, not all is negative. The newly won freedom of speech was mentioned many times by those we interviewed as one of the great liberties people regained after 1985.

> The end of the dictatorship was a blessing. It affected all of us. Before, if you came here with a tape recorder to interview me, I wouldn't have said anything, you know, right? Today it's not that way, a person can talk. It's freedom—we have the liberty to speak.—Maria Fernandes, 66 years old, from Catacumba, now living in the conjunto of Quitungo (2003)

Maria Fernandes got her rights. Regardless of the pros and cons I discuss below, she now has the freedom to speak her mind (at least about matters unrelated to the traffic).

When I was studying grassroots social movements in U.S. cities, I compared the task of poor people's movements to the struggle of the mythic Sisyphus, working mightily to roll the boulder up the mountain, only to find it slipping down again.[7] The status quo is like gravity: it does not need to make an effort to exert its ever-present force—it is hardwired into society's institutions. Time after time, I saw an entire American community fight to preserve its integrity from a highway that would cut the community in two, or to prevent the incursion of a garbage dump in the middle of the neighborhood. Using the community-organizing methods developed by Saul Alinsky (who adapted labor union strategies to community issues), community residents started with small victories that broadened their base of support such that they could take on more challenging issues and win—at least temporarily.[8]

What eventually happened in these U.S. cities when the mobilization was over and no one was paying attention was that things just "rolled along," as it were, and in due time the highways and sewage treatment plants were built according to the original intent. The thing that could not be eroded was the feeling of victory by the powerless over the powerful. This sense of pride was internalized in each person who participated, and nothing could make these persons go back to believing that their cause had no merit. I remember one elderly man I interviewed in San Francisco beaming with pride when describing a confrontational meeting at City Hall. His eyes lit up when he said, "They called me 'sir'!" That was the first time in his life that anyone in a position of power had ever addressed him with respect.[9]

What I saw in postdictatorship Rio reminded me of that moment in San Francisco. There was something in the transition back to democracy that couldn't be taken away, even by the most blatant corruption or inept governance—and that was a sense of entitlement to citizen's rights.

Another major step forward for the favela residents after the dissolution of the dictatorship was recognition of the difference between rights and duties. One of the things I found most distressing in 1969 was the inability of most of the people with whom I lived in the favelas to distinguish between *direitos* (rights) and *deveres* (duties). They generally said that their most important *duties* as citizens were "to obey the law, respect the authorities, and work hard," and that their most important rights were "to obey the law, respect the authorities, and work hard." In other words, in their minds there was no distinction between the two.

In the 2001 interviews, virtually everyone we interviewed in each of the three generations was able to articulate what they thought were their most important rights and duties. The most frequently mentioned rights were access to health care, education and freedom of movement. The rights to work and to receive unemployment insurance were next on the list, followed by the right to be treated with respect and dignity. There were slight variances by generation, with the older people placing more emphasis on unemployment insurance and health care; the children focusing on education and jobs; and the grandchildren prioritizing "freedom to come and go."[10]

In terms of duties, all three generations saw "obey the law" as most important. The duty to "work and meet their professional obligations" was next and, for the grandchildren, "respecting their neighbors" was seen as an important duty as well. The children added the duty to follow through with commitments, and the original interviewees added "honesty and integrity."

The ability to draw a distinction between rights and duties is evidence of a change in people's cognitive maps. The concept of "citizenship rights" only entered common parlance as the dictatorship was winding down, during the abertura. There was a popular movement demanding *Diretos já* ("Rights now!"). *Cidadania* (citizenship) conceived of as a set of entitlements and obligations entered the realm of popular discourse in the ferment of activism just before and for several years after 1985.

But there was not much emphasis on the freedom from want in the citizenship discussion—nor on the rights of the poor to be treated as equals. As Brazilian political scientist Evelina Dagnino explains:

Without the fundamental rights of a decent income, health, education and security, Rio's urban poor will continue as mere cogs in local and regional political machines being greased by new forms of clientelism. The notions of "lack of citizenship" or "new citizenship" never gained much currency among the favelados because their living conditions never permitted them the luxury. Instead, other actors such as NGOs, political parties and academics were the ones that had the leisure to coin new terms for describing what in fact continues to be structural impediments to full participation [of the poor] in the decision-making process for allocating public resources.[11]

The anthropologist James Holston refers to Brazil as an "incomplete democracy." In his view, it was the rapid urbanization in Brazil that caused the "exponential increase in demands on the city and claims to its resources which exhausted traditional notions of citizenship." His research in the favelas of São Paulo revealed an "insurgent citizenship" arising from "struggles over what it means to be a member of the modern state." He describes the changes in the meaning of citizenship as new demands are made that enlarge the scope of the concept, and new forms of exclusion, including exposure to lethal violence, erode those gains. He contends that "the sites of insurgent citizenship are found at the intersection of these processes of expansion and erosion."[12]

The democratically elected political leaders in Brazil have not managed to assure all citizens personal safety, decent pay for decent work, or civil liberties. The legacy of division between masters and slaves is still evident in everyday transactions. Standing in line at any public office, bureaucratic agency, or bank, I notice that when a well-dressed, light-skinned person arrives, it is expected that the "others" will step aside. While becoming less blatant, the expectation of such deference still prevails. Many examples of this are recounted in the autobiography of Benedita da Silva, a black woman born in the favela Praía do Pinto, who rose from community leader to positions on the city council, the national congress, and the senate. Later she became the vice-governor and then governor of the State of Rio and national secretary of social action during the first term of President Lula in 2003.[13]

Whether or not favela residents are aware of their rights as citizens, they remain at the bottom of the totem pole in the political as well as the social and economic arenas. Some discussions in the literature refer to Brazilians' "high tolerance for inequality" as an explanation of how such deep societal divisions could persist. In my view, the persistence of inequality reflects Brazil's long history of exclusion and elitism. If the poor had ever experienced equality or even respect, they would be more likely to protest if it were taken away. As it is, they keep their heads down and go about their business of daily survival.

This is not to say that the urban poor are indifferent to injustice. The reason that their moral outrage does not translate into physical rage—or into political manifestations—is that the view from below lacks potency. The use and abuse of power is still a prerogative of the privileged, and the poor are in no position to take this on. As one woman in Nova Brasília said to me, "Janice, what can we do? …It's not only the policemen, but the judges and the politicians 'way up there' who look the other way and fill their pockets."

This sense of impotence means that while favela residents have embraced the theory of democracy, in practice, democracy has not embraced them.

The Belief-Behavior Disconnect

Despite the broken promise of citizenship and the feeling that government has harmed more than helped, when it made any difference at all, the belief in the ideals of democracy took root among the urban poor—increasingly with each generation.

One striking example is the degree to which the ideal of participatory democracy was embraced. In 1969 and again in 2001 we asked "should decisions be left in the hands of the politicians or should all Brazilians participate?" There is little or nothing in the Brazilian democracy literature that shows the penetration of democratic ideals within stigmatized groups. But I found dramatic evidence to demonstrate that transformation. At the time of the dictatorship only 34 percent of the study participants believed that "all Brazilians should participate." Now, among the children and grandchildren, it is 88 and 90 percent respectively. Figure 8.2 below shows the progression of this shift in attitude.

This finding about the steady increase of belief in an engaged citizenry was reinforced by the responses of the 2003 random sample. Among this group, the percentage saying that "all Brazilians should participate" rose from 34 percent in 1969 to 81 percent in 2003, proving to my satisfaction that the value placed

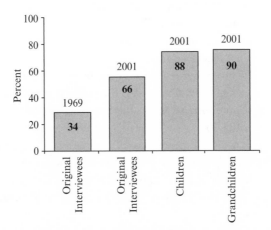

FIGURE 8.2   Belief in Democratic Ideals (% agreeing that "every Brazilian should participate.") comparing percents in 1969 and among the three generations in 2001).

on participation was not limited to the descendents of the people who participated in my original study.

A similar increase in positive responses was found in response to the follow-
up question: "Do you think that you can do something to influence government, or do you think there is no possibility?" The percentage of those who said
yes—that they thought they could influence government—rose systematically
over the generations as shown in figure 8.3.

It would be expected that during the most repressive period of the dictatorship, in 1969, few favela residents would think they could influence the government. The 19 percent of original study participants who said "yes," that they
could influence the government at that time, were likely thinking about their
(sometimes) successful efforts in influencing local government to put in a water
standpipe, lay in a paved stairway up the hill, or provide materials for a drainage ditch. In 2001, 16 years after democracy had been restored, 30 percent of
the original interviewees thought they could exert influence. This number went
up to about 50 percent among their children and grandchildren. The feeling of
empowerment and political efficacy expressed by this upward trend is balanced
by an equally prevalent feeling of powerlessness and inefficacy by the other
50 percent of the children and grandchildren. The same people who strongly
were in favor of all Brazilians participating are split 50–50 on whether such
participation could have any influence on government decisions. The trend is in
the right direction, but experience contradicts hope. These findings provide an
antidote to the retrospective romanticism about authoritarian rule, under which
both the theory and practice of participation were minimal. To borrow a phrase
from Martin Luther King, the favela residents as pseudocitizens are "not where
they want to be, not where they ought to be, and not where they will be, but
they are not where they were."

This increasing belief in political efficacy is all the more interesting in
light of a decreasing faith in the good intentions of government. When asked
whether they think "the government tries to understand and solve the problems of people like you," 61 percent said yes in 1969 and only 38 percent
said yes in 2003. An interesting portrait is emerging that has not been much
noticed—the co-existence of faith that participation can make a difference
and lack of faith in the democratically elected government. As I show later
in the chapter (figure 8.4) this contradiction may be explained in part by the
perception that Brazilians somehow lack the capacity to select good candidates for office, and that it is their own fault when they end up with corrupt
government.

The acid test of these political ideas is in political action. So I wanted to look
at the types and levels of political participation then and now. I found that there
was no clean linear increase in participation as there is in *belief* in participation.
Actual levels of political participation remain low.

Some of those who have been around for awhile, like Alaerte from Nova Brasília, are turned off entirely by the futility of voting. He said,

> I'm not going to vote, for sure. I don't like it. But I have voted in the past. I have been disappointed many times. I think they [politicians] are a band of scoundrels, of cowards. But it doesn't depend on me alone, so I can stay out of it. Just one person [not voting] is no problem.—Alaerte, 65 years old, from Nova Brasília, now living in Campo Grande, in the West Zone, 2004

His comments make sense given the long history of top-down politics and his experience of past disappointments. But voting is only one of many forms of political participation, and he speaks for only his generation. To better understand what types of political actions are taken by what generations and how the past and present compare, I created table 8.1.

My first question was whether differences in participation rates among the groups were age-related or reflected the historic moments of 1969 and 2001. I compared the original sample in 1969 with their children and grandchildren in 2001—who were 16 and older. The voting rates were almost identical between the parents in 1969 (40 percent) and their children in 2001 (39 percent)—which is interesting given that in 1969 the only offices open to popular election were *vereador* (city council) and state legislator. Participation rates in demonstrations were also almost identical (19 percent and 21 percent). In activities related to party politics—signing petitions, attending political meetings or rallies, and working for candidates—the levels of participation in 2001 were three times what they were in 1969 for the same age group. That was one clear result of the return of democracy.

Most striking, however, were the low rates of participation of every type in every group—with the single exception of voting rates for the original inter-

TABLE 8.1   *Political Participation: 1969 and 2001—3 generations (in percentages)*

Did you ever:	1969	2001		
	Original Interviewees	Original Interviewees	Children	Grandchildren
Vote?	40	72	39	7
Sign a Petition?	12	25	31	27
Attend a Political Meeting or Rally?	5	12	18	13
Work for a Candidate?	6	13	20	20
Participate in a Demonstration?	19	15	21	12

Note: The figures for the 2003 random sample show a similar pattern but are even lower.

viewees. This lack of active engagement belies the high rates of enthusiasm for "all Brazilians participating" and "making a difference" reported above. Even the percentage who voted—the most frequent form of political participation—is much lower than would be expected given voting is mandatory for those 18 to 70 years old. (It is voluntary for those 16–18 and over 70).

According to the Electoral Code (passed just after the new Constitution in 1988), Brazilian citizens must show *comprovante de votação* (proof of having voted) to be hired for any *cargo público* (public employment) or to receive a diploma from any public institution. Failure to vote in three consecutive elections results in the annulment of one's *título de eleitor* (voter registration card) and causes problems with the personal identity card that all Brazilians must have and the *cadastro de pessoa física,* or CPF. Possession of a CPF is essential to maintaining a bank account, getting a telephone, ordering goods or services, paying bills, and completing any official or fiscal transaction. In short, those who do not have a CPF card are nonpersons in a juridical sense, as I found out the hard way when I was living in Brazil and trying to manage without one.

A possible explanation for such low voting rates might be that not voting is regarded as a form of protest. But that is not convincing given the option of casting a blank ballot, referred to as *votar em branco* (voting in white). The sense of disenfranchisement among the urban poor must be extreme for them to risk exclusion from government jobs, schools, and other benefits simply by failing to vote.

Knowing that voting rates are notoriously low for young voters, I compared the answers of those ages 16–24 with those 24 and older in response to the question, "Did you vote in the previous election?" Only one in ten (11 percent) of the younger group said yes, compared with about 5 in ten (47 percent) of those aged 24 or older—but a 50 percent default rate on the most basic civic duty is still a sign of distress. Having listened to people in the communities and talked with them at length, I believe that cynicism, rather than apathy, is what keeps them away from the polls. The youth, the best educated, best informed, and most politically savvy of all generations, have the greatest belief in the value of participation, yet they are the least politically engaged. This is the most striking example of the overall finding here, which I call the "belief-behavior disconnect."

WHO PARTICIPATES IN WHAT?

The landscape of political participation at the grassroots level is variegated and changes according to the time, place, and viewer. The high level of community participation I had observed in the favelas in the 1960s seemed to have disappeared by the time I was doing the interviews there in 2001. Our survey included a series of questions about membership (and leadership) in local organizations, so I was able to compare the activities of the original study participants in 1969 with those of their children in 2001 (shown in figure 8.3).

Every type of community association membership dropped to single digits except for religious affiliation, which dropped by only 6 percent (from 53 percent to 47 percent). Part of this was the tenor of the times—locally and internationally. In the favelas, once the struggle against removal and the demands for basic urban services were no longer pressing there was less need for organizing; and as the city became more accessible for recreation, the need for local recreation diminished. In parallel, the international fervor of mobilization that occurred in the 1960s was no longer bringing people together to protest by the mid-1980s, when the dictatorship in Brazil ended. And finally, as I discussed in the previous chapter, the violence in the communities had a dampening effect on all local activities, particularly the Residents' Associations, which no longer represented the residents.

I have long been interested in community associations and in whether participation in them is a substitute for or a preparation for participation in the body politic—or both. By joining a local organization do favela residents became more politically aware, interested, and active outside the community— or does it use up the time available for such engagement?

In order to answer this question and the larger question of what distinguishes the politically active from the others, I created an index of political participation that combined signing petitions, attending political meetings, working for a candidate, and taking part in demonstrations. The index left out voting since it is mandatory. I then tried to determine the characteristics shared by the people who had high scores on this index.

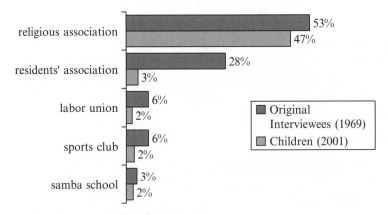

FIGURE 8.3   Community-based participation

I hypothesized that political participation—along with political interest and political knowledge—would be higher for members of local civic organizations; people with dense social networks; those who believed that their own actions (agency) rather than fate, determined life outcomes; optimists; people living in the loteamentos of Caxias (not in favelas) in the 1969 study; and people living in conjuntos, loteamentos, or bairros (rather than in favelas) in 2001. I also guessed that males and whites would be more politically active. Half of these hunches were confirmed by the data analysis and the other half invalidated.

The four that turned out to be correct were: (1) males did participate more than females (although the gap diminished with each generation); (2) people who lived in Caxias loteamentos in 1969 participated more than those who lived in favelas; and (3) people with a proactive (nonfatalistic) mindset—characterized by the belief in agency rather than "fate" or "the will of God"—were more politically participatory; and (4) those who scored highest on the measures of optimism about the future also tended to participate more than their pessimistic counterparts.

The four that proved irrelevant or inversely related to what I had predicted: (1) race made no difference in levels of political participation; (2) living in a favela in 2001—as opposed to a conjunto, loteamento, or bairro in the current time period (2001 and after as opposed to where they had lived in 1969)—made no difference in levels of political participation; (3) membership in secular community organizations made no difference (except that evangelicals participated even less);[14] and (4) social networks had opposite effects on participation, depending on the type of network. Individuals with greater "bridging networks" (external connections with people in diverse walks of life) demonstrated higher levels of political participation while those with more "bonding networks" (internal to the community) showed lower participation.[15]

Whereas race alone did not indicate a significant difference in levels of participation, gender did to some extent, and combining the two was a powerful—if inconsistent—predictor of political engagement. In 1969, white males had the highest participation scores, and black females the lowest. When the same communities were surveyed 34 years later, women had higher participation scores than men (on the same index as in 1969), but lighter skin color remained a predictive factor in political participation.

Three unanticipated factors were found to be strongly related to participation levels: *proximity* of original community to upscale residential areas and the city center; recognition of *stigma* in its multitude of forms; and personal or family exposure to *violence*. Unpacking each of these revealed the following.

Proximity. Those raised in South Zone favelas, such as Catacumba, in the midst of the city's elite, tended toward greater political awareness and participation (and higher SES) than those raised in the working-class areas of the North Zone, including Nova Brasília, or in the even more peripheral, provincial, and parochial Fluminense Lowlands.

Early contact with the middle and upper echelons of society, and with a broader mixture of people through living (or spending time) in the homes of the madames (where their mothers worked as domestic servants or their fathers worked as janitors or security guards), afforded people a broader window on the world and a template for "presentation of self in everyday life,"[16] making it easier for them to "pass" as part of the asfalto and not be pegged as from the morro. A person's identifying pinta (look) involves ways of speaking, standing, walking, dressing, and behaving that is very difficult to emulate if you are from the North Zone or Baixada. The majority of residents from these zones have never been to the city center or South Zone.

Being brought up in the South Zone also created "bridging networks" connecting the favela residents with the know-how (*jeitinho*) for getting things done—and with people they might go to when they were being unfairly treated or needed help. Our study revealed the subtle and powerful effects of proximity, and its lifelong advantages. Variations among the favelas in their size, legal status, or internal structure did not create as much disparity in life outcomes as their locations—nor was the severity of drug trafficking within them a determinant of individual mobility. It was proximity to powerful, affluent people that led to higher rates of political participation and agency among the poor.

Stigma. The stronger the recognition of the many forms of stigma and discrimination in society, the higher was the level of political participation. The pattern for the grandchildren was similar, but their sense of discrimination was *lower* overall. Across the board, those with *high scores on the index of perceived stigma* were more likely to take political action: to vote, sign petitions, attend political meetings and demonstrations, or work for political candidates. These were also the people most likely to believe that "all Brazilians should participate" rather than that "leaving decisions in the hands of the politicians" was best. This might be due to the fact that the wider one's experience is, the harder it is for one to ignore the nuanced forms of exclusion—and the more likely one is to act on one's own behalf.[17]

Violence. The more direct experience of violence a person had had, the less likely that person was to vote or participate in community organizations, but the more likely to take direct political action, such as signing a petition, working for a candidate, attending political meetings or demonstrations, and affiliating with a political party. It would seem that the experience of violence[18] creates disenchantment with electoral democracy and engenders a willingness to take action for change. Those who scored high on the experience of violence index were also less satisfied with their lives and more likely to perceive a lack of unity in their communities.[19]

YOUTH

The youth are the best educated, most knowledgeable, most cynical, and most vulnerable of all of the generations I studied. Between the ages of 14 (when they can leave school) and 18, when they can join the military, is the period of most risk. Child labor laws prevent those under 18 from working, except as interns starting at 16, so there is a period during which it is most tempting to go for the easy money and status of the drug trade. Many still live with their parents at that age, all surviving on the pensions of their grandfathers.

A recent ethnographic study by the Instituto de Estudos do Trabalho e Sociedade showed that youth who are no longer in school and not yet working spend most of their time sleeping, personal grooming, and watching television—when not engaged in activities they would prefer not to discuss with a French anthropologist.

In each successive generation, there is more evidence of self-blame and internalized self-deprecation. This showed up clearly in response to our interview questions about political participation (which revealed increasing alienation and disaffection) and in the perceived failure to elect candidates who might fight for their interests.

As with the internalization of many forms of oppression, alienation from the electoral process has led to increasing self-blame on the part of the urban poor for their failure to elect candidates who might fight for their interests.

As shown in figure 8.4, when asked whether the Brazilian people have the capacity to make wise choices in their selection of candidates, an increasing number say they *do not*. During the dictatorship, when voting was merely a memory, there was more faith in the capacity of the electorate than there is

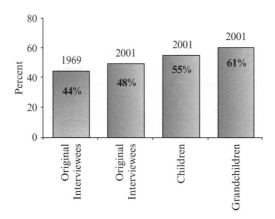

FIGURE 8.4 Lack of confidence in candidate selection. (Increase in the percent of respondents saying that "Brazilians do not have the capacity to make wise elections for their candidates.")

today. Recent experience with electoral democracy has perversely generated *less faith in the ability of citizens to make wise selections in their candidates for public office*.

The roots of the conditions that have led Brazilians to doubt their capacity to elect the right leaders are deep and pervasive. On the one hand, there is little or no accountability on the part of elected officials to their constituents; on the other hand, there are no people's movements sufficiently powerful to make demands on the state. The poor constitute one-third of the voters of the city, so it stands to reason that their mobilization around a policy platform or candidate could be the decisive force for electoral victory.

QUICK FIX?

I see no "quick fix" for strengthening citizenship or building participatory democracy without deep-seated structural reforms and a movement toward a meaningful sharing of power. Even in cities with successful experiences of participatory budgeting, such as Porto Alegre and Belo Horizonte, the poor are not full citizens as long as so many are unemployed and unprotected from police and drug violence in their communities. If the numbers of youth that die each day in the favelas of those cities were white and rich, the voices of their parents would be heard and heeded. Instead, there is the sound of silence.

In my observations over the past five years, the plethora of NGO- and government-sponsored initiatives for training Rio's poor in *cidadanea* (citizenship), "empowerment," and "capacity building," which have met with varying degrees of success, cannot succeed in the absence of real opportunity to exercise these abilities. Giving the disenfranchised knowledge of the full extent of their citizen rights and how to demand them is necessary but not sufficient to give them power or opportunity.

The director of a municipal empowerment training course for women in favelas confessed to being "deeply conflicted" about the work she was doing. "The women in the community are wonderful," she said, "but the program is a kind of tease. It raises expectations and increases frustration, given the lack of job opportunities or channels for exercising political power in real life. The reality these women face after their diplomas are signed and handed out is a dead end."

Her explanation validates the analysis Castañeda has made of "corporatist crony capitalism," as characterized by "unemployment and a corrupt political system institutionalized to protect privilege by perpetuating inequality."[20] This is what the newly trained community women are up against once they have been through the municipality's empowerment course. Inadequate employment, lack of political access, and an absence of protection from violence mean that the poor and uneducated do not enjoy the full benefits of citizenship. Democracy cannot deepen without addressing the enormous inequality that undermines the nature of citizenship for the poor. The words of Louis Brandeis at a critical juncture in the history of democracy in the United States are perfectly applicable to Brazil today: "We can have democracy in this country, or we can have great wealth concentrated in the hands of the few, but we can't have both."

nine

THE MYSTERY OF MOBILITY

In the early afternoon of June 30, 2003, I met up with Edson in front of Nova Brasília, on the congested Avenida Itaoca, just opposite the abandoned Skol Beer Factory. He recognized me right away and said he preferred to talk with me at his brother's house, which was in a safer, more accessible, and *mais arrumado* (more orderly) area of the favela. As a rule, I prefer meeting people in their own homes, where I learn a lot by just looking around, but he said it was too dangerous to *subir o morro* (climb up the hill) to his place. I believed him. This was after my personal brush with the traffic in Nova Brasília, and I had no intention of putting myself at risk again—any more than was necessary to finish the research.

Edson's older brother, Adão, was waiting for us when we arrived. The brothers came from a small town in the interior of the state of Minas Gerais, and both started working at the age of eight. But their lives have taken divergent paths. Adão's house was on the right, about halfway up the hill, along the third entrance to Nova Brasília.

Edson told me that he lives in a precariously constructed two-room shack without a plaster finish or a *laje* (proper roof), along with eight dependents. None of his children are in school or working. He is a *biscateiro* (odd jobber), picking up construction work here and there, with no steady income. He had been a construction worker and was skilled at laying tiles, and he had made enough money at one time to own a small bar, where he sold cachaça (Brazilian sugar cane rum). At that time, he had a car and a savings account and was a big spender. But he got into serious trouble (which he did not specify) and had to flee. He has had several wives and has fathered several children with each of them.

Edson is one of many people I met who live on the edge. He freely admits that this is because he never thought about the future and prefers to live from day to day, thinking mostly about women and fun. He has always spent whatever he has earned without saving anything. His current wife was working but stopped when they married and just "settled in" (*acomodou*). He has no pension because he got angry one day when the social security administration was on strike and he needed medical care, so he stopped making his monthly payments and was cut off. That's when he says he *descaminhou* (lost his way) and his life *descontrolou* (spun out of control).

When I asked him how he manages, he explained, "Now things are really rough, everyone is suffering. I used to get by borrowing here and there from friends and neighbors, but they can no longer help even themselves." He is ashamed to go to the produce markets to pick up leftover produce at the end of the day, saying:

> It's like this. You arrive and there are other people who got there first, and I don't have the courage to stay there picking through the garbage at the end of the fair—would you? How can you when you see little children, shameless, who are there playing with the oranges and tossing them back and forth? For me this is no game.

He had been making ends meet by getting the cesta básica the government distributes to the poor on the basis of necessity. The cesta básica in Nova Brasília is given out monthly through one of the local Pentecostal churches. He explained that when he does not attend the church there, they deny him the food. He is also eligible for Bolsa Família, a national stipend given to families who fall below the poverty line if they meet certain conditions. He also qualifies for the so-called citizens' check, but that comes to a mere 100 reais per month (about US$43 at the time of the interview) and barely lasts a week. He tried moving back to the countryside in his home state, Minas Gerais, but things were even worse there, so he came back to Nova Brasília.

Edson said his brother, Adão, was "more successful in life because he believed in work and planned for tomorrow." At this, they both laughed and said it had always been like that, ever since they were young boys. But hard work and good planning are no guarantee. Their sister, who stayed in their hometown in Minas Gerais, also organized her life around hard work, saving, and planning ahead. But she had a stroke, went blind, and had both of her legs amputated due to severe diabetes. This is where chance and vulnerability enter the picture.

When I asked Edson what made work so hard to find, his brother Adão answered, "O pobre nao tem vez" ("The poor don't have a chance"). He explained:

> Before, there wasn't so much mechanization. Now there are robots to do the work we used to do, and the boss doesn't have to think about anyone. In the Campo Grande garbage dump, which used to employ lots of men, there is now only one worker, a robot, and a computer. Formerly, there were garbage men who threw the trash into the truck. Now there is a machine that scoops it up and dumps it into the truck, so only the driver has a job.

Adão's life is a different story. He lives in a three-bedroom, very well-appointed house with his son and daughter, in what has ended up as a legal loteamento adjacent to Nova Brasília. He was able to move there because he had worked for the owner of that land for nine years as caretaker. Because of his loyalty and consistent vigilance in his work—and his good luck at being there from the beginning—he was able to buy a lot when the owner decided to subdivide and sell. He lives comfortably on his retirement pay from Kibon, the famous Brazilian ice cream company, where he worked as a janitor. He has a carteira assinada and all the documents of official citizenship—birth certificate, identity card, cadastro de pessoa física, marriage certificate, title to his lot, and proof of military service.

Adão's wife passed away three months prior to our meeting, and he missed her terribly. He showed me their bedroom and her things, still arranged on her dressing table and bedside. They decided to have only two children so they could concentrate their resources on providing the best education and opportunities for each. Daisy, the eldest, is studying to be a nurse (which would bring her close to being gente), but her younger brother, Pedrinho, dropped out of school and is in the limbo of neither studying nor working.

Pedrinho spends his days flying his kite from the rooftop and watching television. He is dismissive of his father and threatens to join the drug traffic whenever his father asks him to look for a job or makes any attempt to discipline him.

Adão was thrown into debt by the high cost of his wife's funeral three months earlier, but he has a plan to pay back the money. Life is not easy for him, but he is managing to pay for his daughter's nursing school and to help out his brother Edson by employing him to tile his kitchen and bathroom—floor to ceiling.

When I asked the brothers what they thought accounted for the differences in their lives, Adão said:

There is always one in every family who likes to work harder and wants to get ahead more. All my life I have liked to save money, and I never spent all I earned. If I got 30 contos [an older currency], I would spend 15 and put the other 15 away. I was never interested in women or drink, and my wife and two children were the center of my life.

Edson's response was to laugh good-naturedly, saying, "Adão was always the hard worker and the one who applied himself and planned ahead, while I was more laid-back and content to drink beer with my buddies, rather than focus on studying or working. When I get a *biscate* [odd job] I spend the money right away. I go out, treat my friends, and have a good time."

This narrative illustrates the often-neglected role of individual differences (the fact that siblings have different natures despite being born of and nurtured by the same parents in the same environment) and of chance occurrences, such as the death of Adão's wife, in determining poverty outcomes. Several case studies I present at the end of this chapter highlight individual character traits—together with family norms and values—shared by the most successful men and women in our sample.

WHY MOBILITY IS A MYSTERY

The relative importance of family culture and personal characteristics is one of several problematic issues raised in trying to understand mobility patterns. I use the word "mystery" in this chapter title because even after years of collecting and analyzing the data and looking at it from different angles, answers to the basic questions about the dynamics of mobility remain elusive. The more I look into this dynamic and understand it, the more nuanced and perplexing the findings become. The four questions I set out to address about mobility are apparently quite straightforward:

- Did things get better or worse for the people in the original study and for their children and grandchildren?
- What explains why some people in the favelas moved out and up and some did not? In other words, what factors are associated with residential and socio-economic mobility—moving from favelas into bairros and moving from low to high rankings on standard measures of success?
- Is poverty "sticky" within and between generations? That is, if you were born poor did you stay poor throughout life (intragenerational persistence of poverty) and did children born to poor parents inherit that poverty (intergenerational transmission of poverty)?
- What can personal narratives add to our insights about moving away from, if not out of, poverty, and what roles are played by individual character, family culture, structural change, and luck in this quest to become "gente"?

BETTER, WORSE, OR BOTH?

Starting with the first, most basic questions—did life improve or deteriorate for the study participants and their descendents? The answer is "a definite maybe." Peoples' lives got both better and worse depending on what you look at and how you address the question.

What did emerge clearly from all of my research findings is that upward and downward fluctuations in income and other indices of well-being occurred in small increments, and that changes were neither linear nor did they occur consistently in the same direction. That in itself helps unravel some apparent contradictions. Living on the edge means being vulnerable to frequent reversals and revisions of fortune. The people and families who I have described in the earlier chapters experienced many ups and downs, not only over the 30 years between my two studies, but even during the several years I was in the field conducting this study. Random events—such as illness or the death of a family member, a factory closing, flooding, or the change of power among rival drug gangs—could threaten a family's survival.

Constant fluctuation makes it difficult to give an honest answer to the question of whether life is improving. Another is the conflation of chronological age, phases in peoples' life cycles and structural changes going on in the broader context of Rio, Brazil, and the rest of the world. Each of these is in continual flux, so, as in advanced physics, the frozen moment of observation in itself distorts the reality.

With those caveats in mind, my starting point was finding out whether the people I interviewed decades ago are still living in favelas.

WHERE ARE THEY NOW?

If starting out in a favela condemned one to remain in a favela for a person's entire life, and condemned one's descendants to remain trapped there as well, that would be akin to the totally closed systems of slavery, caste, or apartheid. Brazil and Rio, though infamous for high inequality levels, are not closed systems.

Of the 750 people I interviewed in 1969, 625 lived in favelas; the other 125 lived in similar conditions of poverty and deprivation in loteamentos in the least developed subdivisions of Caxias. These loteamentos, as mentioned earlier, lacked paved roads, electricity, water, and sanitation, and they were spread out on barren land, giving them a forlorn appearance. As much of the land was below sea level, it flooded in the rainy season and turned into a dust bowl in the dry season.

The lots, one after another, were tiny, marked out on the ground with white lime, and devoid of vegetation. The subdivisions I studied at the time were at the farthest edges of the municipality. In many ways, they were less appealing than the favelas, which were built amid some greenery on the hillsides or at the water's edge. But as it turned out, by 2001, the loteamentos had developed into legitimate working-class neighborhoods, and the probability of moving onward and upward was considerably better for those who lived there than for those from a favela.

Of all the people we managed to locate in 2001, almost half had remained in the same community, most often in the same dwelling in which they had been in 1969 or, in the case of Catacumba, in the conjunto apartment to which they were moved in 1970. Table 9.1 shows what percent of each generation (separated by the random and leadership samples), was living in favelas, conjuntos, and bairros as of 2001. The bairros were, for the most part, in peripheral neighborhoods where land values were lowest.

The fact that less than 40 percent of the original study participants were still in favelas in 2001 contradicts the prevailing wisdom in the literature—and among Cariocas—which views favelas as dead ends. It has been assumed that if you are born in a favela you will die in that favela. But the findings shown in the table above indicate that, at least for this group of randomly selected favela residents, comparable numbers of the original group had moved out into bairros (34 percent) as had stayed in the favelas (37 percent). The other 25 percent of the people in my original random sample study group were in conjuntos in 2001. Since none of them had come to the conjuntos by choice, we can assume that if Catacumba had not been removed, those in conjuntos would be about equally divided (as the rest of the sample was) between favelas and bairros. This is an unexpectedly high rate of upward and outward mobility for a city and country perceived as rigidly exclusionary. Another striking point is that

TABLE 9.1   *Where Are They Now? (2001)*

		Favela	*Public Housing Project*	*Legal Neighborhood*
Random Sample	Original Interviewees	37%	25%	34%
	Children	36%	16%	44%
	Grandchildren	32%	13%	51%
Leadership Sample	Original Interviewees	11%	21%	61%
	Children	24%	17%	56%
	Grandchildren	28%	6%	58%

the percentage of people living in favelas dropped slightly for each succeeding generation, while the percent residing in legal neighborhoods increased dramatically. There was also a steep intergenerational decline in the percentage of those living in conjuntos, which can be explained by the fact that, unlike houses in the favelas, apartments cannot be expanded to add the families of married children; they cannot grow as the family grows.

The other unexpected finding that shows up in the table is the erosion of the difference between the random samples and the leadership samples. The difference among the first generation in 2001 is dramatic. Whereas 37 percent of the random sample was still in favelas after 30 years, only 11 percent of the leadership sample had remained. Conversely, 61 percent of the leaders had moved into a legal neighborhood, as opposed to 34 percent of the random sample. That is an accurate reflection of the advantages the leadership sample had. They were disproportionately male, light-skinned, older, and better educated than the random sample, had higher incomes, and were more politically connected and savvy at working the political system. What I found surprising is that they were *not* able to pass on their relatively advantageous position to their offspring.

With each successive generation, there was less difference between the two samples. The children of the random sample moved upward, and the children of the leadership sample moved downward, so that by the grandchildren's generation, they had converged toward the middle and were almost identical. In terms of the percentage remaining in the favelas, the difference closed from a 26-point gap between random and leadership samples among the original interviewees, to a 4-point gap in the grandchildren's generation. Likewise, the difference in the percentage of those who moved to bairros diminished from a 27-point gap in the first generation to a 7-point gap in the grandchildren's generation.

EXPLORING PATTERNS OF RESIDENTIAL MOVES

What was the pathway out of the favelas? Did people go directly to bairros or were they more likely to go to conjuntos first as a stepping stone toward the asfalto?

The year-by-year life histories we collected enabled us to follow each move—showing not only where the people ended up but what pathway they took in getting there. Of interest to both policy-makers and theorists is how frequently the urban poor move and what pattern the moves take. Do those who exit the favelas end up back there, or does each residential move tend to be a step up the ladder? For the original interviewees, we were able to trace each residential move year by year, from birth through 2001 and to determine for each move whether it was a favela, conjunto, loteamento, or bairro. The patterns revealed very few moves and more upward than downward mobility, as shown in figure 9.1.

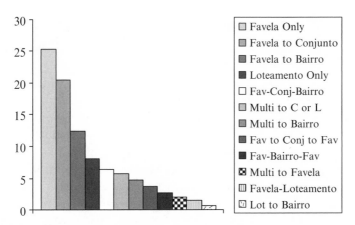

FIGURE 9.1   Residential Mobility Patterns: Original Interviewees, 1969–2001.

I organized the graph by frequency of residential patterns, with the most frequent (being no move at all) on the top. Among those original interviewees who stayed in the favelas, there is little evidence that any of them made horizontal moves from one favela to another.

The next most frequent pattern—moving from a favela to a conjunto—can be attributed to Catacumba's removal and the resettlement of its residents to conjuntos, where they stayed. Since the move was not by choice, the people who fall into this group might be considered another variation of nonmovers. Counter to my expectation, living in conjuntos did *not* make the move to bairros more likely. It was apparently not a training ground for moving up and out, even though conjuntos have a more legitimate status than favelas. More people moved directly from favelas to bairros (12 percent) than moved from favelas to conjuntos to bairros (7 percent), although the difference is small. All other patterns were insignificant. I suspect that if I repeated the study of the same group today, in 2009, a higher percentage would have moved from both favelas *and* conjuntos to bairros to escape the violence.

INTRA- AND INTERGENERATIONAL CHANGES

The value of longitudinal studies is the comparison between "then and now"; the value of multigenerational studies is a comparison of the first generation with their children and grandchildren. Intra- and intergenerational studies are rarely done in squatter settlements, and, as far as I can ascertain, there is no precedent for combining both at any scale beyond a few dozen families.[1]

Changes for the Better

Being an optimist by nature, I begin with the intragenerational and intergenerational improvements—which are considerable. Contrary to the popular notion that the poor are getting poorer, I found a dramatic improvement in many indicators of well-being, including the building materials of the home, the range and access to urban services, household goods, individual consumption, education, and occupation. (Table 9.2 shows intra- and intergenerational gains.)

By 2001, brick homes (as opposed to those made of scrap material, wattle and daub, gains or wood) and access to urban services—even in communities that had not been included in upgrading programs—were nearly universal. Contrast this with 1969, when people used kerosene lamps for light or obtained electricity by illegally tapping into power lines; water was available only at slowly dripping collective spigots at the bottom of the favela hillsides; and sewage ran down the slopes in open channels, overflowing onto pathways and into homes during heavy rains.

TABLE 9.2   *Living Standards, 1969 and 2001, Comparing Three Generations (%)*

	1969 *Original* *Interviewees*	*2001* *Original* *Interviewees*	*2001* *Children*	*2001* *Grandchildren*
Brick home	43	94	97	97
Indoor plumbing	54	76	98	99
Electricity	73	98	97	96
Refrigerator	36	98	97	96
Television	27	93	98	96
Washing machine	0	50	67	63
Air conditioner	0	39	69	68
Telephone line		68	88	89
Car	0	14	29	34
Computer	0	10	22	25
Illiteracy	72	45	6	0
Some/all high school	0	1	29	45
Mean # of years of education	2.37	2.49	7.36	8.88
Nonmanual job (as job held for longest period in life)	6	20	37	61

Note: Impressive gains were shown in housing infrastructure, electro-domestic consumer items, education, and occupation.

Our 2003 interviews, which were with new samples of 425 people from each of the original communities, yielded the same results—nearly universal coverage of brick houses, basic urban services, and infrastructure. This is not the case for any new favela in Rio today, but it is representative of the consolidated favelas that have been in existence since the 1960s or earlier. These consolidated favelas are predominantly located in the North and South zones of Rio and in the Baixada Fluminense.

Improvements were not limited to material conditions. Increases in educational levels were impressive. While 72 percent of the parents of the original interviewees and 45 percent of the original interviewees themselves were illiterate in 1969, only 6 percent of their children and none of the grandchildren were illiterate in 2001. Additionally, none of the original participants or their parents had attended high school, while 45 percent of their grandchildren had—and 11 percent had gone on to university.

What Went Wrong?

Migrants, favela residents, social scientists, and policy-makers alike see education as the key to moving out of poverty. If that were so, the impressive educational gains reported here would have yielded equally impressive increases in income generation and poverty alleviation. But that was not the case. Those who made the greatest sacrifices for their education did not reap the same income returns as those who had the luxury of taking education for granted. The Brazilian economist Valéria Pero compared Rio favela residents with nonfavela residents in terms of their educational and income levels. Her dramatic findings are shown in figure 9.3.

For those who completed only four years of school, the expected income was the same for everyone—Rio residents, favela residents and nonfavela residents. But for every additional year of schooling after those first four, the earnings gap between favelas and nonfavelas widened. For those living in favelas, the more years they continued to study, the greater the gap between what they earned and what their nonfavela counterparts earned.[2]

This finding holds up even when controlled for age, race, and gender. This gap likely reflects differences in educational quality, in the home and community environment and in discrimination in the job market. I have already given several examples of times when favela residents who went on job interviews had their interviews summarily ended or applications turned down due to where they lived.

In light of this, it is no wonder that the favela residents have become disillusioned with education. In my 1969 interviews, almost everyone said that education was "the most important factor for a successful life." By 2001, they cited decent work with decent pay as the most important to factor, with

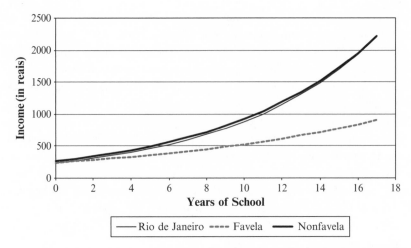

FIGURE 9.3   Income returns to education (2004) are lower for favelas than in nonfavelas. The gap widens with each extra year of schooling. *Source*: Compiled by Valéria Pero from the 2000 Census.

education the second most important followed by health and then income. They specified that the work could be either *emprego* (employment) or *trabalho* (working for oneself). It is telling that they valued work over income, and this was reinforced by my open-ended interviews. Being a worker confers self-respect and dignity that goes beyond the monetary compensation.

This importance of work is one of the central themes that emerged in every aspect of the study. Figure 9.4 is based on answers from the children's generation because they were in the prime of life in 2001 and their sample sizes were

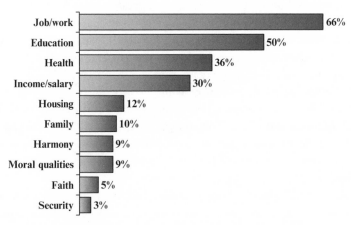

FIGURE 9.4   Key factors for success in life. Children's generation, 2001. *Source*: Catagories derived from answers to open-ended question.

the largest. The same ordinal ranking applies to the answers given by the original interviewees and by the grandchildren—with very little variation in the percentages. Poverty theorists and policymakers might be surprised to see that not only is having a job considered more important than education, but, also more important than health, than income, than housing, and even more important than security. If people place greater value on going to work every day than on their housing, urban services, and personal safety, it is evident that urban policy has been sorely misdirected. Development agencies, national government, and local government alike have been focusing their efforts almost exclusively on housing, on-site upgrading, and land tenure, or on controlling drug sales while what people want is work. I return to this discussion in chapter 11.

Parent-Child Educational and Occupation Comparisons

The gap between income returns to education for favelas and the rest of Rio was confirmed by my own analysis of family trajectories. Having data on three generations for each family enabled me to compare each person with his or her parents. Eliminating anyone not currently active in the workforce, I found that about 60 percent in each generation had better jobs than their own parents— this despite the fact that 85 percent had more education than their parents.

Some of this discrepancy can be explained by the fact that educational requirements for entry-level positions rose faster than the educational gains of the low-income population, impressive as they were. This rising bar applies across the board from manual to nonmanual jobs, from garbage collectors to sales clerks, making it difficult for anyone without a high school diploma to get work and making a university degree necessary to moving into better-paying jobs.[3]

When I was living in the favelas in the 1960s, parents commonly warned their children, "If you drop out of [elementary] school, you won't be able to get a job and you'll end up collecting garbage." Several years ago when I was in Rio, 200 vacancies opened up for garbage collectors. Over 4,000 people applied and a high school diploma was mandatory.

Unemployment has risen citywide since the boom times of my first study. The decline in Rio's economy has made the job market very tight. Among the factors that have led to job loss in Rio are the relocation of the national capital to Brasília; the move of the financial services and cultural/intellectual center to São Paulo; the loss of heavy industry to other parts of Brazil and other countries (deindustrialization); the decline of the port area and the shipping industry; and the loss of tourism and investment due to fear of violence. The consolidation of the built environment and technological advances in construction have eliminated many construction jobs, affecting a large number of poor male workers. Meanwhile the squeeze on the incomes of the middle class and the new regulations giving domestics the right to a minimum wage and the full package of workers rights has—along with new labor-saving household appliances, food take-out services, laundromats, and so on—reduced demand for domestic services. This has meant job loss for many female workers from informal settlements.

Between 1969 and 2003, the percentage of the random samples that had been unemployed for more than six months rose from 32 percent to 51 percent. In 1969, 17 percent of the random sample said they had no income from any source at all; in 2003, almost a quarter of the random sample (23 percent) had no income, more than twice the average for Rio. Favelas had the highest unemployment rates among the various types of poor communities (favelas, conjuntos, and loteamentos clandestinos). Among those employed, favela residents were the least likely to have the more prestigious (though not necessarily the best-paying) nonmanual jobs.[4] As I discussed in chapter 7, the fact that favelas are associated with violence and bandidos makes it even more difficult for those from favelas to get any job, particularly a well-paid job, regardless of educational qualification.[5]

We also found more absolute poverty than we expected in our follow-up studies. In the 2001 interviews 35 percent of the original participants, 18 percent of their children, and 13 percent of their grandchildren said they had gone hungry in the not-too-distant past. Sebastião, one of the original leaders from Nova Brasília, had earned a decent living as a truck driver for the local Coca-Cola bottling factory before it closed in the early 1990s. When I went with Zé Cabo to see him, he was living in a shack in the backyard of his former home, supporting his ailing wife, his daughter, Josilene, and her baby on his monthly pension. Josilene, an attractive woman in her early 30s, had been unemployed for so long that she had given up looking for work. Her father's pension was the only thing standing between her and going hungry and the only source for feeding her little girl.

To summarize, material conditions of life are much better today than they were four decades ago, and educational levels are much higher. But unemployment is also much higher and the educational gains have not translated into proportionally better jobs. The jobs people do get pay what the lyrics to a popular samba call "a salary of poverty," meaning that even among families with a working person, going to bed hungry is not uncommon.

GETTING OUT OF THE FAVELAS

What distinguishes those people and families who made the transition from morro to asfalto from those who, by choice or necessity, did not?

The stories of Jacobi, Margarida, Tio Souza, Nilton, Zé Cabo, Dona Rita, Sebastião, and Djanira provide some sense of what it means for an individual or family to stay in a favela or move to a conjunto or bairro. Among them none moved voluntarily. Marga, Jacobi, Tio Souza, and Nilton were all forcibly removed from a favela to a conjunto, and, among them, two have since moved into bairros—Marga into an apartment in Irajá (in the North Zone) and Jacobi to a western part of the city called Jacarepaguá. Dona Rita moved out to a nearby neighborhood of condominiums but still goes to the favela daily to take care of her store. Zé Cabo moved to the same bairro as Marga but, like her, was forced out by the traffic. Sebastião and Djanira are still in the favela. Collectively, their narratives are compelling, but do not provide a basis upon which to generalize or draw conclusions.

For that we need to look at the data collected from all the original study participants and their descendants. The analysis shows a strong relationship between outward residential mobility (moving from favelas to bairros) and upward social mobility. Those who still live in favelas have significantly lower incomes, higher rates of unemployment, lower educational levels, less access to human services, fewer urban amenities, and less household space per person. They are also more likely to work in manual labor (if they are working) than those in bairros. Likewise, those who have bought land, built houses, or rented/purchased apartments in bairros score much higher on all indicators of socioeconomic mobility, while those living in conjuntos score somewhere in between those living in favelas and those living in bairros.

But this finding tells us nothing about what enabled people to move up and out of favelas. Were those who exited the favelas for bairros better off *before they left the favelas* and therefore able to exit? Or was it that they were fed up with the violence, unattached to extended families, and driven to become gente—thus willing to leave the favela community and take a risk in a bairro, only becoming better off *after their move*? Escaping the stigma of favela life could well have led to—rather then followed from—a higher living standard because it was easier for people, once out, to get jobs, find high-quality schools, and connect to a diverse network of people.

To find out what factors contribute to the likelihood of exiting a favela and moving into a bairro, we used a statistical probability test called a probit model. The analysis revealed three factors that *increased* the likelihood and three that *decreased* the likelihood of a person getting out of a favela. The people who got out tended to be those who (1) had fathers with relatively more education; (2) had more education themselves; and (3) were more knowledgeable about Brazilian politics. These findings confirm what larger studies based on census data have found.[6] We would expect that education (one's parents' and one's own) would be a significant predictor of mobility and that interest in and awareness of politics would reflect this educational advantage.

But they contribute to our understanding by omission. All the other variables that the literature would predict would correlate with getting out of a favela—being male, light-skinned, well-connected, having smaller families, being employed, and earning a good salary did *not* make any significant difference.

The factors that decreased the likelihood of favela exit contributed more to the mobility mystery. The people who stayed tended to be those who (1) owned their homes in the favelas; (2) had a formal job with a *carteira assinada* (signed employment contract) and benefits; and (3) were members of community organizations. All three of these factors also measure well-being, which makes this result counterintuitive. The fact that home owners were less likely to exit favelas contradicts the assumption that those with sufficient resources to own their own homes—as opposed to renting, borrowing, or squatting—would be the very ones who would be able to move out. The home owners were the ones who had invested their life savings in their houses, who had expanded their dwellings to include space for their grown children and their families, and who stood to lose their investment if they left, since the violence had devalued their property. Even if the head of the household was able to move, it was unlikely that he or she was able to afford to buy a space outside the favela that was both large enough and close enough to the city to bring the extended family along. The cost of such a move would be prohibitive or mean giving up work.

The other counterintuitive finding was that people with jobs in the formal sector—that is, those with good salaries, benefits, job stability, and insurance coverage—were *less likely* to exit. Considering income alone, these persons would be the most able to afford to get up and go, but it was the very fact of proximity to their work that made them stay in the favela. The majority of those with carteira assinadas worked long hours and needed to stay close to their workplaces. This explained their reluctance to move to a bairro farther away, which would necessitate spending time and money commuting long distances. Four hours of travel time on top of a 12-hour work day is prohibitive—not to mention the risk of arriving late to work because of a bus breakdown, when three tardy check-ins is cause for dismissal.

Finally, I would have predicted that members of neighborhood associations would be more likely to move out of the favela. The literature is full of theories about high social capital being a good predictor of economic success and likely to provide the necessary resources for upward mobility. After many hours of discussion with my friends living in the favelas it turned out to make sense: obviously (to them) people with close community ties and *raízes* (roots) in the community might be financially able to move out, but they would not want to abandon their communities and all they had fought for over decades. This was the exact situation in which Zé Cabo found himself. And it was why Nilton built his family compound in Guaporé rather then in a bairro somewhere else.

Making sense of this counterintuitive finding confirmed my observation that many people stay in the favelas by choice. A famous case in point is Benedita da Silva who, even after becoming the national secretary of social action, stayed in the favela Chapéu Mangueira, where she has *raízes*. It is why Zé Cabo remained in Nova Brasília after financing land and housing outside the favela for his four grown children. This attachment to one's roots also explains the meaning of the lyrics of many types of music, from samba to Afro reggae to hip-hop to funk. They all proudly praise the very real pains and pleasures of favelas as home. Eleven percent of those in the highest fifth of earnings in our sample chose not to leave the favelas, despite their economic ability to do so.

So which comes first—favela exit or upward mobility?

As in the chicken-and-egg conundrum, there may be no definitive answer. We found a self-reinforcing relationship between favela exit and upward mobility. The favela residents who had greater assets and incomes had more opportunity to move out, and those who succeeded in moving out, especially into bairros, had more opportunity to generate income. In Nilton's case, moving to the conjunto in Guaporé (not nearly as prestigious as any bairro) enabled him to get a job with the Military Police, for which he had been turned down several times while residing in Catacumba.

To untangle the direction of causality between favela exit and upward mobility, we used the socioeconomic status (SES) index—composed of the same elements used in the Brazilian census and household surveys: educational level (number of years in school), consumption of household goods and appliances, and crowding (persons per room). We generated a score for every individual and used the score to compare the well-being of children who stayed in a favela to those who moved to a bairro. To be sure that we were not picking up those children whose parents had moved out and taken them along, we selected only those children born in a favela whose parents still lived in that favela. As figure 9.2 demonstrates, the children who were still living in favelas had negative SES scores (below the average),

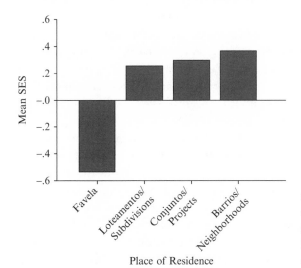

FIGURE 9.2   SES of adult children whose parents (OIs) remained in the favelas according to type of community.

while the children who had moved into bairros had positive scores, with those in loteamentos and conjuntos scoring in between the two.

This demonstrates that, among those children who were born and raised in favelas and whose parents never moved out of the favelas, the ones who never left are at a *distinct disadvantage* and the ones who managed to move out and move into a bairro have a *distinct advantage*. Being in a favela means having teachers who are not as good as the ones who teach in bairros and who only show up 2–3 times a week; having less social support for staying in school; being in a crowded (usually noisy) home with the television on and no room to study or for privacy; not meeting people on a daily basis who have job contacts; and not being hired after a job interview in which an address is required.

IS POVERTY STICKY? BORN POOR, STAY POOR? BORN POOR, CHILDREN POOR?

Daniel, whom I interviewed in Catacumba in 1969, became relatively successful among those in the original sample but remains poor relative to his early childhood. He was born in Ipanema and had maids, a nanny, and all the comforts of the upper middle class until his family became impoverished by his father's drinking and gambling. By the time he was eight years old, his family had lost their house and moved into the favela of Catacumba. Years after they were removed to the conjuntos he managed to save enough to buy a small house in the *suburbios*—the term used for low-income areas on the urban fringe. He has worked as a dispatcher for the informal vans that go from the center of the city out to the various suburbios where most of the lower-ranking workforce lives. His story is one of downward mobility.

Hélio Grande, whose story I pick up again at the end of this chapter, came from extreme poverty in Catacumba and now lives in the famed neighborhood of Gloria. His story is one of "born poor, now privileged." Marga and Nilton were born poor, and are now less poor; Zé Cabo was born poor, got better and became poor again; and Djanira was born poor, and has remained poor. Still, many of their grandchildren—especially the girls—were born poor (or nearly poor), and are no longer poor.

If poverty were chronic and sticky within and across generations, each of these people would be in the same relative position over his/her life span and would have passed their poverty on to their descendents. But that is not the reality I encountered. I found both upward and downward mobility to be in constant flux, with some people doing better than others overall.

The premise and promise of this research is that through understanding more about the endogenous and exogenous factors—or the internal and external conditions—that facilitate upward mobility, it may be possible to strengthen the conditions that make it possible for some to become upwardly mobile. The answer to the question for intragenerational mobility—"is poverty sticky?"— turns out to be "not very." But to answer the question more than anecdotally, we need a way to look at all of the respondents. We did this by using the SES index explained earlier. We could then compare the scores of the original inter- viewees in 1969 with their scores in 2001. There was very little stickiness—the relationship was weak, demonstrating that that the original SES scores for each person were not significantly related to—or predictive of—his or her SES score later in life.

What about intergenerational mobility? Is poverty inherited? Addressing these questions entailed looking at how closely the SES scores of the parents predicted the SES scores of their children and their grandchildren; and again at how the children's scores affected their own children. The answer, as shown in table A.1, is that there was a positive but weak relationship that means that contrary to popular wisdom, the status of parents had little predictive power in determining the status of their children. The single exception was a high cor- relation between the children and their own children. But that finding is arti- ficially inflated, since 22 percent of the grandchildren were still living at home in 2001 when the survey was conducted. In other words, since they shared the same households, their domestic consumption and number of people per room were identical for the children and grandchildren, leaving only education as a differentiator in SES scores between those two generations.[7]

Overall, we concluded that there was a lot more mobility both within and between generations than the literature would have led us to believe. The most interesting negative finding among the comparisons was that the SES scores of the original sample in 1969 were not strongly related to their children's scores in 2001, when they were approximately the same and at the same stage in their life cycle.

There was something else I wanted to check to be sure that this finding about transmission of poverty was reliable. All the calculations I mentioned earlier were done by averaging over the entire sample, which means that ups and downs may have cancelled each other out, causing us to miss the best part of the story. The only way to determine if this was the case was to take each individual separately, comparing the relative status of each person at differ- ent periods of his or her life and relative to his or her own children. We call this "case-by-case analysis" and were able to do it because we had traced these familial relationships in our original questionnaires.

We created transition matrices displaying the movement between the point of origin and the point of destination for each person in terms of their SES scores. We did not address *absolute* mobility in relation to the rest of Rio's popu- lation but *relative mobility* within the group. We divided the group into quin- tiles, using the SES scores and moving from the top 20 percent to the bottom.

For every person who moved up, one moved down. In extremely rigid societies, such as closed caste systems, the percentage of people who change from one quintile to another or whose children end up in a different quintile from their parents is very low. In a fluid social system, however, most people move either up or down relative to the group.

For Rio's favela residents, the degree of movement was fairly high. The intra- and intergenerational transition matrices we created revealed that only 27 percent of the original interviewees remained in the same quintile over the course of their lives, and only 28 percent of their children remained in the same quintile as their parents. Comparisons between mothers and their daughters showed more transmission of relative poverty than comparisons between fathers and sons. There was also a closer relationship between the status of children and their children, for the reasons explained earlier. This confirms the weak intra- and intergenerational transmission of poverty, and it reinforces the finding that Rio's urban poor may be struggling but are not trapped in chronic poverty.

However, it is important to bear in mind that the mobility we are referring to in this section is relative, not absolute, mobility; that upward and downward moves are equal in this type of transition matrix analysis; that most transitions were small, one-step increments; and that even those in the highest SES quintile are still poor in relation to the rest of the city.

The greatest mobility (in the SES index as well as in education, consumption, crowding, income, and occupation separately) is not individual mobility but structural mobility. This refers to the overall raising of the bar on all of those dimensions of mobility in the interval between the late 1960s and the first decade of the twenty-first century. Poverty is not a trap, but much of the improvement that we found was not relative to the rest of society, but the result of a rising tide lifting all boats.

In short, intergenerational transmission of poverty is weak and there is no lifetime condemnation to a particular degree of poverty or to a "stigmatized territory of exclusion," to use Wacquant's phrase. One's fate is not sealed by the position of one's parents or grandparents. The difference between all the favela residents and all the nonfavela residents in Rio is significant, and not easily diminished, but the differences within favelas and among favela residents can be washed out in a generation or less. Among the most successful and upwardly mobile of the original interviewees, the women worked as maids, cooks, box lunch preparers, seamstresses, or vendors; and the men as construction workers, janitors, bill collectors, and office boys. There was also one interior decorator and one picture framer in this group. Most had only one or two children, and most had already left the favelas, conjuntos, or loteamentos for bairros.

Among the children of this group, women's jobs included nurse, hairdresser, florist, cashier, high school teacher, personnel officer, and Military Police officer; the men's jobs included vendor, storekeeper, high school teacher, Military

Police officer, and office worker. In the upwardly mobile subgroup of the children, one-third had no children, one-third had only one child, and the remaining third had two children (with one case who had three). As with the earlier generation, most of the upwardly mobile/successful children lived in bairros, rather than favelas, conjuntos, or loteamentos.

Among the grandchildren of the most successful interviewees, females worked as receptionists, administrative assistants, supermarket checkout clerks, telemarketers, data entry workers, sales clerks, and seamstresses in textile factories; the males worked in the arts (as filmmakers, or in video, graphic design, or performance), owned stores, worked in offices, performed inventory, or were drivers—and one was a real estate broker. Of the upwardly mobile group, 73 percent had no children at all, and of those who did, 80 percent had just one, and the others had two.

It is a bit out of fashion these days to talk about family size since the issue has been usurped by the arguments for and against abortion and a woman's right to choose. It is also widely known that as urbanization levels increase family size decreases (except perhaps in India). We have long understood that the factors behind this fertility drop are urban benefits such as greater educational and employment opportunities for women. Improved medical care for mothers and babies, lower infant and child mortality rates, longer life expectancy, greater access to birth control, and less need for a large family to work the farm (in addition to less pressure on men to demonstrate their virility by fathering large families) also contribute. But we are seeing not only a one-time urban-related drop in fertility but a radical intergenerational decline such that among the youngest cohort in this study, many—like Paty—are deciding against having children at all. This trend has been documented for countries like Italy but—to my knowledge—not in squatter settlements in the cities of developing countries.

NATURE, NURTURE, AND STRUCTURE

The relationships drawn from the survey and life history data can only reveal so much—they do not tell the context or the details of the stories behind the outcomes. To understand the more nuanced qualities that distinguish the "poverty escapers" from the "poverty prisoners," I tried one last approach. We selected the ten most successful and ten least successful among the original random sample, and separately among the leadership sample, based on their SES scores, occupation, and income. We then conducted open-ended interviews with each of them to find out more about their life stories and listen to their personal narratives. The stories of Edson and Adão at the beginning of this chapter emerged from these in-depth discussions. Edson was one of the 10 poorest individuals among all of the original study participants, while Adão was among the 10

TABLE 9.3   *Emergent Themes from Life Narratives*

	Individual	Contextual
Givens	• Drive • Persistence • Skills • Talent	• Proximity to upscale areas • Social networks • Family support (for education, skills/job, etc) • Family culture and values
Choices	• Spouse • Limit number of children • Strategic planning (money, education, etc.) • Learn a trade, start a business, get a job	• Trade-off between living in a favela closer to center, or in a neighborhood farther away

most successful. Together, their stories illustrate how upward and downward mobility can coexist within the same family—adding to the ongoing debates about the relative role of nature and nurture.

Looking at the entire set of these follow-up interviews, I found several themes that emerged repeatedly in different ways. I have divided the factors that appear to affect relative success into *individual* and *contextual* factors and further into *givens* (personality traits or abilities evident at an early age) and *choices* as shown in table 9.3. To the possible dismay of social scientists and policy-makers, I found that random elements of luck and timing accounted for some of the variation in outcomes, making a huge difference in many lives but occurring outside the purview of public policy, civil society, or personal agency.

Shahin Yaqub identified eight "mobility filters" that "distinguish *poverty escapers* from *poverty prisoners,* thereby filtering the escape process."[8] These are parental income, education, gender, race, caste, community, class, and culture. For our interviewees, all of these filters, except caste, played a role, but family culture turned out to be among the most important factors.

The vignettes that follow illustrate many of these traits. They are the stories of Hélio Grande, Maria Giselia, Alaerte Correia, and Nilton—four of the most successful people among the original study participants. Each of them found a pathway away from—if not out of—poverty.

SOCCER, SMARTS, AND FRIENDS: THE STORY OF HÉLIO GRANDE

Hélio is one of the most memorable people I met in my early days in Catacumba. He was 45 years old at that time, a tall, charismatic community leader who was friendly with everyone. He was active in the Residents' Association, the Youth Athletic Club, the samba school, and community events such as dances, picnics, day trips, and so on. He was a great soccer player.

Of all of the people I reencountered, Hélio had experienced perhaps the greatest degree of upward mobility in his life—and in the decades between my two studies. He came from humble beginnings: his father was a construction foreman with incomplete primary school education, and his mother was a housewife, though she had finished high school (which I believe was a critical factor for Hélio's success). Although he only completed junior high school himself, Hélio was one of a very few who succeeded in moving into the South Zone and integrating himself into neighborhood life there. He was president of the neighborhood association of Glória for 14 years—and he became gente.

I interviewed Hélio in his two-bedroom apartment on a tree-lined street in the middle-class neighborhood of Glória.

His home in Glória was a far cry from his shack in the favela. Hélio's success was the result of intelligence, contacts, and luck. He was born in 1922, and at the age of 21 he got married. Someone he knew recommended him for a low-level job as a security guard in the Ministry of Justice in Rio de Janeiro, so he did not need to face public competition (*concurso publico*) for the job. In 1969, he was transferred to Brasília, along with his coworkers, when the national capital was relocated. His wife did not want to go with him, so they separated, and he went with another woman, whom he soon married; they are together to this day. In 1976, at age 54, he retired and returned to Rio to live near his parents, in the suburb of Guadalupe. He had been able to save money in Brasília because he lived in an *apartmento functional* (subsidized apartment for public servants). During the duration of his employment, he continuously sent money to his father in Rio to begin building a house for him, in anticipation of his eventual return. After his return, he sold that house to buy the apartment in Glória—for cash.

In explaining how he had attained this level of success, he said:

> I always managed. I did whatever it took. We never had money ... my family was really poor, there was not enough to eat, and we often went hungry ... but I was never destitute. I always found a way to survive. Whatever sort of work came my way, I always grabbed and did it, and the hardest times passed that way. Success is having luck provide an opportunity and then acting on it. I had health, friendship, and soccer, and I made the rest happen.

Hélio explained that he never felt any type of work was "beneath him," so he was never unemployed for long. He set goals for himself and met them, and he felt that people should go after things they believed in rather than depending on others for their well-being. He said he felt that "consumption" was a vice.

FIGURE 9.5 AND 9.6.   Hélio Grande, from Catacumba, in his apartment in Botafogo, 2005.

His strategy, he said, was to live in a favela while investing his money in property elsewhere when land values were cheap.

Hélio has a son who is a professional soccer player and a grandson who married a Norwegian woman and lives in Oslo. But he is most proud of his daughter, who attended private school, passed the entrance exam to the Federal University of Rio de Janeiro, graduated with flying colors, and has completed two advanced degrees.

> I was able to do for her what I was never able to do for myself; this was my dream. I wanted to be an accountant. Then I wanted to be a lawyer, but I never had a chance to study seriously. And this girl (my daughter) is both: she's an accountant and graduated in law. Can you imagine?

STRATEGY AND SACRIFICE: THE TALE OF MARIA GISELIDA

Maria had the highest SES score in the original random sample. She was living in Centenário, one of the loteamentos in Caxias, at the time of the original study and now lives in a small, spotless apartment in Copacabana. Each of her four children started working at the age of 14, and they helped buy her this apartment after her husband died. Her kids prefer not to live in the South Zone—they've remained in or close to Caxias—and Maria visits them on weekends.

Her family was from the Northeast and valued education and hard work as the keys to success. In her words, they "fought for their lives and ran after any opportunity they could to survive and improve." Maria says that studying, personal drive, and parental support were the critical factors in her success in life.

> I fulfilled my responsibility to raise my kids. I didn't want to leave them with anyone else, so I stayed home with them and didn't work. It was a financial struggle for [my husband and me] to support our kids, but we did it, thank God. I think I raised them well. They haven't disappointed me at all—they make me so happy. The sacrifice I made to send them all to private school was worth it, and they have all worked hard.

Maria Giselia's four children all have good jobs. Her two sons went to law school while working at their father's pharmacy. Once they sold the pharmacy and finished their degrees, they opened a law firm of their own in Ilha do Governador, where they live. They maintain the strong political connections they formed during high school. Maria's younger daughter completed university and is a public servant working as a bank clerk in Copacabana, commuting from Caxias. Maria's older daughter, whom she considers the "loser" of the family, has heart problems and continues to live at the family home in Caxias.

Maria moved to Copacabana in 1989, after her sons sold their father's pharmacy in Caxias and her younger daughter bought the apartment for her. Maria and her husband owned their former home in Caxias, which she now rents out for additional income.

Today, Maria is retired and cares for her older daughter. She also travels when she can. She says that she's able to live on her retirement pay because she was a good financial planner and tucked away money each month during her working life. She made the most money when she started trading in gold jewelry, buying it cheaply in São Paulo and selling it for a profit in Rio. This was lucrative until the value of the dollar rose, along with gold prices. In addition to her current retirement payments and the rent money she receives on the Caxias house, she receives her deceased husband's pension.

FATHER KNOWS BEST: ALAERTE CORREIA, THE BARBER

Alaerte, who had the second highest SES of the original random sample, makes his living as a barber. His wife also contributes to the family income, but the revenue from his barbershop was always the major source. He attributes his success to his father's pushing him to learn a trade:

> My father was 100 percent responsible for [my career/success]. When I was 13 years old, he said, "Son, you're going to go far in life." One of his buddies from back in the countryside had a barbershop near his house. My father asked him to teach me how to be a barber. I said "Oh, dad, I don't have the slightest desire to learn this—I don't want to learn to cut hair, no way. I don't like it." He said, "No, my son, you're going to learn and learn well, because a profession is never a waste." I remember as if it were yesterday. When I was 13, I learned to cut hair, and at 15 I started working in the barbershop. My father's friend didn't like working; he liked soccer and drinking, so I ran the shop alone. At 18, I worked as a barber in the military for a year and eventually opened my own barbershop. If I hadn't learned this trade, I don't know what I would have been. I learned because he wanted me to learn it, he made me learn it; and I can now say that my life is better because of him. He gave me a profession.

Over time, Alaerte has managed to acquire a significant amount of real estate, including an apartment in the conjunto of Fazenda Botafogo, two studio apartments, a house in Campo Grande, a store in the city center, and a piece of land in Fazenda Modelo (on the road to Teresópolis). For Alaerte, having a successful life depends on a solid family structure and a steady salary. And it was finding his trade that made all the difference.

These stories are revealing in their own right, but it's important to understand that the beliefs and behavior patterns we identified among the most successful favela residents are by no means guarantees of success. Some of the people we talked to who were similarly well educated, hard working, and motivated showed downward mobility—leaders and random sample members alike.

NILTON SUMS IT UP

The story of Nilton is one of success, by our standards, but he is a failure according to his own gauge. When I met him in Catacumba in 1969, he was 26 years old and full of promise—bright, motivated, handsome, and one of the few whose parents had succeeded in sending them to private Jesuit secondary school. After the removal to the conjunto in Guaporé, he got a job with the Military Police (he had been repeatedly turned down for similar positions while living in the favela). After his retirement, he became a security guard, and he was most recently a traveling salesman for a company he had worked for some 40 years earlier. His wife had been a seamstress in a textile factory, and after her retirement she continued working from home. Both of his daughters went to private schools and were the first in their community to get desktop computers. One is married and not working, and often stays with her parents when her husband is working late or traveling, because it is too dangerous to be in her own apartment alone. The other (Sabrina, whom we met in the introduction) dropped out of university after she broke her leg in a fall on campus; she became a telemarketer (paid under the table) but had to quit because it was making her deaf. As I mentioned, she has not returned to school.

There are dozens of people whose stories merit telling and whose lives are full of courage and creativity in the most daunting of circumstances. The trope of hope overcoming despair—even when hope did not seem warranted—stands in stark juxtaposition to a saying heard among the poor in another part of the world (Azerbaijan): "Only the well-off can believe in tomorrow."[9]

Is hope really a luxury of the rich? This belief may well represent the deadliest enemy to finding pathways out of poverty. In our many conversations with favela residents, a consistent theme emerged among those who had managed, against all odds, to better their lots in life: a sense of hope. The can-do spirit, the belief that sacrificing and planning can finally pay off—an unquenchable sense of optimism—became self-fulfilling for these upwardly mobile (in aspiration if not yet in reality) favela residents. Among Rio's poor, even the less successful among them, there remains a belief that their day will come.

ten

GLOBALIZATION AND THE GRASSROOTS

Over the next 25 years, virtually all of the world's population growth will be in the cities of developing countries—and most of it will be concentrated in squatter settlements such as the ones I have described here. There will be 19 cities with 20 million or more inhabitants by the year 2021. For that reason, it is crucial and timely to consider the impact of globalization on these marginalized informal settlements.

I begin by taking a critical look at current assumptions about globalization, with an eye toward separating causality from coterminality. In the process I explore not only how the urban poor are affected by globalization but also how much of that effect is due to the way advanced capitalism tends to concentrate wealth (regardless of global influence) and the way new technology tends to replace unskilled workers (regardless of global influence).

Globalization is many things to many people and all things to some people. For example, David Harvey construes it to include "all economic, political, social, cultural, and ideological changes that have occurred with the restructuring of capitalist production."[1] In this formulation, it includes everything, including processes antecedent to today's form of globalization, inherent in it, and consequent to it.

What makes this especially interesting is that the meaning of the term is itself a topic of global discourse.

Despite its polarizing effects in debates on the subject, globalization is intrinsically neither good nor bad. You may love or hate it, but it is here to stay. As is the case with technological advances, it is not going to reverse, nor would that be beneficial. The question is how to permit the "have-nots" among and within countries and cities to partake in the benefits of globalization, rather than simply picking up the tab while becoming increasingly irrelevant.[2]

How does globalization affect the underclass in Rio de Janeiro? To answer this question, I use Erik Thorbecke's definition of the term: "Essentially, globalization means greater integration into the world economy through openness to international trade; international capital movements and labor migration; technology transfer, and the flow of ideas and information."[3]

Each component of this definition has potentially positive as well as negative consequences for the urban poor in Rio:

- *Openness to international trade* may be helpful for favela residents insofar as it reduces consumer prices but harmful in terms of job loss, as capital seeks the lowest labor and production costs, making Rio noncompetitive.
- *International flow of capital* initially helped lower inflation and promote Brazil's 1994 Real Plan, which pegged Brazilian currency to the U.S. dollar. During this period, favela residents were able to buy things formerly and subsequently beyond their means. The real has since increased in value and become more attractive to foreign investors. But a strong currency also raises prices, reducing competitiveness with items made in China, for example.
- *Labor migration*—Brazil has outsourced low-skilled jobs to other countries, leaving fewer jobs for the favela population. Many small business owners and middle-class workers have migrated to the United States to work menial jobs and send home the money they make—but favela residents tend not to be a part of this cycle, due to a general lack of higher education, documentation, and opportunity.
- *Technology transfer*—there is no going back to a precomputer age, and someday, the rise of technology will certainly benefit favela residents—though this change is slow in coming. The stigma of the favelado could be eliminated in the virtual world, where a person's place of residence is unknown and irrelevant. Skill development will be needed, but it is not out of the question that Rio could become a "wired" or "smart" city, generating jobs for people all along the socioeconomic scale.
- *Flow of information*—favela residents are more connected to the world than ever before, through the ubiquity of television and the World Wide Web. The downside is the new sense of inferiority this creates, as Rio's poorest population is bombarded with images of wealth from the United States and Europe.

THE HEART OF THE MATTER: POVERTY AND INEQUALITY

Hardly a day passes without the issue of globalization, poverty, and inequality coming up in newspaper and magazine articles, academic publications, and policy speeches, by both defenders and detractors of the "new world order":

> Rising inequality is the dark side to globalization. [But] no one wants a return to outright protectionism.
>
> PAUL KRUGMAN, *NEW YORK TIMES*, MAY 14, 2007

> An impoverished ghetto of one billion people will be increasingly impossible for a comfortable world to tolerate.
>
> PAUL COLLIER, *THE BOTTOM BILLION* (2007)

> There is mounting evidence that economic growth is less effective in reducing poverty in the face of rising trends in inequalities.
>
> UNITED NATIONS PRESS RELEASE, ASSOCIATED PRESS, FEBRUARY 8, 2007

> Making globalization work for the masses is the central economic issue of the day.
>
> LAWRENCE H. SUMMERS, *FINANCIAL TIMES*, OCTOBER 30, 2006

> Economic globalization has outpaced political globalization. We need collective action to temper capitalism…but we have yet to create the political structures to do so.
>
> JOSEPH STIGLITZ, *US NEWS AND WORLD REPORT*, SEPTEMBER 18, 2006

These quotations, and the articles from which they were excerpted, raise fundamental questions regarding the inevitability of globalization, its costs, and whether its consequences for those excluded may be mitigated or even reversed through the implementation of international agreements or domestic policies.

My five starting premises would be synthesized as follows:

1. *The world is not flat and never was.* The process of globalization over the past several decades has exacerbated preexisting inequalities and divergence. Advanced capitalism has produced "advanced marginalization," whereby those limited to the "space of place" and excluded from the "space of flows"[4] have been reduced from unimportant to irrelevant.

2. *Globalization is not an act of nature.* It is the result of policies that make the market supreme, allowing concentration of capital to trump concern for excluded countries, communities, and citizens. Therefore, changes in policies, rules, and incentives—internationally or nationally—might theoretically

mitigate or reverse the trend toward greater inequality, given sufficient political will.

3. *Globalization is not new,* although advances in telecommunications, information technology, and transportation have increased the speed, volume and extent of flows of capital, labor, information, and ideas.[5] The historical logic of center/periphery in the world system is reproduced at every level, from continents to communities, continually reinforcing the vicious cycle of uneven development or, as Celso Furtado so well put it, "the development of underdevelopment."[6]

4. *Globalization is not unidimensional.* Each of its aspects may have different consequences for different constituencies at different times. It may be good, bad, or neutral, depending on an individual's position in the hierarchy of winners and losers. The results of globalization vary depending on context and specific circumstances, though they are often subject to sweeping generalizations about the wonders or evils of a globalized world order.

5. *Poverty is not reduced sufficiently by globalization* to redress the inequalities exacerbated by it. Poverty levels may have improved in absolute terms in the age of globalization, but the gap between the haves and have-nots has widened. Inclusive growth depends on policy interventions designed to share the fruits of growth with the bottom third of the world's population.

Policy-makers seeking ways to mitigate the human cost of globalization discuss such measures as taxing international transactions, raising stipends and salaries of displaced workers to previous levels, implementing education and job training programs to help people enter the information economy, and various other income redistribution measures that range from the mundane to the utopian.[7] It is unclear whether the political will exists to put these ideas into action or whether the self-perpetuating logic of globalization can be molded by regulatory or contractual arrangements. What is certain is that globalization is not reversible—there is no turning back.

URBAN PLANNING AND GLOBALIZATION

There is a permanent tension between legal and illegal residents of the city, with obvious implications for land use, housing finance, and environmental protection. The race to become a global city casts the urban endeavour as a business, where strategic planning replaces urban planning and profitability replaces the public good. The city has to market itself to compete as a global city, and an undereducated underclass undermines the sell.[8] With this in mind, Rio's poor cannot be studied except within the context of rampant globalization. How have they been affected by today's pervasive globalization of ideas, icons, and identities?

THE URBAN QUESTION

How has the current stage of globalization affected poverty and inequality in urban areas on the periphery of the world hierarchy of cities, particularly in the "slums," squatter settlements, and shantytowns of this study? The prevailing wisdom is that globalization tends to concentrate wealth and deepen inequality within and among cities, countries, and continents.

In fact the relationship is a complex, often contradictory one. The connection between globalization and poverty depends on how broadly we define globalization, how we measure poverty, how carefully we distinguish causality from coterminality, and whose viewpoint we assume.

My question is how the lives of the 40 percent of urbanites living in the shantytowns of Asia, Africa, and Latin America would differ in the absence of our current form of globalization. What would be the impact on poverty, inequality, violence, and voice?

Without a grounded understanding of how globalization affects poverty in specific localities, we cannot hope to refine theory or to transform policy.

THE CASE OF RIO DE JANEIRO

In the years since the end of the dictatorship, Brazil has attained middle-income status by worldwide standards, though much of its population has clearly been excluded. In fact, Brazil has the highest degree of disparity between rich and poor of any large country in the world. As I've shown, the poor of Brazil have been systematically prevented from achieving their full human potential and have been denied the dignity of full citizenship—but I have not yet explored the economic consequences of such a disparity.

Undoubtedly, this level of inequality has set limits on economic growth by depriving the country of the intellectual capital, productive and consumer potential, and political participation of a third of its urban population.[9]

If globalization has a polarizing effect between rich and poor, as I have posited here, then income inequality should have become more acute starting in the 1990s. Income distribution data for Brazil and Rio between 1992 and 2009 indeed shows extreme inequality, but it has decreased over the time period covered by this study.[10] The Gini coefficient is a measure of inequality indicated by a fraction ranging from zero to one, with zero being perfect equality (every person having an equal share of the wealth, income, land, etc.) and one being total inequality (with one person having all the shares). In Brazil, the Gini coefficient varied only slightly (from 0.58 to 0.60) over those 11 years, while globalization by every measure was rising. For Rio, the pattern is nearly identical in the same time period, with the Gini coefficient ranging between 0.55 and 0.58 and ending up at 0.57 in 2003, exactly the same as the national figure.

Poverty figures have also remained fairly consistent or declined. Using United Nations Development Programme definitions of poverty (earning US$2 per day or less) and extreme poverty (earning $1 per day or less), about a third of Brazil's population and about a fifth of Rio's population are in poverty—less than the national average, due in part to the fact that the figures have not been adjusted for purchasing-power parity.[11] The percentage of poor people in Rio declined slightly from 1992–2003, while the percentage of indigent poor increased slightly.[12]

I hesitate to draw conclusions about the consequences of globalization from these statistics alone, as many additional variables are in play, and it is always possible that strong negative and positive effects cancel each other out. But there is no doubt that the economic decline of the city of Rio (absolutely and in relation to the other metropolitan areas) has had a deleterious effect on its inhabitants, particularly on the most vulnerable among them.

During the period of my restudy the city of Rio had lower rates of growth (in GDP/capita) and upward mobility than the city of São Paulo, the state of Rio, all of the major regions of the country, and Brazil as a whole. Although Rio's GDP per capita is relatively high, Rio's cost of living is even higher—and Rio's level of inequality is worse than that of Brazil in general (exhibiting a Gini coefficient of 0.616 compared with 0.593). According to the ratings of the Human Development Index, Rio's quality of life ranges from levels comparable to that of Belgium (in Gávea, an upscale neighborhood in the South Zone, ninth in world ranking) to that of Vietnam (in the Complexo de Alemão, in the North Zone, 108th of 177 countries in the world).[13] This extreme inequality presents an obstacle to social mobility.

ARE FAVELAS CATCHING UP WITH OR GETTING FURTHER BEHIND THE REST OF RIO?

There is ample evidence that globalization has increased inequality among regions and countries in the world, with African nations in danger of becoming "irrelevant" or being relegated to a "Fourth World." If the logic of globalization is one of increased concentration of capital in the richest regions, nations, and world cities, would this logic extend to increased inequality between rich and poor within cities?

The specific question here that is relevant to my study is whether the gap in well-being between favelas and the rest of the city of Rio widened or narrowed between the preglobalized period at the end of the 1960s and the globally embedded first years of the twenty-first century. That is not to say our findings can assert any causal relationship but merely that we can add some empirical data and insight to this discussion.

Looking at the balance sheet of what got better and what got worse in the lives of the urban poor over the past 40 years does not address the issue of inequality. The previous chapter has demonstrated the undisputed improvements in the study communities in terms of collective urban infrastructure and services as well as individual consumption and education. Yet this does not tell us whether inequality in relation to the rest of the city increased or diminished.

In order to reduce inequality, the gains of the favela population would have to *exceed* the gains of the nonfavela population. If the degree of improvement within the favelas was matched by equal improvement in the rest of the city, inequality levels would remain unchanged, despite the notable improvements in the living standards of the favelas. If the premise that globalization deepens inequality is correct, the gap between rich and poor communities in Rio will have become greater over this time period.

To address this issue, we needed to have a representative random sample of the study communities at two points in time—before and after globalization became integral to Brazil's economy. Conveniently for this thought experiment, the first study, in 1968–69, occured during Brazil's protectionist period when "import substitution" was the guiding principle of development. By the time the follow-up interviews were done, with the same people and their descendents, Brazil was among the major players in the global economy. The same was true of Brazil in 2003 when we interviewed a new random sample in the same favela communities. With all of these data, we could examine the before and after conditions to see how people's lives had changed relative to their own earlier condition (pre-globalization); how their children's and grandchildren's lives had changed (in the midst of globalization); and how the communities had changed relative to the city of Rio as a whole.[14]

Using the survey data from Catacumba, Nova Brasília, and Caxias in 1969 and 2003, I was able to compare the profiles of these communities with the profiles of Rio's general population at the time of the closest census. That meant using the 1970 census for comparison with our 1969 sample and using the 2000 census for comparison with our 2003 sample.

The next question was *how* to compare the profiles of the study communities with the census profiles for the city at large. On what basis—using what measures—would it make sense to look for divergence or convergence? We constructed a composite index of socioeconomic status using the same three indicators used by the census: (1) *education* (as measured by the number of years of schooling); (2) *domestic consumption* (as measured by the number of household goods and appliances); and (3) *crowding* (as measured by the number of people housed per room). This yielded a score for each person and an average score for each community, which we then compared with the average score for Rio residents according to the census.

The results were the opposite of what globalization theorists would have predicted. On average, our communities scored lower than those in the the greater city—but the gap between the two was reduced. There was significant upward mobility among favela residents in our three study communities relative to the population of Rio as a whole. In 1969, the average SES score of our sample communities was between the lowest 9–10 percentiles of the population of Rio. By 2003, the average scores of the residents of the same three communities had risen to between the 26th–27th percentiles from the bottom. This means that by 2003, over a quarter of the city's population had lower SES scores than the people in our study communities.

This is a powerful finding, but I had some doubts about its validity. I reasoned that the SES scores for the 2003 sample might be artificially inflated, since there was no reliable way to restudy Catacumba as a place, given that it no longer existed. Using a random sample from the Guaporé and Quitungo conjuntos was the closest approximation, but many people living there had never lived in Catacumba or in a favela, and the overall SES score of the conjuntos was higher than that in the favelas. Likewise, since the Caxias loteamentos had become legitimate neighborhoods due to their legal status, their inclusion in the SES scores may have masked an increased gap between favelas per se and the rest of the city.

To be certain that the closing gap was not an artifact of the sample, I repeated the calculation using *only* the favelas in the study—that is, filtering out the data from the conjuntos and loteamentos and leaving only Nova Brasília and the three favelas in Caxias. The results still showed a distinct rise in levels of living vis-à-vis the city. The average scores of those living in the favelas moved up from between the 9th–10th percentiles from the bottom in 1970 to between the 19th–20th percentiles from the bottom in 2000.

The favelas have a long way to go to reach the mean or median, but the gap is closing. The original study favelas are now in a relatively favorable position compared with newer settlements that have grown up, mostly in the West Zone, in recent years. Although the favelas remain stigmatized and excluded urban places, they do not reflect the inescapable poverty described by the Chronic Poverty Research Group in Manchester,[15] nor did they follow the patterns of advanced marginality described by Wacquant for Chicago ghettos and French banlieu.[16] Instead, there was a gradual improvement in living conditions in the older favelas vis-à-vis the city at large, while more recent migrants filled in the lower ranks of poverty.

One of the reasons for this is that those living in the favelas that already existed in the late 1960s are more likely to be Rio-born, and the Rio-born tend to have higher SES scores than migrants.[17] The hope of a better life in the big city seems to have been fulfilled, both then and now. This is confirmed by perception: 83 percent of migrants in the original 1969 study and 76 percent of those in the 2003 sample said they were "better off than those who stayed behind."

Even using the more stringent measure, one in five Rio residents was living in deeper poverty and worse conditions than the people I have described in the favelas we studied. After following the struggles of Margarida, Zé Cabo, and Djanira, it is disturbing to imagine 1.2 million people living in deeper misery.

But while the composite index of SES scores shows a closing of the gap, its component parts—education, household consumption, and crowding—may not. It is possible that the creation of an overall index obscured areas in which the gap was increasing. So we looked at each of the three components individually.

Educational level comparisons reinforced our conclusion. While the years of schooling attained by our study population remain lower than Rio's general population, the gap has diminished dramatically since the first study. In 1969, the people in our sample had an average of 2.1 years of schooling—only a third of the Rio average of 6.1. In 2003, those in our sample averaged 7.3 years of schooling, while those in Rio's general population had 8.8 years, narrowing the difference between the two groups from 4 to 1.5 years of education over the 34-year span.

Table 10.1 shows the structural gains in education, as well as a tendency toward narrowing the gap between our sample and Rio's population as a whole. The most notable change is that in 1969, 42 percent of our random sample *had no education at all*, as compared with 11 percent in the city of Rio. By 2003 only 4 percent of our sample and 1 percent of Rio's population had not attended school, showing both structural gains and convergence. The percent of those completing elementary school only had dropped to about half of previous levels and there was no siginificant difference between our sample and the Rio average. In high school the difference is only 4 percent. College attendance is the big divider, however. The fact that 6 percent of our sample has reached university is a promising sign, even though it is only one-third of the 18 percent in the city at large.

A similar narrowing of the gap between the population of the consolidated favelas and the rest of the city shows up in data measuring household crowding/density. In 1969, the average number of people per room in our sample was 1.96, as compared with almost 1.10 in the city—almost double. By 2003, the density in the study communities had dropped to 0.84 per room, while the city density dropped to 0.76—not eliminating the gap but clearly reducing it.

This convergence is, as shown in table 10.2, most apparent in the consumption of domestic goods. By 2003, many favela households owned appliances that did not exist or were only available to the upper classes at the time of

TABLE 10.1   *Comparison of Education Levels between Study Samples and Rio Municipal Average*

	Years of Education (in %)			
	1969 Study Sample	*1970 Rio Census*	*2003 Study Sample*	*2000 Rio Census*
None	42	11	4	3
Elementary	50	50	32	23
Jr. High	6	9	27	21
High school	2	24	30	34
University	0	6	6	18

the original study. Such things as refrigerators, televisions, washing machines, air conditioners, and video players went from luxury items to basic household goods in favelas. As table 10.2 shows, the only notable differences between our 2003 random sample and the city as a whole in 2000 were in ownership of microwave ovens, cars, and computers.

Fifteen percent of those in our 2003 study communities owned computers, as compared with 26 percent in the city in the same time period—a difference of only 11 percent. The biggest gap showed up in the number of people who owned a car or truck: 42 percent of Rio's residents versus 18 percent of the study community residents owned a vehicle. The favela residents also spend a higher percentage of their disposable income on food and a lower percentage on housing as compared with municipal averages. In stigmatized communities, there is a strong quest for status through possessions. Regardless of household income, a favela family cannot buy acceptance, legitimacy, or title to their land,

TABLE 10.2   *Comparison of Household Consumption Levels between Study Sample and Rio Average Municipal*

	Domestic Goods (in %)			
	1969 Sample	*1970 Census*	*2003 Sample*	*2000 Census*
TV	26	70	97	99
Refrigerator	31	73	97	98
Radio	75	84	94	97
Washing machine			60	65
Air conditioner			35	38
Video viewer			57	71
Microwave			23	37
Computer			15	26
Car / Truck	1	19	18	42

so they invest in home improvements, domestic appliances, and personal status symbols.

This high rate of consumption and the convergence toward the norm was not what we expected in light of the literature on the poverty trap or globalization. Even looking at those consumer categories where a relatively large gap exists, it is impressive that 60 percent have washing machines, 35 percent have air conditioners, 23 percent have microwave ovens, 18 percent have motor vehicles, and 15 percent have computers.

One clearly positive aspect of globalization is the Internet, which has given the urban poor access to the information society and connected them through e-mail to people they might never otherwise have had an opportunity to meet. About a fifth of homes in our study communities have broadband Internet connection, supplied through the Residents' Associations for a fee. The rest access the Internet through computers that have been donated to the associations themselves or cybercafes in the favelas or nearby. Many nonprofit organizations in Rio provide computers and computer skills training in favelas or make computers available for community use at their offices around the city.

Online work strikes me as great opportunity for favela residents—a way to avoid the issue of stigmatization, as the worker cannot be traced to a geographic location any more than a call from a cell phone can be traced to a luxury apartment or a squatter shack. I see cell phones as an avenue for job-finding, bill-paying, and Internet use.

This reduction in inequality for the communities I studied reflects the cumulative benefits of urban life for that segment of the population living in the older, more consolidated favelas. But the same gains do not exist for the newer favelas, where the gap is similar to that of our communities in the 1960s. But the improvements in the consolidated communities are real and are confirmed by the residents' assessments of their class status. In 1969, 10 percent of our sample considered themselves "middle class" or better; in 2003, this figure had doubled to 20 percent. In the multigenerational interviews done in 2001, even more of the original interviewees—27 percent—categorized themselves as middle class or higher, as did 16 percent of their children and 27 percent of their grandchildren.

THE PERSPECTIVE OF THE POOR

What does globalization look like from the perspective of the poor in Rio de Janeiro? To address this question, we asked our study participants, "How has globalization affected your life?" The interviewers recorded the answers exactly as spoken, and the results reported here are based on the first answers each person gave. The responses did not differ significantly by gender, race, birthplace, current community, or socioeconomic status.

The overwhelming majority of respondents across all three generations said that globalization had not made any difference. In their words: "Things are the same"; "There wasn't any change"; "It had no direct effect."[18] The percentage giving this response declined with each generation (though it remained the majority response throughout) from 85 percent of the original interviewees to 59 percent of the children to 52 percent of the grandchildren expressing the opinion that globalization had made no difference in their lives. These percentages coincide with increasing educational levels. This result is surprising, given that much of the programming and products shown on television are "made in the USA," and by the time of the second study, almost everyone, regardless of generation, reported watching television every day.[19]

Among the minority who reported that globalization *did* affect their lives, the responses tended to validate the academic literature on the subject. We found both negatives and positives:

- *Negatives:* In every generation, the most frequently mentioned effects of globalization were a tighter labor market, increased unemployment, a decline in financial security, lower salaries, and less purchasing power. The percentages of those citing these factors varied from a low of 6.8 among the original interviewees to a high of 19.7 among their children.

- Among the original interviewees, the second most frequent response was that globalization "creates economic dependency on other countries" or "makes us slaves to the global economy." Fewer than 5 percent of the total sample gave these answers—mainly, leaders who had experienced the struggles of the 1960s and 1970s and tended to be more politicized than the random sample.

- *Positives:* Children and grandchildren mentioned that globalization produced "improved life in general," "improved access to information and communication," and "improved technology, such as cell phones and computers." These answers did not come from the original study participants; 7 percent of these responses came from their children, and 24 percent from their grandchildren.

- The next most common answer was that globalization prompted "higher requirements for study, knowledge, and certification," which can be seen as positive or negative.

- Only the children and grandchildren mentioned this final factor: "facilitated purchase of imported products."

In follow-up, in-depth interviews with the most and least successful individuals from the original sample, we found that those who saw globalization as beneficial often mentioned reduced prices of imported goods, while those who saw it as detrimental made the connection between globalization and cheap imported goods leading to the loss of manufacturing jobs, citing layoffs and factory closings. They reported that displaced workers were never told whether their factory was going out of business, relocating to another area of Brazil, or moving to another country where both labor and production were cheaper.

I asked Sebastian—one of the former leaders in Nova Brasília, now living a hardscrabble life with his family on the outskirts of Caxias and suffering from Parkinsons's disease—what made work so hard to find these days. He answered, "The poor don't have a chance" ("O pobre não tem vez"), and went on to give his account, quoted earlier, of how jobs once done by several men had been taken over by a robot at the Campo Grande garbage dump.

Others speculated that international competition has raised the standards of production and thus the bar on educational and skill requirements for job entry, which would help explain why their educational gains have not been sufficient to break through to the most professional, prestigious, and highly paid jobs.

Two other considerations that arose in regard to globalization's impact were the new visibility of the consumer culture and the havoc wreaked by the international arms and drugs trade. Ubiquitous television images of a global consumer society have created new needs, especially among young people. The constant bombardment of images of status goods and markers of prestige (unattainable by everyone in the poor communities except those engaged in the drug trade)[20] has created a pseudo–reference group for youngsters. They feel deprived in relation to what they see.[21]

Local nonprofit organizations such as Afro Reggae and Nós do Morro have tried to reinforce the cultural identities of Afro Brazilians and of favela dwellers, but for the most part, the status symbols continue to be international brand-named shirts and sneakers, along with cars, motorcycles, cell phones, and pagers. As I mentioned earlier, I have seen young people wearing multiple pagers and cell phones (that do not work) as prestige signifiers. When the message of the global media is "You are what you own," the young urban poor begin to look to drug lords as their role models.

Other negative impacts attributed to globalization include homogenization, disrespect of local and national cultures, and lack of stewardship of natural resources. In the rush for jobs and profits, many cities have entered a race to the bottom—in terms of tax incentives and labor costs—combined with a universalized Western cultural and architectural veneer. As such, they have welcomed polluting factories and toxic dumping that do not meet the standards applied elsewhere, while failing to generate the jobs needed for those entering the labor force.

The lack of work has caused great uncertainty among the younger generation in Brazil. As reported at a UN panel on February 14, 2008, young people in Brazil are increasingly unable to get a foothold in the global labor market while job security is being eroded for the rapidly aging workforce.[22] Unemployment in Brazil has increased significantly since 1995, despite robust economic growth averaging 3.8 percent annually from 1998 to 2008 and a 16.5 percent increase (to 2.9 billion) in the number of people with jobs. Even for those who are currently working, employment is becoming less and less secure. According to Mario Barbosa, of the Brazilian Ministry of Work and Employment,

> Stiff competition under increased globalization has led to reduced job security, a reduction in job-related benefits, and a diminished role for organized labor. Precarious working conditions are now the rule rather than the exception. [Squatters and] migrants...face discriminatory treatment in the workforce that leads them to accept short-term contractual employment.[23]

The rising violence I discussed in chapter 7 is another manifestation of globalization. As Jailson, the founder of the observatório of Favelas explained "The main way that international trade is destroying the lives of Rio's poor is through the vast international market for drugs (particularly cocaine) and the imported supply of sophisticated arms (many from the United States), which the drug traffickers use to intimidate the police and take control of communities and the city."[24] His view was that if there were an international embargo on arms sales to Brazil, the violence and death rates would drop dramatically. Arms from the United States, Israel, and Russia account for the vast majority of those used in homicides by both police and dealers. The impact of open trade on the ease with which arms (and drugs) can enter the country is not negligible. The greater permeability of borders and the increased volume of imports and exports make it easier to move smuggled goods in both directions.

THE ROLE OF FOREIGN INVESTMENT

Our survey included one other question that sheds light on the changing perception of globalization from 1969 to 2003. In order to discover how people viewed the role of foreign companies in Brazil, the survey asked people to complete the statement "Foreign companies are in Brazil in order to..."; we then coded their responses according to the three categories (1) help Brazil to progress; (2) take care of their own interests; and (3) exploit the Brazilian people. (These options were not read to the interviewees—rather, their answers were recorded in full and then coded.) The valid percentages, based on the 85 percent who answered in 1969 and the 95.5 percent who responded in 2003, are shown in table 10.3.

Between 1969 and 2003, there was a decline in the percentage of favela residents who perceived global investment as positive. This may reflect not only the increased presence of foreign companies (and increasing difficulties for favela residents in getting jobs at such companies) but also the overall climate of skepticism about who benefits from international investment. In 2003, forty-five percent gave the most neutral response (to take care of their own interests),

TABLE 10.3   *Perceived Reasons for Foreign Companies to Be in Brazil*

Foreign companies are in Brazil in order to:	1969		2003	
	Frequency	*%*	*Frequency*	*%*
Help Brazil's progress	188	36.9	253	21.7
Take care of their own interests	191	37.5	522	44.8
Exploit Brazilians	131	25.7	391	33.5
Total	510	100.0	1,166	100.0

while over one-third saw the foreign companies as exploitive, taking advantage of Brazil's low wages, long hours, and less restrictive health, safety, and environmental regulations. The percentage who said they believed that foreign investment creates jobs and attracts capital that will grow Brazil's economy and eventually benefit the poor dropped by almost half. Still, one-fifth of the 2003 sample saw foreign investment as "helping Brazil." Further analysis is needed to explore the income, education, occupation, race, gender, and age of those who gave each answer.

In short, from the viewpoint of the urban underclass, globalization is seen as mostly irrelevant, and among those who do perceive an impact, only slightly more point out the negative effects than those who see the positive. It would seem, therefore, that the five premises listed at the beginning of this chapter are sound: globalization, if not deepening poverty per se, has certainly deepened inequality.

The issue of changes in living conditions again raises the question of how any contextual changes—whether at the international, national, or city level—materially affect the lives of the poor, regardless of whether they perceive the effects or not. Are those who fail to see the effects of globalization on their lives reflecting "false consciousness" or naïveté—or an accurate assessment of reality?

MICRO IMPACTS OF MACRO CHANGES

One of the major goals of our longitudinal research project was to see how the changes in the lives of the poor we followed correlated with changes in Brazil's politics, economy, and public policy. We used several approaches to explore these connections.

The study traced the chronology of benchmark changes in the economic, political, spatial, and policy contexts of Brazil as a whole and Rio specifically.[25]

To see if various periods coincided with fluctuations in the lives of favela residents, we used the year-by-year life history data we had collected and attempted to map periods of individual (and collective) upswings and downswings for such variables as unemployment, types of job, educational attainment, number of children, degree of crowding, and location/type of residence.[26]

We also asked each interviewee to specify the best and worst periods of his or her life in terms of economic well-being, employment (one's own and contributing members of one's household), and assets and overall financial security. We then plotted the timing of these periods against the opening of trade, the booms and busts of the Brazilian economy, and major policy changes—and against the poverty variations indicated in the life history data. No clear pattern emerged.

This lack of a correspondence between macro-level changes and changes in the lives of those we interviewed might be attributable to gaps in the interviewees' memories or their failure to make connections between larger trends and family fates. Likewise, it could be due to simple methodological flaws and/ or to the overwhelming number of intervening variables. We did, however, find two clear personal repercussions of structural or policy changes.

The first was in patterns of employment. Our life history data provided year-by-year occupational histories and for those working we asked whether they were formally employed (with a carteira assinada), self-employed, or doing odd jobs (biscates) on an irregular basis. The distinction between manual and nonmanual labor was the indicator that revealed the most consistent picture over time.

For each calendar year, we looked at the type of work perfomed by people between the ages of 16 and 31. Combining the life history data changes for each person in all three generations and in the new random sample revealed a progressive transition from manual to nonmanual occupations from 1954–2003. Figure 10.1 shows the results.[27]

The marked decline in the percentage of working-age favela residents doing manual labor and the concomitant rise in nonmanual labor are a direct reflection of structural changes in Rio's job market, which, in turn, was affected by national and international labor market trends. These shifts are undoubtedly a result of advanced capitalism and the globalization of labor, capital, information, and technology.

A second clear pattern also emerged from our interviews. As a result of the Real Plan, which tied Brazil's national currency to the U.S. dollar so as to curb inflation and increase global competitiveness, there was a consumption bonanza among the urban poor as their purchasing power rose and prices remained constant.

While many respondents had never heard of the Real Plan by name, they spoke about this one-time opportunity to acquire consumer durables at deflated prices. Family after family in each of the low-income communities proudly

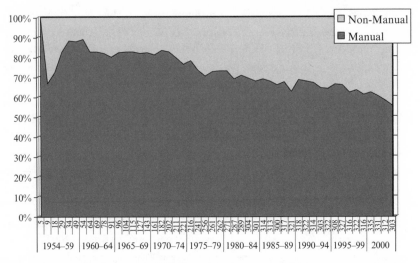

FIGURE 10.1   Decline in manual jobs and rise in nonmanual jobs, 1954–2003, based on life history matrices collected in 2001 and 2003. *Source*: Graph points represent the percentage of 16–31-year-olds who were working in each year, divided between manual and nonmanual, so they add up to 100%. The numbers of interviewees for each year is shown along the bottom axis. We include 1954–1960, but the numbers of interviewees who met the criteria in each of these years was under 50—too low to be significant.

showed off heavy wooden furniture, large television and sound systems, washer/ driers, and air conditioners, saying, "If we had not bought this when we did, we would never have been able to afford it again."

Despite these two suggestive findings, it was difficult to detect systematic reflections of macro changes in the lives of the favela residents. Personal upheavals such as illness, death, divorce, or loss of a job; natural disasters, such as floods and fires; and community-wide crises from forced resettlement to the closing of a nearby factory, school, or clinic, to the drug wars tended to obliterate (or at least obscure) the effects of larger but more removed changes. The uncertainties of daily life for people on the margins are so huge that they can hardly cope on a moment-to-moment basis, and there is no safety net to help them bounce back from crises.

IS GLOBALIZATION A DOUBLE-EDGED SWORD
OR A TWO-SIDED COIN?

Our study provides evidence of both positive and negative changes in the lives of favela residents between the preglobalization era and the current globally integrated era. Conditions have improved in many areas, but not all. The favela communities have become physically more integrated into the urban fabric as the city has expanded around them and transportation improvements have shortened commuting time. Infrastructures, services, access to domestic goods, and educational levels have improved. Although unemployment rates have risen, those who are working are more likely to be in "routine nonmanual" jobs, considered more respectable than blue collar jobs—although the pay is often lower and the hours longer.

The gap in living conditions between the study sites and the rest of the city has narrowed, not widened, on several quality-of-life indicators. This apparent catching up of the informal city with the formal appears to contradict the logic of globalization, which would predict that the poor become poorer, wealth would concentrate upward, and inequality would increase. On the other hand, such gains as the urban poor have made cannot be attributed to globalization. There are too many factors at play to determine cause and effect. The most recent migrants, who are now the poorest, do not share in the urban amenities accrued by those who came earlier. At present (2009), the new West Zone favelas have conditions similar to those in the study favelas in the late 1960s.

We know that city life offers more opportunity than rural life; that education, health, and incomes rise while birthrates drop; and that the diverse contacts made through "bridging networks" are extremely useful—sometimes life-saving. Following Granovetter's findings on "the strength of weak ties," it is no surprise that the longer a person is in the city, the greater the advantage.[28] Thus, with or without globalization, we would expect gains in living standards across time and generations. The argument that globalization hastened the rate of cityward migration would be spurious in the case of Rio, since the most rapid growth occurred during the 1950s and 1960s under the isolationist policies of import substitution, before globalization.

The complex relationships between poverty, inequality, and globalization for the case of Rio force us to look beyond the facile positions and ideological platitudes that often dominate the discourse. Unless nation-states and cities can forge an alternative social contract with the poor who service their needs, build their cities and homes, and produce and consume their products, the pattern of stunted development, missed opportunities, and wasted resources will continue to be self-replicating and self-fulfilling. What is needed may be a direct challenge to the comfortable culture of privilege that perpetuates itself at the expense of the common good.

eleven

REFLECTIONS ON PUBLIC POLICY

When I was a girl, my grandmother, who immigrated to New York in 1904 from a shtetl outside Kiev, would tell me, only half in jest: "Rich or poor, it's good to have money."

This saying has come to mind as I have been thinking about the policy implications of my Rio research. In addressing the urbanization of poverty and the marginalization of the poor I keep coming back to the question of livelihoods. As important as housing and urban services—even stipends—may be for improving the quality of life in the favelas of Rio, the people who live there would prefer to have work. In their world, no higher sign of respect can be paid to a person than to say that he or she is a worker, particularly a hard worker (*muito trabalhador*).

Above all, the residents of Rio's favelas want the opportunity to earn fair pay for decent work. When interviewed, they say they do not care whether their earnings were from *emprego* (employment in a formal job) or *trabalho* (self-employed, informal work). Their view is that given the opportunity to earn their living, they could solve most of their other problems on their own. I can imagine them smiling and nodding in agreement with my grandmother's saying. But for most of them, it is not only "good to have money" but even better to have a job. By being a worker, they become somebody.

What has often been seen pejoratively as a "culture of poverty" is not a culture at all but a pragmatic response to coping with harsh reality. If the urban poor had the opportunity to use their energy and skills to earn a decent living—as happened when the Indians in Vicos, Peru, became landowners—their purported self-defeating beliefs and behaviors would disappear as well as those excuses to justify their exclusion. Their values mirror those of the bourgeoisie, rather than set them apart.

One challenge of addressing the policy implications of a complex study such as this one is finding a meaningful level of discourse between systemic issues—such as the nature of capitalism, the persistence of poverty, or the tradition of exclusion—and the specific manifestations of those issues, such as lack of affordable housing, high unemployment, and appalling rates of lethal violence. The overarching questions of human rights, citizen rights, and the right to the city go beyond public policy to the need for negotiation of a new social contract between citizens and the state. Civil society, the collection of associations and people's organizations that occupy the space between the state and the market, is the arena in which Brazilians and Cariocas have been working to carve out such new arrangements—but there are no simple solutions and participation in itself is not a panacea.

I have divided this chapter into three sections. In the first one I review the evolution of public policies toward Rio's favelas from the 1964 military coup until 2009, tracing the turnaround from removal to upgrading. In the second I lay out three distinct approaches to thinking about policy initiatives. In the final section I focus on specific research findings and their policy implications in five areas—housing, land tenure, income generation, violence, and citizenship. The chapter concludes with some overall reflections based on listening to and learning from the people living on the edge.

As I described in chapter 2, the issue of favelas and other forms of informal settlements arose with the "urban explosion" that resulted from the "flood" of rural migrants to the big cities of Latin America, Asia, and Africa during the post–World War II period. Relatives and hometown friends followed the early pioneers into the cities and settled beside them in shantytowns, where they were close to jobs and urban amenities. The people who came were the most highly motivated among their compatriots in the countryside. These pioneers had both the vision and the means to seek a better life and wider horizons.

In response to this urban influx, all manner of policies and programs have been tried to stem the tide of cityward migration and limit city size. Failing to limit urban growth, the "gatekeepers" of the city—the planners and policymakers whose image of the city was one of order and beauty—were appalled as the informal settlements expanded outward into the urban periphery, upward into forested hillsides, and inward, densifying existing communities with new units built under, above, behind, and beside the initial dwellings. Toehold communities mushroomed into veritable squatter cities of their own.

In their hysteria over the swelling shantytowns, policy-makers failed to see that these communities were not problems but solutions to the lack of affordable housing.[1] The concept of the house as a thing or commodity began to give way to the concept of "housing as a verb,"[2] a process. Poor families built incrementally, buying a few bricks at a time, stacking them in the backyard and improving their homes as their resources permitted.

In addition to shelter, these self-built dwellings were, and continue to be, used for commerce, storage, service provision, light manufacturing, and meeting places of secular or religious nature. Sweets, drinks, cigarettes, matches, and other assorted items are sold from front windows; restaurants or bars with metal tables and chairs are set up outside, next to pool tables; beauty salons, barber shops, day care centers, evangelical meeting rooms, and Afro-Brazilian terreiros exist alongside a myriad of small manufacturing ventures within—and in front of—the houses. While many of these enterprises serve the local population (such as car and motorcycle repair, dressmaking, and baking), others are linked into national and even international companies as locations for off-site sweatshops. This cottage industry or "putting-out system" ties the informal settlement into the formal production process. For example, large car manufacturing plants have used the cheap labor of squatters working in their own homes to upholster car seats. The manufacturers (or their intermediaries) deliver raw materials—such as leather, stuffing, and buttons—to the homes and pick up the finished product, at which point it is sent for assembly with other parts that may have been made in other countries.

Those who enacted public policies to remove squatter settlements and relocate residents in social housing complexes did not consider the importance of the dwellings in earning family livelihoods. Such policies were equally indifferent to the importance of reciprocity and exchange networks in helping the poor cope with crises and calamities.

Thinking about how to integrate the morro and the asfato to the benefit of all depends on the way poverty is understood. Viewing the basis of poverty as deviant behavior, moral turpitude, or just plain laziness implies one line of policy. Viewing poverty as a systemic problem implies very different solutions. The tendency toward "blaming the victim"[3] has never led to a single useful policy. On the contrary, like debtor's prisons or criminalizing the poor, it has only made things worse.

SECTION ONE: EVOLUTION OF FAVELA POLICY IN RIO—FROM
RAZING FAVELAS TO RAISING FAVELAS

For a century, public policy responses to the favelas of Rio followed the model of "cutting out the cancer" from the healthy urban territory. In Rio, from the appearance of the first "favela" in 1897 through the last years of the dictatorship in 1985, public policy toward squatter settlements focused on their removal.

Ridding the city of squatters was the policy response to the (unfounded) view that favelas posed a threat to the city. In addition to the perceived criminality and immorality of the favela residents—categorized as the "undeserving poor"—there was also widespread fear that favelas were hotbeds of communism capable of fomenting revolution. It was the nightmare of the Right and the dream of the Left that the urban poor would be the vanguard of a popular uprising.

Despite all efforts to the contrary, favelas continued to grow, and to grow more rapidly than the rest of the city. Their growth, a combination of "pull" factors attracting people from the countryside to the city and "push" factors arising from landlessness, servitude and droughts in the Northeast, reflects the absence of housing alternatives. Even as I write these words, there is no affordable shelter for the millions of people living in favelas or for those who are about to arrive. With the return to democracy in 1985, and a quarter to a third of Rio's (voting) population living informally, the idea of on-site upgrading entered the policy discourse. The concept of upgrading or urbanizing favelas included opening up access roads for emergency vehicles, paving the main internal roads, replacing muddy slopes with concrete stairways, installing electrical, water, and sanitation systems, along with garbage collection and street lighting, and, in some cases, dredging sewage-filled canals and streams or building cable cars to transport people and goods up to the tops of communities.

Insofar as favelas were not considered part of the city, upgrading was not an option, but the times—and ideas—were changing. The idea of servicing favelas in place, seeded by research and writing in the 1960s about the potential for integrated workers' communities and the dire consequences of squatter removal,[4] was reinforced by the failure of "urban renewal" in the United States.[5] Some pilot projects were instituted in Rio, and the government gained experience such that by the mid-1990s it was possible to begin a large-scale upgrading program.

Despite this 30-year lag time between research/knowledge and policy/action and the fact that most favelas have not been urbanized, Rio is still in the forefront among cities worldwide. As of 2009, many local governments including those of Mumbai, Delhi, Dhaka, Johannesburg, Nairobi, Bangkok, Jakarta, and Cairo continue squatter eviction programs.[6] The political and financial costs of providing housing for hundreds of thousands of displaced persons are often the only deterrents to the bulldozer.

The story of favela policy in Rio is not entirely linear, but it does reveal an overall consistency of effort to rid the city of favelas up through a turning point around 1980.[7]

The following section provides a guide to the institutions, issues, and individuals involved in this policy shift.

The Players and the Policies

The policies to condemn, contain, discourage, and dismantle the first favelas in Rio from their inception at the end of the nineteenth century through the military coup in 1964 are described in chapter 1. The continuing policy history from 1964 to 2009 becomes ever-more complicated as new agencies (with new acronyms) are created while the old ones remain. This practice is part of what Brazilians sarcastically call the government's full employment policy. As a result, any serious discussion of favela policies in Rio warrants demystifying the myriad agencies and approaches involved—a service I endeavor to provide in the following pages.

1. Removal and Failure of "Popular Housing" to Reach the Poor: 1964–1970s BNH-Banco Nacional de Habitacão

In 1964, Brazil's National Housing Bank was created with the express purpose of financing the construction of low-income housing, referred to as "social housing" or "popular housing." The source of capital was the FGTS—Fundo de Garantía de Tempo do Serviço—Brazil's social security fund. Employees paid 8 percent of their monthly salaries into the fund, and the contributions were matched by employers, creating a vast account that became a model of housing finance in its time.

The housing financed by BNH was, in fact, too expensive to be popular or social. For many reasons, including unrealistically high standards of construction and underestimated costs of land, materials, infrastructure, and labor, prices per unit vastly exceeded what the poor could afford. The typical project consisted of "core" or "embryo" houses built on individual plots of land, with sufficient room for expansion as families grew. Public funds—the retirement savings of all the workers in the country—went to subsidizing housing for the middle-class, not the poor.

The priorities of favela residents and those of funders and politicians were diametrically opposed. For poor families the highest priorities were affordability (which meant incrementally building their own homes on-site as their earnings permitted), proximity to work and schools, access to urban services and security against eviction. The rest they could do themselves through "sweat equity," that is, contributing their labor individually and collectively. After all, they were the construction workers who built the city.

For government and BNH officials the main thing was the photo-op—at a ribbon-cutting ceremony in front of rows of colorfully painted little houses. They wanted rapid completion of the finished houses and rapid cost recuperation. Distance from the city or availability of public transportation were of no concern—they wanted the cheapest land possible. Thus the mismatch.[8]

CODESCO-Companía de Desevolvimento Comunitarío The Company for Community Development, started in 1968, was a radical counterexample to BNH, demonstrating the viability of upgrading favelas on-site. It was organized by a group of architects, economists, and planners who convinced the governor, Rio state, Negrão de Lima, to authorize a pilot project in three favelas—one on a hillside, one in a swamp, and one on flat, dry land. Community residents, although not given land title, were given assurance that they would not be removed. Long-term, low-interest loans were made available for building materials (purchased in bulk), and construction tools and equipment were shared. The state government brought in heavy machinery to widen the main access roads for emergency vehicles and installed basic urban infrastructure—water, sanitation, and electrical wiring; and created open space for schools, clinics, and soccer fields. The families whose shacks had to be taken down to make room for these public works were compensated with new homes in the same community.[9]

Little by little—as time and savings permitted—the wooden and scrap barracos were transformed into distinctive family homes and the communities evolved into thriving working-class neighborhoods, indistinguishable from their surroundings. Figures 11.1 and 11.2 show how the barracos looked in 1968 and the way one of the houses looked when I visited 15 years later (see figure 11.3).

Despite its popular success and promise of a low-cost, long-term solution to the integration of Rio's favelas into the urban context, CODESCO did not continue after 1969, when the three pilot projects were completed. The national

FIGURE 11.1   Barracos in 1968 before CODESCO began upgrading work.

FIGURE 11.2   Barracos in 1968 before CODESCO began upgrading work.

government remained firmly committed to favela eradication, and Rio's governor could not go forward with this approach.

The one goal that CODESCO could not achieve was legalizing land ownership in the favelas, an issue that remains unresolved to this day. Competing
claims of ownership, an outmoded system for resolving land disputes (requiring
each parcel to be adjudicated separately), and the absence of instruments for

FIGURE 11.3   Family improved houses on the same lot 15 years after CODESCO.

wide application of *usucapião* (Brazil's version of squatter's rights) account for an enormous backlog of cases.

CHISAM—Coordenação da Habitação de Interesse Social da Área Metropolitana As the national-level program to rid Rio of its favelas, CHISAM had the military might, political clout, and financial resources to prevail. From its inception in 1968 until its demise in 1975 it removed over 100 favelas, destroying more than 100,000 dwellings and leaving at least half a million poor people without their homes. The eradications were systematic and relentless, targeting the South Zone favelas first, where land values were the highest, and then continuing into the North Zone. The displaced families were relocated to distant conjuntos where they were placed—depending on their income levels—in one-room barracks, core houses, or conjuntos.

COHAB-GB—Companhia de Habitação Popular do Estado da Guanabara COHAB-GB, the state housing company, was the co-partner of CHISAM in the removal-and-resettlement process. In the early 1970s the city of Rio was still delineated by the former Federal District, and it comprised the State of Guanabara, separate from the State of Rio de Janeiro. By 1974 COHAB-GB had built 32 conjuntos with 40,277 units meant to house 215,000 displaced persons. In 1975 the states of Guanabara and Rio were fused into a single state of Rio de Janeiro, and functions of their housing companies were taken over by a new organization named CEHAB-RJ (Companhia Estadual de Habitação do Rio de Janeiro). CEHAB-RJ's mandate was to continue the eradication of favelas.[10]

The World Bank played a leading role in promoting on-site upgrading, starting in Dakar in 1972, at least 10 years before any national or local government undertook such a progressive initiative. It was the World Bank that fought to convince the Brazilian National Government to try on-site upgrading of favelas and "sites and services." On-site upgrading meant the installation of basic urban services—water, sanitation, electricity—in the squatter communities to serve the dwellings people had built for themselves; sites and services anticipates the future arrival of cityward migrants by providing urbanized subdivisions with individual plots of land for each family to build its own home. Such measures lower the cost per unit dramatically as compared with retrofitting the water and sewerage pipes around and under existing favela dwellings.

I saw for myself, as a consultant on a World Bank mission to Rio in 1978, how difficult it was to convince the BNH to adapt any project that would lower housing costs sufficiently to meet the needs of the poor. To get the Brazilians to try the alternate approach, the World Bank team made the approval of a large traditional "low-income" housing loan contingent on the inclusion of at least one upgrading and one sites-and-services project.

Promorar and Projeto Rio: The creation of Promorar in 1979 signaled the beginning of the sea change I referred to in the introduction to this chapter. It was a national-level program to urbanize favelas built in areas at risk of flooding. Most of these were *palafitas* (shacks built on wooden stilts) at the edge of the bay. This was the first project to provide structurally sound housing for squatters on-site since the aborted CODESCO experiment. In Rio, it began in the Complexo do Maré and was called "Projeto Rio." It was later replicated in five other favelas after proving successful.

Systematic favela removal slowed down after 1973 and stopped after 1975. What made the eradication policy fall out of favor? Did something cause CHISAM to go broke? Was there a change in the political tides with the beginning of the *abertura,* the political opening to democracy? Certainly the government did not change its attitude toward favelas overnight and become committed to a diverse urban landscape.

Removal/resettlement policies had cost the government dearly in both political and monetary capital. Calculations of cost recovery from the inhabitants' gradual purchase of the conjunto apartments were overly optimistic, and the political hostility of the removed squatters had not been fully anticipated. New conjunots could not be built fast enough to match the demand created by favela removal, and the conjuntos became a management and maintenance nightmare. Due to corruption in the construction process and lack of budgeting for maintenance, the conjuntos started to deteriorate within six months of completion (with water and sewerage leaking through the walls), and the supposed green areas became muddy garbage dumps emitting an awful stench. (See photo of Conjunto de Quitungo in chapter 3.)

Another factor was CHISAM's closing in 1975. While it had been successful in removing favelas, it had been a total failure in removing the causes of favela growth. In the late 1960s and the1970s, Brazil entered a high-growth period known as the "Economic Miracle," which brought more migrants than ever streaming into Rio. Jobs were abundant but salaries low, so the only place for the new workers to live was in favelas. The government realized it was fighting an uphill battle and since most of the families in the conjuntos were unable to meet their monthly payments, the state was unable to recover its costs.

In an attempt to create cash flow, the BNH began to finance large private construction companies to build housing for the middle and upper classes and to cut its support for the conjuntos. With no new conjuntos to receive displaced people from the favelas or from other conjuntos, it was pointless to continue evictions.

2. Mobilization and Experiments with Upgrading: The 1980s

Once democracy was restored in 1985, it became politically unrealistic to promote large-scale favela eradication since close to a third of the Rio electorate was living in favelas or other types of informal housing. At the same time, the federation of favela associations began to join forces with labor unions, student movements, and opposition political parties to demand their rights and push for direct elections and the creation of a National Assembly to write a new constitution.

In 1979, the Catholic Church created a grassroots outreach called the Pastoral da Favelas, which provided free legal assistance to favelas in their fight for land tenure. This effort (which grew out of the tradition of Liberation Theology and the mobilization of Base Communities—Comunidades Eclesiásticas de Base) had a legal assistance service that fought for land ownership. Their actions halted 17 evictions through lawsuits and organized legal defense committees that were set up in 33 favelas.[11]

This happened at about the time that Israel Klabin became Rio's Mayor and UNICEF helped to fund an ambitious program to urbanize Rocinha, one of the largest favelas in Brazil and in all of Latin America. The project was done with the unpaid labor (sweat equity) of the favela residents and became a point of reference for the future. In 1982, Leonel Brizola was elected governor of the State of Rio, with strong backing from favela residents. He had been a progressive politician who had to leave the country during the military dictatorship, and he returned to Brazil when political amnesty for the exiles was declared.

All of these changes took place as the dictatorship was winding down, during the process known as the abertura. During this period, the municipal and state governments undertook several initiatives to upgrade favelas. Although there was no immediate successor to CODESCO, the experience had set a precedent, so that after the return to democracy in the mid-1980s, a series of variations on CODESCO followed, including local and state government initiatives, *Project Mutirão* (Collective Self-Help) and *Cada Família Um Lote* (Each Family a Land Parcel).

Projeto Mutirão (1983–84), was the first initiative to compensate residents for their sweat equity in the upgrading of their own communities. The project started with construction of sanitation infrastructure and eventually included roads and community centers. The municipality paid the favela workers the minimum wage. This project was the first of several municipal-level interventions aimed at urbanization, and the lessons learned were essential to the larger scale projects that followed. Projeto Mutirão installed infrastructure in portions of 15 favelas, including Rocinha, the largest favela in the South Zone.

Cada Família Um Lote: Launched in 1983 by Governor Brizola, this was the state government's equivalent of the municipality's Projeto Mutirão. Its goal was to provide *land ownership,* water, and sewerage to 1 million poor families in the state. This project fell far short of that goal, but it did succeed in granting some 23,000 title deeds and upgrading two favelas in the city of Rio. It also contributed to a change in mentality and to the practical experience of how to incorporate favelas into the formal city.

In 1985, the year democracy returned in Brazil, the city's *Five-Year Plan* proposed that the favelas be fully incorporated into the city and receive all neighborhood-level services including formal recognition of their existence, street paving, street lighting, door-to-door mail delivery, and daily garbage collection. The five-year plan never went beyond the planning stage due to a political crisis that paralyzed the city of Rio.[12]

3. Urbanization Reaches Scale: 1990s–2007

In the 1990s, the Plano Director (Master Plan) for the city of Rio picked up the thread of the dormant five-year plan, stipulating the inclusion of favelas in urban services. The tax collection system had been decentralized, so the municipality had a new source of revenue with which to fund upgrading projects in favelas.

During the first mandate of Mayor Cesar Maia (1993–97), several particularly heavy rainstorms again caused flooding and erosion in the hillside favelas. Dozens of homes were washed away in these torrential rainstorms, and untold numbers of community residents were killed. The homes that remained were inundated with sewage as the open sewage canals overflowed with rainwater. In response, the city government initiated the Reforestation Program.

Reflorestamento-Mutirão Remunerado (Reforestation-Remunerated Self-Help): This program involved planting rapidly growing edible vegetation such as fruit trees and vegetables on the topmost areas of the favela hillsides, with the triple functions of fixing the soil against erosion, discouraging new settlement further up the hillsides, and improving nutrition. To prevent human waste from mixing with rainwater canals and overflowing during the rainy season, the city installed closed sewerage pipes, leaving open canals for rainwater only. Additionally, the program had an educational component involving health and nutrition and internships for youth, who could also work at off-site greenhouses.

Reforestation was a clear departure from the exploitative practice of expecting or requiring unemployed favela residents to provide free labor for government projects in their communities. For the first time at a large scale, the municipality agreed to pay community workers rather than oblige them to "volunteer." Local residents with the requisite skills were given priority in hiring for these jobs, and the community had input into (although not control over) certain management and design decisions.[13]

Favela-Bairro, Phase I (1994–2000): With the experience of the Reflorestamento Program, the municipality was ready to undertake a more ambitious initiative. In 1994 they launched Favela-Bairro, with the goal of integrating the favelas into their surrounding neighborhoods through infrastructure upgrading, public works, and design elements such as public plazas at the entrances to the communities. Fifteen favelas, ranging in size from 500 to 2,500 dwelling units, were selected for the first round. There was an open competition for the contracts. The city government worked with the Brazilian Institute of Architects on the request for proposals and the (anonymous) selection of 15 winners. Each selected team was assigned to one of the 15 favelas. In that way, some of the youngest and most innovative firms—such as Arquitraço—were able to try

FIGURE 11.4   Reforestation Project, 1987. Edible plants, bushes, and trees grow on the hillside above this favela.

their hands in this uncharted territory, and a variety of approaches could be tested and compared.[14]

Once the project started, the city government sought support from the Urban Division of the Inter-American Development Bank, and by 1995 had secured a five-year grant of $180 million dollars with a commitment of further funding dependent on outcomes. The Caixa Econômica Federal also recognized the potential in the program and entered with federal funding. A more formalized bidding process was developed, requiring specification of costs and timeframes.

Favela-Bairro took Rio's experience with remunerated self-help a step further, not only paying workers but hiring program managers from the community members who already had experience in favela upgrading. By the end of the first phase, 52 favelas and 8 loteamentos irregulars had been beneficiaries of the program.

Favela-Bairro Phase II (2000 to 2005): Over the next five years the project was continued, adding an additional 62 favelas and 24 loteamentos, which brought the total number participating to 114 favelas and 24 loteamentos. The work plan included project components in education, health, skills training, and community development and also projected experiments with microcredit, income generation, and property rights recognition. But these components made no headway at all.

A ten-year anniversary celebration of Favela-Bairro was held at the Inter-American Bank headquarters in Washington, DC, in 2005 to much acclaim. It was recognized as the most ambitious squatter upgrading program in the world.

Upgrading Continues (2005 to 2008): Project completion was delayed in some of the favelas when contractors gave up and walked away from the job, having miscalculated the cost of the work or the difficulty of the working conditions. The city continued to add favelas to the program with the knowledge that funding for Phase III had been approved by the Inter-American Development Bank (IADB). By 2008 Favela-Bairro had reached a total of 168 favelas and loteamentos—affecting over half a million people.

Inspired by this success, the city spun off two upgrading projects of its own: one called Bairrinho, for small favelas with fewer than 500 units and the other, Grandes Favelas, for those with over 2,500 units. Work has already begun in several of the largest favelas such as Rocinha in the South Zone, Jacarezinho in the North Zone, and Rio das Pedras in Jacarepaguá,or the West Zone.[15]

One of the most interesting experiences in this regard is the Celula Urbana (Urban Cell) in Jacarezinho, developed by Lu Petersen in collaboration with the German Bauhaus-Dessau Foundation. European architects and designers who visited favelas found a visual reference to the walled medieval city in the narrow, winding streets, the densely clustered buildings, and the individually built dwellings blending into a coherent visual style. A team from Germany worked with the Rio team to design a plan that would open up the densest areas to light and air, create a central open-space to anchor community gatherings and provide better access to the rest of the city.

The plan includes a modernistic three-story community center designed with space for the Residents' Association, a concert hall, meeting rooms, computer classrooms, art studios, and a video lab. The idea is that the center will act as a magnet for community activities and its tower will be visible from all parts of the community. Households in the most dense and airless locations (some without windows or light aside from the front door) will be relocated within the community to humanize living conditions and reduce health hazards, particularly respiratory disease. A *passarela* (walkway) over the main highway will open up access to an underutilized territory for development of an educational center and small business incubator. Thus far, the project has created one square block of this urban cell and is now being run by the state government, with funding from the national Accelerated Growth Program.[16]

Favela-Bairro, Phase III (initiated 2008): Funding for Phase III was held up for nearly three years by political party rivalries between the city and federal governments and concerns about Rio's overextended debt capacity (whose limits are set as a percentage of net revenues). The city managed to obtain a waiver because the funds were going to an ongoing project, not a new one. The terms of Phase III were negotiated between the IADB and Mayor Cesar Maia before his term was over, and the funds were released in 2008. By 2009 work had begun in six more favelas, and many others had completed project preparation and were ready to begin work.

The list of favelas to be included and their order of priority had been approved at the beginning of Phase I by the city council, so the ones next in the pipeline had been working with the municipality to get ready.

Several evaluations, both internal and external, had been conducted on Favela-Bairro, and the planning for Phase III took the constructive suggestions into account—while trying to avoid becoming a catchall for everyone's favorite issue. Increased emphasis was placed on social investments such as day care centers, education for youth and adults (offering high school equivalency certification), computer courses, after-school cultural and sports programs, and violence mitigation. The violence mitigation approach will be incremental and will target domestic violence, order in the streets (such as fines for littering), and include sports and skills training to young men ages 4–21. It will also encourage the communities to identify "hot spots" of violence and provide them with resources to do their own diagnostic of the problem, establish baseline data, and monitor the impact of the programs.

As my research also showed, the evaluators of Favela-Bairro did not see much interest in or demand for microcredit in the favelas, so that idea was dropped. The most worrisome aspect in my assessment is that along with these proposed social programs there will be a monitoring of favela growth, which may include containing walls such as those shown in the photograph of Santa Marta in chapter 1.

Did Favela-Bairro Bring the Morro and Asfalto Closer?

As impressive as upgrading 168 favelas may be, that number represents only 16.5 percent of the 1,020 favelas in Rio as of July 2009.[17] There is a long way to go and a lot to be learned both from what worked and what might have worked better.

When I was conducting the field research during 2001–2003, Phase I of Favela-Bairro had already been completed and Phase II was well underway. I was surprised to discover how few of the 2,200 people we interviewed had heard about Favela-Bairro or knew anything about it. True, none of the favelas I worked in had been part of the project, but I would have thought it would have been a topic of discussion within all favela communities. There was evidently little or no coverage of the program in the news, and the only publicity I saw was a small, unimpressive exhibit at Santos Dumont, the Rio domestic airport. I still wonder whether the lack of publicity was part of a larger strategy to limit expectations, the result of a limited budget for outreach, or simply an oversight.

I was interested in Favela-Bairro, and I visited dozens of the project communities between 1999 and 2008. In each one I spent time talking with residents, interviewing current and former community leaders and generally observing what was going on. I reasoned that the favelas that had participated in earlier upgrading experiences, starting with CODESCO, would be more prepared to take advantage of the project and better able to mobilize community participation. I was wrong. Too much time had passed, and the people who had been involved in and who carried the institutional memory of previous projects had been marginalized by the new leadership installed by the drug traffic. In many instances I found that the records of past meetings and community events had been destroyed or disappeared or that the entire Residents' Association building had been set on fire by the new directors.

Nonetheless, there was a buzz of excitement and activity centered around the on-site construction offices in the communities where the work was in progress. In newly completed favelas the physical and visual improvements were impressive: litter-free streets, clean-flowing water in the canals and small rivers, open plazas, look-out points at vistas, paved roads, and street lighting. I saw well-designed multiunit homes full of light and air for families whose houses had to be moved to make room for the public works. There were day care centers, women's sewing cooperatives, televised courses (which grant credit through a local teacher), and permanent stalls and shops for street vendors. The before and after visuals were impressive. Some of the favelas, including Parque Royale (shown in figures 11.4 and 11.5) became "poster children" for the program.

FIGURES 11.5 AND 11.6   Favela Parque Royale on the Ilha do Governador close to the campus of the Federal University of Rio de Janeiro, before and after Favela Bairro. Images courtesy of the Secretary of Housing, Rio Municipal Government, 2004.

In the aftermath of the upgrading the results were dramatic in all participating communities.

Some communities had fought to preserve a small historic chapel or a place of symbolic significance and had won. The drug traffic seemed to have evaporated and residents were proud and optimistic. The only complaint I heard during my first round of visits was that families were responsible for connecting the utility lines from the roads to their own homes. In some cases the households could not afford to do this or installing utilities meant digging up living room floors, which residents had finished using costly hardwood flooring.

When I returned to the same favelas on later visits however, reality had set in. Things were different in each place, and some of the work teams had involved the community more than others—but for the most part, I saw that the residents did not feel a sense of *ownership* over the improvements that had been made. Once the presence of the government dissipated with the closing of the community construction offices, people told me that things began to deteriorate and revert to their earlier conditions. People who had had jobs with the construction were unemployed again; others had lost their livelihoods when their work areas (for car repair or metal recycling) were "regularized," meaning moved or closed.

The newly dredged, cleaned, and lined waterways with clear flowing water that I saw a few years earlier had reverted to the public garbage and sewage receptacles they had once been; the internal plazas were not much used, and the ones facing the street were not well maintained; garbage and graffiti were everywhere; and the drug traffic had returned. In one case, the ancient shade tree in the small green area where the elderly sat to cool off and relax had been cut down and the greenery paved over as a way to eliminate hiding places for the traffic. In its stead there were blue, yellow, and red high gloss metal chairs, benches, and minimalist play equipment that became burning hot in the sun, making the convivial gathering place unusable.

These observations notwithstanding, the quality of life in the favelas that were part of Favela-Bairro was significantly better than in those that had not been reached by the program. The fact that they had been beneficiaries of public investment gave those communities greater assurance that they would not be removed, even though land title issues remained unresolved. The installation of urban infrastructure made every aspect of life easier and healthier. And the experience of having been the object of government attention for the duration of the construction period gave the community a sense that they were no longer invisible in the eyes of the government. Feeling that they were recognized was an intangible but important change.

Critics of Favela-Bairro had anticipated "white expulsion," the term used for the program's gentrification (to distinguish it from the forced evictions of earlier times). They argued that once urban services and a degree of legitimacy reached the favelas, they would become more desirable, real estate prices would rise, and residents, instead of remaining in place and benefiting from these improvements, would be tempted to sell to buyers in higher income brackets and start over in worse favelas further away. In my observations, this did not happen, or if it did, it was on a very small scale. First, there was not much demand for buying in favelas that were not close to the center and South Zone (whose prices were already inflated); second, people were accustomed to living in their communities, had friends, relatives, and support networks there and perhaps jobs nearby so there was not much interest in moving out—especially into unknown favelas further away. The profits to be made selling would be insufficient to buy in more desirable locations, much less to move to the asfalto.

Room for Further Improvement

In hindsight, it is easy to find things that might have worked better. Favela-Bairro was a bold leap forward but it was not "the best." There are no "best practices," only practices that are better than others at a particular time and place. Once an innovative idea reaches implementation and then becomes routinized, its internal contradictions present new challenges to be addressed.[18]

In the case of Favela-Bairro, regardless of how much was spent on urban infrastructure, paving pathways and roads, dredging and cleaning canals, building open plazas and introducing urban design elements, it did not succeed in integrating the favelas into their surrounding neighborhoods. There is no doubt in anyone's mind where the asfalto ends and the morro begins.

The economic manifestation of this spatial divide is clear from the data comparing average incomes of favela and nonfavela individuals in Rio. Average incomes in South Zone neighborhoods are five to six times greater than in neighboring favelas. Even in the mostly low income West Zone, nonfavela incomes are 1.5 times greater than in favelas. The stigma attached to living in a favela runs too deep to be obliterated by appearances. In the eyes of most residents of surrounding neighborhoods, favelas remain "subnormal agglomerations" rather than "areas of special interest," their new designation in urban planning jargon.

While both phases of Favela-Bairro included a social investment component that, on paper, included income generation, very little was accomplished in these areas. Even day care centers built as part of the program found themselves without funding for staff and thus remained empty and closed. Since the project was focused primarily on building, the subcontractors involved were mostly architects and engineers, and the work was done by construction companies. It is not surprising that the physical components trumped the social ones.

The financing bodies were likewise more experienced in large-scale infrastructure projects than in social investment, so they tended to prioritize the former. So-called soft development, which includes social, educational, cultural, and local economic development (and funding for qualified teachers, skills mentors, and day-care workers), tends to be more labor intensive, more place specific, more difficult to evaluate, and less likely to show visible short-term results.

I wonder whether spending the same amount of financial and administrative resources over the past 15 years on "upgrading" the earning capacity of the residents (and on other priorities they have articulated) would have had greater impact on their integration. The closer they become to working-class communities, the easier such integration will be—and the residents believe that their visual appearance, urban services, and safety will follow from their ability to earn their own income.

Even in terms of the physical upgrading, several people who live in the least accessible parts of their communities said that the urban infrastructure and services did not reach the poorest part of the favela where they live.

For me, the greatest cause for concern is that there was little sense of community pride or ownership once the construction crews left the sites and the project offices were closed. This bespeaks a lack of community engagement in priority-setting and decision-making. The best intentioned and most experienced professionals, nonprofit directors, or community leaders cannot speak for the residents, and unless the residents have an influential voice in the process and outcomes, they will remain "clients" rather than "players."

The Presence of the State

The issue of community control remains to be resolved, but the sense of abandonment that occurred with the closing of the on-site offices during construction has begun to be addressed by the city government. By 2004 new city government offices had been set up around Rio, each serving several Favela-Bairro communities. These offices are called POUSOs, or Posto de Orientação Urbanistica e Social (Urban and Social Orientation Centers). They are staffed by a handful of architects, engineers, and social workers who are there during working hours and attend to people on a drop-in basis.

One of the POUSO's functions is to provide favela residents certificates of occupation, called *Habite-se*, which give holders the right to own their homes and a permit to live in them despite the fact that residents do not own the land upon which their homes are built. This document does not have juridical standing as far, but it does accomplish two goals: it gives the families an increased sense of legitimacy and consequently the freedom to invest in their dwellings, and it provides a way to prevent housing deterioration by making the issuing of the document contingent on an analysis of the structural soundness of each dwelling. Although the idea was a good one, there were too few POUSOs to make a difference and the program was weak and underfunded.

This is about to change. The third phase of Favela-Bairro anticipates a POUSO in every one of the participating communities, starting with 56 new ones, 30 of which are fully funded. The POUSOs will maintain a government presence in each favela after the construction phase is completed and will serve as the focal point for social projects. They will include social assistance referral centers (Centros de Referencia de Assistencia Social-CRAS), which will refer people to the appropriate agencies for family support. A process of monitoring and evaluation is being created to provide an ongoing feedback loop for learning what is working and not.[19]

SECTION TWO: ANGLES OF APPROACH TO POLICY-MAKING

Policy Cannot Solve All Things for All People

There are limits to what may be accomplished through public policy. The way Brazil is inserted into global markets at the transnational level may fluctuate and the way personality traits are expressed at the individual level may change over time, but in both cases they are largely beyond the reach of policy interventions.

At the global level, flows of capital, labor, information, and ideas are not controlled by any overarching authority or policy-setting institution. The images that reach the favelas through the Internet or television give them access to ideas from the world over, creating new "needs" for contemporary status symbols while technological advances displace unskilled labor.

At the other end of the spectrum are individual differences, personality traits, and family characteristics that are beneath the radar of social policy. Even within the same family, our study showed, some siblings did much better over the course of their lives than others. Ascribed characteristics such as skin color or gender and acquired characteristics such as educational level or occupation exist alongside differences in intelligence, appearance, charm, and enthusiasm. Interviews with the most successful survivors in our sample showed that traits such as persistence, optimism, and the ability to plan ahead enabled some to take advantage of opportunities that came their way and to pursue opportunities that others might not have perceived.

Between these two extremes lies what Manuel Castells has called the "space of place."[20] My research over the past four decades has shown that proximate events such as a factory closing or an outbreak of dengue fever have greater impact on family well-being than most local or national public policies. Central location within the urban fabric and daily contact with a diversity of middle- and upper-class people, such as the residents of Catacumba enjoyed, confers a lifetime of advantage. The networks and contacts made in the course of simply living and working in the South Zone were of direct help in getting work.

Favela residents who made such contacts could use the address of their boss or *patroa* to give their children access to the good public schools and better health care in wealthier neighborhoods. They could also look to financially successful people as models for how to dress, speak, and comport themselves. Locating poor families amid the rich and building social networks across classes are not easily attained through policy instruments.

In the space of place, people live their lives and raise their families. They are the ones best equipped to find the niches for action between the market and the state or in the interstices between the global and the individual. Experience has shown the vital importance of their knowledge and "know-how" (as well as "know-who") in problem-solving, yet it is rarely sought. Even when participation of local residents is mandated, they are rarely heard or heeded. This is an arena of practice, not policy.[21]

Knowledge and Agency

There is never a simple one-to-one correspondence between research findings and policy recommendations. Understanding the changing reality of marginality in Rio's favelas is a formidable task unto itself. Deeper understanding of the issues covered in the preceding chapters does not determine how best to address them.

Even so, it would be cowardly to avoid examining the research findings from this study with an eye toward their policy relevance. If the empirical and ethnographic evidence is not used to inform the debate about what is to be done, we will be stuck with our existing understandings, beliefs, and positions.

Three Approaches to Public Policy

I see three distinct ways to deal with the challenge of integrating marginalized populations into the city: (1) place-based approaches, (2) poverty-based approaches, and (3) universal approaches. Place-based approaches target defined *territories of exclusion,* such as favelas, conjuntos, or irregular loteamentos. Poverty-based approaches target individuals or families that fall below a defined poverty line, regardless of where they live. Since not everyone living in favelas is poor and not every poor person lives in a favela, this approach implies that some favela families would not be eligible for this type of program and some nonfavela families would be eligible. Universal approaches are those that apply equally to everyone in the city or country, regardless of location, property title, income, or assets. The three approaches are not mutually exclusive—they are each an essential piece of the puzzle. I address them below as they apply to the case of Rio.

Place-based approaches target stigmatized communities as a whole without distinguishing among the income levels of the inhabitants. They include all upgrading and community development programs mentioned in the policy history section of this chapter. These programs, whether they revolve around housing improvements, urban infrastructure, social services, or local economic development, are defined and delineated by a territorial boundary.

Favela-Bairro is the culminating example of this approach. Earlier in this chapter I discussed the strengths and weaknesses of Favela-Bairro and its potential evolution in its next phase. My specific research findings about housing and land use are presented in the concluding section of this chapter.

The poverty-based approach in Brazil is Bolsa Família, a national program that provides low-income families with a monthly stipend, deposited into a debit account. It grew out of several separate programs begun during the presidency of Fernando Henrique Cardoso and has been consolidated and extended during the two terms of President Luis Ignácio Lulu da Silva. In many ways the concept is akin to the long-debated "negative income tax," except that the stipends—called Conditional Cash Transfers, or CCTs—are provided only upon fulfillment of certain obligations, such as school attendance, prenatal care, infant inocuations, and/or elder care.

This program serves the dual purposes of helping low-income families meet their basic needs, while encouraging them to invest in the health and education of the next generation. Critics contend that it is really a large-scale political patronage system designed to secure votes for the Labor Party and perpetuate dependence on government beneficence. It may be both, but it has already succeeded in reducing national inequality levels.

The CCT system works through the female heads of households, who are considered most likely to use the stipends for their families' basic needs. A stipend is provided for each child who remains in school. This removes the incentive for parents to take their children out of school to help support the family, particularly in the countryside. There are additional stipends for the care of elderly family members, regular doctor visits, and so on. Although the amounts received are modest, the payments have had a notable impact, particularly in the rural areas. In the poorest states of the Northeast, up to 70 percent of families are being helped through the program. Nationwide, as of January 2009, Bolsa Família was benefiting over 11 million poor families—about one-fifth of the national population.[22]

The absolute number and percent of beneficiaries is much lower in the cities than in the countryside, since eligibility levels are set at the same level for the entire country, rather than adjusted for differences in cost of living. As of 2007, Bolsa Família had reached 139,000 of 1,370,000 families in Rio de Janeiro, fewer than one in ten.[23]

If it has not already been done, the implication of this finding would be to adjust the eligibility level for Bolsa Família according to purchasing power parity, which takes the cost of living into account. This is already done in setting the minimum wage for different regions. The adjustment in eligibility for Bolsa Família, if determined not by income levels but by the cost of a standard *cesta básica* (basket of goods), would mean inclusion of a much higher percentage of urbanites. In Rio, even selling candy, shining shoes, or performing clown acts for cars at traffic lights generates higher cash earnings than living on the land, but may not mean a higher standard of living.

The other policy implication is the need to tailor and target program components to the specific needs of each age group: children, adolescents, adults raising families, and the elderly. I would imagine this too is already being done.

Universal approaches address such individual issues as the right to safety, decent housing, and equal protection under the law. The "right to the city" includes the freedom to use public space, to move about at will, to participate in the job market, to be treated with respect, and to have a voice in decisions about the city's future. Workers rights were instituted by Getulio Vargas, president of Brazil from 1930–45. These include the pension system, the minimum wage, and the right to organize labor unions. The pension system is currently the major source of support, if not the only source, for many of the original study participants, who in turn support their children and their grandchildren. In response to the survey question "Who is the politician who has most helped you and people like you?" the most frequent answer was *not* the Rio mayor responsible for Favela-Bairro but Getulio Vargas, whose worker protections often make the difference between living and starving.

Participatory budgeting is another good example of a universal approach. It was initiated in Porto Alegre in the early 1990s when the Labor Party was elected with the pledge to make city government transparent and accountable. The city budget allocations for capital improvements, maintenance, and service delivery are broken down by neighborhood and made public so that each neighborhood can see what it is receiving relative to every other neighborhood. Initial meetings are held within the neighborhoods to set priorities for the coming year's budget. Then meetings are held among and between the neighborhoods to negotiate which needs are most pressing in which localities Rather than the expected competition, Rebecca Abers, who studied the process, discovered the emergence of what she calls "negotiated solidarity." She documented the way a spirit of collaboration emerged once needs were compared among communities.[24] Although there have been differences in the degree of decentralization and participation in Porto Alegre as the city government has changed over the past 15 years, the concept has caught on and been adapted by many other cities in Brazil (starting with those controlled by the Labor Party) and by many cities all over the world, who have formed a network for mutual support and exchange of experiences.[25]

The Three Approaches Combined

In some cases all three of these approaches come together. Brazil's Growth Acceleration Program, known as the PAC (Programa de Aceleração do Crescimento) is one such program. It was launched in 2007, during a time of high rates of economic growth and a large national surplus. It combines place-specific investment in favela upgrading, poverty-based investment in new housing construction for families with fewer than five minimum salaries, and universal-based elements of economic growth, job creation, and income redistribution. Its stated objectives are "to reduce income inequality in Brazil through poverty reduction and the inclusion of millions of citizens in the formal job market" and to make long-term improvements in infrastructure that will be conducive to business investment.[26] In Rio, the focus is on urbanization of the large favelas, building affordable housing and thereby stimulating the growth of the construction industry.

The president himself travelled to the Morro de Alemão to announce the program, generating great excitement and high expectations. When I was in Nova Brasília in October 2008 work had already begun widening the main entrance road into Nova Brasília to install large-diameter sewerage pipes. Most people I spoke with knew about the PAC although no one was clear on how long it would last or whether it would end up as yet another unfulfilled promise.

The plan for the area includes a cable car to connect the more remote parts of Nova Brasília to bus lines and a rail station on the main road and building subsidized low-income apartments on the site of a nearby abandoned factory.[27]

The skepticism of my favela friends was not without basis. The global recession has already lowered Brazil's growth projections for 2009, and the PAC work schedule is already behind its targets. On June 3, 2009, *Business News Americas* reported that a recent study found only 3 percent of PAC projects had been completed in two years. The following day they reported the government correction that as of April 30, 2009, 14 percent of the 2,446 projects being monitored had been completed—not an encouraging sign.[28]

The policy benefits of combining the three approaches would be the ability to coordinate and supplement rather than overload or overlook. But promising all things to all people is not a road map for success. Many component programs and policies are already in place in each of the three categories, but they are rarely considered in concert. The result is that even the boldest policies are not reaching their full potential. For example, if upgrading of favelas and conjuntos was coordinated with Bolsa Família to help individual families meet their basic needs, and if job and income generation initiatives of the PAC were worked out by local residents, each program would build on the other rather than remaining in its separate silo. And as long as we are in the subjunctive— if this were part of a city-wide participatory budgeting process that included city residents in the setting of priorities, the invisible people might start to become visible.

In thinking about the way to combine the three approaches and refine the planning process, I would take into account such issues as:

- *Time frame.* What measures can be taken in the short, medium, and long terms?
- *Agency.* Which citizens, civil society organizations, public sector agencies, and private businesses would be required to initiate, and implement, each measure?
- *Collaboration.* What type of partnerships would be needed among the stake-holders and how could they develop mutual trust?
- *Scaling up.* How could successful initiatives, often birthed at the grassroots level, be brought to scale without compromising the integrity that made them work?
- *Obstacles and opponents.* What barriers might be faced, which groups might be threatened or institutions opposed—and how to overcome these barriers and threats?
- *Windows of opportunity.* What openings might occur, in the political context, for moving forward and how to take advantage of them?[29]
- *Sharing approaches that work.* How can solutions that have worked in one context be useful in similar circumstances elsewhere, and how can the peer-to-peer exchange that makes this work be fostered?[30]

SECTION THREE: RESEARCH FINDINGS AND THEIR
POLICY RELEVANCE

Among the many issues that arose in my interviews with community residents, nonprofits, local, national, and transnational policy-makers, and scholars (1) informal housing; (2) land tenure; (3) jobs and income generation; (4) drugs and violence; and (5) citizenship and the right to the city.

Informal Housing: Favelas, Conjuntos, Loteamentos

Several unexpected findings turned up in my study. While some of my conclusions in *The Myth of Marginality* are as true today as they were when the book came out in 1976—such as the asymmetric insertion of the poor into the city system—I have since reversed my view on some of the book's recommendations, based on what I have learned from taking a longitudinal approach.

This shows how misleading project evaluations can be, particularly as they are usually conducted shortly after program completion. It is also a sobering reminder that research done at a single point in time—which includes nearly *all* research—may not provide a sound basis for policy guidance.

Two areas in which this new study necessitates a revision of my earlier findings are the long-term benefits of living in favelas and conjuntos and the importance (or not) of land tenure for favela residents.

Conjuntos turned out to be an advantage in the long run, rather than the disaster that the residents had experienced and I had observed in the short term. In *The Myth of Marginality*, based on hundreds of interviews I conducted in the conjuntos in 1973 just three years after the removal of Catacumba, I argued that putting people into the North Zone conjuntos was an unmitigated disaster. I reported how it had disrupted every aspect of life for the families. The stories I heard, some of which I have quoted in earlier chapters, were horrendous. My observations and conversations affirmed that the move had been devastating to the health and well-being of the residents. Their family incomes declined to half of former levels at the same time that they assumed paying monthly installments on their apartments and fees for urban services (which had been free in the favelas). Transportation to and from work, which had also been free as it was primarily done on foot or bicycle, cost as much as a quarter of previous family income, such that only one person per family could afford the commute to work in the South Zone. In Catacumba, men had typically supplemented their primary incomes with a second job or freelance work on evenings and weekends. Women took in laundry for the madames in the nearby neighborhoods and sent their children to deliver the washed and ironed clothing. Children did *biscates* (odd jobs) after school and on weekends, also contributing to the family income.

Bus fare from the conjuntos to work cost the equivalent of a fourth of a typical monthly salary, which meant that only the main wage earner could afford it. The trip added almost two hours each way onto 10-hour workdays and necessitated rising before dawn to stand in line for a place, even standing up, on the bus. Anyone arriving late to work could easily be fired on the spot, so none of these workers could risk it.

Worse still, the monthly payments for the conjunto apartments had been calculated on the basis of surveys of total family incomes *before* the move. They were much too high to be sustained on the shrunken family earnings after removal. Those who fell into arrears were at risk of being sent to triage houses (described in chapter 3). Community leaders were not relocated with the rest, so as to avoid any mobilization, and no one ever found out where they went. Families, friends, and neighbors were separated according to income and number of children. Moved from being surrounded by supportive networks, families found themselves living next to people they had never met. Many suffered from stress-related diseases, and dozens died.

Schools, clinics, day care, commercial space for those who had supported themselves through selling or sewing from home, recreation areas for the youth—none of these urban amenities for which these families had come to the city existed in the conjuntos.

The transition was indeed devastating, and many of the old-timers are still "grieving for a lost home."[31] It took quite a while for the benefits of the move to become apparent. If I had not returned three decades later, I would never have known that, on balance, moving from favelas to conjuntos turned out to be advantageous for most people, and for their children. Over time, making monthly payments for the apartments, for water and electricity, and having a legitimate street address conferred a sense of pride and legitimacy on people that had been inaccessible to them in the favelas. They also had an easier time getting jobs once they had legal addresses to use. It is true that there is little room for expansion to accommodate new family members in the conjuntos and that they do not have the status of the asfalto, but overall those in the conjuntos have done better than those who stayed in the favelas, in terms of jobs, income, education, and level of consumer goods (i.e., the components of SES), as well as in overcoming stigma. This is not to say that if they had become landowners in Catacumba that they would not be better off than they are today. There is no reliable way to test that theory, although I did try.[32]

What I can report is that after the initial shock and adaptation, many people felt a personal pride in having prevailed and gone on with their lives; and for their children, being raised in a conjunto rather than a favela conferred clear advantages. Access to jobs and urban amenities improved over time as the city expanded northward and public transportation improved. In the long run the most pernicious aspect of Catacumba's removal was the dehumanization of the process—the act of forcing people out of their homes. Freedom of choice and of movement might arguably be denied to criminals, but not to law-abiding citizens whose only "crime" is their poverty.

In the conjuntos, the problems of unemployment, drug-related violence, inferior schools, and absence of health services and recreational spaces were similar to the conditions in the favelas. Although the conjuntos were government projects they were not maintained nor protected by the state. And the promise of apartment ownership is largely unfulfilled to this day.

Ownership was a driving force in the development of the conjuntos. The monthly apartment payments were calibrated to repay costs such that after 25 years, the buildings would be totally owner occupied. It has not worked out that way. Our 2003 sample survey in the conjuntos of Guaporé and Quitungo, where the former Catacumba residents had been placed, showed that less than 40 percent of those living in the conjuntos had official title to their apartments. The other 60 percent were living there informally—half of them with no title at all and the other half with "informal title"—not legally recognized. (See figure 11.7 for details.) After more than thirty years the majority were living in a state of limbo, one step closer to legality than those in favelas, but not part of the formal city.

This points out the commingling of legal and social status. While the conjunto buildings are similar to private sector housing developments for the middle class, the fact that poor people live in them means that the residents remain marginalized and therefore the community remains stigmatized.

Loteamentos Versus Favelas—A Theory Tested

Also surprising among the findings of my follow-up study was that the loteamentos distant from the center of Caxias turned out to be a better option in the long run than centrally located favelas, although they seemed worse in 1969. At that time, the municipality of Caxias was in the early stages of development. The center and its surrounding neighborhoods were urbanized, but the peripheral areas were sparsely populated subdivisions that were legal but not urbanized. The grid of paved roads, electricity, water, and other urban services did not extend to these areas. The small plots of land could be purchased or rented for very little—providing an alternative to squatting. Using a quasi-experimental research design, I selected half of my sample from the three favelas where families had decided to invest the little money they had in food, shelter, and education and live rent-free on unused lands. The other half of my sample was composed of people who had decided to buy or rent a lot in one of five subdivisions and therefore had less to spend on other needs. Five years later, when my first book came out, it appeared that the favela option had been wisest. People in Vila Operária in particular had built a thriving neighborhood with a strong Residents' Association and a new school and had raised money for professional teachers. And, as described in chapter 5, they had been granted the right to remain on the land.

The loteamentos, on the other hand, had high turnover, as many occupants were renters, and the residents had weak or no community organizations or Residents' Associations. They typically did not know their neighbors, did not have much local commerce, did not hold parties or dances for the school children, and in general seemed to have the problems of the poor without the solidarity to see them through.

The view from 40 years hence is the opposite. The municipality of Caxias has had one of the highest growth rates—in economic and population terms—in the metropolitan region, and all of the loteamentos have been paved, provided with infrastructure, and incorporated into the rest of the city with equal legal standing, despite their residents' lower incomes. Among all of the subgroups of the study, the people who were originally from the Caxias loteamentos had the greatest social mobility and the highest quality-of-life and SES scores.

The lesson here is that *legality counts*. Low-income communities exist on a continuum of legitimacy, and the closer a community is to legal status and legal documentation of that status, the more likely are its residents to be treated as people who can act on their own behalf.

On the other hand, *place counts* as well—and the two are not usually coterminous. One of my study findings is that being exposed to middle- and upper-class people on a daily basis conferred a lifelong advantage on the residents of Catacumba—even though they occupied the land illegally. Knowing how to speak, act, dress, and behave like a South Zone person and having the network of contacts that studying, playing, and working in an upscale neighborhood makes possible was of great value in every aspect of life.

The policy considerations appear contradictory. It is ideal to have legal status and to live in the midst of an upscale part of the city, but only the rich can afford that combination—which is precisely why they are so adamant in their opposition to coexisting with favelas. What can be done?

One answer would be to find a way to integrate new low-income housing into multiclass, multiuse neighborhoods. Spatial segregation (ghettoization) is self-defeating and self-perpetuating. Land banking by the municipal government and the use of acquired land for subsidized housing are ways to integrate social classes geographically, which we found is so useful for upward mobility. The use of eminent domain by the city to acquire properties not being used by their owners would minimize speculators holding land off the market for higher sale at a later date, reduce sprawl, and provide space for social purposes such as low-cost housing, schools, parks, small business incubators, and job-training centers. The use would be determined by the need to complement current use patterns.

Since the demise of the BNH in 1985 there has been no national housing policy, no housing finance policy, and no urban policy in Brazil. The Caixa Econômica, which replaced many of the functions of the BNH, has not been in the business of housing finance. They have limited programs for upper-middle-class housing and for civil servants. But almost all real estate transactions in Brazil are made "a vista"—the full price paid in cash at the time of the sale. In some cases, buyers need to begin payments on apartments based solely on floor plans, before or during the building construction.

There have been several small affordable housing projects financed by municipal governments. During my research in 2004–08, I visited some attractive new municipal housing projects in Rio and Caxias that were targeted to families earning 3–6 minimum salaries. They were designed following the principles of the "new urbanism"—high density, low-rise buildings as opposed to large apartment buildings or detached houses. I went with Djanira to visit two of these communities in Caxias, outside the city, which were gated communities with guards and designated for civil servants.

The project in downtown Rio, called Morar no Centro (Living in the Center), created in-fill housing meant to be affordable. I was charmed when I visited it. The city acquired dilapidated old buildings among lovely family homes on tree-lined streets and renovated each one, converting them into several small apartments (or larger when several adjacent properties were available for purchase). Families earning 1–6 minimum salaries were eligible, but preference was given to small families at the higher end of the range, meaning that 92 percent of the people I interviewed would be excluded.

On my way to the Tom Jobim International Airport in Rio in June 2009, I learned from the taxi driver, who lives in a favela, that this may be changing with a new housing finance program for families earning 1–3 minimum salaries. This was confirmed by a piece in the *Financial Times* just a few days later. On July 2, 2009, the paper reported on a new government program called *Minha Casa, Minha Vida* (My Home, My Life) intended to expand home ownership and boost growth in the construction industry. According to the article, the Caixa Econômica will invest US$31 billion in subsidies for home purchases, for families who can prove they have a steady income. Loans will be repayable in monthly installments over 20 years, and they will be supplemented by land donations from state or municipal governments. Construction is expected to start in 2010, and I will be eager to see whether the program succeeds in keeping payments low enough to serve favela families with steady incomes.[33]

Policy implications from these research findings and observations would suggest that the government should:

1. Provide choices. Given that millions of Rio's citizens are currently priced out of the formal housing markets and that continued favela sprawl into the forests and wetlands is unwise, a wide range of alternate affordable housing options— including renting, leasing, house-sharing, and housing finance for single and multiple-family housing and condominiums—would make sense. Depending on trade-offs between financial conditions, closer proximity, and space needs, families may have different needs at different times. The options might range from sites and services, to workers' vilas (or temporary shelters), to the gated condominiums I saw in Caxias, to dense high-rises on major transportation corridors and rental units within large homes.

2. Invest in people. If as much had been invested in human capital as in physical infrastructure in Rio's favelas, we would see a different situation today.

As the old Chinese proverb says:

> If you are planning for a year, sow rice.
> If you are planning for a decade, plant trees.
> If you are planning for a lifetime, educate people.

Adapted to the urban setting this would mean that community upgrading projects might partner with an array of other agencies (and incorporate an array of existing programs) starting with day care and preschool and continuing through (full-day) primary and secondary schools, high quality cost-free pre-vestibular courses (preparation for university entrance exams), and all the way to training for jobs. All this would be done with the support of buddy systems, mentoring, and incentives for success.

In the communities we studied, we saw that boys from 14–18 years old had the highest risk of death and the least to do with their time. School attendance is mandatory through age 14, and employment or military service only begin at 18, so there is a four-year void. Ironically, the laws passed to prevent the exploitation of child labor have instead prevented teenagers from starting an occupation, and hence from gaining experience and staying out of the drug traffic.[34]

3. *Give the community control.* In my experience, when community residents have a decisive voice in project planning, implementation, management, monitoring, and maintenance, the success rates are higher and the costs are lower. If responsibility is put in their hands and they are respected as experts on matters of their own lives and communities, they will be the ones to struggle with hard decisions and agree on trade-offs among competing priorities. They will then have a stake in the project and its outcome and determination to maintain and protect their investment.

4. *Bring the city to the favelas.* The municipal government needs an ongoing street-level presence in each community, preferably employing community members as managers. A selection process could identify interested residents in each community who are qualified to serve as on-site city ombudspersons. Those hired would receive training, be paid a monthly salary, and have direct phone and Internet access to all city agencies so they could solve many local problems on the spot. The idea is to change the face of the local state from that of the antagonistic policeman to the problem-solving public servant. If the new plans to bring POUSOs and referral centers to each favela go forward, it would go a long way toward achieving this goal.

5. *Consider the conjuntos.* Why not initiate a "Conjunto-Bairro" Program in the housing projects to upgrade their physical, social, and safety conditions and integrate them into their surrounding neighborhoods? The only improvement the government has made in the conjuntos in 30 years has been painting outward-facing building facades, just prior to elections some years ago. Abandoned by the state and avoided by private investors, the conjuntos have become more like favelas with the added disadvantage that they have large parcels of non-defensible space between the buildings, making them more dangerous.[35] Perhaps the conjuntos have been easier for the government to ignore, since they are not visible from the upscale urban areas, do not occupy invaded land, and have not organized to make demands.

6. *Control clandestine subdivisions.* Currently the clandestine or irregular loteamentos have the highest growth rate and living conditions that are among the worst in Rio. Newly arrived families are often conned into buying small plots of land in hidden subdivisions by fraudulent developers. Their modus operandi is to open up a narrow dirt road and clear lightly used cattle grazing or agricultural lands, usually small areas within enormous land holdings that are not patrolled. Lots are laid out and sold to new migrants with the promise of roads, water, electricity, and other amenities. Once the payment is made and the false "title papers"

produced, the developer disappears, the migrant families are stranded in the middle of nowhere, and the government is faced with removing the families and providing housing for them or bringing urban services to these remote areas.

Rogue developers could be discouraged from further incursions if landowners were held accountable for patrolling their property lines (and given the option to sell parcels to the city), if the government deployed the helicopters now used for favela surveillance to identify new settlements, and if the profiteers were brought to justice.

7. Anticipate continuing migration. Without advance planning for receiving newly arriving migrants, all upgrading projects and alternative housing solutions will be outpaced by uncontrolled growth. The time is ripe to reconsider sites and services. Government might use its right of eminent domain to acquire periurban land, subdivide it into housing plots; designate areas for open space, community facilities, schools, soccer fields, and commerce; and install the urban infrastructure before anyone settles there—much less costly than retrofitting urban services to an existing settlement. Families buy or "lease" the lots at minimal costs, with long-term financing toward purchase, and build their homes incrementally as their situation permits.[36]

8. Direct urban growth and mitigate sprawl. Public investment in housing as well as incentives for private developers should be concentrated in the direction of desired city expansion and in proximity to jobs and public transportation. In Rio one promising area for such development is along the Avenida Brasil, which has many parcels of vacant land and abandoned factory buildings. Its centrality makes it a promising location for conjuntos, cooperatives, condominiums, and other affordable housing options.

From what I understand, there will be strong demand for low-income housing in the West Zone of Rio, around the steel industry complex being expanded by the Companhia Siderurgica do Atlantico. They are investing a billion dollars in the project and expect to hire 50,000 new workers. The overall plan, projected over ten years ago, is to create a new urban hub, with the modernized port of Sepetiba as the shipping node.

Land Tenure and Home Ownership

Without doubt the most contradictory finding of this longitudinal study is that land tenure is largely irrelevant to the favela residents in Rio today. This is exactly the opposite of what I found in my earlier study and passionately defended in my earlier book.

Granting land title to the favela residents was the strongest policy recommendation I made in *The Myth of Marginality* and was a unifying thread throughout the book. The thrill of field research is the discovery that things which seemed immutable can and do change. My frustration was that by the time the policy community picked up on the importance of land ownership (and in some cases made it their mantra) the moment when it could have made a decisive difference (at least in Rio) had passed, and a new reality was in place.

This research confirmed the benefits of legality and legitimacy. But the fact that the life of inclusion is better than the life of exclusion does not necessarily imply that if favela residents were given land title without any other changes in their circumstances, they would join the ranks of the included. Giving individual title documents to residents of a community whose overall right to occupy the land remains contested is an empty gesture.

A case in point is the community of Caju near central Rio. Because it was located on federal lands that have been given to the city, the residents have received title papers. In fact, with much pomp and circumstance, titles have been handed out by at least two city administrations—with little to show for it. Eagerly I set up a visit to Caju, notebook and camera in hand, to interview community residents and leaders. The community has the visual charm of other small hillside favelas where residents take pride in painting and maintaining their homes. There was no indication that life in Caju was at all different from life in a comparable community without title. The residents thought it was humorous that each mayor wanted to be shown in the newspapers giving them property papers, and that the politicians expected expressions of gratitude. They told me they would be a lot more grateful to have jobs.

Theoretically, getting title to the property under one's home would be a plus. Practically, it is no longer of concern to favela residents. The right to *usucapiao*—ownership after continuous occupation for a fixed period of time ("adverse possession")—has provisions for both individual and collective cases, but is only applicable on privately owned land. Most favelas were able to remain in place after initial settlement precisely because there was no private owner to kick them out. Today, there are infinite legal complications for each parcel of land, often involving multiple claimants, competing documents and contradictory precedents.[37] So no simple solution exists for regularizing ownership for the 1,020 favelas in Rio at this time. For the people I interviewed, it is a moot point. De facto tenure has existed since the return to democracy almost 25 years ago. The fear of removal ended 10 years before that when the eradication policies ended. Once party politics returned, with the direct vote for mayor and governor, any public act against the million (or more) informal residents became a political liability. The investments in Favela-Bairro starting in 1994–95 made residents feel even more secure.

As a former president of the Residents' Association of Cantagalo (one of the remaining South Zone favelas) said: "We already have possession of our land. Aren't we living here? It's obvious that a title document in our hands would be great, but only if it came together with urbanization, with concrete improvements in our living conditions." The newsletter of the Federation of Residents'

Associations, *Favelão*, recommended that the residents "demand urban infra-structure and basic urban services before land title, or you will end up paying for nothing more than you now have for free."[38]

That is not to say that favela residents would refuse land title if offered. Eighty percent of those I interviewed said they would like to have legal owner-ship of their property but only if it did not mean incurring land taxes and ser-vice fees—especially since they will still be excluded from the respect and urban amenities enjoyed by other property owners in the city of Rio.

A policy idea here is to allow a grace period during which property taxes are waived and then gradually phased in if title is conferred. The second point is that if and when land and service taxes are imposed on favela communities, they should be entitled to the same package of services and the same quality of services as any other area of the city. That means not just better schools, health centers, and garbage collection but protection from violence and extortion as well.

One might imagine that without land ownership, it would be impossible to own, buy, sell, rent, or inherit homes. On the contrary, all of these transactions are thriving in Rio's favelas. There is a flourishing real estate market where real estate and land transactions proceed "as if" both the dwellings and land were legally owned.

Within the communities ownership is fluid. Most of the first-generation migrants (representing 80 percent of the original study participants) built their own homes and consider themselves owners, although they have no title papers. Members of their extended families who live with them likewise have no documents—nor do their children when they inherit the house. In all these situations people perceive themselves as owners. In cases where the adult chil-dren started families of their own and bought or rented a home in the com-munity, they may or may not have proof of that transaction. When I ask people about this, they say that sometimes the two parties write out an agreement by hand and shake on it; sometimes they go to the residents' association, fill out a form with all the details of the sale, sign it in front of witnesses, and have it signed and stamped by the president of the association; and sometimes they take the signed papers from the residents' association to a *cartorio* (registry) to have the transaction registered. But even this is not a legally recognized docu-ment. It has no juridical standing.

In our questions about home ownership, we relied on people's perceptions. They responded in one of three ways: no title, informal title, or official title. We did not run an independent check to see what kind of "official" or "informal title" they may have had. Because not all people from the original sample and their descendants remained in favelas, we had the extraordinary opportunity to compare the perceived ownership status in three types of communities rang-ing from extra-legal (favelas) to quasi-legal (conjuntos) to fully legal (bairros).

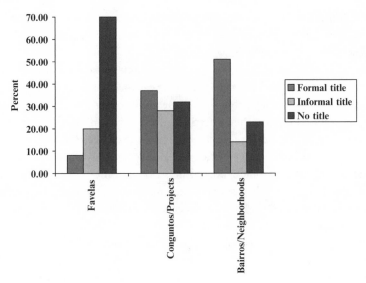

FIGURE 11.7   Self-reported home ownership in favelas, conguntos, and barrios, 2001.

There were too few people in loteamentos to bust the findings since we divided them by the three ownership categories. My guess, based on all the analysis of other variables, is that the profile could be similar to that in the conjuntos. The results are shown in figure 11.7.

As expected, the favelas have the lowest percentage of residents with official title to their homes and the highest percent with no title at all. The barros have the highest percentage with official title and the lowest with no title, but—contrary to expectation—only 50 percent of these barrio residents have official title. It was equally surprising to see that 22 percent of people in the bairros have no title at all. I did not expect to see this in the asfalto. Conjuntos, as expected, occupy an intermediate position between favelas and bairros, with much lower ownership and higher informality than I would have thought. It occurred to me that a large number of those who said they had no title at all might be renting, but renters (official and informal) accounted for only 10–15 percent of all non-owners. What remains to be seen is whether the 20 percent of favela residents who claim to be homeowners have any legal standing as such and, if so, under what circumstances they received title and if it made any difference. For the government who anticipated owner-occupancy in all conjunto apartments, the fact that under 40 percent of residents have title papers might cause them to rethink how conjuntos are managed and who is benefiting. Of those families who managed to get from the morro to the asfalto, perhaps the half that still do not own would be eligible for the new Minha Casa, Minha Vida Program.

TABLE 11.1   *Intergenerational Differences in Home Ownership in Favelas, Conjuntos, and Barrios*

	Original Interviewees	Children	Grandchildren
Favela	9	9	0
Conjunto	44	31	19
Bairro	59	44	4

I began to wonder whether some of the ownership findings might be illuminated by looking for generational differences. I imagined that grandchildren who had more education, better jobs, and greater Internet access would be more likely to have legal title to their homes. The analysis proved me wrong. On the contrary, as shown in table 11.1, the original interviewees were the most likely to be owners, the children next most likely, and the grandchildren least.

Home ownership decreased from generation to generation in all three types of communities. Interestingly, the steepest declines occurred among those living in conjuntos and bairros—dropping from 59 percent, to 44 percent to 4 percent. The tiny fraction of home owners in the favelas has remained at the same insignificant level.

Thinking about the families I know best gave me some insight into this intergenerational decline in ownership. Many of the children and grandchildren have been unable to acquire sufficient savings to rent or buy a home, particularly because purchase requires full payment in cash and there has been no mortgage system available to them. For example, Margarida's four daughters and grandson, all of Jacobi's children and grandchildren, one of Nilton's daughers, Zé Cabo's son and granddaughter and Djanira's son and granddaughter all live with their respective parent/grandparent. Some are still students, like Diana; others, like Sabrina, are just starting to work, and even the most successful, like Patricia, who are earning well, are renting. Among those in Patricia's generation who have moved into bairros in the formal sector, 20 percent are renting.

Perhaps the most telling finding of the ownship analysis is the dramatic effect it has on socioeconomic status within each type of community. In the favelas, as shown in figure 11.7, all renters worse off than all owner, but the degree of difference between *unofficial renters* (those with documents) and *official owners* (those who reportedly have title papers) is extreme. And this divergence is even more extreme when conjuntos and bairros are added.

The comparisons above make the point that the people who are official owners in a legitimate neighborhood are highly likely to have high scores on the SES index, meaning relatively high education, purchasing power, and living space. But these comparisons say nothing about the direction of causality. We

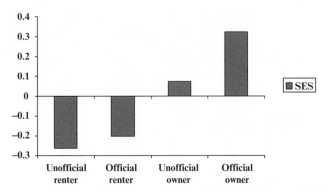

FIGURE 11.8   Socioeconomic status differences among formal and informal owners and renters in favelas, based on the new random sample of 1,200 in the study communities, 2003.

have learned from interviewing those at the two extremes that in most cases, the capacity to purchase a home in a bairro, as Zé Cabo, Jacobi, and Hélio Grande have done is the first step up the socioeconomic ladder and that living there provides additional advantages. In short, there is little dispute that "rich or poor it's good to have money."

What is in dispute is the importance of land and home ownership in moving out of poverty. One of the main reasons academics and international development agencies give for focusing on ownership is that it enables people to use their homes as collateral for loans. In the case of Rio's favelas, that is a spurious argument. The people have no interest in using their homes as collateral. This is not unique to Rio. I found the same disinclination in the yards of Kingston, Jamaica; the villas de miseria in Buenos Aires; the gececondu in Istanbul; the kampungs in Jakarta; the barong-barong in Manila and in shantytowns from Nairobi to Mumbai. The premise of Hernando de Soto that home ownership will release capital and free the entrepreneurial spirit[39] is not widely shared among the urban poor. In my experience people living on the edge are extremely reluctant to risk their most important asset on loans. As most cannot count on any steady source of income, they do not want to incur debt.

In Rio's low-income communities there was little or no interest in microcredit for the same reason. The people in our study borrowed money from a variety of informal and formal sources. They report that interest rates in the formal sector are prohibitively high and that they are not always treated well in their dealings with formal sector financial institutions. They certainly do not want to risk losing their home in order to borrow money. The major reason they gave my study group for borrowing money was to "repay other debts," followed by "pay for basic necessities." Less than 1 percent mentioned borrowing to start a new business or to improve their homes.

This intertwining of the informal and formal city, the legal and illegal, the legitimate and illegitimate is a fact of life for Rio's poor. If ownership is considered important by experts and external agencies, pathways toward it need to be "soft" and easily negotiable for those who have learned to be suspicious about the intentions of state officials and institutions. As the data above indicate, the rates of legal home ownership are low in conjuntos and bairros as well as in favelas. Issues of land and housing ownership cannot be separated from the broader concept of the right to the city. Who is the city for? And whose interests is it meant to serve?

Jobs, Work, Income Generation

While multilateral aid agencies including the World Bank, the Inter-American Development Bank, UN-Habitat and the Cities Alliance; bilateral agencies and local, state, and national governments have been focused on squatter upgrading and land regularization, the people who live in the favelas have been focused on *jobs*—more broadly, on income generation or "livelihoods." The residents are clear that their integration into the rest of the city depends more on their earning ability than on the design engineering of their communities. They suffer more from the stigma associated with being a favela resident than from the lack of land title or urban services. Private enterprise has already found in them an excellent market for the consumption of collective and individual urban services. There is no good reason why favelas cannot become working-class communities and communities of workers.

There is no cumulative experience in job creation comparable with that of on-site favela urbanization. Knowing that remunerated work is the greatest need does not imply knowing what to do about it. With the global recession adding millions to the ranks of the unemployed and underemployed, this is not a problem unique to Rio's favelas or to Rio in particular.

Some proposed responses deal with ways to create jobs in the areas of each city's comparative advantage; others deal with ways to prepare job seekers for the growth sectors of the economy. In this regard, the public sector needs to make common cause with the private sector, as well as with the excluded citizenry.

Strategically, does it make sense to try to hold onto manufacturing jobs when the costs of production outside Rio are much lower? Would retarding the use of labor-saving technologies in production, construction, or business services be more than a stopgap measure? Is there untapped entrepreneurial talent waiting for start-up capital to launch new businesses? Would raising the minimum wage (as Brazil has just done) or lowering the legal working age help or hurt the marginalized population?

Tactically, how can those who have the requisite skills be matched with "clients" looking for workers to do jobs—small or large? How can technical schools and job training programs be tied directly to the needs of employers and businesses? And even if the skills-need matches are made, what can be done to nullify the stigma of a favela address or personal appearance that signals such?

Several measures considered "pro-poor" have had unintended consequences. For example, raising the minimum wage in Brazil, which is a step in the direction of basic dignity, ends up causing many people to lose their jobs and others to be demoted from formal to informal status (to save money), depriving them of workers' rights and protections.

In Rio, after a protracted struggle to distance housecleaners and nannies from the patronizing attitude of their employers and the legacy of slavery, domestic work was professionalized in 1989. Domestic workers won the right to the minimum wage, a month's paid vacation, and the so-called "decimo terceiro" (thirteenth)—an extra month's pay at the end of the year. As a result, many households that had formerly supported a full-time live-in housekeeper (often with her young children) switched to hiring that same person one day a week at the new rates. For many of the women in the favelas, this meant competing with others to find four other days of work and losing the free room and board they and their children had enjoyed during the week—and losing the chance to use the *patroa*'s (boss's) address and to register their children at the good neighborhood schools.

Laws raising the legal working age to 18 have had similar unintended consequences, such as making drug traffic more appealing for youth who want to start earning their own money. A recent op-ed piece in the *New York Times* pointed out that the global movement against sweatshops contrasted sharply with the aspiration of the garbage pickers in Cambodia.[40] For the garbage pickers, to be able to work in a sweatshop, out of the blazing sun and with the security of a guaranteed wage, was a dream to work toward. How can the universal issues of decent pay, protection of children, or improved work conditions be reconciled with the fact that in reality these measures sometimes result in more hardship for those most in need?

The PAC, as far as I know, does not stipulate giving priority to local residents who are unemployed, nor does it specify procurement of supplies from local vendors, even though such measures would make good sense. It was initiated in 2007, when Brazil had accumulated a large surplus for investments, and it was ambitious in scope, promising a million new homes by 2011. The 2008–09 economic crisis has put a damper on the proliferation of these plans, but it is too early to tell whether it will go forward or whether the jobs created in cities will go to the urban poor.

On the worker-preparedness side, Brazil tried a national program—Primeiro Emprego (First Job)—that was launched in 2004. For at-risk youth, getting one's first job is a critical step on the path to future employment—particularly since it provides the chance to get a signed carteira de trabalho which is a prerequisite for future jobs, particularly in the formal sector. The program was supposed to coincide with the period when youth finish or leave school and are not yet working so that joining a drug gang would not become the default option in the absence of alternatives.

Primeiro Emprego pays a stipend to program participants, along with transportation and lunch costs. Program management is decentralized to nonprofit organizations in each city. In Rio, each of a half dozen selected NGOs was assigned to one area of the city and encouraged to develop its own curricula and teaching plans so that alternative approaches could then be evaluated. The major problem was that the courses trained the youth for service or manufacturing jobs that did not exist. With no job offers forthcoming, the graduating students ended up working at fast food chains or at other low-paying jobs or entering the traffic. If employers had been consulted on what skills they needed in future hires or what vacancies they had, the program might have trained students to fill those needs.

More problematic, several teachers who worked in the program reported that most of the students who signed up had no interest in learning the skill set being offered—be it photography, hair and nail care, accounting, or starting a business. Instead, students came to class in order to receive the stipend. One of the teachers in the program told me that of the 25 students in his class, only 3 or 4 paid any attention. To overcome this, a program would have to put hundreds of young people from favelas and conjuntos into jobs with a future and publicize the successes on television and in the communities. Almost every young person I interviewed, including those who were involved in the traffic, said their preference was to find "decent" work. They can recognize useful skills training for real jobs, and they also know the early death rates for youth in the traffic.

School supplement programs for favela youth are proliferating.[41] One project that I visited in 2005 was called *Projeto Aplauso* (Project Applause) after the entertainment magazine that initiated it. The project also benefits from the support of several private companies. This joint venture took over an abandoned *galpão* (warehouse) near the Rodaviaria (the central city bus terminal), to which young people from 17 favelas have easy access. It provided high quality training in arts and crafts, music, dance, drumming, carpentry, sewing, and embroidery. Equally important was that the project gave hundreds, perhaps thousands, of youngsters an alternative to joining the traffic.

They had a place to go, something useful to do, linkages to well-known artists and entrepreneurs and a sense of belonging. There were periodic open houses and performances to which potential employers, talent scouts, government and corporate sponsors, and the general public were invited. As far as I know, Galpão Aplauso is still in existence, being supported largely by contributions from private companies.

Locally initiated programs within the favelas have also captured the rapt attention of the youth. The video and webmaster training studios in the favela of Jacarezinho; the computer programs, arts, capoeira, and baking programs run by Roda Viva in the favela of Borel; the theater group Nós do Morro in Vidigal; the census research group, prevestibular preparation courses, language training, arts/cultural groups run by CEASME (Centro de Estudos e Ações Solidárias da Maré, or Maré Solidarity Action and Study Center) in the Complexo do Maré; and similar on-site programs are filled with enthusiastic participants.

I was impressed with the local economic development strategies being formed by a group of residents from the favela of Cidade de Deus who have been working for several years in collaboration with committed professionals, business leaders, and NGOs. They are engaged in a series of monthly breakfast meetings they call Livre Pensar Social (free social thinking) held in the center of Rio at the offices of the Caixa Econômica Federal. The group selects topics of greatest importance to them and invites speakers to give presentations at each meeting followed by questions and discussion. The level of debate at the meetings I attended is highly informed, lively, and sophisticated. No one turns them down. This is one venue where anyone invited will be taken seriously and where ideas are likely to be translated into social action. Every two weeks community meetings are held in the Cidade de Deus. The last time I was there, in 2007, they had started several small income-generation projects including dressmaking, sewing, and confections cooperatives, a crafts fair and a local flea market. They were planning to purchase an abandoned storage facility to convert into a small business incubator and were setting up women's support groups. They are learning by doing as the Chinese proverb says:

> Tell me and I will forget.
> Show me and I may remember.
> Involve me and I will understand.

Looking elsewhere for income generation models, a nongovernmental approach that has had some success in Bangalore took the approach of connecting workers in squatter settlements with job needs in households or businesses. LabourNet matches employers and workers, through a call center and a web-based interface. Workers pay a small membership fee for job placement, access to training, access to health insurance, and an identification card. The identity card allows them to open a bank account and to present credentials of reliability. Job openings are broadcast to LabourNet members through text messages so that interested and available parties can respond instantaneously. By being associated with a recognized institution, these workers can command higher wages than they would otherwise. LabourNet has already registered close to 5,100 workers and run training workshops for over 900 of them.[42]

Rio might also adapt the concept of enterprise zones and empowerment zones from England and the United States. The idea is to encourage businesses to invest in low-income communities, designated "enterprise zones," that offer financial incentives such as reduced taxes and relaxed regulations. In "empowerment zones," businesses receive employment credits (or wage credits) for each person they hire from designated low-income communities. These programs have stimulated economic growth and employment in a targeted way in declining areas within cities, with a fair degree of success.[43]

In terms of employment one idea that has worked well elsewhere is massive investment in workforce education, computer literacy, and communications infrastructure, including provision of free wireless Internet access in targeted areas of the city. Andre Urani initiated a program of this type—called Rio On-Line—when he was secretary of labor in the first administration of Mayor Cesar Maia, but it was not carried forward by the following mayor.[44] In June 2009, I attended a meeting of Rio Como Vamos? (Rio, How're we doin'?), a collaboration started in 2007 among nonprofits, businesses based in Rio, and interested individuals to generate reliable data on key issues facing the city, open up a discussion about these, and set goals and benchmarks to stimulate actions—from the neighborhood to the city to the metropolitan level. It seems like a very promising initiative, but time will tell.

Research conducted by the Mega-Cities Project (a transnational nonprofit) working in 21 of the world's largest cities documented many innovative approaches already underway that address environmental regeneration and income generation simultaneously. One of these was started in the Zabaleen community (the traditional trash collectors) in Cairo. Two major problems—too much garbage and too few jobs—were turned into a solution when they began separating out raw materials from the garbage and creating saleable products from each. The metal was made into engraved trays; the fabric into quilts, placemats, and accessories; the plastic into sandals and shoes; and the rubber into hoses. Instead of receiving a few cents per ton from an intermediary for separated garbage, the community members received the value of the crafts work they had done. This enabled them to move out of the garbage dump into apartments, to move their children out of the donkey carts into schools, and to begin to erode centuries-old caste ostracism.

In the South Bronx, in the days when properties were abandoned and land was cheap and plentiful, a community group grew mushrooms and herbs in a greenhouse on an abandoned lot and sold their produce to high-end restaurants. In Harlem, the Environmental Benefits Program trained and paid community residents to serve as environmental monitors of both private and public facilities in the neighborhood, using fines levied for infractions to pay their salaries. Some cities passed stringent air quality rules enforced by high fines, which created an incentive for the creation of new "green" businesses and the use of less polluting vehicles; other cities passed new home construction ordinances, opening up markets for new businesses in everything from building materials, roofing, windows and doors, paints, carpeting, insulation, and gray water reuse to solar heating. The city of Curitiba, Brazil, is well known for its many ecological measures and public works projects, including using recycled spaces for new businesses or educational and cultural centers; giving free bus tickets to squatter residents for each bag of garbage they bring down to the garbage truck; and creating a bus system, called the "surface metro," which has gotten 28 percent of the population out of their cars, reduced air pollution, and provided hundreds—if not thousands—of jobs in the process.[45]

The "greening of the city" creates jobs in alternative energy, reforestation, environmental cleanup, and green industries. Passing strict environmental laws provides a market for the manufacture and sale of green energy, green buildings, and green transportation, creating new jobs in the process. A recent article, "Greening the Ghetto," describes a nonprofit organization based in Oakland, California, that is bringing green jobs "into the hood" and expanding the reach of the environmental movement.[46] Van Jones, author of *The Green Collar Economy*, speaks of solar panels, wind turbines, and home weatherization programs being both deployed and made in the ghetto and bringing jobs and profits to the ghetto, while lowering the cost of living.[47]

To my mind, green jobs, green products, and green infrastructure are highly promising areas for public policy and local community action in the favelas of Rio—and informal settlements elsewhere in the global South. Our entire urban infrastructure was invented in a brief 12-year period at the end of the nineteenth century, before we were aware of the limitations on natural resources. No basic changes have been made since. The systems are linear, so food, water, and energy flow through our cities and into the waste stream. A circular system would turn the output of each process into the input for the next one. The concept of "resource-conserving cities," which I first came across in the early 1970s,[48] has become much more technologically and politically feasible in the intervening decades. The greatest opportunity to create sustainable systems will be in those cities of the global South, whose infrastructure is not yet fully in place and whose services now exclude large portions of their populations. I can imagine favelas being used to "leapfrog" from nineteenth-century to twenty-first century technologies and to experiment with different alternatives. The workers who create and install the new systems would become highly desirable in the job market, as upscale home owners and apartment buildings decided to install green technologies.

The main message of job creation or job preparation is that only with the involvement of the residents of the informal communities can solutions emerge. Their experience, knowledge, and commitment are essential to finding solutions, implementing them, and learning from mistakes along the way. Any public policy without local commitment is highly unlikely to achieve success.

Drugs, Arms, and Violence

The use of "recreational" drugs is not intrinsically different from the use of alcohol, cigarettes, or prescription medications. All societies throughout history have found some means of altering states of consciousness, entering into religious states, or escaping from reality. As I have already discussed, the problem for the people I work with in Rio is the violence surrounding the acquisition and sale of these drugs. Each of the ingredients in the toxic stew of violence in Rio contributes to the death toll and the fear that has turned lives of poverty into lives of tragedy. The victims of this tragedy are disproportionately young men and boys. Many of them enter the traffic knowing they will not live to be 25, if that.

The level of violence appears to rise with the level of youth unemployment. If a concerted effort were made to open up job opportunities for the 14- to 24-year-olds who are at high risk, many lives would be saved, and the concept of a future would have meaning for them. Mandatory schooling ends around age 14 and legal work or military service begins only at age 18, so youth experience four years of being in between. At that age, the parents do not have a great deal of control and the adolescents do not have a great deal of self-control, so the situation is volatile at best.

One of the findings of this study is that the young men are willing to work but not if the work is demeaning, the conditions degrading, and the pay indecent. Whereas their grandparents, original migrants to Rio, were happy to do any type of work for any level of pay, their children and their children's children expect more. They are not gente humilde from the roça (countryside) but astute observers of the urban scene into which they were born. Many would rather gamble with glory and death than be humiliated by a boss or paid a "wage of hunger." Earning so little that they have nothing to show for it at the end of each month is simply another form of disrespect. They get enough of that outside the workplace, just by being dark-skinned young males who live in favelas or conjuntos.

Moreover, the need fulfilled by the drug gangs is not only for money to purchase status symbols and attract the most desirable young women but also for the sense of identity and belonging. For young men who are treated as worthless, if not criminal, to be valued as part of a group is worth a lot. That is why Afro Reggae has been so successful.

Afro Reggae is a nonprofit organization, a social movement, and an ideology. Its mission is to keep kids out of the drug traffic by giving them a way to express themselves through music and dance. It provides a connection to Afro-Brazilian history and culture, using theater, celebrating heroes of resistance, and teaching capoeira, drumming, songwriting, dance, and other performing arts. Members have access to medical care and social workers. Afro Reggae started in the favela of Vigario Geral, in the wake of a series of deaths and the establishment there of the Casa de Paz (House of Peace). From the beginning, Afro Reggae has been independent of and unwilling to be intimidated by the competing drug gangs. The film *Favela Rising* gives a compelling portrait of the organization's work and the drama of its survival.[49]

One of the reasons Afro Reggae has not been wiped out is that gang members themselves see the beauty of it: they want an alternative, if not for themselves then for their children. They hear truth in the words of the Afro Reggae songs. They hear protest. They hear the details of the injustices, and they hear the telling of their own frustrations and hopes. Junior, the founder of the group, says Afro Reggae is about "culture, social responsibility and creativity. These days if you really want to change a situation, you first have to change people's self-image in that situation."[50] The group's internal organization borrows from the hierarchy and stringent disciplinary codes that characterize the drug gangs. Members become passionately committed, not just to their colleagues and to a critique of reality but to acting to change that reality.

Modeled as an alternative to selling arms and drugs or using extortion, Afro Reggae sustains itself through its business as a production company. As Junior explains, they have excellent connections and earn money by staging shows at the biggest venues with the biggest stars. They create jobs in the favelas through a cooperative that handles their product line, merchandizing, recruiting, marketing, and publicity.

The movement is so compelling that they were hired by the city of Belo Horizonte, the capital of the state of Minas Gerais, to bring policemen and favela residents together over drumming and singing, so as to open a dialogue between the two groups.

The anthropologist and criminologist Luiz Eduardo Soares captured the essence of the issue when he said:

> We have to offer youth at a minimum what the drug trade offers: material resources, of course, but also recognition, a sense of belonging and of value.... No one changes if he or she thinks that they are worth nothing. Do we want to exterminate poor youth or integrate them?...Pardon and give a second chance also means forgiving ourselves and giving ourselves a second chance, as a society. Wouldn't it be great for us to have a chance to escape from the horrible guilt of having abandoned thousands of children to the fate of picking up a gun?[51]

The discussion of alternatives for youth is only one element of violence reduction. Each of the 10 ingredients in the toxic violence stew would ideally be addressed in an integrated manner. For example:

1. Favelas and conjuntos would become included in the scope of state protection against violence rather than remaining the targets of state-sanctioned violence.

2. Inequality levels would begin to shrink with the jobs and cash transfer policies.

3. If cocaine were legalized, regulated, and taxed, the sales points would no longer need to be hidden within favelas.

4. Drug gangs and networks would be weakened by lowered prices for cocaine; by the elimination of police, judiciary, and political complicity; and by retaking control of the prison system.

5. The purchase of weapons would become more difficult with the imposition of registration requirements and high tariffs on imported weapons, disarmament campaigns, and protocols to track weapons confiscated by police.

6. Police reform would include police deployment to "hot zones" of violence using geographic information systems; improved pay and promotion for exemplary action averting violence; improved communications and equipment for record keeping, accountability, and monitoring; conflict mediation training; and zero tolerance for police brutality, with a hotline for anonymous reporting.

7. Implementation of the rule of law would take place decisively, transparently, and equally for all.

8. Members of militias, who are all employed public servants, would be subject to loss of job or pension if found participating in extortion or extrajudicial use of lethal violence.

9. The entire city would mobilize in solidarity with the favelas to demand jobs and justice, in the same way the "Rights Now!" movement did at the end of the dictatorship.

10. A mass media campaign would be launched, distinguishing between "bandidos" and favela residents and reporting on studies demonstrating that "hardline" police brutality and "crackdowns" reduce rather than increase public safety. I can imagine a "Carioca of the Week" newspaper column and television spot highlighting people from the communities, city government, state police, businesses, or NGOs whose ideas or actions have helped make Rio a more peaceful city.

Obviously, these ideas are easier written about than accomplished. The list simply underscores the depth and breadth of the violence problem and the fact that the primary drug consumers are not favela residents.[52]

One issue frequently raised by favela residents is the culpability of drug users. There is no war on poverty in Rio, it is a war on the poor. The fact is that the poor are killed with impunity while the rich "playboys" suffer no consequences from buying and using the cocaine that is sold by a fraction of the community residents. If Rio's wealthy residents were really concerned about their city and their safety they could stop buying and using cocaine rather than continuing to blame the victims. Rio has the highest cocaine consumption of any city in the world. If the local markets dried up, the city would become a lot safer.

Citizenship and the Right to the City

Personal legitimacy, not land or housing legitimacy, is what is at stake in the city. As long as favela residents are perceived as marginals, no urbanistic upgrading, skills training, or police reform will succeed in integrating the morro and the asfalto, the favela and the bairro. There are no tested policies for how to extend personhood to include the poor. The passport to urban citizenship should be a right, not a privilege of the rich, but that is not yet the case.

One of the findings of my study is the importance of documents and documentation in moving from invisibility to visibility. Many more official documents are needed to be a participating member of society in Brazil than in the United States. One must have a birth certificate; a cadastro de pessoa física; carteira de identidade (identification card); a marriage license; a carteira de trabalho, preferably assinada (signed by your employer in a formal-sector job); a voter registration card; a military service card; and paid bills documenting possession of a fixed residence.

Our research project created an index counting each document as one point and found a strong relationship between how well each person was documented and their socioeconomic status (and income). This finding suggests that it would be useful to expand the Balcao de Direitos program that Viva Rio started in Rocinha, which helps people obtain required documents within their own community. It took me weeks to get a cadastro de pessoa física—even with lots of professional help and a bank account in Brazil; most wealthy people have these and hire a *dispachante* (a professional who is paid to take care of the bureaucratic red tape involved in any official transaction) to wait in the lines for them if they need to make some adjustment.

There are yet other deterrents to poor people obtaining documentation. One woman I met said she had not taken her son to be registered because she was ashamed of their clothes—they did not have the kind of clothes needed to *sair na rua* (go out into the street of the formal city). Others say they lack the bus fare.

The issue of documentation would be a powerful and manageable place to start. Making it easier for favela residents, the urban poor in general, and average Brazilian citizens to obtain the documents necessary to be treated as full citizens of the polity would go a long way toward alleviating certain forms of exclusion. People need an address and door-to-door mail delivery, and streets in favelas need to be named and the buildings numbered. Such residential identification measures have been attempted, but the traffic has opposed them as they think it makes it easier for police to locate them. There is an episode of *City of Men* that shows this issue brilliantly.

My research revealed that the return to democracy in Brazil brought neither inclusion of the poor nor bargaining power to poor communities. The incursion of the drug traffic into the favelas only made matters worse, but the fundamental problem was that the democratic transition was, to use Holston's phrase, "incomplete." Comfortable, worn patterns of corruption, cronyism, and clientelism resurfaced once the rigid controls of the dictatorship were relaxed and party politics returned. The only pathway to recapturing the city of Rio from the violence and chaos caused by the drug traffic is to complete the democratic transition with transparency, equality under the law, and accountability for lawlessness. As long as corruption dominates decisions, there can be no faith in the fairness of government, and that space will be filled by some alternate power system for resolving disputes and maintaining order.

The "right to the city" as a collective right derives from the concept of the French sociologist Henri Lefebvre. The idea incorporates all of the individual rights in the Universal Declaration of Human Rights passed 60 years ago and adds a spatial dimension.

In Brazil, the movement for the right to the city began as a series of local discussions leading up to the drafting of the "Estatuto da Cidade" (City Statute) for inclusion in the new 1988 Constitution.[53] For two years leading up to the Constitutional Convention, there were daily demonstrations in Brasília drawing together whichever group of citizens and organizations had a stake in the chapter of the proposed Estatuto da Cidade being debated on that day. A Rio-based NGO, along with many other NGOs around the country, played a coordinating role in drafting and circulating the articles of the proposed Estatuto da Cidade.

Among the proposed provisions of the Estatuto da Cidade were the "law of adverse possession" in urban areas (*lei de usucapiao urbano*), guaranteeing collective rights to the regularization of informal settlements; the stipulation that each city of over 20,000 must prepare a *plano diretor* (master plan) with city residents' full participation; and the creation of a democratic administration for each city of that size, through community policy councils, steering committees, public debates and consultations, conferences about subjects of urban interest, popular initiatives for proposed laws, plans, and urban development projects.

The Estatuto da Cidade's proposed provisions also include protections of human rights, property rights, the right to personal safety, housing rights, health rights, educational rights, the right to earn an honest living in decent working conditions for a decent wage, the right to a secret ballot, the right to a voice in decisions affecting one's life, and the rights to freedom of movement, speech, and assembly.

A newly created Ministry of Cities, formed under Lula's Labor Party presidency, organized and funded assemblies in large cities around the country to discuss the Estatuto da Cidade. After several major assemblies, culminating in the last quarter of 2008, the principles, implications, and action plans were made clear and a broad consensus reached. The idea for establishing programs similar to Estatuto da Cidade has now caught on—and been further elaborated—in cities in South Africa and elsewhere.[54]

However, according to one of the original organizers of this process, the outcome of all the "participatory effervescence" has been disappointing. She said that in the past year or so, many of those most closely involved concluded that the process had led to an "institutionalization of social movements," turning them into an auxiliary of progressive government and that not many concrete changes had resulted from the master plans that emerged from all of the public meetings.[55]

This was a disappointment to me but not a surprise. I had already seen such processes come to the same ends in Madrid, Copenhagen, London, New York, and many other places.[56]

Many of the original supporters of this open process concluded that its relative lack of success was due to the way capitalism is structured around urban real estate, combined with the Brazilian heritage of clientelism and patrimonial privilege. These forces ended up co-opting the leadership of the social movements and reaffirming the unequal city. Proponents of Estatuto da Cidade see the issues of land use and property ownership as the core of the resistance to change. One person I spoke with said that the Estatuto da Cidade served to market the Brazilian case in terms of the "rhetorical discourse," but after eight years it was never really put into practice or connected with on-the-ground reality. This was true in all the cities of Brazil without exception. On its official website, the Estatuto da Cidade still sounds wonderful, but there is no mention of outcomes beyond the initial series of meetings that were held. I wonder what lesson those who participated in those meetings, perhaps acting as citizens for the first time, will take away from this. One hopes it will be a determination to create a stronger independent power base, but I fear it may lead to reluctance to engage in further participatory exercises.

One thing that would help greatly to strengthen civil society in Brazil would be changing the tax laws to make individual and corporate donations to social organizations tax-exempt, as they are now for artistic organizations. The lack of such a provision is a legacy from the dictatorship that hangs on in the legal structure of the nation. Immediately after the end of the dictatorship, there was a blossoming of community organizations, labor unions, Catholic base communities, and Communist Party cells within the favelas, with links to NGOs, unions, and political parties in the greater city. This moment of awareness and activity in civil society only lasted for a few years before it began to dissolve and fragment under the pressures of partisan competition, co-optation, and the takeover of community associations and Residents' Associations by the traffic. If a mechanism for funding nonprofit agencies similar to that in the United States could be established, there would be a better chance of "building power, building community, and building people."[57]

REFLECTIONS

Counterproductive Incentives

My research has shown that the failure to implement promising ideas is due not lack of funding, lack of technical capacity, or lack of know-how but to *counterproductive incentive structures* that sabotage forward movement. There are no incentives for collaboration across sectors, classes, and levels of government or even for power holders merely to listen to the voices of the poor. Elected officials benefit from short-term, visible results that help them get reelected, even though most problems need long-term solutions. While continuity is essential for successful policy outcomes, the tendency is to dismiss anything "not invented here" and start over. Business rewards risk and invests in research and development in the search for innovation, but in government it is safer to continue with an ineffective policy than to try an innovation that might fail.[58]

Likewise, the international development agencies, often the trendsetters as well as funders of poverty-alleviation policies, promote staff members for pushing as much money out the door as quickly as possible, rather than experimenting with innovative, site-specific, and culturally appropriate solutions that are more likely to meet the needs of a local population. Participation may slow down the process in the early stages, but it is the only way to elicit the intelligence of those who are experiencing the problem so as to enable its success in the long run.

VAUGHN FAMILY CENTER IN LOS ANGELES

One example at the grassroots level reveals how changing the incentives changed the reality. The San Fernando Valley in Los Angeles is a low-income area whose population is composed largely of immigrants from Central America. The local school ranked among the worst in California. Every day, the children came home to their parents with pink slips of paper from their teachers, listing infractions or failures. Many of the parents did not speak English, and none knew what to do with their children except to punish them, which seemed only to make matters worse. Yoland Trevino, one of the mothers, came up with the idea of giving the children yellow slips every time they did something right. The school principal and teachers agreed to try it. Each time a child got to school on time, or arrived in a clean school uniform, or passed a quiz, another yellow slip was signed and sent home.

The next step was to open a small canteen in the school where students could bring in their yellow slips and convert them into points. Depending on the number of points they earned, they could get anything from a pencil or notebook to a backpack or transistor radio. The parents and teachers contributed the money, and they created the Vaughn Family Center. Each day, a different group of mothers volunteered to bring lunch to school, so the teachers and parents had a chance to talk together. There were many people with skills who were unemployed and many who could not afford to take their children to a dentist or doctor, so they decided to set up a service and skills exchange.

Each community member wrote down all the things they could teach or provide—sewing, cooking, Spanish language lessons, babysitting, yard work, plumbing, construction, and so on. They also listed what they needed. A barter economy was established in the entire community. A local currency that could be earned and spent was created. The entire region was included and began to mobilize around the school—which became a charter school. The achievement records five years later were among the highest in the State of California.[59]

Nonreformist Reforms

Short of improbable scenarios, there are any intermediate efforts that might be undertaken to improve the conditions of life in the morro and—for that matter—in the asfalto? In short, the goal is to improve what might be called "the real city," the one that does not respect theoretical boundaries and is produced by the ever-shifting commingling of formality and informality. Would it be possible to identify "system-challenging innovations"—initiatives that redefine problems and solutions, contest the rules of the game, and include different players at the table?[60] The past half century of failed attempts to reduce urban poverty and resolve the issue of squatter settlements is testimony to the need for new ways of thinking. In considering this, I think of Andre Gorz's concept of nonreformist or transformational reforms, those that alter the logic of the system and change the balance of power.

The knowledge and wisdom of the marginalized population are essential to successful problem solving and policy-making. Inclusion of the informal sector will release valuable resources for production, consumption, and citizenship that the city needs to thrive. Even the best policies and programs will require popular as well as political mobilization and will ultimately depend on the degree of willingness to consider the underlying issues of resource allocation and redistribution.

Despite the many policy and programmatic efforts discussed in this chapter, the "urban question" remains unresolved.[61] The failure to create a shared commitment to the city as a place existing for all—to accept socially and politically the existing economic integration of the city of the rich and the city of the poor—continues to disrupt the peace, despoil the environment, limit economic growth, and destroy the potential for convivial urban life.

Sharing Approaches That Work

The city of Rio, like all the megacities in which I have worked, is full of innovative solutions to problems of income generation, housing, and the environment, but no one knows about these because they mostly occur on a small scale and are not publicized. The idea would be to identify these and build on them by either scaling up into public policy or reaching out from community to community. If the poor made common cause with the middle class and rich against the violence and drug traffic, they would have the power to affect public policy. We have found it very powerful in the Mega-Cities Project to share innovative solutions that have proven successful in other communities, cities, and countries and to use the prestige of international exchange to bring in new ideas without political opposition. A survey of the foremost urban leaders in Rio, Mexico City, New Delhi, Lagos, London, and New York conducted by the Mega-Cities Project with Roper Starch International showed that 96 percent of leaders (in government, business, labor unions, nonprofits, community-based organizations, academia, and the media) saw the urban problems they faced as similar to those of other megacities; 94 percent said it would be beneficial to share information about problem solving with these cities; 11 percent considered themselves knowledgeable about solutions elsewhere.[62] They often ended up contracting with costly consultants or "experts" who offered preformulated solutions rather than learning about much more practical initiatives that had proven successful in similar places.

The bottom line is a redefined social contract based on the commitment to a just city, a diverse city in which rights apply to all. The population of Rio de Janeiro's formal city will have to join forces with with the population of the favelas in order to create the leverage for transforming the policies and practices that are part of the problem. The mindset and values of the formal city may have to catch up with the new reality of the "real city." "Us and them" may have to evolve into a larger "we." Without a doubt, widespread popular support, social mobilization, and political will are needed to forge a unified city out of a divided city.

twelve

THE IMPORTANCE OF BEING GENTE

Janice, when I first met you I thought that if I married well, if my wife and I both worked hard all of our lives, if we had only two children, and if we sent them to private schools and kept working after retirement, that I would become gente. But now, 30 years later, after doing all of that, I am light-years away.

NILTON (GUAPORÉ, 1999)

The marginalization of Rio's poor is so extreme as to exclude them from the category of personhood. What came up over and over again in my conversations and interviews was the desire to be or to become gente (literally, to be or to become a person).[1] The term *gente* means "somebody"—a *person,* a *human,* and to be gente is to be accorded the dignity and respect that is automatically conferred on the "we" of the human community and denied to the "they."[2] The term points to the circumstances in which the poor simply do not exist in the mental map of the wealthy. Much like Ralph Ellison's "invisible man," favela residents go through life "in search of respect," the phrase Philippe Bourgois used so aptly used as the title of his book on selling crack in a New York City ghetto.[3] Human rights may not apply here.

The unlikely metamorphosis from a "nobody" into a "somebody" is the human drama that creates the compelling appeal of the popular Indian movie *Slumdog Millionaire.* The film, which won several Oscars in 2009, tells the story of a homeless chai wallah (tea server) who is forced as a child to flee a Mumbai shantytown when his mother is killed by religious zealots. In the course of various adventures in his struggle for survival, he learns some odd facts that enable him to win successive rounds and finally the top prize of the Indian

FIGURE 12.1   The open plaza at the entrance to Favela Vidigal, on Avendia Niemeyer, showing the bright turquoise ceramic tiles inscribed with passages from the Declaration of Human Rights. (Created by the children in the community as a public art project with François Shein)

version of the television quiz show *Who Wants to be a Millionaire?* The show's host begins by mocking and humiliating him, progresses to unfairly tricking him, and finally has him arrested and tortured, in the belief that he must be cheating, since such a lowlife could not possibly have as much knowledge as this chai wallah appears to have. Despite the Bollywood ending, with the boy becoming a millionaire hero and getting the beautiful girl, there were protests in India over "slum voyeurism" and over the term "slumdog." Clearly, the film's glamorization of its hero's intelligence, tenacity, creativity, and fidelity to his true love does not compensate for the use of such a derogatory term—a term that denies personhood.[4]

I first heard the word *gente* used to mean "a person" in 1963 while living in Arembepe, the fishing village in Bahia that I mention in the preface. The custom for announcing oneself when visiting another's home was to clap your hands loudly at the front door and yell out "Tem gente?" ("Anyone home?"). What caught my attention was that when the woman of the house came to the door, the question was repeated—"Is anyone home"? She said her husband was out on the *saveiro* (fishing boat). She was home, but she did not count as anyone.

The country folk who migrated to the city were not much concerned about their status. They were proud of having survived the journey, finding a place to live, and being able to support themselves and their families. But living in a favela was sufficient to put them in that "no one" category. I heard the term used again when I witnessed thousands of people unwillingly taken from their homes and thrust into garbage trucks for transport to the conjuntos. Removal was an assault on their personhood. "All we wanted was to be treated like gente," they said.

Being treated as less than human in everyday transactions at banks, government agencies, and public offices deepens and reinforces the we/they divide inherent in the "myths of marginality." The nonperson status was sealed during the military dictatorship and in its aftermath by the state's failure to protect favela residents from lethal violence committed by the traffic and police. This became a vicious cycle, reproducing the behavior of deference and self-deprecation, which in turn reinforced the mark of nonpersonhood. As the anthropologist-criminologist Soares has put it, "to move forward, [we] need to recognize that favela residents are humans whose entire lives have been lived in terror. They have never experienced what it feels like to be a full–fledged citizen and have never had their personhood affirmed."[5]

The meaning of "gente" is fluid. Within the favela, people often use the word to mean "we" or "us," as in the statement "A gente tem medo de sair" (We are afraid to go out). Or they might use the phrase "gente boa" to indicate a good, honest person—to vouch for someone. If they say "Janice é gente boa," they mean "She is okay, she is a good person, one of us."

Within the favela, everyone has personhood. The divide is between honest, hardworking family folks and *malandros* or *bandidos*. The *Collins English-Portuguese, Português-Inglês Dictionary* defines *malandro* as a "double-dealing, cunning, street-wise crook" or simply a "lay-about." *Bandido* means bandit. It is the way people in the communities refer to the drug dealers—bandidos, or marginals. However bad the malandros and bandidos may be, the people in the favelas still accept them as people.

Being gente is not a static state. It is a relational condition that may vary for a single person over time or according to the eye of the beholder. For someone born to wealth, it is never a question. It is part of the urban condition of the underclass, a way the affluent distance themselves from those less fortunate and reinforce their sense of being above the rules.

This is encapsulated in the often-used phrase of intimidation, "Você sabe com quen está falando?" (Do you know with whom you are speaking?)[6] The implied threat is that any person of means has the political clout to rise above the law, and will make trouble for the lowly bureaucrat being addressed if he or she is unwilling to bend the rules or look the other way in deference to the superior status of the speaker.

The cases that follow illustrate a range of circumstances along the continuum of being gente. Zé Cabo's story illustrates the impermanence of becoming gente and how easy it is to lose it. Dona Rita's story shows that money is not enough if you do not have the requisite appearance. Claudia has the appearance but is only a snap decision away from losing all. Sebastião had a good run at it, but now it is too late—as he says, "the time has passed."

ZÉ CABO: THE IMPERMANENCE OF BEING GENTE

Zé Cabo acted like and was treated like gente in the military and as the respected elected leader of Nova Brasília in its early days. He tells with pride of walking into city government offices and being recognized. He was not made to sit in the waiting room of the humble petitioners, who would be received in order of appearance until the end of the day and then sent on their way. Vereadores called him "Sir." They knew he could easily bring 20 busloads of residents to town hall and cause a scandal if there were any wrongdoing or mistreatment. Zé's dignity of bearing and detailed knowledge of every aspect of community needs and resources made him his community's definitive source of intelligence and authority.

Yet today, having been driven out of Nova Brasília by the drug gangs, he is living in an isolated, half-finished house in a place where no one knows him. No one knows what he achieved. He is nearly broke after paying his son's and his own medical bills and having purchased or built homes for two grandsons, one son, and one daughter from his first marriage and two daughters (plus their young children) from his second marriage. His granddaughter Patricia, the one family member who is completely gente, is concerned about his health but will neither visit him in the North Zone nor invite him to visit her in Copacabana. The gulf is wide. I imagine that she would prefer not to expose her favela roots. In her eyes, her grandfather is gentle and generous but not gente.

DONA RITA—MONEY IS NOT ENOUGH

It also takes more than money to be seen as gente. Rita owns two stores along the main road in Nova Brasília, several trucks, a nice house in a middle-class neighborhood, a beach house, and at least one car. Yet the clerks in a central Rio eyeglasses store would not serve her because of her appearance. Her clothing, shoes, hairstyle, and demeanor signaled that she was from the North Zone and therefore unlikely to be able to afford any of the frames. She had to demand to see the glasses and open her purse and show about US$1,000 in cash in order to get the salesgirl to unlock the showcase. She has a lot more money than most university professors but is not gente, nor is her son. Perhaps her grand-daughter, who is studying nursing while helping her father in the shoe store, will become gente—it is not yet clear.

Cariocas can instantaneously determine who is gente and who is not. This identification of "otherness" is based on tacitly agreed-on assessments of wealth, occupation, education, type of community, and overall appearance. All of these visual cues combine into what Brazilians call a pinta da pessoa: "the way the person comes across," or as Goffman put it, "their presentation of self in everyday life."[7] As I discussed in chapter 6, speech, body language, bearing, manner of dress, skin color, and self-assurance are all social signals separating the outcast from the entitled. But sometimes they are misleading.

CLAUDIA: LOOKING LIKE GENTE IS NOT ENOUGH

Claudia is a well-dressed, blonde, 30-something salesperson in the Fashion Mall, the elegant shopping mall in Sao Conrado, where some of Rio's richest families live. To see her, one would think she is gente. On the basis of her man-ner of speech, dress, and overall appearance—her subtly highlighted hair, pol-ished nails and fashionable clothing and accessories—she has the look of gente. Yet what is not visible is the fine line that separates her from nonpersonhood. She does not have a formal work contract, with the benefits and worker protec-tion that a contract implies. Her wages are low (and go primarily to keeping up appearances), her hours are long, and her job is contingent on the whim of the store owner. If she gets sick and misses work, she forfeits pay, while racking up medical costs; or if her bus breaks down (or is attacked—a common occurrence on the North Zone lines) she may be fired for missing work or for arriving late more than three times. She lives in an apartment building right in front of a favela, and although it is legal, it is considered part of the favela. If she loses her job, she won't be able to pay her rent, will lose her apartment, and will have nowhere to go. This happened to a friend of mine who was robbed just as she had withdrawn her rent money from the bank. She was never able to make it up. There is no leeway.

If having local status, assets, livelihood, and the requisite appearance is not enough to ensure being a person, neither is exiting the favela and moving into a conjunto or legal neighborhood. Tania Maria, a social worker for the Rio city government is a well-educated professional who conveys the demeanor of and is considered gente regardless of her government salary (which is low), of what she is wearing, or of her brown skin color. But Zé Cabo's daughter, Wandelina, who was a school librarian and lives in Santa Cruz, in a condominium of detached houses for government employees, speaks and acts not unlike the way she did when she was growing up in Nova Brasília and is often not treated as gente.

SEBASTIÃO: TOO LATE TO BECOME GENTE

Sebastião Daniel, from Nova Brasília, was a community leader in the 1960s and 1970s. He had a good job as a truck driver for a construction company and rose to become the dispatcher for all building materials. He moved to Nova Brasília in 1955 and within a decade was described as "king of the community."

He fought with local governments on behalf of poor people, holding elected officials to their campaign promises.

Currently, he is living in abject poverty next door to his former home in Nova Brasília. He is supporting a sick wife and seven other family members on his pension and a monthly basket of staples he gets from the church. When asked the biggest problem he is facing at present, he answered, "Getting milk for my grandson." When I asked him what should be done to help the poor, he responded that whenever he encounters anyone in need he gives him whatever money he can.

The worst aspect of his life, he said, is that he can no longer work and has to "ask for things." He is nearly blind and very hard of hearing, but said if someone would give him a truck, he'd drive it and earn money. He added, "I thought I would become gente someday, but my time has passed."

POOR AND RICH IN PEOPLE'S HEADS

In terms of perception, what it means to be rich and poor in Brazil corresponds closely with what it means to be gente or not. In October 2002, Unilever, a multinational consumer product conglomerate, contracted the Fundaçao Getulio Vargas to conduct market research among low-income Brazilians in an effort to better understand their potential customers. The results of the opinion survey were reported in *Valor Econômico*, a Brazilian newspaper, on March 18, 2003. The following lists show people's responses to the question about what it means to be poor and to be rich in Brazil.[8]

WHAT IT MEANS TO BE POOR

- Take the bus
- Be disrespected by the police
- Have to work to survive
- Have a boss
- Only buy what's on sale at the supermarket
- Have to wait on a line at the bank
- Believe that one's destiny depends on God
- Hit your children
- Need to move to improve life

WHAT IT MEANS TO BE RICH

- Use jewelry
- Have relatives or friends in the government
- Wash your dishes in a dishwasher
- Study in a university
- Be corrupt/rob public funds
- Buy things in the supermarket without looking at the prices
- Have employment but not have to work
- Eat out in restaurants
- Always buy your favorite brand products
- Attend a gym or sports academy

In her autobiography, Benedita da Silva, who was born and raised in a Rio favela and became national minister of social action, defined being poor as having only one set of clothing and washing it each night; not having enough food for the children; satisfying their hunger with a fried mixture of water and manioc to swell the stomach; sending them to sleep with cloth tied tightly around their bellies to reduce the hunger pangs; sending them from door to door at the end of the month to ask for food or money; and using motor oil for cooking because it costs less than cooking oil.

As Regina from Catacumba told me, "We are nobodies. Our houses are no-place. We cannot use our own address to enroll our children in school. We have to give the address of the madame in order to get our children into decent schools, get medical care, or get a job." Her daughter added: "The rich don't want the poor living near them or going to school with them—only serving them. They prefer us to remain invisible."

Identity for favela residents, aside from characteristics of age, gender, and color, is constantly being defined and redefined in the struggles over inclusion/exclusion and marginalization/integration. It says a lot about life in Rio that being a human being (gente) cannot be taken as a given for a third of the city's residents, and that the educational and job opportunities that would change that are not readily available.

The lack of opportunity for the poor is—in itself—a form of dehumanization and oppression that makes it impossible for a person to fulfill his or her full potential. MV Bill said in an interview: "Putting people in subhuman conditions in the favelas—that's a form of violence. Kids from the favelas attend state schools [and] have to work to help their families as well. Therefore, favela kids never have good enough education to get into public universities. They never have a chance. Those places go to middle- and upper-class kids from private schools."[9]

The internalized lack of self-esteem, inevitable for youth who are never treated as respectable people, is conducive to teenagers dropping out of school, having unprotected sex that leads to early pregnancies, and joining drug gangs. At least in the gang, the adolescent boys feel important and powerful. They are armed, they have cash; they wear expensive shoes, shirts, and jewelry; they may have a motorcycle, and they attract the attention of the most desirable young women. It is not hard to imagine a teenager being willing to risk early death for the chance to experience the respect and deference that ordinary people take as their birthright.

As Luiz Eduardo Soares has said, "in the end, there is a hunger more profound than physical hunger: the hunger for affection, recognition, self-esteem."[10] For those not born to it, higher education, professional occupation, and prime location within the urban geography are the best markers of being gente. The people from the favelas who became famous athletes, singers, models, movie stars, or politicians began to be treated as gente and to act like gente, and then they were gente. Examples run from Pele, the soccer star, to Gilberto Gil, the famous composer-singer who became an environmental activist, local politician, and then national minister of culture; and Benedita da Silva, who became the first black woman governor and then Minister of Social Action. But these are all exceptions to the rule.

The relationship between poverty and personhood in Latin America, and particularly in Brazil, was forged in the history of colonialism and slavery and fine-tuned under various authoritarian regimes, most recently the 20-year military dictatorship. Full enjoyment of universal rights for those without property and wealth has been "a sometime thing," to borrow from *Porgy and Bess*. This legacy has made it possible for educated and otherwise civilized people to slip into regarding favela residents as "other," while still maintaining a positive image of their own humanity. They feel good about treating their household help "as part of the family" (that is, paternalistically) as long as both sides are clear on the power hierarchy and behave by the rules of the game.

In the words of Evelina Dagnino, a renowned Brazilian political scientist, "being poor means not only economic, material deprivation but also being subjected to behavioral norms that imply a complete lack of recognition of poor people as bearers of rights."[11] She goes on to say that this "absolute absence of rights" means suppressing human dignity. When people internalize that self-image of unworthiness, they signal it in their demeanor, behavior, speech, and body language, which—in turn—signal permission to the "alpha" to exclude, exploit, even abuse. Edward Telles, refers to this suppression of human dignity as "incivility," adding that within this cultural complicity, being poor becomes a "sign of inferiority, a way of being in which individuals become unable to exercise their rights."[12]

The society convinces itself that the poor are poor because they are lazy, unreliable, and inferior—not through any societal injustice or inequality of opportunity. The fault lies with the victim. In *The Myth of Marginality* I refer to this as a "specular" relationship, in which the "mirror on the wall" does not reflect back the truth but the more comfortable image that the rich—the fairest of them all—have earned their privileges through their innate superiority. They have worked hard for it, and they deserve it. There is no guilt in this scenario.

The normalization of the social division between gente and nongente is evident in all social interactions, even on the beach. Aside from the usual class and race distinctions at various *postos* (sections) of the South Zone beaches—Copacabana, Ipanema, and Leblon—there are the ambulatory beach vendors. They come by bus from favelas in the distant *suburbios*, carrying all manner of food, beach accessories, handicrafts, and souvenirs. A *New York Times* article, "Drawing Lines across the Sand," reported an interview with one vendor who said: "Sometimes you get these groups of really hot upper-class babes putting down their boyfriends or talking about their sex lives right in front of you. It's like you're not even there, like you are invisible or not a person."[13]

Similar stories of lack of personhood are found elsewhere. In a shantytown on the outskirts of Durban, South Africa, a woman named Shamita Naidoo says "she often wonders whether anyone really ever sees her. She also wonders the same thing about the hundreds of people living around her, in tiny tin shacks perched underneath gum trees on a nearby hill. 'Sometimes…it seems like we are all invisible.'"[14]

On the other hand, ambulatory vendors on Rio's South Zone beaches, the men in the sidewalk kiosks that sell cold drinks and snacks, and even taxi drivers, give their goods and services to anyone who looks like gente, trusting them to repay them at a later date. I have seen a woman selling bikinis and beach cloths called *cangas* let a tourist take several away to try on at the hotel, without asking for a cent. The food stall owner will provide lunch and drinks to tourists in front of the Cesar Park Hotel (who have not brought cash to the beach) and trust them to return and pay up the following day.

Diametrically opposed to this is the fact that the favela residents hired by the fancy hotels to provide beach chairs, towels, lifeguard service, and security to the hotel guests are followed all day by high resolution surveillance cameras and may not be paid anything but bus fare and a lunch sandwich. They are expected to earn what they can from tips alone. These are the people most likely to share their sandwich with you if they happen to be taking their lunch break and you are nearby.

MULTIPLE KNOWLEDGES AND SENSE OF SELF

If those lines in the sand are erased and the favela youth are able to develop a sense of self-worth and self-respect, it will be that much more difficult for those who wish to keep them in a subservient position. Many programs run by nonprofit organizations in the favelas incorporate aspects of affirming this inalienable right of personhood. Some, such as the Committee for the Democratization of Information Technology (CDI), founded in 1995 by Rodrigo Baggio, do this by bringing information technology and computer access/training into the favelas. Others, such as Viva Rio, have programs such as "Favela Tem Memória," an oral history project that favela youth work on with elders, or favela correspondents, who write weekly columns on what is happening in their communities. Other programs, for example those of the Centro de Estudos e Ações Solidárias da Maré in the favela of the Complexo do Maré, run prevestibular courses, train and hire youth to conduct door-to-door censuses of their communities, teach English and French, and offer theater, video, film, dance, creative arts, music, and capoeira programs for youth.

One NGO program, Roda Viva, creates support groups for mothers while providing day care for their children. Another of their activities deals directly with youth, preteens, and adolescents before they have given up on themselves, internalized their nongente status and entered the drug trade or prostitution. I was especially struck by a group leader who was using Paulo Freire's approach to consciousness raising (*conscientização*). This was combined with computer courses that actually taught literacy and writing skills under the guise of teaching computer skills.

A discussion group I observed in the Morro dos Macacos provides an excellent example of reinforcing personhood. It started with the usual noise, commotion, joking, and jostling as the young people arrived, coming up the steps on the side of the Residents' Association and into the meeting room. Along three of the walls were makeshift wooden desks, with a computer on each one. After I was introduced, the facilitator asked for a minute of silence for each person to think about what they knew and what knowledge they had to share. They began to quiet down. Then he told this story:

Three people traveling together came to a river and asked the boatman to take them across. He readily agreed, and when they were on their way, the first passenger, a lawyer, asked him if he was familiar with Brazilian law. When the boatman humbly admitted that he was not, the lawyer replied, "Then you are *perdido* [doomed, lost]—without that knowledge, you can be nothing." The second asked the same about mathematics, and on hearing the boatman knew nothing of this, repeated, "Then you are perdido—without knowledge of math, you are nothing." The third, a schoolteacher, said, "Surely you know how to read and write." "No," said the boatman. The schoolteacher replied, "Then you are perdido."

Suddenly a huge tidal wave came up the river and tipped over the canoe. The boatman turned to his passengers in concern, and seeing them being swept along downstream yelled out, "Do you know how to swim?" "No," they said; "We never learned." "Then you are perdido," he replied.

Before this anecdote, the kids were looking uncomfortable and bored. When he came to the end, they were paying rapt attention and looking pleased and astonished—they had never considered that they, too, might have valuable knowledge based on their life experience. This was one small step away from drug dealing, and one small step toward thinking of themselves as gente.

FAVELA TOURISM, OR "POORISM"

Not all roads lead to gente, and not all relationships between the morro and the asfalto will help people bridge that gap. Some forms of contact serve only to reinforce the nonpersonhood of the favela residents.

The recent favela craze that has expressed itself in many ways has done nothing to reinforce the residents' sense of identity and worth. On the contrary, it has brought favelas into the spotlight of a wider audience not as repositories of knowledge or of people with the capacity to revitalize Rio's flagging economy or fragile ecology but as an exotic curiosity of poverty—as a voyeuristic pleasure with the subtext "Better them than us." Is this the modern-day equivalent of the European fascination with the "noble savage"?

The faddish buzz about favelas could not even be imagined in 1968 and had not yet blossomed when I returned to pick up the research in 1999. However, it has grown rapidly in the years since then, with its heady mixture of forbidden otherness, romance, danger, drugs, music, and the new industry of funk balls.

While favela residents fear leaving their houses to go to work, favela tourism is burgeoning, giving new and ominous meaning to the old saw "It's a nice place to visit but I wouldn't want to live there." The appropriation of the culture of the poor by the privileged, known variously as "reverse snobbery" or "slum-ming," is not new. What *is* new is the scope and scale of it that today's globally networked society allows. Notable visitors to the now famous (or infamous) favela of Rocinha include the queens of Sweden and Denmark, Princess Diana of England, Bill Clinton, Mikhail Gorbachev, the Pope, and President Ignácio Lula da Silva.

Now, in addition to taking the cable car up to Sugar Loaf and the tram to Corcovado, tourists can stop by one of the city's elite hotels or go online to sign up for an "authentic" favela tour. A broad menu of options includes going safari-style in an open Jeep, traveling by air-conditioned minivan, or embarking on a walking tour. Details are easily found at Ipanema.com, in the "Rio de Janeiro Favelas Guide," or in the "Gringo Guides." Favela Tours, one of the earliest companies in the business, now takes more than 5,000 people into the favelas each year. There is no tinge of shame in this commodification of favela life.

As an indication of how romanticized favelas have become, a recent BBC News article featured photographs of a happy young American couple spend-ing their honeymoon at a bed-and-breakfast in Rocinha, conveniently situated on the hills above the South Zone.[15] It's no accident that of all the favelas, Rocinha has become the most popular among tourists. Its views are spectacu-lar, surpassing those from the nearby Sheraton and Inter-Continental hotels. Every NGO wants to work in Rocinha, and every government program wants a pilot project there—while most of the other 800 favelas in Rio receive almost no attention from either. The book *Sorria, Você Esta na Rocinha* (Smile, you are in Rocinha) describes it this way:

> It seems like a dream, a delirium, a vision, something crazy: seen from afar with its millions of flickering lights, the Favela of Rocinha looks like a gigantic flying saucer recently landed on a Rio hillside. It's as if an unidentified flying object improbably parked there to attract the curiosity of anyone trying to grasp the meaning these luminescent signals are sending to the city.[16]

Being objectified like exotic wildlife on a safari or extraterrestrials on a visit to Planet Earth does not go unnoticed by the favela residents. Though the tours are marketed as bringing money into the communities through sales of drinks, snacks, and art, and supporting educational and recreational programs, this is not the way it works. The local luncheonette where the vans stop for cold drinks and the arts-and-crafts stand where tourists are given time to purchase souvenirs are obliged to pay a steep kickback to the tour enterprise and to the narco-traffic. Favela tourism ultimately profits the dominant drug gang of the moment and reinforces their control over the people in the community.

Wanting to experience these favela tours for myself, I took one in 2004. The guide, assuming no one spoke Portuguese, simultaneously romanticized and denigrated the residents. When it came time for a "home visit" to see a dwelling from the inside, I could see the entire family filing out the back door just as the group began getting off the bus. Every precaution was taken to ensure that no one could talk directly with an actual resident.

The small sums of money that make it through to the residents are always welcomed, so there is disagreement over whether to commend or criticize this tourism. Unfortunately, the poorest favelas, the ones that have not benefited from NGO or government programs and that have the greatest need for income, are not on the tour circuit at all. They are too distant, too dangerous, and devoid of picturesque views.

According to my last count, only 8 of the 1,023 favelas in Rio (as of 2007) attract tourism: Rocinha (56,400 residents), Vidigal (9,400), and Vila Canoes (1,600) are the most popular. Ipanema and Copacabana have four favelas left (Pavao-Pavãozinho, Cantegalo, Morro de Cabritos, and Ladeira de Tabajares), and Leme has two (Babelonia and Chapéu Mangueira). The Botafogo hillside favela of Santa Marta (sometimes erroneously called Dona Marta) has a long history of spirited leadership and community mobilization as well as stunning views of the city, which may attract foreign visitors. The worldwide image of favelas is based on a tiny number of particularly well-located communities with views that in any other city would be the prerogative of the super-rich.

The local Rio population does not share this favela fascination. In fact, most do everything possible to avoid entering the very neighborhoods where their own maids and handymen live (with the exception of those who go to buy drugs or to attend funk balls or samba schools). In *City of Walls*, Caldeira writes about the lengths to which the rest of the local society will go to feel protected from what they fear from the favelas—gated communities, security systems, round-the-clock armed guards.[17] When I recently attempted to visit a musician friend in an upscale community, I had to walk over a moat while being filmed, show identity papers to an armed guard, and have written authorization to enter the building if she was not there to let me in. When I walked down residential streets in the older parts of the city, I saw that the gardens in front of the apartment buildings were fenced in by iron grates. Old people sat in folding chairs reading their newspapers, taking in a bit of sun, and watching the street activity from behind bars. These upscale new fortresses, built to keep undesirables out, make those inside feel like prisoners. It's not exactly conducive to the conviviality of urban life. Meanwhile, favelas are turning themselves into gated communities as well, with the addition of grates over many windows and doors.

Just how undesirable is it to live near a favela? Apartments on streets with entranceways into favelas are available for rent or sale at about half the rate of comparable places elsewhere. Clearly, "favela chic" does not extend to living near one.

FAVELA CHIC

If favela tourism began in 1992, when Marcelo Armstrong started the first favela tour, then worldwide favela chic started in 1995, with the opening of the Parisian bar Ubercool. Frommer's review gushes: "No other nightclub in Paris succeeds at satirizing and respecting Brazilian-ness as effectively as this one…attracting good-looking, trendy men and women who come to dance, flirt, and chat in any of a dozen languages." London's trendy East End was next. The *Time Out* guide commented in 2008: "There's a definite carnival feel to the place, with bric-a-brac strewn around the tatty, lived-in interior intended to bring to mind a real Brazilian favela and funky Brazilian beats on the sound system." Then came a Tokyo restaurant called Favela, serving nouveau Brazilian cuisine along with Brahma, the common Brazilian beer, at 10 times the usual Brazilian price. Finally, New York City got in on the act with Miss Favela, a restaurant that opened in Brooklyn in the spring of 2008 and Favela Cubana in Greenwich Village in 2009.

The term "favela chic" is ensconced in the lexicon of international fashion, food, nightlife, art, and music. The favela's image of otherness, its authentic aesthetic, and its libidinal energy have captured the imagination of the global elite. But how does this homage to the favela compare with the real thing? For starters, "bric-a-brac" and "tatty" are not words I would use to describe homes in a favela. Most are immaculate and in a constant process of improvement and/or expansion, being the main or only assets of their owners. In the consolidated favelas (the older ones that have continually expanded out and up), most houses have glazed tiles on the floor and on the walls of their kitchens and bathrooms; comfortable couches and polished coffee tables in the living-room; and formal bedroom sets of dark wood— as well as most of the electrical appliances found in an upper-middle-class home. Most favela residents are so fastidious that before there was running water or paved steps, they would go down to the street barefoot, wash their feet in the collective spigot, and then put on their shoes.

Favela fascination does not stop with nightlife or exquisitely designed replicas of supposedly tawdry shacks. Artistic representations are popping up in the most unexpected places. In 2005, the Luxembourg metro station in Paris was transformed by an enormous installation of favela photos, elaborated on with quotations from favela residents and aficionados (including one by me). The architecture/design installation "Favelité," by Françoise Schein, Laura Taves, Pedro Rivera, and Pedro Evora, was on exhibit for several months, and was intended to show something of value and beauty in the favelas as well as to raise the consciousness of Parisians regarding their own privilege vis-à-vis the deprivation of others.

There is no question that for artists and architects especially, there is a certain beauty in Rio's favelas. With their variegated colors, interesting angles,

FIGURE 12.2   Favela Installation at the Luxembourg Metro Station in Paris.

and creative use of materials, favela structures can be seen as exemplifying the mantra of the new urbanism: Low rise, high density—made visually interesting by an absence of standardization.

Consumer items related to the favela craze get even crazier. Havaianas, the colored rubber flip-flops that are popular in favelas and cost about US$3.50, are selling in fashionable London boutiques for US$170. If that weren't absurd enough, a "favela chair" created by Italian designers Fernando and Humberto Campana in 2003 seems to cross over the line from homage to insult. It is said to sell for US$4,025, but may be purchased online at the sale price of only US$2,985. The advertisement for it states: "The 'Favela' chair is constructed piece-by-piece from Pinus, the same wood used to build the favelas, and every piece is hand-glued and nailed."[18]

This certainly puts a new twist on Oscar Lewis's idea of a "culture of poverty," which he mapped out as a set of behaviors and beliefs passed down from one generation to the next, perpetuating the poverty cycle. In counterpoint to that, today a highbrow cultural phenomenon of simultaneously imitating, mocking, and exalting the poor has taken hold.

The pejorative perception of favelas has taken different forms, but has only worsened with the entrance of drug and arms trafficking within their territories. Revenues from the profits of favela chic bars, restaurants, dance, music, fashion, and design have not reached the favela communities, while they fill the pockets of the rich in Europe—and to a lesser extent in the United States.

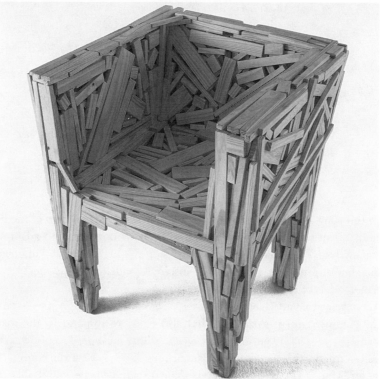

FIGURES 12.3 AND 12.4   A favela (photo by author) and the Favela Chair, designed by Fernando and Humberto Campana in 1991. (Image taken by Andréas Heiniger)

THE RESPONSE FROM INSIDE

Within the favelas, the response to favela chic is mixed. Songs about favela pride turn the derision and commodification upside down. The lyrics of local rap, hip-hop, funk, Afro Reggae, and samba songs spin the meaning of favela into a point of pride and insurgent identity, as in the popular songs "Eu sou favela" (I am favela) and "Minha favela" (My favela). This has a lot to do with the crossfertilization of Afro Brazilians and the Black Pride movement in the United States. But make no mistake: if the word *favela* has been reappropriated by favela residents, it remains a term of derision in the rest of society.

MINHA FAVELA (MY FAVELA)

Favela that witnessed my birth
Favela that holds my roots
I open my heart and sing my love for you.

You smile during the day and cry at dawn
Embrace and love all who are born,
When they are killed, you cry and mourn

Only those who know from the inside
Can ever understand
Your beauty and your beast
Here I can be happy at the very least.

How is it our people who work so hard and are so good,
Are seen as marginals, best killed if they could?
I think that society must have very bad vision.[19]

In this song and others, favela residents have turned the energy of the place around, jujitsu style, embracing the derision of the outsiders and adapting it for themselves. They enjoy seeing on television the high-fashion combination of glamour and trash couture they've inspired, modeled by the most famous fashion models of Brazil.

The favela residents have ridden the wave of favela chic in music, sarcastically commenting in their lyrics but also ready to respond to the market demand. There is a CD entitled *Favela Chic*, whose local producers are cashing in on the trend while simultaneously attacking the naïveté of the concept. The first cut, "Manda O Som DJ!—Favela Chic" (Send over the sound, DJ) starts with the seductively taunting voice of a man, clearly a favela resident, saying "You must be crazy—You think favelas are chic…come on, stay awhile…see for yourself…here favelas are not chic, not in the least."

In a similar response, the favela theater group Nós do Morro (We of the Favela), which made its name revealing the traumas of favela life from within, started writing and performing plays about the seamy side of the spoiled rich kids who come to the favelas seeking thrills and drugs. The play I saw, which took place on a favela rooftop (*lage*), told the story of several of these confused young people, in search of emotional connection and meaning, who had rented the lage for a wild drug party.

The only sympathetic character in the play was a favela resident hired by these teenagers as their security guard for the night. The play made audiences uncomfortable—and not just from sitting on the metal folding chairs arranged around the stage area. They had gotten their tickets from hotel concierges or on the Internet, had been picked up at the Sheraton Hotel by minivans, and had been driven up into the heights of the favela of Vidigal. At the entrance to the favela was an amphitheater covered in turquoise tiles spelling out the Declaration of Human Rights—a project that had been completed by favela children under the supervision of Belgian artist Francoise Schein. The Declaration is a clear statement of rights, but the residents of Vidigal clearly do not share in these rights.

How are the people living in Rio's favelas to react to the existence of "favela chic" fashion shows in Paris, while their sons or brothers are being murdered over Nike shoes? How are they to feel about the favela chic chair, the price of which could finance a business start-up, when their daily struggle involves choosing between buying medicine for a diabetic spouse or milk for a baby grandson?

FAVELAS ARE NOT PARADISE

To say that the word "favela" and its connotations are "problematic" would be a gross understatement. Every issue relating to favelas is fraught with projections, contradictions, and misunderstanding. However they are seen by outsiders, the favelas of Rio remain stigmatized places of fear within a city struggling to redefine its economy and identity, within a highly unequal country not yet able to provide equal protection under the rule of law.

If my earlier work showed the positive side of favelas and argued for their right to remain, this new study shows how marginality has evolved from a myth to reality. The marginalization of the urban poor became a self-fulfilling prophecy, as does the denial of the right to personhood. When you take away self-esteem, how can you develop human potential?

At the other end of the spectrum, the glorification of favela residents as models of utopian sustainability (by the likes of Stewart Brand) does as much disservice to them and the challenges they face as does their vilification by the media and their objectification by profiteers. It is appalling to read that favelas are now being touted as the solutions to environmental problems, overpopulation, and housing shortages.[20] The notion that they are protected and provided for by a "parallel power" of benign drug lords is as offensively false as the earlier stereotypes of their inability to adapt to urban life.

Globalization has transformed the local job market; world-class images have defined local "needs"; and international drug and arms traffic have remade local settlements into violent traps for the disenfranchised. This is not a model for emulation or for achieving a sustainable planet.

The direction for going forward would be to make common cause between the morro and the asfalto on the issue of economic growth and jobs, without despoiling the environment that is Rio's source of local pride and international tourism. There is mutual benefit to be had in this new formulation. Insofar as Rio's financial and natural resources are being stretched to their limits, the answer must be found by cultivating the one resource that is abundant and underutilized in the city—its people.

Booker T. Washington, who was born into slavery in 1856 in the then Confederate State of Virginia, rose to become president of the Tuskegee Institute in Alabama. It was then a college for "Negroes," and Booker T. Washington was the ardent promoter of its existence and of economic opportunities for its graduates and all who were being held back by racial discrimination.

In 1895, in a speech he gave at the Cotton States and International Exposition in Atlanta, Washington mixed black pride and southern pride by encouraging blacks to stay and work in the South (rather than migrate to the North) and whites to value this contribution to a thriving local economy. His speech to a mixed audience was upbeat but not without an ominous warning. In it, he said, "We shall contribute one-third to the business and industrial prosperity of the South, or we shall prove a veritable body of death, stagnating, depressing, retarding every effort to advance the body politic."[21]

AGENCY AND OPTIMISM

Despite all, the people in the favelas have by no means given up hope. Nor have they resigned themselves to the obliteration of their right to be part of the human community. Cariocas, as Rio natives are called, are perpetual optimists. This came out strongly in their assessments of the progress they had made in their own lives and in their expectations for the future. They were less optimistic about the future of their communities, their city, and their country. The majority saw themselves as having exceeded their own aspirations, and surpassed the expectations that their parents had for them. Only one-fifth reported their lives turned out worse than they had expected.[22] There is a positive relationship between optimism and successful life outcomes and between perceived satisfaction and actual well-being on the individual level.

Given the constraints faced by favela residents, I was eager to see how those I interviewed in 1969 and again in 2001 perceived their opportunities for success in life, and how that differed from the perceptions of their children and grandchildren. In their view, do they have the same chance of succeeding in life as any other person, or did they see their chances blocked by a closed system that denies their existence as gente?

In our questionnaire we asked one of the classic questions about class consciousness: "Do you think that your child and the child of an *homem de negócios* (businessman), have the same chance to succeeed in life *(vencer na vida)*?" After all the talk of exclusion and stigma, I would have predicted that most parents would say *NO!* But I would have been wrong. Around six in ten people in both time periods and in all three generations said *YES*: 56 percent of the original sample in 1969; 57 percent of them in 2001; 62 percent of their children and 57 percent of their grandchildren. After verifying that the question was correctly understood and that the answers were valid, I began to search for the meaning of this consistent answer. My interpretation is that the respondents had so thoroughly internalized the fiction of equal opportunity that to say their children had less than a fair chance would be to admit their failure as parents rather than the result of a closed and unjust system. That helps explain the absence of anger or rebellion among most community residents. Their self-esteem is so low that they blame themselves for any failure in upward mobility.

I also asked several direct questions about class. People reported having moved up and down the class ladder at different stages in their lives. Some said they were now in the *classe pobre* (poor class), but a generation ago, when they were public functionaries or truck drivers, they considered themselves part of the *classe media* (middle class). Study participants from the older generation often commented that they no longer saw a middle class. "Agora só tem duas classes—rico e pobre" (Now here are only two classes—rich and poor), they said, with "a huge chasm between them."

Despite the striking improvements in the material conditions of life, the poor feel ever further from being gente. It appears as an ever-receding mirage on the horizon. Perhaps as the grandchildren finish their schooling, their high unemployment rate will drop, and more will enter formal sector jobs with benefits. Secure jobs with good pay would be one way to close the gente gap.

Dona Rita is skeptical, although she does hold out hope for her granddaughters, who are studying teaching and nursing. Her son has already raised them where she lives—outside the favela. That gives them a better chance, she says. After pointing out certain improvements in Nova Brasília over the past several years, she gave a sigh and added: "Favela é favela e ainda tem preconceito" (A favela is still a favela and there is still prejudice against us). She added, "It raises doubts in people's minds if you give an address here—you have to give a false address to be treated fairly."

PERCEPTIONS AND PROSPECTS

Insofar as perceptions affect sense of identity and behavior patterns, the way individuals look at their own situation is an essential aspect of breaking out of the poverty trap. Mobility is a relational concept, and it is always defined through comparison to others. As the literature shows, people's outcomes in absolute terms are often not as important to their sense of well-being and degree of hope, or a sense of how they are doing relative to their own past, their own aspirations, as the expectations their parents have had for them. They also assess their progress in terms of others in their family, their community, the place from which they came, their colleagues at work, and so on. Even television characters become a kind of reference group against which people assess their own sense of deprivation.[23]

In the questionnaire, we explored this by asking the respondents what they thought it meant to have a "successful life" (*uma vida bem sucedida*). Using their own definitions, respondents were then asked to place their current lives on the rungs of a ten-step ladder.[24] Six questions followed with each answer marked on a rung of the ladder relative to where they had positioned their own lives in the current moment.

The positive responses to six of these questions are shown in table 12.1.

Despite all of the disappointments and setbacks discussed throughout this book, the table shows that most people across all generations (close to 60 percent) ranked their current lives as better (on a higher rung of the ladder) than they had been in the past decade(s). But most felt that their children's lives were worse than their own–probably due to the fear and violence they live with (since we have seen that education and material conditions

TABLE 12.1 *Perceptions of Progress toward a Good Life*

	% RESPONDING "BETTER" OR "MUCH BETTER" TO EACH COMPARISON					
	Q1: My life now vs. 30 (10) years ago[a]	*Q2: My life vs. my parents' lives*	*Q3: My kids lives vs. my life*	*Q4: My life vs. my expectation*	*Q5: My life vs. my parents' expectation*	*Q6: My family vs. other families in community*
Original Interviewees	59	53	43	48	58	41
Children	60	35	44	52	49	27
Grandchildren	65	27	47	52	50	19

[a] We asked about 30 years ago for original interviewees; and 10 years ago for children and grandchildren.

have improved with each generation). The children's assessment of their lives relative to their parents' lives is increasingly negative for each successive generation. Over half of the original sample ranked their lives as better than their parents,' but only 35 percent of the children and 27 percent of the grandchildren said the same. To put it the opposite way, 73 percent of the grandchildren ranked their lives as worse than their parents'. They are torn between the out-of-school/out-of-work dead end on the one hand and the short-life-expectancy-for-those-in-the-traffic dead end on the other. No wonder their parents' lives seem enviable in comparison.

In the same vein, the grandchildren show the greatest sense of relative deprivation in response to the question comparing their family with other families in the community (the right-most column of the table). Eighty-one percent of the grandchildren felt their families were worse off than others around them; as compared with 73 percent of children and 59 percent of original interviewees. A material explanation for this might be that half of the grandchildren live in legitimate bairros where indeed they may be among the lowest-income families, while two thirds of the original sample still live in favelas or conjuntos where they may be among the more established. The trend for the younger generation to have achieved the most and feel the least satisfied may reflect what Graham and Pettinato call the "frustrated achievers" syndrome in new market economies, whereby those who are doing the best by objective measures are the least satisfied.[25] However, there was little variance in the way the different generations viewed the ways that their own lives had evolved relative to their own expectations and relative to their parents' expectations—they were fairly evenly split between those who felt they had surpassed expectations and those who felt disappointed. The notable exception was that the lives of the original interviewees more often exceeded the presumably modest hopes of their parents and less often exceeded their own greater expectations.

What this seems to point to is that even as progress is being made at the material and educational levels, the goal of breaking out of poverty—of becoming gente—is a moving target, always elusive and out of reach. The closer you get, the more excluded you feel, and the grandchildren who by objective standards are the closest to being working or middle class are the ones who feel the farthest away. Economic achievements are not overcoming the marginalization, disrespect, and exclusion that the poor experience, despite indicators that they are now less poor.[26]

How, then, do they see their progress over the past several years, and how do they see their prospects for the future? I asked these two questions in the 1969 interviews and in the 2001 interviews with the original study participants, their children, and their grandchildren. From generation to generation, the percentage saying "better" or "much better" rose steadily over time, from a low of 24 percent among the original interviewees in 1969 to 46 percent among the same people in 2001; to 63 percent among their children; to a high of 73 percent among their grandchildren.

Despite the economic miracle of the 1960s and the major achievement of moving to Rio, the people I interviewed in 1969 had a rough time. Just over half said their lives were better five years earlier. That percentage went up by the time we reinterviewed them in 2001 and rose steadily among their children and grandchildren. In fact, violence, drugs, and lack of jobs notwithstanding, the percent of children who said their lives were improving was over two and a half times that of their parents. Something good must be happening. Perhaps it has to do with the exit from favela life The move made by the original interviewees from countryside to city and their integration into urban life as squatters must have been more arduous than the move from favelas (or conjuntos) to bairros.

We also asked "Will your life be better in the next five years?" In 1969, only 12 percent answered "better" or "much better," while 66 percent answered "worse" or "much worse." By 2001, 64 percent of the original interviewees, 88 percent of their children, and 95 percent of their grandchildren thought their lives would improve in the next five years.

So despite all, hope is alive and thriving as depicted in figure 12.5.

Whatever generalization you make about favelas can be contradicted by a counterexample. If you show their vibrant side, you risk romanticizing poverty. If you dwell on the violent side, you obscure their vitality and you risk propagating wrong-minded stereotypes and stigma that residents battle every day.

FIGURE 12.5   Favela children ready and eager to build the city of tomorrow.

Everything in a favela contains its opposite. If you think favela tourism is an exploitation and commodification, you are not respecting a potential source of cash coming into the community. If you take a moralistic stance vis-à-vis the drug traffic, you ignore the fact that those involved may be supporting their families on the money they earn. But…what use is a new bedroom air conditioner when most young men don't live past 25 or 30? It is a complicated situation that resists simple conclusions. Only through prolonged involvement can the deeper truths revealed by my 40 years of observation, analysis, and reflection be teased from the myriad of conflicting meanings and messages.

Poverty and exclusion are plastic, changing with changing times over each generation—and they are by no means a simple function of attaining better goods and services (although these represent a major step forward). Each generation has faced different challenges. For the original migrants, the move to the city, the exchange of rural poverty for urban poverty, and developing the ability to survive in the new milieu was the challenge. It was in itself a major leap forward to establish a bridgehead or toehold in the big city.[27] Their collective struggles created a sense of community solidarity not shared by the following generations.

For the children, born in the city, the quest was for higher education, for getting out of the favelas, and for a sense of recognition and respect. In the grandchildren's generation, educational attainment is high; over half are living in legal, legitimate neighborhoods; and the level of consumption of household goods is close to the municipal average. Their particular challenges are finding work (over half are unemployed), avoiding being killed, and finding respect. An economist looking at census data might not even perceive that this generation has risen out of poverty: sadly, within the current context of Rio de Janeiro, these young people are still disenfranchised, dismissed, and considered expendable. Regardless of all the favela residents' achievements over three generations, most of the youngest generation would not be considered gente today. They do not feel included in the life of Rio. In my interviews I found that even the ones with jobs in the formal sector who owned cars and computers felt obliged to act *subservient* and *deferential* toward *o senhor* or *a madame*. This is how a historically unequal society maintains the superiority of the rich without risking the revolt of the poor.

On the morro in Canudos, where Antonio Conselheiro, the Counselor, led his flock nearly a century and a half ago, the favela bushes remain. The favelas above and around Rio and other cities remain, too. Will they be treated as the Counselheiro's flock was treated? Will they be slaughtered? They are now so many more in number than they were then. Unless we can overcome the fear of otherness and mutually engage in the struggle against need, repression, disrespect, and violence, there will be no urban future for the rich or the poor.

appendix 1

RESEARCH METHODS AND CHALLENGES

As you can imagine, the process of finding the original study participants after thirty years was fraught with challenges. It was like being a detective, searching out clues, going to the places where I had last seen each person, following up leads, running into dead ends, and trying alternative tacks. It was also an enlightening process in itself—and a joyous one when I found each person. In reconnecting with these individuals and families—more of them than I ever dreamed I would find—I discovered just how strong and long lasting the community ties within favelas can be, even in the absence of physical proximity. For years, without telephones or email, and without bus fares for visits, people managed to stay in touch by word of mouth. They knew where their friends and former neighbors had gone, how their health was, and which of their family members still lived in the area.

OBJECTIVES OF THE LONGITUDINAL RESEARCH

In 1999 when I embarked on the restudy for this book, my objectives were stated as follows:

- To better understand the intra- and intergenerational dynamics of urban poverty
- To explore the changing mythology and reality of marginality
- To trace life history patterns against macro political and economic transformations
- To test the mediating effects of civil society and social networks
- To see the impacts, if any, of local, national, and international public policies implemented since the original study

I matched each objective with a broader goal and with the tasks necessary to accomplish the research, and laid out the products and outcomes for each part of the work. The way these connect to each other is shown in (table A1.1).

TABLE AI.I *The Dynamics of the Urban Poor and Implications for Public Policy*

Goals	Objectives	Tasks	Products	Outcomes
• To understand the dynamics of urban poverty and mobility	• Trace the life trajectories of favelados over 30+ years	1. Commission Longitudinal Trend and Policy Studies	• Longitudinal data on the life trajectories of Rio's favelados for use in other studies	• Larger knowledge base on the factors that shape and perpetuate urban poverty
• To explore the effects of public policy on low-income individuals, families, and communities	• Identify coping mechanisms and survival strategies for overcoming poverty	2. Review Literature and Secondary Data	• Capacity building: trained residents in documenting their own reality	• Clearer understanding of the role local, national, and international policies play in lives of the urban poor
• To trace life history patterns against major political and economic transformations and urban evolution	• Train and employ favelados along with university students for research team	3. Relocate Original Interviewees or Their Families and Descendants	• Input into official documents, e.g., World Development Report	• Increased capacity and self-esteem of favela residents, community organizations, local nonprofits • Informal policy-makers at local, national, and international level
• To test the mediating effects of civil society and social networks	• Evaluate the impact of public policy on the urban poor in Rio, contrasting targeted and untargeted policies	4. Draw New Random and Leadership Samples in Original Communities	• Photo documentation showing then and now	• Improved allocation for urban research, policy, and practice
• To better inform decision-makers concerned with the urban poor	• Identify milestones in the political, economic, and urban changes in Brazil	5. Select Policy-Specific Upgraded Favelas for comparison	• Policy implications derived from research findings	• Creation of methodology for use in other longitudinal and panel studies of urban poverty and mobility

- Explore the role of NGOs and community-based associations
- Convene stakeholders and policy meetings to test results and disseminate findings

6. Prepare and pretest survey instruments
7. Conduct field interviews
   - Multigenerational
   - Site-Specific
8. Contextual and historical research
9. Coding of life history data, questionnaires, and interview results
10. Data verification and analysis
11. Draft report for feedback
12. Present findings at Rio, Brazil, and international meetings
13. Revise final report
14. Dissemination to targeted audiences

- Publication in journals, edited volumes, and newsletters
- Book

- Where political will exists, higher probability of policy success
- Learning community to share knowledge and advocate for change focused on upgrading and urban poverty

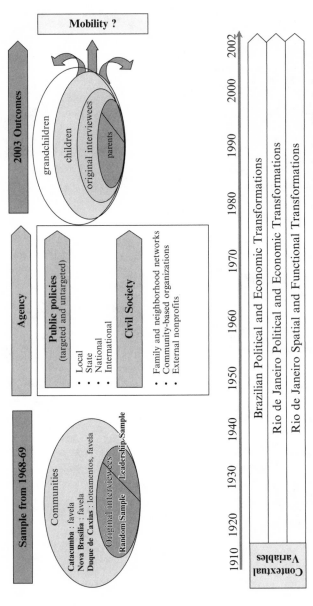

FIGURE A1.1 Conceptual framework for longitudinal multigenerational study in the favelas of Rio de Janeiro.

CONCEPTUAL FRAMEWORK

The conceptual framework I used in addressing the study goals and objectives and in guiding the analysis is diagrammatically depicted in figure A1.1, which I also discussed briefly in chapter 9.

The fundamental question is what happened to the residents of the three original communities in 1968–69 over four decades as compared with their (largely rural and illiterate) parents and as compared with their urban-born, better-educated children and grandchildren. It looks at how public policy and civil society may or may not have influenced the changes over this time period and within the larger context of transformations in Brazil and in the city of Rio de Janeiro.

MIXED METHODOLOGIES

The study was optimistically ambitious in scope. I am not sure I would have had the courage to start it if I had realized how many years it would take. But I wanted to trace the life trajectories across the four generations and knew that this had never before been done in any systematic way for the urban poor. With the help of colleagues and the invaluable assistance of local residents, I combined qualitative and quantitative methods, including direct observation; in-depth (open-ended) interviews; a participatory process to collectively recreate the history of each community (DRP); and survey questionnaires plus year-by-year life histories gathered from interviews with a total of 2,182 people. All of these were used to compare with the original questionnaires, life histories, and open-ended interviews conducted in the earlier study, and to compare with census and household survey data from the same points in time. With this mixture of methods I was able to shed light on the issues of transgenerational transmission of poverty, inequality, and exclusion, and to explore social mobility in a highly unequal society.

PROBLEMS CONFRONTED

Among the problems we faced were (1) finding the original interviewees and verifying their identities (having used first names only in our original study led to many false leads in the beginning); (2) establishing contact with and cooperation from family members of original participants who had since died; (3) gaining access to the communities (permission to conduct the study) in the face of increasing control by drug gangs; (4) formulating a revised questionnaire that would be comparable to the original one but comprehensible and relevant in the current moment; (5) recreating the contextual histories of the three communities; (6) dealing with selective memory and memory loss; and (7) testing for potential bias resulting from any systematic differences between the people we found and those we did not find.

THREE PHASES OF THE STUDY

The study was divided into three phases, an exploratory phase (to test the feasibility of finding the original interviewees); a multigenerational interview phase that looked at the same people and their descendents over time; and a community study phase, looking at a new random sample in the original study sites.

Phase I: Exploratory Research

In assessing the feasibility of finding original participants and working with them in the restudy, we conducted a series of open-ended and semistructured interviews with some of the "survivors" from the original sample, collecting their personal narratives and exploring how they tended to describe their experiences, how much they recalled, what they identified as benchmarks in their own lives, and the lives of their communities, and what meaning they assigned to certain words, concepts, and images.

Phase II: Implementation

Next, we reinterviewed 262 out of the original 750 study participants and a random sample of their children 16 years or older (394 out of 1,005). We then moved on to a random sample of their grandchildren, 16 years or older. We decided to include grand-children, despite the fact that there were fewer of them, because we suspected that some of the mobility that the original generation seemed to expect for their children when they decided to migrate to the city was only beginning to show up in the grandchildren's generation.

This phase also included contextual interviews and participatory collective recon-struction of community histories (using DRP), as well as leadership interviews with old and new leaders in which we touched on struggles of the past, challenges of the present, and what has changed over time. We were fortunate enough to capture some of the key moments in these interviews on videotape, including a scene in which three former lead-ers of Catacumba returned to the site of where their homes had been (now an abandoned park) and recalled growing up there and the politics that had led to their eviction.

Phase III: The New Random Sample

The next step was to select new random samples from the original communities and apply the same survey techniques to them, so that we might compare the communities at two points in time, as well as assess and mitigate any bias that might result from the particular subsample we were following. We interviewed 400 people randomly selected in each of the communities and 25 local leaders from each community.

We also identified the ten most and least successful individuals from the random sample and from the elite sample and conducted open-ended interviews with these 40 individuals, searching for clues as to what factors may have contributed to their dispa-rate positions in life.

And finally we created multigenerational portraits of selected families, visiting each member of each generation. We were concerned about how the selection of random children within a family could affect our perceptions of the next generation. To address this concern, I selected several of the leaders and random sample individuals whom I knew well in each of the three communities, and I visited the homes and/or workplaces of as many of their siblings, children, and grandchildren as possible. It was while doing this that I created the family trees showing the size of each family along with the education and occupation of each family member. . Getting to know the children and grandchildren better was essential to the stories I have told in this book.

CONCEPTS OF POVERTY, INEQUALITY, MARGINALITY, EXCLUSION, AND MOBILITY

We have based our understanding of these terms and their relationship with each other not only on the excellent existing literature cited throughout this book, but on the way they are used and understood by community residents themselves.

In short, throughout both the original study and the follow-up we have used a multi-dimensional perspective, incorporating social, cultural, political, and economic components into our understanding of what it means to be poor, disenfranchised, excluded, and stigmatized. The ideas of choice, freedom, citizenship, voice, dignity, rights, and responsibilities have all emerged in the process.

INDICATORS

Although our work is based on multigenerational life trajectories, we have limited data on the parents of the original interviewees (place of birth, level of education, and principle occupation). Our robust data begins with the original participants and continues through a randomly selected sample of their children and grandchildren. Our questionnaires included sections addressing the following areas:

- *Basic Data:* We started with basic information on the education, occupation, contribution, and participation of the entire family group and of each household member.
- *Year-by-year life histories matrix:* We tracked changes in residence, occupation, education, family status, and (from 1969 on) health, in order to understand life fluctuations and detect periods of upward and downward mobility in both absolute and relative terms.[1]
- *Domestic economy:* Questions were included about the household's assets and income sources, the nature of the residence, the collective urban services the household used, and the monthly expenditures of the household unit.
- *Social capital:* Questions were included about friendship and kinship networks (nature, extent, and frequency), membership in associations, and participation in community activities.
- *Violence, police, drug traffic, and personal security:* Questions about these concerns were added to the section on the use of public space in the original questionnaire.
- *Perceptions about public policy:* We asked questions about persons' political perceptions and participation; perceptions about public policy and citizenship; and contacts with various levels of government.

- *Social mobility:* We asked some of the questions used by Graham and Birdsall and included the ladder from the Latino Barometro.[2] We asked about persons' aspirations and expectations (their own and those their parents had for them) and how each person compared his or her own status to that of various reference groups—siblings, other community members, and people outside the community. We also asked perception questions about exclusion, stigma, and discrimination, and how some of those have changed over time.

THE LESSONS WE LEARNED

Along the way, we encountered problems of many types, including conceptual, methodological, technical, and logistical ones. It's useful to go into a bit more depth about a few of them, along with the ways we attempted to overcome them, for the sake of others embarking on panel studies under similar circumstances. (A set of longitudinal panel studies in the squatter settlements of different cities and countries would indeed be a powerful resource for addressing the unanswered questions that my studies have raised.) The most important problems we encountered, how we approached them, and what we learned from them are as follows.

Relocating Original Interviewees

We faced several serious difficulties in relocation, including the fact that 30 years had passed; that one of the communities had been removed and the residents scattered into several public housing projects; and that in the interests of confidentiality during the height of the dictatorship, we had asked only for first names (except among those in the leadership sample).

Our approach. I started by recontacting and visiting my closest friends in the communities and the families with whom I had stayed during my time there. I had maintained contact with them over the years and was able to find them easily and ask for their help. It was readily obvious from the start of Phase I that university students would have an impossible time trying to relocate the families, so we composed teams of community residents, many of them children or neighbors of original study participants. We developed a training program for them and a form of remuneration based on hours worked and on successful location of original participants.

They started at the original address, and if the person was no longer there, asked for any leads or information. (It is interesting that 50 percent of those we found were either in the same house or in the same neighborhood, so that made our task easier.) If no information was known, they went to the neighbors on both sides and the opposite houses. If no one remembered the person or family, they went to the various community organizations, churches, local hangouts, and so on. We even created posters with the name of the study, saying "We want to find you again," showing a photo of me in 1969 and a drawing that had been used on the cover of the Portuguese edition of my book (knowing that some of them had seen it), and giving our office address and phone number.

We made it as easy as we could for the original participants to contact us, with the help of announcements on local community radio stations and in local newsletters— although the results of these efforts were limited.

What we learned. We were surprised by our success: The percentage of people that had relocated was highest for the community where we expected it to be lowest (Catacumba, which had been removed in 1970) and lowest for the place we expected it to be highest (Caxias, where half the interviewees were land owners). The reason, we discovered, was the strength of the local social networks. The Catacumba residents had fought so many collective battles for water, electricity, sanitation, street paving, and finally against removal that they had more powerful bonds with one another, despite their geographic separation. Those in the loteamentos had not participated in collective struggles for urban services, had not formed as many community organizations, and therefore did not know their neighbors as well. When a family moved out, the sale was simply a market transaction, and few kept in touch with them. What's more, many of the names and street numbers in these neighborhoods had been changed—and even some of the names of the neighborhoods themselves. Favelas retain a living memory that private property does not.

This phenomenon explains the results charted here. Clearly, we had a much greater success rate with the leaders, not only because we had their last names, but also because they tended to be widely known.

Dealing with Original Interviewees Who Had Died

We were able to locate the families of many of the original participants who had passed away. What we did in this case was to fill in the life history matrix by interviewing the person's spouse and oldest children to reconstruct his or her residential, occupational, educational, family, and health histories. Of course, we could not apply the questionnaire in these cases, but we did include all of the children in our running list of the next generation, and sampled them proportionately.

Verifying the Identity of the Relocated Individuals

In the middle of our interviewing process, we discovered a daunting problem. As the data from the life histories and questionnaires were being checked for consistency before coding and digitizing the results, we noticed that some of the information did not match the profile of the original person interviewed. Some were the wrong age to have been included in the original sample; others showed a birthplace of their mother or father that did not match data we had, and so on.

Our approach. Once we realized that there had been some misidentification of respondents, we halted the coding and systematically reviewed each person identified, using key variables for determination. We found 45 falsely identified individuals, all with the same first name as the original respondent. Two modifications were made in our procedures, as follows. (1) We used the data from the life history matrices from 1969 to crosscheck the validity of each of the people identified thus far. (2) We added

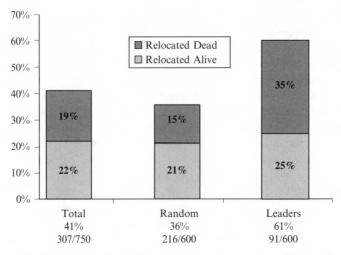

FIGURE AI.2   Relocation of original interviewees. Success rate of finding the original interviewees between 1999 and 2001, in total and for each community; indicating those found living and those who were deceased.

several additional pieces of information about each original respondent to the packet of information we gave to the field team, so that they might have a higher rate of accuracy in their identifications.

What we learned. This revision cost us precious time and money, so we recommend that future researchers utilize a rigorous verification process from the beginning. Ultimately, we crosschecked the key information (the age and gender of each child as well as the date of marriage) on each questionnaire, calling on the interviewees for clarification whenever we encountered inconsistencies.

Access to the Communities and the Problem of Violence

Without a doubt, the biggest change we found when we returned to the urban neighborhoods was the presence and power of drug gangs that vied with one another for control of the favelas and engaged in armed battles with the police. The challenge of this violence was the greatest one we faced, and most difficult to overcome. Its most important negative effects were as follows. (1) Many of my researchers (even those from within the community) were unwilling to participate in the study, and many others dropped out. For example, the traffickers noticed that one of our team members, a resident of the Quitungo housing project, was visiting several apartments every day and began to suspect she was spying for the authorities. She was threatened and forced to resign from the project. (2) Several families of original interviewees had moved out of their communities altogether, fearing they'd be caught in the crossfire. Some had been in Nova Brasília all of their lives but had fled to their families' or spouses' hometowns; others had lived in the conjuntos for 30 years, since the relocation, but had left to rent apartments in outlying neighborhoods, fearing that their children would become involved in drugs if they stayed. (3) No one was able to enter the communities on days when the gangs were carrying on armed battles or the police had decided to conduct a raid, causing many delays in our fieldwork. (4) There was a high rate of refusal to answer questions about violence. The rates of "Do not know/Do not want to answer" in questions related to dealers, police, or violence was up to 40 percent on some questions, compared with almost zero on most others. About 10 families would not even provide us with the names or locations of their children, fearing they might be involved with the traffic.

Our approach. We understood that our study involved dangerous work, and we took the danger quite seriously. Very carefully, we attempted to negotiate access to the communities through the leaders of the Residents' Associations (most of whom were placed in leadership roles by the drug lords) and to visibly identify all team members as such, for their protection. Each researcher was given a "kit" including a bright turquoise T-shirt with the Mega-Cities logo; a name tag that was worn around the neck, with a photo ID, the name of the study, the name of the researcher, the office telephone number, and so on; and a letter signed by me explaining the study and identifying the interviewer by name as part of the research team. We called potential interviewees each morning, to ask if it was safe to come and see them, and when there was a doubt, we rescheduled the interview.

What we learned. Although we were careful, we understood that unexpected things happen. For future studies, we recommend sending interviewers in pairs and keeping them in close touch with field supervisors at all times. (The ubiquity of cell phones should make that much easier today.)[3]

Perfecting the Questionnaire

An effective questionnaire had been the cornerstone of our original study, and was just as important when we went back. Our dilemma was how much to update it. As we developed the questionnaire, scrutinizing its content, language, and underlying theoretical constructs, we became concerned that some topics that had arisen in open-ended interviews we had recently conducted were absent from the original questionnaire, most notably violence. In addition, some topics that have figured prominently in recent literature, for example household composition and authority, had not been covered in great detail in our earlier study. Some of our phrases and words now sounded archaic and inappropriate. Our challenge was to revise the instrument so that it would provide an effective basis for comparison between then and now, as well as between our study and other current ones in the field. (These included Moser's longitudinal study of household responses to poverty and Birdsall and Graham's work on social mobility.)[4]

Our approach. After consideration, we eliminated the original questionnaire's section on attitudinal modernity and updated certain words and phrases so as to keep the questions clear and comprehensible. We added several sections, including one on violence, and a matrix of household composition and contribution, along with more information about the expenditure patterns of the family. We also used the ladder of social mobility recommended by Birdsall and Graham. The result was a very long questionnaire that included 124 questions in addition to the life history matrix. It took over two hours to apply—and not surprisingly, we found that although the original participants seemed content to go through it, their adult children often became impatient. We considered shortening the questionnaire for the next generation but decided against this, for fear it would impair comparability.

What we learned. We would not use such a long questionnaire again, though we gained valuable insights from each section. In my original study, I did a second pretest of the questionnaire after the results from the first one were incorporated—and perhaps we should have done this again. During the course of our interviews, we realized that we had sacrificed exact comparability when we had reworded the questions, so for the random samples in Phase III, we went back to the original questionnaire, staying as faithful as possible to all of the items we retained.

Creating a Contextual Questionnaire

We prepared a contextual questionnaire based on the one I had developed for the original study, and applied it to community elders and the original leaders. It proved very problematic for the second study, as each of the respondents had a different perspective on the history of the community and remembered different events as important. Coherence and reliability became challenges we could not overcome, even with the help of newspaper accounts from the time. (It turned out that the favelas were rarely mentioned in the papers, except when one was removed.) Books and dissertations proved equally unhelpful.

Our approach. We needed a collective memory in order to reconstitute the history of each community and crosscheck dates and events. We didn't want to impose what we considered the benchmark events in each place's history onto people's personal stories, but to see them from the residents' point of view. We decided to employ a DRP, an event in which we brought several members of the community together to collectively interpret their own reality and concerns. We created an enormous time line that covered an entire wall, marking only key calendar dates starting with 1920, showing where 1968 would be, and going up to the present year. We let the participants fill in all the other years and the events they felt were relevant.

Participants were given pads of sticky notes and invited to write on them what they considered the most important events in the life of their community and place them on the time line. They ended up creating several crosscutting categories: urban services, housing, drugs and violence, natural disasters, major political events, and so on. There was much discussion and argument about exact dates and names—and suddenly people began to overcome their shyness and start having fun with the task. We took notes, made videotapes, and ultimately used the brown paper scrolls and sticky notes to write up the community histories.

What we learned. The people know best, and together they know more!

Memory

One of the major difficulties in studies done over such a long period of time, is the fallibility of memory and its selective nature, a problem that was worsened by the advanced age of most of the members of our original sample. Memory is constantly being reconstructed—and we were asking people to remember in some detail the many residential, occupational, and educational changes they'd experienced over 30 years. Our goal was nothing less than trying to capture the messy ups and downs of real life and the way challenged people have coped with crises, not for a handful of people but hundreds of them, across several generations. These data are difficult to collect, to code, and to analyze.

Our approach. We discovered that the life history matrix worked quite well as an entry point into the interviews, encouraging the interviewer and interviewee to sit side by side and fill in the changes together, going back and forth in time and across categories. One item, such as the birth of a child, might help jog memory of other items, such as place of residence; likewise, a move to a new place was often associated with a change of job or lack of work. It became an enjoyable collaborative exercise, using triangulation to help fill in memory lapses. Our real challenge was in determining how to interpret the data, especially how to control for normal changes in the life cycle. Thus, the year of a life event (including the all-important date of entry into the workforce) and the person's age were both considered in each interpretation of upward or downward mobility.

In addition, we were grappling with the fact that many changes make life neither better nor worse—they are simply trade-offs maximizing different things at different times. For example, leaving the favela for a peripheral neighborhood cannot always be considered a step up. (Consider the case where someone has left not by choice but out of fear of violence, and has found himself terribly lonely and isolated in his new setting.) Similarly, a move from a salaried job to working for oneself cannot necessarily be considered a step down. (Suppose she is earning the same amount or more in the informal sector and has more freedom and flexibility.) These are some of the issues we considered in interpreting our data.

What we learned. We found that the richer the data and closer they were to reality, the harder it was to draw simple conclusions or find coherent patterns. In light of that fact, our qualitative data and personal narratives loomed larger in importance as we worked to interpret our results.

BIAS

While it seemed an achievement to locate over one-third of our original sample after three decades, there was still the risk that the two-thirds *not* located would present an entirely different picture, either much better or much worse, and that we would therefore be unable to generalize from our findings. To this considerable risk of bias we added the possible distortion inherent in the fact that the people we found tended to be the youngest of the original group.

Our approach. In an attempt to quantify our bias, we compared three groups using the original 1969 data: (1) living original participants who had completed questionnaires in both time periods; (2) dead original interviewees for whom we had reconstructed life histories; and (3) all those from the original study we could not find. Despite age and community biases, we found the three groups to be fairly homogeneous, and that gave us confidence that we had managed to find a relatively representative sample. There was a slight tendency among the group we found toward higher family income, more access to services, more children, and more integration into their communities—but these differences were not significant. We were left wondering whether those who remained in the same communities and so were easiest to find were simply the failures who couldn't make it out or the successes who did not end up on the streets.

We made an effort to answer this question with in-depth interviews of all the original participants we had located. I made trips to Joao Pessoa, Natal, Brasília, Belo Horizonte, São Paulo, and Porto Alegre for the purpose, even if there were only one or two individuals in those places.

What we learned. I learned that without this step we would have had no idea just how difficult life was in the countryside and how deep the poverty there could be. Many who left the favelas came back after finding no work and no way to survive; others got bored and came back to be part of the life of the big city again. Those who stayed and prospered were able to join with other family members to open shops and services or were able to live inexpensively on retirement and pensions.

What we planned to do but could not. We had planned to add two more elements to the study design: (1) a quasi-experimental design testing the effects of favela upgrading policies and removal; and (2) a study of the new favelas and clandestine subdivisions in the West Zone.

The first idea was to select favelas that could serve as a loose control group—insofar as they had the exact opposite histories of policy interventions from those we studied. We would then be able to compare the lives of the residents in those communities with the lives of the residents in our original communities. For example, we wanted to select a South Zone favela as similar as possible to Catacumba (in 1968), but that had *not* been removed and to find a North Zone favela similar to Nova Brasília (in 1968) that had *not* been ignored by government upgrading programs, but on the contrary had been the beneficiary of several such projects from CODESCO to Cada Familia um Lote, to Mutirao to Favela-Bairro.

The last step was to look at the newer favelas and loteamentos in the West Zone to see how they compared with the North and South zone favelas when I first studied them. Time and money ran out before these two final steps were taken—but I am still interested in seeing what they would reveal and collaborating with students or colleagues who wish to explore this.

appendix 2

ANALYTICAL FRAMEWORK FOR ASSESSING SUCCESS

DIMENSIONS AND CORRELATES OF UPWARD MOBILITY

Whereas most of the original study participants and their second- and third-generation descendants made considerable progress toward improving their lives, only a handful made it into the upscale South Zone of the city or landed professional jobs. Out of 883 people across all three generations, only 6 of the original interviewees, 13 of their children, and 3 of their grandchildren had achieved living standards that would characterize them as gente—*people,* rather than invisible, disposable beings.

How did these few manage to get ahead? Was it sheer luck and happenstance or are there patterns in attributes, attitudes, and/or behaviors that increased their probabilities of success? How would we measure the concept of "getting ahead" or achieving "successful" outcomes relative to the group as a whole?

In thinking about those who have been successful, we can look to the Catacumba resident who became part of Brazil's Olympic rowing team and his son, who is now in medical school—or Benedita da Silva from Babylonia, or Pelé, or any number of sports and music stars.

As successful outcomes go far beyond the standard per capita family income, I expanded the way that I measured success to include (1) economic mobility, as measured by socioeconomic status and individual income; (2) geographic mobility, as measured by exit from favelas into legal neighborhoods; (3) political mobility, as measured by citizenship/participation; and (4) psychological mobility, as measured by aspirations, satisfaction, and perceived mobility relative to various reference groups (see figure A2.1).

The findings based on this analytical framework reveal the interactions among these factors and the way they can create an upward spiral linking SES and incomes with agency, civic and political participation, and optimism.

The questions behind this analytic approach are: What comprises success in moving away from poverty and exclusion, and what factors–endogenous and exogenous—affect a person's chances of success? The analytical framework (shown in figure A2.1) presents a systematic way to explore the relationship between the "givens," for example, independent variables such as age, gender, race, origin, and household composition; "mindset," for example, attitudes such as fatalism, optimism, agency; social capital, for example, bonding and bridging; and five varieties of successful outcomes.

The first thing to notice in the diagram above is that I have defined successful outcomes along multiple dimensions—so that the dependent variable is a composite measure. I used the socioeconomic status index (SES) and income as two aspects of economic success; favela exit as a sign of spatial integration, citizenship as a measure of political integration, and satisfaction as a measure of perceived wellbeing. When I tested each of these dimensions of success against each other, I found strong significant correlations among them that held up across all of the generations and both time periods. The single exception is that political participation was significantly correlated only with SES and not with any of the other measures, which may be due to the low level of political participation and lack of variance.

In looking for patterns based on each person's ascribed characteristics, we found that age and the stage a person was at in his or her life cycle influenced attitudes and outcomes in the expected direction, favoring the young or those in midcareer; and that being male (or in a male-headed household) conferred distinct advantages. Youth and maleness also correlated positively with intervening variables such as agency and optimism, which led to greater success—thereby compounding the gender advantage and creating a "virtuous cycle." Those who had advantages to start with were able to take advantage of them to keep improving relative to the rest of the group, whereas those less fortunate were generally unable to catch up.

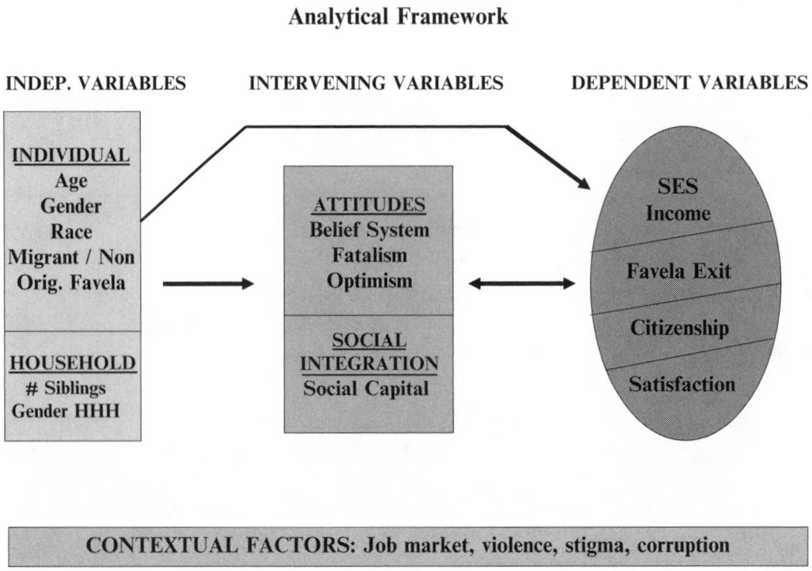

Analytical Framework

FIGURE A2.1   Framework for data analysis on five outcome measures.

Race, on the other hand, made surprisingly little difference within this low-income population.[1] Underclass status seems to have trumped skin color, confirming what the interviewees had reported: the stigma of poverty (signified by favela residence) weighed more heavily than the stigma of race. The other strong findings were that those born in Rio (versus those who were migrants) had higher SES scores in all three time periods (1969, 2001, and 2003) and that those with smaller families scored higher in SES, income, and satisfaction.

Whereas *white males* were the most "successful" by outcome measures, *mulatto females* (followed by mulatto males and black females) were most *upwardly mobile*. In terms of original location, the most successful were from the *subdivisions in Caxias* (who started out slightly better off than those in favelas), but those from the *favela of Catacumba* (in the midst of the upscale South Zone) had the highest mobility. While education was a determining factor in successful outcomes for the original sample, those who went from the lowest to the highest quintiles over their lifetimes were not the most educated among their peers—some were illiterate, and many had low or no schooling. (It was in the mobility of their children and grandchildren where education—especially university education—made a notable difference.)

As for intervening variables, fatalism was negatively correlated with successful outcomes across all generations. In other words, people who believed that what happened to them was a result of destiny or fate (versus hard work) or that Brazil's future depended on God or luck rather than on the work of the people or good government were less likely to be proactive in seeking out opportunities, less likely to have a strategy

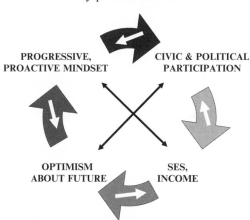

VIRTUOUS CYCLE
2-way positive correlations

PROGRESSIVE, PROACTIVE MINDSET   **CIVIC & POLITICAL PARTICIPATION**

OPTIMISM ABOUT FUTURE   **SES, INCOME**

BEING MALE, WHITE AND YOUNGER GIVES OVERALL ADVANTAGE, BUT ABOVE RELATIONSHIPS HOLD CONTROLLING FOR RACE, GENDER AND AGE

FIGURE A2.2   Virtuous Cycle: Positive relationship between progressive and practive mindset, civic and political participation; socioeconomic status and income; and optimism about the future.

for getting ahead, and thus less likely to succeed. (This, in turn, reinforced their passivity and fatalism—creating a vicious cycle.)[2]

Conversely, optimism about the future[3] was positively correlated with socioeconomic status and political participation, most notably among the children of the original interviewees. Using a series of questions to measure perceived satisfaction with one's life, we discovered that, across all generations, those who felt most satisfied also scored highest on the optimism measures. They also exhibited a proactive rather than a passive mindset, and took action in dealing with community or family problems rather than waiting to see if things would improve.

The relationship between social capital and successful outcomes was determined by the *type* of networks, the memberships, and the socializing behavior of the individuals. Those with greater "bridging networks" (external) had significantly better outcomes in SES, income, and political participation than the average, and those with greater "bonding networks" (internal) had worse outcomes.[4]

On the issue of satisfaction, there were clear differences among the generations. For the people interviewed in the first study, community unity was highly important, but it made little difference for their descendants. Only for the children's generation was socioeconomic status a strong factor in satisfaction; and for the grandchildren, the most important factors were indebtedness (the more debt, the more satisfied—which may seem surprising, but I will explain) and title to one's house (as opposed to land title, which was a separate variable).

From living with the families and knowing the grandchildren as well as I do, I can explain the apparent paradox of more debt leading to greater satisfaction. The debt is consumer credit, and consumption is the badge of prestige for the young. They buy everything, from cell phones to sound systems to shoes and shirts, on "time," paying in multiple installments that include staggering amounts of interest—sometimes totaling several times the price of the item. The more they owe, the more they have to show off, the better to impress their friends and approximate the images they see on television. This leads us to the broader question of how people assess their own progress and future prospects. In short, this creates a virtuous cycle—an upward spiral. Figure A2.2 depicts this spiral of upward mobility that I found for those who were moving away from poverty.

The findings represented here show that agency (a proactive mindset and engagement in civic and political life) was closely related to optimism about the future and, in turn, to higher income and socioeconomic status. This held true regardless of age, race, or gender. However, being a young, light-skinned male conferred a distinct advantage but not enough to determine positive outcomes on the five facets of success.

INTERGENERATIONAL TRANSMISSION OF SUCCESS

The question of how much of life success is determined by the degree of success of one's parents (raised in chapter 9) is relevant here. What if birthplace, number of siblings, type of community, beliefs, behaviors, and social networks were all irrelevant in explaining differential life outcomes because they were predetermined by the degree of success of the parents? This would indeed be the case in a caste system. To test this with our data, we used the individual socioeconomic status scores of parents and their children. It enabled us to see the extent to which any individual's SES score is determined by (or could be predicted) by his or her mother's or father's score. As described in chapter 9, we found very little relationship between the scores of parents and children. In short, there was no evidence of intergenerational poverty or relative success. The coefficients for each type of parent-child match are shown in table A2.1 below.

TABLE A2.1 *Intra- and Intergenerational Transmission of Poverty as Measured by SES Scores (based on comparing each individual with his or her own children)*

Intragenerational	
• Original interviewee 1969 and 2001	0.275

Intergenerational	
• Original interviewees in 1969 and their children in 2001	0.358
• Original interviewees in 2001 and their children in 2001	0.314
• Children in 2001 and grandchildren in 2001	0.498
• Original interviewees in 1969 and the grandchildren in 2001	0.239
• Original interviewees in 2001 and the grandchildren in 2001	0.09 (not sig)

Note: This shows positive but weak relationships for each pair. The only strong correlation is between the status of the children and the grandchildren.

notes

PREFACE

1. This was a summer program for 13- to 15-year-old girls organized by Leon and Frannie Sciaky, who had moved to Oaxaca after their progressive school was shut down
   and they were exiled from the country during the McCarthy era.
2. Alan Holmberg debunked the theory of a self-defeating culture of poverty by showing that the only thing needed to change the "backward" values and passive behavior
   of the Indians who worked on a hacienda in the Peruvian highlands was to buy the
   land and give them the ownership. Instead of taking several generations to score
   higher on the "Modernity of Man Index" (Alex Inkeles), it took only the time needed
   for the workers to believe that the land was actually theirs.
3. In Brazil the word "interior" connotes not distance from the coast but distance from
   "civilization." This unusual opportunity for undergraduate research was part of the
   Cornell-Harvard-Columbia-Illinois Summer Field Studies Program in Anthropology, funded by the Carnegie Foundation.
4. Arembepe later became an international hippie destination hangout; it was eventually destroyed by a chemical plant just up the coast. The two other study sites (both
   within half a day's walk) were Jaua, an even smaller fishing village, and Abrantes, an
   agricultural village arrayed around an open square where a single record was continually blasted over loudspeakers, celebrating the recent arrival of electrical power.
5. This is one of the reasons the Paulo Freire method as described in his book *The
   Pedagogy of the Oppressed* (1973) was so appealing and so powerful. It started with
   the "meaning" of the key words people used most often (their core vocabulary) and
   instead of sounding out the syllables, it helped associate the word in its entirety with
   a picture of the designated object that they could recognize and name. The symbol—
   a set of letters—and the object were shown together on slides Freire made up and
   projected with a generator for power.
6. The doctoral dissertation research was funded by grants from a Woodrow Wilson
   Teaching Fellowship.

7. See Jane Jacobs (1961).

8. See Nancy Scheper-Hughes (1992); Richard Benjamin Penglase (2002).

9. When something personal was confided, such as the infidelity of a husband, I would stop taking notes, but the women would say "Write, write that down—it's very important."

10. Janice E. Perlman (1976); Janice E. Perlman (1977).

11. A brief window of opportunity opened in 1981, when a small group at the World Bank—Richard Webb, Doug Keare and Ana Maria Sant'Anna—became interested in doing comparative restudies of earlier surveys in Lima and Rio squatter settlements, looking at the extent to which the lives of their inhabitants were influenced by macroeconomic and political changes or public policies in their respective countries. The bank funded a 2-week study trip to Rio to test the methodology of finding the original interviewees, but the project came to an abrupt halt when Richard Webb was called back to Peru to become governor of Peru's Central Bank.

12. Tim Campbell at the World Bank Institute took the initiative for this study and followed it through to its conclusion. Greg Ingram, who headed the Research Committee of the World Bank at the time, took the risk of supporting the study, despite the scepticism of many of his peers.

13. Professors Carlos Weiner and Pedro Abramo were my local partners on this, along with three of their graduate students.

INTRODUCTION

1. Four percent have completed some university schooling and another 4 percent of the children have earned a university degree.

2. Encyclopaedia Britannica Online, s.v. "Brazil," www.britannica.com/EBchecked/topic/78101/Brazil (accessed June 24, 2008).

3. Ministério do Planejamento, Orçamento e Gestão, and Instituto Brasileiro de Geografia e Estatística (2000).

4. This was done in two stages: (1) selecting households using a random numbers table, after mapping and numbering each household, and then (2) selecting individuals systematically (1 in every 2.5) from a running list of every household member between 16 and 65 years old. That way, rather than ending up with a sample of households, I was able to get a random sample of residents in the communities. Some households had more than one person included in the sample and others had none.

5. The idea of including an "elite" sample came from my work with Professor Frank Bonilla at MIT, who was conducting a large-scale study in Venezuela and creating a simulation that could play out future scenarios.

6. The life history matrix was inspired by the work of Jorge Balán, Harley Browning, Elizabeth Jelin, and Lee Litzler (1969) in Monterrey, Mexico.

7. For a complete description of the method see J. Perlman (1974).

8. Janice E. Perlman (1976b); the book won the C. Wright Mills Award in that year; was published in Portuguese by Editora Paz e Terra, São Paulo, Brazil, in 1977; and was released in paperback in the United States in 1977.

9. As Javier Auyero (1997), 508–12, puts it, "Almost three decades ago, in what would later become one of Latin America's most original and controversial contributions to the social sciences, a group of sociologists tackled…the escalation of urban marginality. Working within a structural-historic neo-Marxist perspective, they recovered the notion of 'marginality' from the realm of modernization theories…which focused on the lack of integration of certain social groups into society due to their (deviant) values, perceptions and behavioral patterns. Marginal groups, according to this approach, lack the psychological and psychosocial attributes that were deemed necessary to participate in 'modern society.…Marginality was thought to be the product of the coexistence of beliefs, values, attitudes and behaviors of a previous, more traditional' stage of development."

10. Even Frantz Fanon (1965), 104, in *The Wretched of the Earth,* speaks of the "uprooted peasants circling aimlessly around the city" as a natural source of revolutionary activity.

11. I could not find the perfect phrase or shorthand to refer to the original interviewees. In some of the charts, I have used OIs as an abbreviation for Original Interviewees; while in other places I variously use "original study participants," "original sample," or "respondents." I find all of them uncomfortable, cumbersome, and disrespectful to the individuals who gave of their time and trusted me with their stories and answers to my questions. However, I have not yet found a term I like, so I use these terms with this disclaimer.

12. There are many panel studies, but very few in urban shantytowns, in part because conditions for such a study are nearly prohibitive. No street addresses, registries, or official records of "slum" populations exist, and people tend to use nicknames because so many have the same names. It was a risk to conduct research in what the rest of the city has always considered a no-man's-land, but today that risk has increased exponentially with the rise of drug trafficking and the violence among gangs and police. It is not surprising that this study took so many years to complete under these conditions.

13. Some studies have used proxy panels to address issues of social mobility. They attempt to create matched cohorts using census data rather than following actual people over time. See the excellent work of François Bourguignon, Francisco H. G. Ferreira, and Marta Menendez (2003) at the World Bank and that of Sonia Rocha (1997) and Ricardo Paes de Barros, Ricardo Henriques, and Rosane Mendonça (2001) in Rio de Janeiro.

14. For more detail on the ways we tested for bias, see appendix 1.

CHAPTER 1

1. Although the Morro de Provência is considered to be the first favele, the favela of Santo Antonio emerged around the same time and in the same manner. Three other settlements date back even further (to 1881): Quinta do Caju, Mangueira (different from the one of samba school fame), and Serra Morena. These areas were first settled by Portuguese, Spanish, and Italian workers. See Mariana Cavalcanti (2007).

2. Mariana Cavalcanti (2007), 31; Carlos Lessa (2000), 201.

3. Marcelo Baumann Burgos (1998).
4. Mariana Cavalcanti (2007).
5. Loïc J. D. Wacquant (1996).
6. Zuenir Ventura (1994).
7. Conferring legal land tenure to squatters remains problematic, and will likely be embroiled in legal proceedings for the foreseeable future, despite the relevant sections of 1988 Constitution, the City Statute, policy/planning provisions for squatters' rights (*uso capiao*) and eminent domain—and efforts by international agencies. Official documents called "Habite-Se" were distributed to residents of the favelas that were upgraded through Favela-Bairro project by the Municipal Secretary of Urbanism, giving them a title to their own house even though they do not own the land beneath it. (Interview with Alfredo Sirkis, Municipal Secretary of Urbanism and Environment, March 31, 2004.) According to Lu Peterson, the Municipal Special Affairs Director, some of the Favela-Bairro participants do not want land tenure to be legalized as they do not want to pay property taxes and they feel secure in their land use as is. When asked why they are not interested in using land title as collateral for loans, they repeatedly say that they do not want to assume any loans without a sure way to repay them, which means steady work, which most do not have.
8. Pedro Abramo (2001; 2003a; 2003b); Pedro Abramo and Suzana Pasternak Taschner (2003) and Janice Perlman (2010).
9. Aside from those few living on the streets, poor people live in *loteamentos clandestinos* (irregular subdivisions), conjuntos (public housing projects), *villasor avenidas* (small alleyways lined on both sides with rows of one-room rentals with shared facilities) and the traditional *corticos* (old houses divided up with one family per room) or *cabecas de porco* (workers' housing built as barracks).
10. Data given to me by Andre Urani during a conversation at the Instituto de Estudos do Trabalho e Sociedade (Institute for the Study of Work and Society) in 2008.
11. According to a speech by Rio's mayor, Cesar Maia, on the tenth anniversary of Favela-Bairro in September 2004. See the website of the Instituto Pereira Passos for updates. A third phase, long delayed by political and economic frictions between the national government and the city of Rio, is about to begin as this book goes to press.
12. Favela-Bairro is the most ambitious and extensive squatter upgrading program that has been implemented in Latin America (and perhaps the world). It is funded by the Inter-American Development Bank, with contributions from the National Caixa Economica and local municipal government. According to Jose Brakarz, the brilliant creator, promoter, director, founder of the program within IBD, the third replenishment includes provisions to include the larger favelas, to attend to social development and job creation and to encourage greater citizen participation (personal discussion, January 2009). I discuss this further in chapter 1.
13. In fact, the devalued properties proximate to favela entrances have gradually come to be considered as part of the morro although they are technically and legally on the asfalto.
14. Teresa P. R. Caldeira (2000).
15. See article on this by João H. Costa Vargas (2006).

16. Tio (Uncle) and Tia (Aunt) are terms of respect and endearment used to address older people.

17. Labels like *slum* need to be contextualized to make sense. Students I took on a study abroad seminar spent several days with pavement dwellers in Bombay before coming to Soweto Township in Johannesburg. They were amazed at the good conditions of the apartheid-period workers' housing—disappointing our hosts, who expected they would be appalled. Several men shared a room, and there was only one bathroom and one kitchen per floor, as compared to living on a sidewalk against a stone wall. In a parallel situation, when Brazilian youth from the favela were invited to stay in the South Bronx with the Ghetto Film School students, they thought they were living in luxury—until they were told they were in one of the worst "slums" in New York.

18. See discussion by Nancy Youman (1991).

19. Launched in 1999 by the Cities Alliance under the joint sponsorship of the World Bank and the UN Center for Human Settlement (UN-Habitat). See Alan Gilbert (2007).

20. The MDGs were set in 2000 in discussions among 187 nations and were signed by 147 countries, who committed themselves to collectively reaching eight overarching goals (with 18 specified targets) by the year 2015. Goal 7 is "Ensure environmental sustainability." See www.un.org/millenniumgoals.

21. United Nations Human Settlements Programme and Global Urban Observatory (2003).

22. See Hoskins (1970), on the origin of the word "*slum.*"

23. *The New York Times* described the cholera epidemic as "hitting hardest in the poorest neighborhoods, particularly the slum known as Five Points, where African-Americans and immigrant Irish Catholics were crowded in squalor and stench," and, as Kenneth Jackson pointed out in the same article, "exposing more than ever the city's divisions of class, race and religion." Jackson continued, summarizing the prevailing attitude of the day as the classic "blaming the victim—if you got cholera it was your own fault. As the article pointed out, in the same vein, the Martin Scorsese film *The Gangs of New York* refers to the "low life" in the "sinkhole" of New York City. See John Noble Wilford (2008).

24. To use the terms Charles J. Stokes (1962) used to distinguish passing through on the way up from being left behind apparently in a "no exit" situation. These terms have often been used to contrast communities of immigrant groups to New York City (or the U.S. in general), with communities of African Americans who appear trapped in ghettos from one generation to the next. Empirical research is needed to address this issue lest it fall into an unexamined stereotype.

25. David Satterthwaite in correspondence with the author, May 8, 2009. See also Special Issue of *Enviroment and Urbanization* (1990) which covers housing submarkets in different cities; and *Squatter Citizen* (1989).

26. Licia do Prado Valladares, Lidia Medeiros, and Filippina Chinelli (2003).

27. See McCann (2006).

28. See, in order of mention, João Costa Vargas (2006), Richard Benjamin Penglase (2002); Marcos Alvito (2001); and Marcelo Baumann Burgos (2002).

CHAPTER 2

1. The terms *global South, shantytown, squatter settlement, slum,* and *informal sector* are each laden with the baggage of connotations and implications that make them problematic.

2. United Nations Department of Economic and Social Affairs (2008).

3. Mark Lewis (2007).

4. Janice E. Perlman and Bruce Schearer (1986).

5. See Daniel Howden (2007).

6. Janice E. Perlman (1993; 1990); Janice E. Perlman and Molly O'Meara Sheehan (2007).

7. Actually, it shifts to the "real city," in which the formal and informal are interdependent.

8. UN-Habitat (2008).

9. Alfredo Lattes, Jorge Rodríguez, and Miguel Villa (2002).

10. United Nations Department of Economic and Social Affairs (2008).

11. Slowing urbanization rates mean a cumulative decline in (1) the rate of domestic rural-to-urban migration, (2) the rate of immigration of foreigners directly to cities, and (3) the natural rate of population growth in cities. Africa, which has remained the least urbanized region, will have the highest urbanization rates in the coming decades. See United Nations (2000); Alfredo Lattes, Jorge Rodríguez, and Miguel Villa (2002), 2; Marcela Cerrutti and Rodolfo Bertoncello (2003).

12. United Nations Human Settlements Programme (2003); Eduardo Lopez Moreno and Rasna Warah (2006).

13. David de Ferranti et al. (2004).

14. Valéria Pero (2004).

15. The sources used for the facts and figures in this section unless otherwise indicated: United Nations Department of Economic and Social Affairs (2008); F. E. Wagner and John O. Ward (1980); Edésio Fernandes (2007), 203; Valéria Pero (2004); and World Bank (2007).

16. Ricardo Neves (2003), 66.

17. According to Sonia Rocha (2000) and (2003). She clarifies, "While the percentage of those in poverty in rural regions has remained consistently higher than the percentage in urban regions, *urban areas continue to contain the majority of the country's poor* (Rocha, 2003, p. 135 emphasis mine).

18. According to the World Bank's statistics (elaborated by IPEA), the percentage of poor persons in Brazil is typical of countries with only one-third of Brazil's per capita income.

19. Valéria Pero (2004).

20. São Paulo favelas are quite different from those in Rio, in terms of their location, organization, and political engagement, as James Holston (2008) describes in his book *Insurgent Citizenship.*

21. Estado da Guanabara (1973).

22. Sergio Besserman and Fernando Cavalliere, Instituto Pereira Passos (2005). See also Ayse Pamuk and Paulo Fernando A. Cavallieri (1998); Paulo Fernando A. Cavallieri (2005).

23. IBGE: Instituto Brasileiro de Geografia e Estatística (2000).
24. See www.observatoriodefavelas.org.br. Also Bryan McCann (2006).

CHAPTER 3

1. Ironically, Jacobi was thrown into the same jail years later—not for religious reasons, but for his work as a journalist during the dictatorship.
2. See Fernando Morais's excellent biography, "Olga."
3. Gordon Parks (1978), 24.
4. Gordon Parks (1978), 120.
5. Gordon Parks (1978), 122–23.
6. The photographs were taken by Luis Blanc and the two architects were Gilda Blanc and Heloisa Coelho. They also made a count of the number of people per household. The house numbers were picked by a random number table and marked in the map in red ink circles. This map hangs on the wall in my office so when I look up from my writing, there are the houses, now long gone.
7. Field notes, August 12, 1969.
8. Gordon Parks (1961).
9. It is not clear whether in 1967, when Catacumba succeeded in getting the police station they wanted, the residents still felt as positively about it as they had about the idea six years before.
10. The Yellow Line was built by the city government during the first mandate of Mayor César Maia, but inaugurated when his successor, Luiz Paulo Conde had become mayor. It links the growing and wealthy Barra de Tijuca to Avenida Brazil going through the North Zone. It gave the North Zone access to the South Zone beaches (much to the dismay of many South Zone residenets) and improved access from the low-income area of Jacarepaguá (where Jacobi lives, and where the Cidade de Deus is located) to the Centro. The Red Line, connecting Rio to the Baixada, was built by the state government with federal support, and opened just in time for the 1992 Earth Summit, making the trip from the international airport to the city much more convenient. The new government also benefited the Complexo do Maré with the creation of a park—later the site of the Vila Olímpica. These changes are among the few that the favela population sees as one of the improvements since the dictatorship ended.

CHAPTER 4

1. The 2007 national development program, PAC (Programa de Aceleração do Crescimento), includes plans to turn some of these abandoned factory sites into low-income housing and to use others for social programs, job training, small business incubators, and other types of economic development programs. Community residents are skeptical about government promises, but still hopeful that this time will be different. PAC has plans for one million units of affordable housing nationwide.

2. For greater detail on the sampling process see Perlman, *Myth of Marginality* (1976) and *Methodological Notes on Complex Survey Research Involving Life History Data* (1974).

3. According to Zé, the only people who were ever removed in Nova Brasília were 12 families who occupied land belonging to a textile factory, Tuffy. They were transferred in 1965 to another area inside the community.

4. Under the PAC, there are plans to use the site of the closed Coca-Cola factory for a housing project for low-income families who make at least one minimum wage. If this happens, it will be the first government housing program to reach that segment of the population.

5. There is disagreement as to how many favelas and which ones are part of the Complexo de Alemão. According to a UNICEF-funded research project conducted by Centro de Promoção da Saúde (CEDAPS), a nonprofit research center, there are 12 favelas; according to the Instituto Pereira Passos, using the IBGE 2000 census data, there are 10. The CEDAPS study lists 3 favelas (Grota, Parque Alvorada, and Armando Sodre) that do not appear in the Instituto Pereira Passos study, and the Instituto Pereira Passos study lists one (Joaquim Queiros) that CEDAPS does not.

6. V. Hugo (2007).

7. The Report for UNICEF was done by the Centro de Promoção da Saúde (CEDAPS), (2003).

8. There are several complexos in Rio at this time, including the Complexo do Maré (9 favelas, population 114,000); Complexo do Jacarezinho (6 favelas, population 36,500); and Rocinha, which is a single favela occupying its own regional district in the South Zone (1 favela, population 56,400). These figures were given to me by the former director of the Instituto Pereira Passos, Sergio Besserman, based on the 2000 census which is the most recent one. They are conducted every ten years by the Brazilian Institute of Geography and Statistics, IBGE.

9. Grota, an older favela started in 1928 as a cattle farm.

CHAPTER 5

1. *Vila* refers to a settlement, often a group of houses around a courtyard or along both sides of an alleyway.

2. The two states were fused in 1979 and together became the new State of Rio de Janeiro, a move that remains controversial to this day.

3. José Claudio, interview with author, 1999.

4. The family history was compiled in 2005 and reflects people's ages at that time.

5. Many of the women I interviewed distinguish between the number of babies they gave birth to and the number who survive, but she did not volunteer the information, so it is possible that she had more.

6. To mention just a few examples: the son of the church janitor in Copacabana now has his own construction business and owns several apartments there; another young man now has a thriving picture-framing business in Ipanema, near the Praça General Osorio; and one of the community leaders became a bank assistant in Brasília and now lives in Botafogo with his wife and his daughter, who is an accountant and lawyer.

CHAPTER 6

1. "Eu Sou Favela" was composed in 1994 by Noca da Portela and Sergio Mosca. Lyrics quoted in Jane Souto de Oliveira and Maria Hortense Marcier, "A Palavra e (needs accent) Favela," in Zaluar and Alvito (1998), 102 (translation mine).

2. For contemporary references to people as dirty or as "social diseases," see Benigno Trigo (2000).

3. "Favelas of Guanabara" (mimeo), Rio de Janeiro, Fundação Leão XIII (1968).

4. See Janice E. Perlman (1976b), chaps. 7 and 8, for a fuller discussion of this topic.

5. Janice E. Perlman (1976b), 195.

6. Janice E. Perlman (1976b), 250–59.

7. Many of those I interviewed said they had purchased their expensive household items, such as hardwood bedroom sets or living room furniture or, in some cases, even cars, during the period just after the Real Plan, when their was worth more and added that if they had not bought those items at that time, they would never have been able to afford them.

8. United Nations Development Programme (2003); IPEA-Instituto de Pesquisa Econômica Aplicada (1999).

9. An excellent source for more detail on this is L. C. Queiroz Ribeiro and E. Telles (2000), 80.

10. Helen Icken Safa (2004), 6, identifies this as a trend for Latin America: "structural adjustment severely limited governmental spending—resulting in the decline of the public sector and privatization of public services on which many of the urban poor depended. It also froze wages and employment; contributing to the expansion of unregulated jobs in the informal sector for the self-employed and subcontractors to the formal sector." Elizabeth Leeds (1996) shows how this is related to the increasing unemployment in Rio and to the appeal of drug trafficking.

11. I divide the informal economy into two parts, distinguishing between illicit activities and illegal ones. Illicit practices are not officially registered, do not pay taxes, pay their workers in cash without benefits and/or occupy space–on the street or in buildings—not designated for such use. The illegal part of the informal economy includes the more lucrative businesses such as drug and arms dealing, blue or white collar crime, organ sales, and indentured servitude.

12. According to Peter M. Ward (2004), 2, since 1970 Latin American countries have tended to shift from largely patrimonial and undemocratic states toward more democratic, but downsized governments, off-loading welfare systems to local governments and NGOs.

13. Sueli Ramos Schiffer (2002), 226, states that "in practice, this means losing some basic guarantees [such as] health assistance...extra month's pay (the *decimo terceiro* or 13th month), paid holidays, retirement benefits and severance pay that have been in effect since the 1940s for formal sector jobs as a form of compensation [for] poor wages."

14. I am using the word *toxic* in the sense that Wolfgang Sachs uses it in his 1992 book, *The Development Dictionary*. The original title of that volume was to be, "A Dictionary of Toxic Words."

15. Naila Kabeer (1999) describes social exclusion as "the phenomenon of being 'locked out' of participation in social life as a result of the active dynamics of social interaction rather than as a condition of dependence stemming from some anonymous processes of impoverishment." She uses it as a multidimensional concept in which "factors of power relations, agency, culture, and social identities come into play, an environment in which individuals do not have access to public resources, [and] as a result they are able to contribute but not able to receive." This is what I described earlier as asymmetrical integration. For an earlier discussion of social exclusion in Brazil see Paulo Singer (1997).

16. For example, Sophie Bessis and Roskilde Symposium (1995) propose that the difference is that poverty is studied by economists while exclusion is studied by sociologists; S. Paugam (1995) asserts that social exclusion is the paradigm allowing our society to become aware of its own dysfunction; Peter Townsend (1985) claims that social exclusion has "strengthened approaches to poverty by involving the lack of fundamental resources and the inability to fully participate in one's own society"; and Cecile Jackson (1999) distinguishes between "structural and individual exclusion."

17. Marcio Pochmann et.al. (2004).

18. See Amartya Kumar Sen (1999), and other works, including those by Raj M. Desai and Wolfensohn Center for Development (2007); Mercedes Gonzalez de la Rocha (2001); Deepa Narayan-Parker and Patti L. Petesch (2002).

19. Marcus Melo (2002), 379.

20. Loïc J. D. Wacquant (1996).

21. For more on CCTs, see Valéria Pero and Dmitri Szerman (2005); François Bourguignon, Francisco H. G. Ferreira, and Phillippe G. Leite (2002).

22. Neither the minimum wage nor the currency exchange rates have remained static during the period of this study. As of February 2009 the minimum wage was about 400 reais per month and the dollar was worth around 1.9 reais. This puts the minimum wage in Rio at about 200 dollars per month (www.blogloco.com/r-465-novo-salario-minimo-2009/).

23. Loïc J. D. Wacquant (1996).

24. Pedro Abramo (2001).

25. See Joan M. Nelson (1969).

26. Recorded on the album *Traficando Informação* (1999).

27. MV Bill, whose real name is Alexandre Baretto, is in his midthirties. He has coauthored two bestselling books in Brazil: *Falcão: Meninos do Trafico* (2006) and *Cabeça de Porco* (2005).

28. See Jane Souto de Oliveira and Maria Hortense Marcier (1998).

29. See Luke Dowdney (2003).

CHAPTER 7

1. Alexei Barrionuevo (2008), A6. See also Monte Reel (2007), A1.

2. Edgar Pieterse (2007), 13.

3. Conrad Kottak, now a preeminent professor and author, was in Arembepe and Abrantes in the early 1960s. We were both on the undergraduate Columbia-Cornell-Harvard-Illinois Summer Field Studies Program in Anthropology. His

research consisted of showing photographs of faces to Brazilians and asking people to identify the racial term for each. He found about forty different terms used and very little agreement about how they were used.

4. Reported by Larry Rohter (2004), A3.
5. V. Hugo (2007).
6. "Rio de Janeiro," s.v. Nationmaster.com, accessed November 30, 2008.
7. Liana Leite (2008); Demétrio Weber (2008). Comparisons between violence rates in Latin America and Europe show that a youth in Latin America has 30 times greater probability of being murdered than a youth in Europe. The mortality rate among youth in Latin America is 43.4 per 100,000 versus 7.9 per 100,000 in Europe.
8. Ignacio Cano (2004).
9. The HDI for Complexo de Alemão is 0.587, Gabon is 0.637; Cape Verde 0.722. In some European countries, the index is almost double that of Rio's favelas, e.g. Norway (0.927), Belgium (0.923), and Sweden (0.923). The HDI of Brazil as a whole—0.792—places it sixty-ninth among the world's 177 nations. See V. Hugo (2007) and "Rio de Janeiro," s.v. Nationmaster.com.
10. For more on this, see Alba Zaluar, Clara Lucia Inem, and Gilberta Acselrad (1993). 78; Elizabeth Leeds (1996); Daniel Katz (2008).
11. MV Bill, interview, Leros, June 2005, www.leros.co.uk.
12. For more detail on this see Elizabeth Leeds (1996), 52–56; Luke Dowdney (2003), 25; and Moises Naim (2005).
13. See Marcelo Lopes de Souza (2005).
14. See Elizabeth Leeds (1996), 52–55; Daniel Katz (2008).
15. Elizabeth Leeds (1996), 56; Daniel Katz (2008); Luke Dowdney (2003), 27–39.
16. Luke Dowdney (2003), 31, 39.
17. A more detailed breakdown of the roles in the drug traffic is provided by Louis Kontos and David Brotherton (2008), 15–20.
18. Interview with Ignacio Cano, 2001.
19. "Rio de Janeiro," Nationmaster.com.
20. See James Holston (2008).
21. L. Wacquant (2008), 12. Wacquant cites Nilo Batista (1998), 77, as the source of the concept of "criminal policy as the shedding of the blood"; see also David J. Hess, Roberto A. DaMatta, and Sidney M. Greenfield (1996), 7–8, 22–27, and Ken Auletta (1982) on the assumption that the underclass operates outside the boundaries of society.
22. L. Wacquant (2008), 14.
23. Gary Duffy (2008).
24. See Colin Brayton, "Rio De Janeiro: GatoNet, Alt.Public.Transport Worth R$280 Million a Year," in the New World Lusophone Sousaphone (weblog), August 27, 2008; http://tupiwire.wordpress.com/2008/08/27/rio-de-janeiro-gatonet-altpublictransport-worth-r280-million-a-year/. The numbers are only estimates. Conversion rates fluctuate daily. I have used a 2:1 ratio, reais to dollars to arrive at the dollar estimates.
25. The title of this section is from the title of a book by David Caplovitz (1963), The Poor Pay More: Consumer Practices of Low-income Families.
26. These expressions come from the classic work of Gilberto Freyre (1956).

27. Daniel M. Brinks (2006), 213.

28. I reference this phrase from Janet L. Abu-Lughod (1994).

29. In the last weeks of 2006, for example, the *New York Times*, the BBC, Reuters, and other news sources carried stories about the "wave of gang violence" that swept over Rio to protest the inauguration of the new state governor elected on a platform of "cracking down on crime and violence." These actions were coordinated by a drug kingpin from within his prison cell and were carried out citywide as a way to demonstrate that the traffic, not the government, was in control. When the federal police were called in to help, the operation was ineffective, and the symbolism backfired, reminding people of the military police during the dictatorship rather than giving them a sense of security.

30. For more on this, see Daniel Katz (2008); Luke Dowdney (2003), 70–72; Enrique Desmond Arias (2006); Robert Gay (2005).

31. Brazil 2008 Crime & Safety Report: Rio de Janeiro (July 8, 2008), Overseas Security Advisory Council (OSAC).

32. None of our study communities was controlled by a militia during the period from 1999–2007, but by 2008 they had taken over some functions in Vila Operária in Caxias and were in a tense standoff with the traffic.

33. Gary Duffy (2008).

34. Notes from the DRP (Rapid Participatory Diagnosis) meeting on December 2001, which our research team organized for the collective reconstruction of the community history of Catacumba and the Quitungo-Guaporé conjuntos.

35. See Janice Perlman "It All Depends: Buying and Selling Houses in Rio's Favelas," January 2010, Report for IHC, Washington D.C. (available at www.mega.cities.net) See also Pedro Abramo (2003a; 2003b); Pedro Abramo and Suzana Pasternak Taschner (2003).

36. Notes, DRP meeting, December 2001. In December 2008, I heard that the state government had gotten rid of the traffic in the favela Santa Marta, which has a long history of struggle and independence. When I visited there in June 2009, there was the UPP: a police station on top of the hill, where specially trained *policies pacificadores* (peace-keeping police) maintained a constant presence in the community and kept dealers out. The community residents were overjoyed at their regained safely and freedom but were upset about the huge wall that was being built around their community as part of the same plan.

37. Interview with Nilton, Guaporé, 1999.

38. Interview Nova Brasília, July 29, 2002.

39. V. Hugo (2007).

40. The changes in religious affiliation over the 40 years did not show the massive conversion to evangelicalism that the popular press would lead us to believe. The biggest change was a decline in the number of people who considered themselves Catholic—and among those who no longer did, half had become evangelical in one form or another, and the other half said they "had no religion." Among the grandchildren's generation, the majority reported having "no religion."

41. See Mercedes Gonzalez de la Rocha (2001).

42. See Robert D. Putnam (2000); Robert D. Putnam, Robert Leonardi, and Raffaella Nanetti (1993).

43. See Mark Granovetter (1983).
44. Marcelo Lopes de Souza (2005).
45. Patrick Neate and Damian Platt (2006).
46. M.V. Bill (2006).

CHAPTER 8

1. Interview with Tio Souza at his apartment in Padre Miguel, July 2004.
2. The question was "Did the end of the dictatorship and the return to democracy have any major impact on your life?" In a more detailed breakdown, of the entire group of original interviewees, 17 percent said they did not know, and 66 percent said no impact, leaving only 18 percent who said it made any difference at all in their lives. This is an astonishing finding contradicting the academic literature and the perceptions of policy-makers, NGOs, and activists who believed that the return of democracy would be a great boon to the underclass.
3. Scott Mainwaring (1999; 1995) and Juan Forero (2004).
4. Enrique Desmond Arias (2006a).
5. Teresa P. R. Caldeira (2000).
6. This system was explained to me by Dona Rita and her daughter Simony in Nova Brasília, October 3, 2008.
7. See Janice E. Perlman (1983a).
8. See Saul David Alinsky (1969; 1971).
9. See Janice E. Perlman (1983b).
10. Among all three generations, health care that is accessible, affordable, and professional emerged as a high priority, confirming my observations of how dreadful the Rio public hospital system had become. I often heard the phrase, "the hospital is where people go to die." There is no "parallel power" providing health service through the drug gangs.
11. Evelina Dagnino (2003), 5.
12. See James Holston (2008).
13. See Benedita da Silva, Medea Benjamin, and Maisa Mendonça (1997).
14. The lack of relationship between civic and political participation may be due to the exceedingly low levels of membership in local associations in 2001 as opposed to 1969. Every type of community association membership dropped to single digits except for religious affiliation, which nonetheless dropped by percent from 53 percent in 1969 to 47 percent in 2001.
15. This disputes Robert Putnam's famous thesis that the bonding networks are related to greater political and economic integration; see Robert D. Putnam, Robert Leonardi, and Raffaella Nanetti (1993). We found clear differences among the communities: People in Caxias—where the favelas, the loteamentos, and the rest of the municipality are virtually continuous—and Catacumba—in the middle of the South Zone—had the highest levels of external networks; while Nova Brasília had the lowest (and the highest internal networks). The forced relocation of the favela of Catacumba to the Quitungo and Guaporé conjuntos, which was devastating in 1970, has proven beneficial as the residents of the conjuntos have many more ties to people and institutions outside the community. The community unity in favelas that

played a critical role in absorbing new migrants in the beginning, eventually held some people back from moving out and up.

16. Erving Goffman (1959).

17. This is a good sign, if it means that those who are most aware of the myriad forms of exclusion are the most willing to take action. The question was "Do you think discrimination exists regarding [a list of items drawn from the pretest]?" The order of the original interviewees' answers was as follows: living in a favela (84 percent); skin color (80 percent); appearance (74 percent); being a migrant (60 percent); and gender (53 percent). The answers of the children and grandchildren were almost identical. The index gave one point for each type of stigma recognized, as each presents a barrier to participatory democracy.

18. We created a "violence index" from the question "Have you or anyone in your family been a victim of robbery, mugging, physical attack, homicide, breaking and entering, police extortion, other forms of extortion, and/or rape/sexual abuse?" Each affirmative answer added one point to the index for that person and we correlated that index with several variables measuring different types of participation.

19. Interestingly, we found no correlation between the violence index score and gender, race, age, community of origin, interest in politics, belief in participation, thinking Brazilians have the capacity to select good candidates, or seeing the class system as closed.

20. Jorge G. Castañeda (2006).

CHAPTER 9

1. In the United States most panel studies are conducted with populations that are easy to track, such as Ivy League undergraduates, nurses or nuns. The closest parallel to this study is the work of Edward E. Telles and Vilma Ortiz (2008), in *Generations of Exclusion: Mexican Americans, Assimilation and Race*, which followed a large sample of Mexican Americans in Los Angeles and San Antonio across generations. The data from the original study of migrants from Mexico, conducted in the late 1960s, was found in an abandoned corner of a library at UCLA and Telles was able to locate the same people and interview them and their descendents. Given that Telles did not conduct the original study himself, this wonderful book does not describe how people and their communities changed beyond the statistical results of his survey. Caroline Moser also did an interesting restudy of a squatter settlement in Guatemala, but it was limited to a small number of families in a single small settlement she had studied decades earlier. My restudy was the inspiration for several later restudies funded by the World Bank and the British Aid Agency.

2. See Valéria Pero (2002b and 2004a).

3. For more detail on this see Estanislao Gacitúa-Marió and Michael J. V. Woolcock (2008) Estanislao Gacitua-Mariô Michael J. V. Woolcock and Instituto de Pesquisa Econômica Aplicada and (2005).

4. Those reporting "no income" or "not working" are not necessarily unemployed or looking for work. They include housewives, students, retirees, and anyone being supported by someone else, such as parents, children, spouses, etc. Favelas had the

highest proportion of people not working (39 percent); then bairros (30 percent) and conjuntos (27 percent). Dividing those who were working into manual and nonmanual occupations showed the bairros had the highest percent of nonmanual (40 percent); the conjuntos next (34 percent); and in the favelas least (only 21 percent). There is a clear hierarchy among these types of communities.

5. According to Karen Moore (2005), social exclusion and "adverse incorporation" interact so that people experiencing discrimination and stigma are forced to engage in economic activities and social relations that keep them poor. Shahin Yaqub (1999) discusses this form of exploitation as the plight of the working poor.

6. Gacitúa-Marió and Woolcock, (2008 and 2005).

7. The coefficients for these correlations are as follows: between the original interviewees in 1969 and 2001: 0.275; between the original interviewees in 1969 and their children in 2001: 0.358; between the original interviewees and their children in 2001: 0.314; between the children and grandchildren in 2001: 0.498; between the original interviewees in 1969 and the grandchildren in 2001: 0.239; and, between the original interviewees and the grandchildren in 2001: 0.09.

8. Shahin Yaqub (1999), 19.

9. Quoted in Deepa Narayan-Parker (2005), 3.

CHAPTER 10

1. See David Harvey (2003).

2. Discussion with Wanda Engel Aduan, October 2009.

3. See definitions and discussions in Machiko Nissanke and E. Thorbecke (2005; 2007a; 2007b).

4. For more on the concept of advanced marginality see Loïc J. D. Wacquant (1996; 1999). The idea and terminology for "space of flows" as opposed to space of places comes from the seminal work of Manuel Castells (2000).

5. Some scholars argue that globalization is *not* linked with advanced capitalism, and is *not* a consequence of policy pressure to follow the Washington consensus, but is the "manifestation of an age-old drive natural to the human spirit…the urge to profit by trading, the drive to spread religious beliefs, the desire to exploit new lands and the ambition to dominate others by armed might—all had been assembled by 6000 BC to start the process we now call globalization" (see Nayan Chandra, 2007).

6. Celso Furtado (1964; 1982).

7. On this see Kenneth F. Scheve and Matthew J. Slaughter (2007).

8. See Otilia Arantes, Carlos B. Vainer, and Ermínia Maricato (2000).

9. See Merike Blofield (2007) for comparisons with Latin America in general.

10. In Brazil, less than 1 percent of the national income went to the bottom 10 percent of the population, while close to 50 percent went to the top 10 percent of the population. The percent going to the lowest decile ranged in a narrow band from a low of 0.6 percent (in 1993, 1996, and 1997) to a high of 0.8 percent (in 2002), with all other years staying constant at 0.7. The top 10 percent of the population likewise had a narrow range and high degree of consistency over the decade, with a high of 48.6 percent (in 1993) to a low of 45.8 percent (in 1992) and 46–47 percent in all other years.

11. The highest percent of Brazilians under the poverty line over this period was 41.7 percent (1993), and the lowest was 32.7 percent (1998), with 33–34 percent in all other years, showing no strong globalization effect at the macro level. For Rio, the rates declined slightly between 1992 and 2003 (26.6 and 23.4 percent, respectively) accompanying an increase in the percent in extreme poverty.

12. See David de Ferranti, Guillermo Perry, Francisco Ferreira, and Michael Walton (2004) and Estanislao Gacitúa Marió, Michael Woolcock, and Instituto de Pesquisa Econômica Aplicada (2005).

13. The average per capita income of the upscale neighborhood, Gávea, is 2,140 reais per month, more than 12 times the average of the Complexo de Alemão where Nova Brasília is located, where the average is 177 reais per month. In 2000, when this was calculated, the exchange rate was 2.7 reais to the U.S. dollar.

14. We identified the geographical boundaries of the original communities as follows. For Catacumba, we sampled from all the building blocks within the official perimeter of Quitungo and Guaporé, the two housing projects where most people had been relocated after the favela's removal. For Nova Brasília, we used the map of the community made in the original study to delimit the perimeter of the area of interest (a detailed analysis of each street, pathway, and alley was done during several field visits in order to complete this task). We then mapped the streets and alleys within the community so as to update our 1969 map (which had been based on the aerial photograph and verified by a team of two architect-planners, Gilda Blank and Eloisa Coelho). In the case of Caxias, we used city maps and compared them with the 1969 research map to establish the perimeters of each favela and loteamento. Using these maps, fieldworkers walked each street and created more detailed maps showing internal alleys and the location of each entrance to a dwelling—or multiple dwellings (some behind the visible houses).

15. Maia Green and David Hulme (2005); Karen Moore (2005), 16.

16. Loïc J. D. Wacquant (1996).

17. In 1969, 43.7 percent of our sample was born in Rio state, and in 2003, 71.5 percent. In both cases, those born in Rio had significantly higher SES scores than migrants.

18. A rising percent from each generation (from 3 percent to 22 percent) said they "did not know" or refused to answer. All percents reported are "valid percents" after the removal of this group.

19. As self reported, 90 percent of the original interviewees, 98 percent of their children, and 97 percent of their grandchildren watched television on a daily basis, as compared with 37 percent in 1969. This is consistent with the findings in 2003 of 97 percent of the new random sample in the three study sites having "watched television daily or almost daily."

20. Young men and women explained to me that they turned down job offers on the basis of calculating how long they would have to work in order to buy brand-name clothing or shoes—after deducting their transportation and lunch costs.

21. Studies have shown that perceived satisfaction is more a function of one's position relative to one's reference group than of one's own absolute income, socioeconomic status, or upward or downward mobility. The reference group could be created by international images of teenagers on television.

22. Panel discussion on Youth and Employment at the UN Commission on Social Development, Department of Economic and Social Affairs, New York, February 14, 2008.

23. Remarks by Mario Barbosa, International Affairs Advisor from the Brazilian Ministry of Work and Employment, at Panel on Youth and Employment at the UN Commission on Social Development, Department of Economic and Social Affairs, New York, February 14, 2008.

24 Interview with Jailson, June 2009.

25. We looked at starting periods and lag periods of place-targeted programs (such as on-site upgrading focused on the territory of favelas, clandestine lots, or public housing), poverty-targeted programs (such as the early conditional cash transfers, based on poverty measures regardless of place of residence), and universal programs (such as changes in the minimum wage or access to credit that applied to all citizens but would affect the people in our sample directly).

26. Income was not included as a variable in the life history matrix, as prior studies have shown lack of recall, reliability, and validity.

27. In each year, the sample is composed of different people. As the years progress from 1960 to 2003, new individuals enter the sample (when they reach age 16) and others leave the sample (once they turn 32). (When the number of subjects for any year became less than 50, we discontinued the sequence.) We used the life history matrices starting with the current year and tracing each change in occupational status from 2003 back to the first job at or after 16 years of age.

28. Mark Granovetter (1983).

CHAPTER 11

1. Janice Perlman (1976); Marcelo Baumann Burgos (1998); Victor Vincent Valla (1985).

2. John F. C. Turner (1972).

3. William Ryan (1971).

4. Charles Abrams (1964; 1965); John F. C. Turner (1968; 1969; 1972); John F. C. Turner and Robert Fichter (1972); Anthony Leeds and Elizabeth Leeds (1970); Luciano Parisse (1969); Lisa Redfield Peattie (1968); Janice E. Perlman (1975).

5. The razing of "slum" housing in the inner cities of the United States and relocation of their former residents into large public housing projects created so many problems that such prize-winning projects as Pruit Igoe in St. Louis and Cabrini Green in Chicago eventually had to be demolished.

6. For further discussion see Neal Pierce (2008). For recent squatter evictions, see http://www.google.com/search?sourceid=navclient&aq=3h&oq=&ie=UTF-8&rlz=1T4SUNA_enUS253US255&q=squatter+eviction (downloaded July 23, 2009).

7. Three factors made the shift possible. First was the appointment of Mayor Israel Klabin by Governor Chagas Freitas, who was independent-minded and opposed favela removal. Klabin created the Municipal Secretariat of Social Development, the first city agency whose mandate was helping Rio's poor. Second was the creation of Promorar (a national program under the last dictator, Joao Figueiredo), which provided federal funding for "Projeto Rio" to upgrade the stilt houses built out into Guanabara Bay in the favelas of Maré. Third, and perhaps least recognized, was the electrification of Rio's favelas by Light (Servicos de Eletricidade), the Canadian-

Brazilian joint venture electric company that operates in the Rio municipalities. For the favela leadership, this was a benchmark, insofar as they were tasked with mapping the favelas and organizing the residents who would become the new paying customers of the company. This prepared a cadre of leaders in each favela who knew the extent of their communities better than anyone and who later became leaders of social mobilizations. (Interviews with Mario Brum, Jan. 7–8, 2008. For more detail on the history of favela policy see Brum 2006.)

8. The diagram illustrating this mismatch can be found in my 1987 article, "Misconceptions of the Urban Poor and the Dynamics of Housing Policy Evolution."

9. The three CODESCO favelas were Mata Machado, Morro Uniao, and Bras de Pina. Among those who worked on this were Silvio Ferraz, Carlos Nelson, Silvia Wanderley, Gilda Blank and Olga Bronstein. For more on CODESCO, see Carlos Nelson Ferreira dos Santos (1971; 1980; 1981; 1983); Carlos Nelson Ferreira dos Santos and Olga Bronstein (1978). See also Gilda Blank (1980); Janice E. Perlman (1976b).

10. Official figures show that as of December 24, 2005, the Rio state public housing agency was administering 200 conjuntos, 131,615 social housing units, and 22,306 lots. An estimated 700,000 people or more were living in these projects. See the Projects Registry (Cadastro de Empreendimentos) of CEHAB-RJ; Directory of Housing Projects. See also the website for Favela tem Memória, http://www.favelatemmemoria.com.br/.

11. See Ralph della Cava (1988) and Bryan McCann (2008).

12. The crisis occurred when the first elected mayor, Saturnino Braga (elected in 1985) found himself caught between a hostile governor, Moreira Franco, and a hostile City Council loyal to the Governor, Leonel Brizola. The government refused to release funds to the city, and the City Council in turn refused to approve any spending, so urban projects ground to a halt. This coincided with the huge floods in 1988 which destroyed dozens, even hundreds of favela homes and killed many people. As a consequence all city funds went to cleanup, reconstruction, and temporary housing.

13. A case study of the Reforestation Program, "Reforestation in Rio's Favelas, Rio de Janeiro, Brazil," by Marlene Fernandes, is available at the Mega-Cities Project website at http://www.megacitiesproject.org/publications_environment.asp.

14. At the time Favela-Bairro was initiated, Cesar Maia was mayor, Luiz Paulo Conde was Secretary of Planning, Sergio Magalhaes was Secretary of Housing, Wanda Engel Aduan was Secretary for Social Action, and Lu Petersen was project director. Lu had been part of every favela upgrading program since CODESCO.

15. The sections on Favela-Bairro and the programs it inspired, as well as the plans for Phase III, have integrated my own observations, readings, and interviews, and been informed by personal interviews with Jose Brakarz, most recently on July 22, 2009. Jose Brakarz, Senior Urban Development Specialist at the Inter-American Development Bank, has been the driving force behind Favela-Bairro since its inception. For more details see Brakarz (2002) and Andrea Vianna, (2005).

16. For more on the Celula Urbana see Lu Petersen (2003). The agreements with the Bauhaus group were signed in 1991 and 2001. As of 2009 the program is being run by the state government, which has also taken over the upgrading of the other large favelas. The funding comes from the federal government and is channeled through Governor Sergio Cabral rather than Mayor Eduardo Paes because of party affiliation.

17. Data from *O Globo*, July 19, 2009. For entire article, see http://oglobo.globo.com/rio/mat/2009/07/18/cidade-do-rio-ja-tem-mais-de-mil-favelas-756879298.asp.

18. Elsewhere I have written in more detail about the perils and pitfalls of the notion of "best practices" (see Perlman and Sheehan [2008]) and on the life cycle of urban innovations. On the life cycle of innovations, see Robert Yin (1981) and for its application to mega-cities see Elwood Hopkins (1994).

19. Interview with Alfredo Sirkis, Municipal Secretary of Urbanism and the Environment, June 2004, and site visits to several POUSOs with Tania Castro, project director.

20. See distinction drawn by Manuel Castells (1993) between the space of flows and the space of place.

21. For a deeper discussion of knowledge and influence see Roz Lasker and John Guidry (2009).

22. For more on Bolsa Família, see Lavinas et al. (2008). Also www.ric.org/iniciativa/pdf/wp7.pdf.

23. The Rio city (municipal) population in 2007 was 6,200,000 or about 1,370,000 families, of whom close to one-third are living in poverty. Interview with Fernando Cavaliere at the Instituto Perreira Passos, May 2009.

24. See Rebecca Abers (1998) and the many other publications she has written on this topic since.

25. See Yves Cabbanes (2004) on the expansion of participatory budgeting through a network covering several countries. He has played an active role in convening this network and bringing the mayors together at the World Urban Forum in Vancouver in 2004.

26. For more details on the PAC, see www.brasil.gov.br/pac/ and www.vivafavela.org.br.

27. On Avenida Itaoca, near the entrance to Nova Brasília, dozens, perhaps hundreds of families, are already living in the shells of abandoned factories, without running water or electricity—just to escape the violence of the drug traffic in the Morro de Alemão. This is especially true for the poorest families, who live on the highest parts of the hillside and face the greatest danger while going up and down to school or work. These sites would be ideal locations for high density conjuntos that would blend seamlessly into the surrounding urban fabric.

28. See *Business News Americas*, Wednesday, June 3, 2009, and Thursday, June 4, 2009. www.bnamericas.com/.../Study: and www.bnamericas.com/.../Govt.

29. John Kingdon's case studies on agenda-setting in public policy have shown the importance of anticipating such windows of opportunity and being able to respond to the moment with: (1) a ready and interested general public; (2) tried and tested solutions to the problem at issue already documented and on the shelf; and (3) a broker who knows the appropriate decision-maker and knows where the tried-and-tested solutions can be found and can bring the solutions to the key person during that narrow window of opportunity in the flow of the political process (1984).

30. See www.mega-cities.net for case studies of 40 such innovation transfers and the methods used to broker such exchanges, led by the community wishing to adapt the solution to its own reality (the import model) rather then by an institution that has funded the transfer of that solution to other places that may not be interested (the export model).

31. See Marc Fried (1963), on "grieving for a lost home" in the case of urban renewal in a Boston neighborhood.

32. I did try to test the "counterfactual" conjecture ("what-if" hypothesis) by selecting a favela in the South Zone that was as similar as possible to Catacumba in 1970—with the single difference that it had not been removed. I then planned to compare the life histories and current life conditions of the former Catacumba residents (now living in conjuntos) with those of the South Zone favela residents. I intended to do this through matched pairs, controlling for age, gender, race, and educational level, as well as for the profile of the communities as a whole. Once I started working on this, however, I realized that there was no way to set up such a quasi-experimental design that would yield reliable results. There are simply no communities that could be considered comparable. The specifics of the community histories, locations, political relationships, and other factors could easily lead to strong but spurious conclusions that were unrelated to the removal and relocation issue.

33. See article on Minha Casa, Minha Vida by Jonathan Wheatley (2009).

34. Interviews with Wanda Engel Aduan, September 2008 and October 2009. For further details on her ideas, see Wanda Engel Aduan (2006).

35. For more on defensible space see Oscar Newman's book of that title (1972).

36. Some sites and services experiments included core houses (*casas embrião*) on each plot, which proved too expensive for newly arriving migrants and too remote and small to attract favela residents. To bring prices down the project may consist of a raised cement floor at the center of each lot serviced by a "hydraulic wall" that contains the water and electricity connections.

37. Interview with Arlindo Daibert, Diretor do Centro de Estudos, Procuradoria Geral do Município do Rio de Janeiro (Director of Policy Studies, Office of the Attorney General, Rio de Janeiro), September 2008.

38. Newsletter *Favelão* quoted by Mario Brum in discussion with author, January 26, 2009.

39. Hernando de Soto (2000).

40. Nicholas D. Kristof (2009). The documentary film, *Garbage Dreams*, makes this point about Cairo's Zataleen.

41. Brazilian schools operate two sessions per day; the children attend either in the morning or the afternoon. There is little for them to do for the other half-day, which leads to missed educational opportunities and ample opportunity for getting into trouble. When Brizola was Governor of Rio State, he tried to change that by creating CIEPS schools that would serve the students full-time, including providing meals, sports facilities, lunches (often the only hot meal the children had all day), locker rooms with showers, and basic health care. The new school buildings with their signature modern design were meant to fulfill the unmet needs of low-income students that the rest of the city children received as a matter of course.

42. Brian English, personal communication, January 22, 2009. LabourNet is one company of the Scale-Up Program at CHF International.

43. Sir Peter Hall developed the concept in 1979 during the Thatcher government, inspired by free-trade zones in Singapore and Hong Kong, and the idea was picked up the same year by Representative Jack Kemp (R-NY).

44. Some aspects of the work have continued under the auspices of IETS, the nonprofit Instituto de Estudos do Trabalho e Sociedade (Institute for the Study of Work and Society), which Urani created after he left office.

45. For case studies of 40 such innovation transfers and the lessons learned and for more detail on the poverty-environment nexus, see "Environmental Justice: Case Studies Mega-Cities" at www.mega-cities.net."

46. Elizabeth Kolbert (2009).

47. Van Jones (2008).

48. I first heard of "resource conserving cities from Prof. Richard Meier my colleague in the Department of City and Regional Planning at University of California, Berkeley. See Richard Meier (1974).

49. Film Directed by Jeff Zimbalist and Matt Mochary, 2005.

50. Quoted in Patrick Neate (2003), 199–200. See also Neate and Platt (2006, 2010).

51. Luiz Eduardo Soares, an anthropologist and university professor was the Coordinator of Public Safety in Rio de Janeiro (1999–2000), National Secretary of Public Security (2003), directed a public security think tank in the municipality of Nova Iguaçu and is currently Secretary for Violence Prevention there. His films *Notícias de uma guerra particular* and *Tropa de elite* (based on his book *Elite da Tropa*) are reference points for discussion in this field. He also coauthored *Cabeça de Porco* with MV Bill and Celso Athayde (2005). Quotation from an interview with Luiz Soares, July 6, 2005, available at the website of Dreams Can Be Foundation; www.dreamscanbe.org/controlPanel/materia/view/433, accessed December 20, 2008.

52. For more on these issues, see Teresa P. R. Caldeira and James Holston (1999); Elizabeth Leeds (2007); Ignacio Cano and Nilton Santos (2001); Leonardo Marino (2008).

53. See Instituto Pólis (2002); Edésio Fernandes (2007).

54. See Edgar Pieterse (2007) and Caroline Kihato et al. (2006).

55. Personal correspondence, March 2009.

56. Perlman in Susskind (1983).

57. For more on "building power, community," and people see Perlman (1976a; 1978; 1979; 1983a; 1983b).

58. Alan Altshuler and Marc Zegans (1990).

59. For more details on the Vaughn Family Center and other successful bottom-up initiatives in low-income neighborhoods in New York and Lost Angeles, see Janice E. Perlman and Elwood M. Hopkins (1997).

60. Janice Perlman (1990).

61. See Manuel Castells's seminal book of that name (1977).

62. For more details on the survey, see Global Leaders' Survey, www.mega-cities.net.

CHAPTER 12

1. Nilton was one of the most intelligent and well educated of the Catacumba residents at the time I was living there. He was the person who most fully understood my research and was most helpful to me. Today, he lives in a house he built just beside the apartment blocks of the Guaporé conjunto.

2. Although derived from the same Anglo-Norman French root *genterie,* the Brazilian term *gente* is not the equivalent of the English *gentry*. "Gentry," according to the

Oxford English Dictionary, refers to "people of good social position"…to a sense of "superiority of position, birth or rank," such as "the landed gentry." In Brazilian Portuguese, the word means "person," "someone who counts" regardless of wealth. For further translations and definitions, see *Collins English-Portuguese, Português-Inglês Dictionary* (New York: HarperCollins, 2001), 165.

3. Philippe I. Bourgois (1995).
4. See Fareed Zakaria (2009), 42.
5. From interview with Luiz Eduardo Soares, July 6, 2005, available at the website of Dreams Can Be Foundation; www.dreamscanbe.org/controlPanel/materia/view/433, accessed December 20, 2008. Soares exposes in the documentary *Noticias de uma Guerra Particular* the complicity between the police and drug dealers, as well as the vulnerability of the police officers—and the fact that most of them come from the same lower-class background as the dealers they are so eager to kill.
6. Brazilian anthropologist, Roberto da Matta wrote his now famous piece, "*Você sabe com quem está falando?*" in 1979.
7. See Erving Goffman (1959).
8. This list taken from a chart entitled "Pobre e Rico na cabeça das pessoas" (Poor and Rich in people's minds), part of the Pesquisa FGV-Opinião para Unilever (2003), quoted in Ricardo Neves (2003), 79.
9. Quoted in Patrick Neate (2003), 191–92.
10. Luiz Eduardo Soares interview (2005).
11. Evelina Dagnino (1998).
12. Edward E. Telles (1994).
13. Larry Rohter (2007). Ralph Ellison titled his 1952 novel, *The Invisible Man*.
14. Quoted by Lara Farrar, in "Slums offer surprising hope for tomorrow's urban world," June 11, 2008, CNN, London (CNN.com).
15. Steve Kingstone (2003).
16. Julio Ludemir (2004).
17. Teresa P. R. Caldeira (2000).
18. Favela chair, www.mossonline.com/product-exec/product_id/31681 (accessed April 16, 2008). Image shown with permission of designers.
19. The original lyrics in Portuguese can be found under "Favelas do Brazil," www.youtube.com. Translation by author.
20. See Farr for CNN interviews with Stewart Brand and Robert Neuwith. Stewart Brand, who started the *Whole Earth Catalogue* and published it from 1968–72, is president of the Long Now Foundation, concerned with solving long-term problems. Robert Neuwith is a journalist/author (2005).
21. Quoted in Kelefa Sanneh (2009), 28.
22. This corresponds with all the research I have done in squatter settlements the world over. The bottom 20 percent are either too poor, too elderly, or too sick to participate in any self-help program. They are the ones needing social assistance and stipends rather than loans for housing or small business start-ups. It appears that in the Rio study, they are the fifth who said their lives were "worse than they expected."
23. See chapter 10, note 24, and John Cassidy (2006).

24. Ten-step ladder approach from Nancy Birdsall and Carol Graham in periodic surveys for *LatinoBarometro*. See Nancy Birdsall and Carol Graham (2000), 234–48.

25. See Carol Graham and Stefano Pettinato (2001).

26. See discussion of inequality and mobility in Estanislau-Gacitúa Marió and Michael J. V. Woolcock (2008).

27. John Turner used the term "bridgehead" (1972) in describing settlement patterns of migrants to Lima and Santiago.

APPENDIX I

1. On the collection, analysis, and use of life histories, see Balan, Jorge, Browning L., Jelin, Elizabeth, Lee, "A computerized approach to the processing and analysis of life stories obtained in sample surveys." *Behavioral Science*, 14, n. 2, 1969, pp. 105–120.

2. BirdSall, Nancy, and Carol Graham. *New Markets, New Opprotunities? Economic and Social Mobility in a Changing World.* Washington DC: The Brookings Institution, 2000.

3. I was almost killed myself, one sunny day while waiting for the people to arrive for the participatory community history reconstruction in Nova Brasília. The meeting was set for a Sunday at the Residents' Association and had been approved, but while waiting I decided to take pictures of some of the same places I had photographed 30 years ago. Soon I was surrounded by angry young men, well armed, and wanting my camera. Evidently I had taken pictures of some prohibited areas without knowing it. Because two of the community residents on their way to the meeting intervened, and we went to the Residents' Association where the President was able to speak for me, they only took my film, not the camera. But a group of them were waiting for me 6 hours later at the end of the day's meeting, and I had to be put into a taxi in a big hurry.

4. Moser, Caroline, *Confronting Crisis: A Comparative Study of Household Responses to Poverty and Vulnerability in Four poor Urban Communities.* (Washington, DC: The World Bank, 1996).

APPENDIX 2

1. Only in the grandchildren's generation, was there a correlation between lighter color and higher SES, but no significant relationship between skin color and any of the other outcome variables. The correlation would show up strongly if the entire Rio municipality were included.

2. Other "fatalism" questions include: Can a man be good without having religion? and Should couples try to limit their number of children or accept what comes?

3. The questions were: In the next five years, do you think life in (Brazil Rio de Janeiro, your community, your own life) will be much better, somewhat better, somewhat worse, or much worse? The optimism index was calculated by giving one point for each positive answer (either somewhat or much better).

4. Networks were measured by the geographical proximity of the four closest family members or friends of the interviewee. Internal networks were considered "high" if 3–4 friends or family members lived inside the interviewee's community; low networks consisted of 1–2 friends or family members; and no internal network meant that one's closest family and friends lived outside the community. The same logic was applied to external networks. High meant 3–4 friends/family members lived outside the community; low was 1–2. The correlations between internal and external were significant and negative. See Granovetter (1973).

references

Abers, Rebecca. 1998. Learning Democratic Practice: Distributing Government Resources through Popular Participation in Porto Alegre, Brazil. In *Cities for Citizens: Planning and the Rise of Civil Society in a Global Age,* ed. Mike Douglass and John Friedmann, 39–65. Chichester, UK: Wiley.

Abramo, Pedro. 2003a. Eu Já Tenho Onde Morar: A Cidade da Informalidade. In *A Cidade da Informalidade: O Desafio das Cidades Latino-Americanas,* ed. Pedro Abramo and Suzana Pasternak Taschner, 1–11. Rio de Janeiro: Livraria Sette Letras: FAPERJ.

———. 2003b. *Mobilidade Residencial no Rio de Janeiro: Considerações Sobre o Setor Formal e Informal do Mercado Imobiliário.* Rio de Janeiro: Federal University of Rio de Janeiro.

———. 2003c. Uma Teoria Economica Da Favela: Elementos Sobre o Mercado Imobiliario Informal Em Favelas a Mobilidade Residencial Dos Pobres. In *A Cidade da Informalidade: O Desafio das Cidades Latino-Americanas,* ed. Pedro Abramo and Suzana Pasternak Taschner, 198–225. Rio de Janeiro: Livraria Sette Letras: FAPERJ.

———. 2001. *Mercado e Ordem Urbana: Do Caos à Teoria Da Localização Residencial.* Rio de Janeiro: Bertrand Brasil.

Abramo, Pedro, and Suzana Pasternak Taschner, eds. 2003. *A Cidade da Informalidade: O Desafio das Cidades Latino-Americanas.* Rio de Janeiro: Livraria Sette Letras: FAPERJ.

Abrams, Charles. 1964. *Man's Struggle for Shelter in an Urbanizing World.* Cambridge, MA: MIT Press.

———. 1965. *The City Is the Frontier.* New York: Harper and Row.

Abu-Lughod, Janet L. 1994. The Battle for Tompkins Square Park. In *From Urban Village to East Village: The Battle for New York's Lower East Side,* ed. Janet L. Abu-Lughod, 233–66. Oxford: Blackwell.

Aduan, Wanda Engel. 2006. The Elusive Quest for Equality: Interview with Wanda Engel Aduan. *IDBAmérica: Magazine of the Inter-American Development Bank* [database online], www.iadb.org/idbamerica/index.cfm?thisid=3865 (accessed March 5, 2009).

Alinsky, Saul David. 1971. *Rules for Radicals: A Practical Primer for Realistic Radicals.* New York: Random House.

———. 1969. *Reveille for Radicals.* New York: Vintage Books.

Altshuler, Alan, and Marc Zegans. 1990. Innovation and Creativity: Comparisons between Public Management and Private Enterprise. *Cities* 7 (1) (2): 16–24.

Alvarez, Sonia E. 1993. "Deepening" Democracy: Popular Movement Networks, Constitutional Reform, and Radical Urban Regimes in Contemporary Brazil. In *Mobilizing the Community: Local Politics in the Era of the Global City,* ed. Robert Fisher and Joseph M. Kling, 191–219. London: Sage.

Arantes, Otilia Beatriz Fiori, Carlos B. Vainer, and Ermínia Maricato. 2000. *A Cidade do Pensamento Único: Desmanchando Consensos.* Petrópolis, Brazil: Editora Vozes.

Arias, Enrique Desmond. 2006a. The Dynamics of Criminal Governance: Networks and Social Order in Rio de Janeiro. *Journal of Latin American Studies* 38 (2): 293–325.

———. 2006b. Trouble en Route: Drug Trafficking and Clientelism in Rio de Janeiro Shantytowns. *Qualitative Sociology* 29 (4): 427–45.

Auletta, Ken. 1982. *The Underclass.* New York: Random House.

Auyero, Javier. 1997. Wacquant in the Argentine Slums: Comment on Loic Wacquant's "Three Pernicious Premises in the Study of the American Ghetto." *International Journal of Urban and Regional Research* 21 (3) (September): 508.

Balan, Jorge, Harley L. Browning, Elizabeth Jelin, and Lee Litzler. 1969. A Computerized Approach to the Processing and Analysis of Life Histories Obtained in Sample Surveys. *Behavioral Science* 14 (2): 105–20.

Barrionuevo, Alexei. 2008. In Rio Slum, Armed Militia Replaces Drug Gang's Criminality with Its Own. *New York Times,* June 13, 2008.

Barros, Ricardo Paes de, Ricardo Henriques, and Rosane Mendonça. 2001. *A Estabilidade Inaceitável: Desigualdade e Pobreza no Brasil.* Rio de Janeiro: Instituto de Pesquisa Econômica Aplicada.

Batista, Nilo. 1998. Politica Criminal Com Derramamento De Sangue. *Discursos Sediciosos: Crime, Direito e Sociedade* 3 (5–6).

Bearak, Barry. 2004. Poor Man's Burden. *New York Times Magazine,* June 27.

Bessis, Sophie, and Roskilde Symposium. 1995. *From Social Exclusion to Social Cohesion: A Policy Agenda: The Roskilde Symposium, 2–4 March 1995.* Paris: UNESCO.

Birdsall, Nancy, and Carol Graham. 2000. *New Markets, New Opportunities? Economic and Social Mobility in a Changing World.* Washington, DC: Carnegie Endowment for International Peace: Brookings Institution Press.

Blank, Gilda. 1980. Brás De Pina: Experiência De Urbanização De Favela. In *Habitação em questão,* ed. Licia do Prado Valladares, 17–47. Rio de Janeiro: Zahar Editores.

Blofield, Merike. 2007. *Proposal for the Observatory on Inequality in Latin America.* Mimeograph. Miami: Center for Latin American Studies, University of Miami.

Bourgois, Philippe I. 1995. *In Search of Respect: Selling Crack in El Barrio.* Cambridge: Cambridge University Press.

Bourguignon, François, Francisco H. G. Ferreira, and Phillippe G. Leite. 2002. *Ex-ante Evaluation of Conditional Cash Transfer Programs: The Case of Bolsa Escola.* Washington, DC: World Bank.

Bourguignon, Francois, Francisco H. G. Ferreira, and Marta Menendez. 2003. *Inequality of Outcomes and Inequality of Opportunities in Brazil.* Washington, DC: World Bank

Development Economics Office of the Senior Vice President and Chief Economist and Development Research Group Poverty Team.

Brinks, Daniel M. 2006. The Rule of (Non)Law: Prosecuting Police Killings in Brazil and Argentina. In *Informal Institutions and Democracy: Lessons from Latin America*, ed. Gretchen Helmke and Steven Levitsky, 201–26. Baltimore: Johns Hopkins University Press.

Brum, Mario Sergio Ignácio. 2006. O Povo Acredita Na Gente: Rupturas e Continuidades no Movimento Comunitário Das Favelas Cariocas Nas Décadas de 1980 e 1990. Master's thesis, Universidade Federal Fluminense.

Burgos, Marcelo Baumann. 2002. *A Utopia da Comunidade: Rio das Pedras, uma Favela.* Rio de Janeiro: Editora PUC, Edições Loyola.

———. 1998. Dos Parques Proletários Ao Favela-Bairro: As Políticas Públicas Nas Favelas do Rio de Janeiro. In *Um século de favela*, ed. Alba Zaluar and Marcos Alvito, 25–60. Rio de Janeiro: Fundação Getulio Vargas Editora.

Cabbanes, Yves. 2004. Participatory Budgeting: A Significant Contribution to Participatory Democracy. *Environment and Urbanization* 16 (April): 27–46.

Caldeira, Teresa P. R. 2000. *City of Walls: Crime, Segregation, and Citizenship in São Paulo.* Berkeley: University of California Press.

Caldeira, Teresa P. R., and James Holston. 1999. Democracy and Violence in Brazil. *Comparative Studies in Society and History* 41 (4) (October): 691–729.

Cano, Ignacio. 2004. *O Impacto Da Violência Em Rio de Janeiro.* Rio de Janeiro: Universidade do Estado do Rio de Janeiro.

———. n.d. *Police Oversight in Brazil.* Working paper. Rio de Janeiro: UERJ. www.altus.org/pdf/b_ic_en_pdf.

Cano, Ignacio, and Nilton Santos. 2001. *Violência Letal, Renda e Desigualdade no Brasil.* Rio de Janeiro: 7 Letras.

Caplovitz, David. 1963. *The Poor Pay More: Consumer Practices of Low-income Families.* New York: Free Press of Glencoe.

Cassidy, John. 2006. Relatively Deprived: How Poor Is Poor? *New Yorker*, April 3, 42.

Castañeda, Jorge G. 2006. Latin America's Left Turn. *Foreign Affairs* 85 (3) (May–June): 28.

Castells, Manuel. 2000. *The Rise of the Network Society.* Vol. 2. Malden, MA: Blackwell.

———. 1997. *The Power of Identity.* Malden, MA: Blackwell.

———. 1993. Why the Megacities Focus? Megacities in the New World Disorder. Paper presented at the seventh annual Mega-Cities Coordinators meeting, Jakarta, August 1–9, see www.mega-cities.net, *Environmental Justice* for full text.

———. 1977. *The Urban Question: A Marxist Approach.* Cambridge, MA: MIT Press.

Cavalcanti, Mariana. 2007. Of Shacks, Houses, and Fortresses: An Ethnography of Favela Consolidation in Rio de Janeiro. Ph.D. diss., University of Chicago.

Cavallaro, James, and Anne Manuel. 1997. *Police Brutality in Urban Brazil.* New York: Human Rights Watch.

Cavallieri, Paulo F. A. 2005. Favelas in Rio: Data and Changes. In IPP [online database]. www.citiesalliance.org/doc/features/slum-electrification-workshop/favelas-rio.pdf (accessed March 1, 2009).

———. 2003. *The Situation of Children and Adolescents in the Complexo de Alemão.* UNICEF.

Central Intelligence Agency. 2009. *The World Factbook 2009.*

Centro de Promoção da Saude (CEDAPS). 2003. The Situation of Children and Adolescents in the Complexo da Alemão. New York, UNICEF publication.

Cerrutti, Marcela, and Rodolfo Bertoncello. 2003. Urbanization and Internal Migration Patterns in Latin America. Paper presented at conference "African Migration in Comparative Perspective," Johannesburg, South Africa, June 4–7.

Chandra, Nayan. 2007. *Bound Together: How Traders, Preachers, Adventurers, and Warriors Shaped Globalization*. New Haven: Yale University Press.

Dagnino, Evelina. 2003. Citizenship in Latin America: An Introduction. *Latin American Perspectives* 30 (2) (March): 3–17.

———. 1998. Culture, Citizenship and Democracy: Changing Discourses and Practices in the Latin American Left. In *Cultures of Politics, Politics of Cultures: Re-visioning Latin American Social Movements,* ed. Sonia E. Alvarez, Evelina Dagnino, and Arturo Escobar, 459. Boulder, CO: Westview Press.

da Matta, Roberto. 1979. Você sabe com quem está falando?, in *Carnavais, Malandros e heróis*. Rio de Janeiro, Zahar Editores.

de Ferranti, David, Guillermo Perry, Francisco Ferreira, and Michael Walton. 2004. *Inequality in Latin America and the Caribbean: Breaking with History?*. Washington, DC: World Bank.

de la Rocha, Mercedes Gonzalez. 2001. From the Resources of Poverty to the Poverty of Resources? The Erosion of a Survival Model. *In Mexico in the 1990s: Economic Crisis, Social Polarization, and Class Struggle*. Special issues, pt. 2. *Latin American Perspectives* 28 (4, July): 72–100.

Della Cava, Ralph. 1988. The Church and the *Abertura* in Brazil, 1974–1985, Working Paper #114. Queens College, the City University of New York, November.

De Souza, Marcelo Lopes. 2005. Urban Planning in an Age of Fear: The Case of Rio de Janeiro. International Development Planning Review 27 (1): 1–19.

Desai, Raj M., and Wolfensohn Center for Development. 2007. *The Political Economy of Poverty Reduction: Scaling Up Antipoverty Programs in the Developing World*. Washington, DC: Wolfensohn Center for Development at the Brookings Institution.

de la Rocha, Mercedes Gonzalez. 2001. From the Resources of Poverty to the Poverty of Resources? The Erosion of a Survival Model. In Mexico in the 1990s: Economic Crisis, Social Polarization, and Class Struggle. Special issues, pt. 2, *Latin American Perspectives* 28 (4) (July): 72–100.

Desai, Raj M., and Wolfensohn Center for Development. 2007. *The Political Economy of Poverty Reduction: Scaling Up Antipoverty Programs in the Developing World*. Washington, DC: Wolfensohn Center for Development at the Brookings Institution.

Diamond, Larry Jay. 2005. Empowering the Poor: What Does Democracy Have to Do with It? In *Measuring Empowerment: Cross-disciplinary Perspectives,* ed. Deepa Narayan-Parker, 403–25. Washington, DC: World Bank.

Dowdney, Luke. 2003. *Crianças do tráfico: Um Estudo De Caso De crianças Em violência Armada Organizada no Rio de Janeiro*. Rio de Janeiro: 7 Letras.

Duffy, Gary. 2008. Vigilantes Take Over Rio Shanty Towns. 2008. BBC News. http://news.bbc.co.uk/2/hi/americas/7283640.stm (accessed June 28, 2008).

Dugger, Celia W. 2004. To Help Poor Be Pupils, Not Wage Earners, Brazil Pays Parents. *New York Times*, January 3, 2004.

Escobar, Arturo. 1995. *Encountering Development: The Making and Unmaking of the Third World.* Princeton, NJ: Princeton University Press.

Estado da Guanabara. 1973. *Faveladas Removidas e Respectivos Conjuntos.* Rio de Janeiro: Secretaria de Planejamento e Coordenação Geral do Estado da Guanabara.

Fanon, Frantz. 1965. *The Wretched of the Earth.* New York: Grove Press.

Fernandes, Edésio. 2007. Constructing the "Right to the City" in Brazil. *Social and Legal Studies* 16 (2): 201–19.

Fernandes, Marlene. 1998. Reforestation in Rio's Favelas. In Perlman, Janice, *Environmental Justice: The Poverty/Environment Nexus in Mega-Cities.* Available at www.megacitiesproject.org/publications_environment.asp.

Ferranti, David de, Guillermo Perry, Francisco Ferreira, and Michael Walton. 2004. *Inequality in Latin America and the Caribbean: Breaking with History?* Washington, DC: World Bank.

Ferreira, Francisco, H. G., Phillippe Leite, and Julie Litchfield. 2008. The Rise and Fall of Brazilian Inequality: 1981–2004. *Macroeconomic Dynamics* 12 (S2): 199–230.

Forero, Juan. 2004. Latin America Graft and Poverty Trying Patience with Democracy. *New York Times,* June 24.

Freire, Paulo. 1973. *Pedagogy of the Oppressed.* New York: Seabury Press.

Freyre, Gilberto. 1956. *The Masters and the Slaves (Casa-Grande e Senzala): A Study in the Development of Brazilian Civilization.* New York: Knopf.

Fried, Marc. 1963. Grieving for a Lost Home. In *The Urban Condition: People and Policy in the Metropolis,* ed. Leonard J. Duhl. New York: Basic Books.

Fundação Leão. 1968. *Favelas of Guanabara.* Mimeograph. Rio de Janeiro: Fundação Leão.

Furtado, Celso. 1982. *A Nova Dependência: Dívida Externa e Monetarismo.* Vol. 2a. Rio de Janeiro: Paz e Terra.

———. 1964. *Dialética do Desenvolvimento.* Vol. 2. Rio de Janeiro: Editôra Fundo de Cultura.

Gacitua-Marió, Estanislau, and Michael J. V. Woolcock. 2008. *Social Exclusion and Mobility in Brazil.* Washington, DC: World Bank.

———. 2005. *Exclusão Social e Mobilidade no Brasil.* Brasília: Instituto de Pesquisa Econômica Aplicada.

Gay, Robert. 2005. *Lucia: Testimonies of a Brazilian Drug Dealer's Woman.* Philadelphia: Temple University Press.

Gilbert, Alan. 2007. The Return of the Slum: Does Language Matter? *International Journal of Urban and Regional Research* 31 (4): 697–713.

Goffman, Erving. 1959. *The Presentation of Self in Everyday Life.* Garden City, NY: Doubleday.

Goirand, Camille. 2003. Citizenship and Poverty in Brazil. *Latin American Perspectives* 30 (2): 226–48.

Graham, Carol, and Stefano Pettinato. 2001. *Happiness and Hardship: Opportunity and Insecurity in New Market Economies.* Washington, DC: Brookings Institution Press.

Granovetter, Mark. 1983. The Strength of Weak Ties: A Network Theory Revisited. *Sociological Theory* 1: 201–33.

Green, Maia, and David Hulme. 2005. From Correlates and Characteristics to Causes: Thinking about Poverty from a Chronic Poverty Perspective. *World Development* 33 (6/6): 867–79.

Harvey, David. 2003. *The New Imperialism*. Oxford: Oxford University Press.

Hess, David J., Roberto A. DaMatta, and Sidney M. Greenfield. 1996. The Brazilian Puzzle: Culture on the Borderlands of the Western World. *American Anthropologist* 98 (2): 458.

Holston, James. 2008. *Insurgent Citizenship: Disjunctions of Democracy and Modernity in Brazil*. Princeton, NJ: Princeton University Press.

———. 1999. *Cities and Citizenship*. Durham, NC: Duke University Press.

Holston, James, and Arjun Appadurai. 1999. Cities and Citizenship. In *Cities and Citizenship*, ed. James Holston, 1–18. Durham, NC: Duke University Press.

Hoskins, W. G. 1970. *The Making of the English Landscape*. London: Penguin.

Howden, Daniel. 2007. Planet of the Slums: UN Warns Urban Populations Set to Double. *Independent*, June 27.

Hugo, V. 2007. The Assault on Rio's Favelas and the Growth of State Repression in Brazil. In International Committee of the Fourth International (ICFI) [database online]. www.wsws.org/articles/2007/jul2007/fave-jo5.shtml (accessed December 14, 2008).

Instituto Perreira Passos (IPP) 2008. Planning Department, Rio de Janeiro (Unpublished documents).

Instituto de Pesquisa Econômica Aplicada. 1999. *Caracterização e Tendências Da Rede Urbana do Brasil*. Campinas, Brazil: Universidade Estadual de Campinas, Instituto de Economia.

Instituto Pólis. 2002. *The Statute of the City: New Tools for Assuring the Right to the City in Brasil*. São Paulo: Instituto Pólis.

Jackson, Cecile. 1999. Social Exclusion and Gender: Does One Size Fit All? *European Journal of Development Research* 11 (1): 125–46.

Jacobs, Jane. 1961. *The Death and Life of Great American Cities*. New York: Random House.

Kabeer, Naila. 1999. The Concept of Social Exclusion: What Is Its Value-added for Thinking about Social Policy? Paper presented at conference "Re-visioning Social Policy for the Twenty-first Century: What Are the Key Challenges?" University of Sussex, England. October 28–29.

Katz, Daniel. 2008. Bala: The Institutionalization of Extrajudicial Violence by the Police of Rio de Janeiro. Undergraduate honors thesis, Political Science, University of California, Berkeley.

Kihato, C., B. Ruble, and P. Subrirós. Forthcoming. *The Challenges of Urban Diversity: Inclusive Cities versus Divided Cites: A Comparative Approach to Rethinking the Public Domain and Public Stage*. Washington, DC: Woodrow Wilson Center.

Kingdon, John W. 1984. *Agendas, Alternatives, and Public Policies*. Boston: Little, Brown.

Kingstone, Steve. 2003. Rio Shanty Town Becomes Tour Spot. BBC News [database online]. http://news.bbc.co.uk/go/pr/fr/-/2/hi/americas/3247709.stm (accessed April 16, 2008).

Kolbert, Elizabeth. 2009. Greening the Ghetto. *New Yorker*, January 12, 22–28.

Kontos, Louis, and David Brotherton. 2008. *Encyclopedia of Gangs*. Westport, CT: Greenwood Press.

Kottak, Conrad. 2006. *Assault on Paradise: The Globalization of a Little Community in Brazil*. Boston: McGraw Hill.

Kristof, Nicholas D. 2009. Where Sweatshops Are a Dream. *New York Times*, January 15.

Lasker, Roz Diane, and John A. Guidry. 2009. *Engaging the Community in Decision Making: Case Studies Tracking Participation, Voice and Influence*. Jefferson, NC: McFarland.

Lattes, Alfredo, Jorge Rodríguez, and Miguel Villa. 2002. Population Dynamics and Urbanization in Latin America: Concepts and Data Limitations. Paper presented at Seminar on New Forms of Urbanization, Bellagio, Italy, March 11–15.

Lavinas, L. et al. 2008. Combinando o Compensatório e o Redistributiuo. Rio de Janeiro IBASE.

Leeds, Anthony, and Elizabeth Leeds. 1970. Brazil and the Myth of Urban Reality: Urban Experience, Work, and Values in "Squatments" of Rio de Janeiro and Lima. In *City and Country in the Third World: Issues in the Modernization of Latin America*, ed. Arthur J. Field, 229–70. Cambridge, MA: Schenkman.

Leeds, Elizabeth. 2007. Serving States and Serving Citizens: Halting Steps toward Police Reform in Brazil and Implications for Donor Intervention. *Policing and Society* 17 1(3): 21–37.

———. 1998. Cocaina e Poderes Paralelos Na Periferia Urbana Brasileira Ameacas a Democratizacao Em Nivel Local. In *Um século de favela*, ed. Alba Zaluar and Marcos Alvito. 1st ed., 233–76. Rio de Janeiro: Fundação Getúlio Vargas.

———. 1996. Cocaine and Parallel Polities in the Brazilian Urban Periphery: Constraints on Local-level Democratization. *Latin American Research Review* 31 (3): 47.

Leite, Liana. 2008. Brasil é Quarto País em Mortes de Jovens. *Bulletin of the Observatório de Favelas*, December 3. www.observatoriode-favelas.org.br.

Lessa, Carlos. 2000. *O Rio de Todos os Brasis: Uma Reflexão em Busca de Auto-Estima*. Rio de Janeiro: Editora Record.

Lewis, Mark. 2007. Twenty-first-century Cities: Megacities of the Future. Forbes.com [database online]. www.forbes.com/2007/06/11/megacities-population-urbanization-biz-cx_21cities_ml_0611megacities.html (accessed June 11, 2008).

Lopes de Souza, Marcelo. 2005. Urban Planning in an Age of Fear: The Case of Rio de Janeiro. *International Development Planning Review* 27 (1): 1–19.

Lopez Moreno, Eduardo, and Rasna Warah. 2006. The State of the World's Cities Report 2006/7: Urban and Slum Trends in the Twenty-first Century. *UN Chronicle* 43 (2): 24.

Ludemir, Julio. 2004. *Sorria, Voce Esta na Rocinha*. Rio de Janeiro: Editora Record.

Mainwaring, Scott. 1999. Patronage, Clientelism and Patrimonialism. In *Rethinking Party Systems in the Third Wave of Democratization: The Case of Brazil*, ed. Scott Mainwaring, 175–218. Stanford, CA: Stanford University Press.

———. 1995. Brazil: Weak Parties, Feckless Democracy. In *Building Democratic Institutions and Party Systems in Latin America*, ed. Scott Mainwaring and Timothy Scully, 354–98. Stanford, CA: Stanford University Press.

Marino, Leonardo. 2008. Para Entendermos as Origens da Violência Policial no Rio. *Observatório de Favelas*, March.

McCann, Bryan. 2006. The Political Evolution of Rio de Janeiro's Favelas: Recent Works. *Latin American Research Review* 41 (3): 149–63.

Meier, Richard L. 1974. *Planning for an Urban World: The Design of Resource-Conserving Cities*. Cambridge: MIT Press.

Melo, Marcus. 2002. Gains and Losses in the Favelas. In *Voices of the Poor: From Many Lands*, ed. Deepa Narayan and Patti Petesch. Washington, DC: World Bank.

Ministério do Planejamento, Orçamento e Gestão, and Instituto Brasileiro de Geografia e Estatística. 2000. *Censo demográfico 2000: Características Gerais Da população*. Rio de Janeiro: IBGE.

Moore, Karen. 2005. *Thinking about Youth: Poverty through the Lenses of Chronic Poverty, Life-course Poverty and Intergenerational Poverty*. CPRC Working Paper 57. Manchester: Chronic Poverty Research Centre, University of Manchester.

Morais, Fernando. 1985. *Olga*. São Paulo: Editora Alfa-Omega.

Moser, Caroline. 1996. Confronting Crisis: A Comparative Study of Household Responses to Poverty and Vulnerability in Four Poor Urban Communities. Washington, DC: World Bank.

MV Bill, Celso Athayde, Frederico Neves, Central Unica das Favelas (Brazil), and Som Livre (Firm). 2006. *Falcão Meninos do tráfico*. Rio de Janeiro, Brazil: Som Livre.

Naím, Moisés. 2006. *Illicit: How Smugglers, Traffickers, and Copycats Are Hijacking the Global Economy*. New York: Random House.

Narayan-Parker, Deepa. 2005. Conceptual Framework and Methodological Challenges. In *Measuring Empowerment: Cross-disciplinary Perspectives*, ed. Deepa Narayan-Parker, 3–38. Washington, DC: World Bank.

Narayan-Parker, Deepa, and Patti L. Petesch. 2002. *Voices of the Poor: From Many Lands*. Washington, DC: World Bank.

Neate, Patrick. 2003. *Where You're At: Notes from the Frontline of a Hip Hop Planet*. London: Bloomsbury.

Neate, Patrick, and Damian Platt. 2006. *Culture Is Our Weapon: AfroReggae in the Favelas of Rio*. London: Latin American Bureau. (Penguin Books, 2010).

Nelson, Joan M. 1969. *Migrants, Urban Poverty, and Instability in Developing Nations*. Cambridge, MA: Center for International Affairs, Harvard University.

Neuwirth, Robert. 1991. "I'd Rather Be Poor in Rio: Interview with Janice Perlman. New York, *Newsday*. October 31.Viewpoints section.

———. 2005. *Shadow Cities: A Billion Squatters, a New Urban World*. New York, Routledge.

Newman, Oscar. *Defensible Space: Crime Prevention Through Urban Design*. New York, Macmillan.

Neves, Ricardo. 2003. *Copo Pela Metade*. São Paulo: Negócio.

Nissanke, Machiko, and Erik Thorbecke. 2007a. A Quest for Pro-poor Globalization. In *Advancing Development: Core Themes in Global Economics*, ed. George Mavrotas, Anthony F. Shorrocks, and World Institute for Development Economics Research. New York: Palgrave Macmillan.

———. 2007b. *Linking Globalization to Poverty*. Helsinki: World Institute for Development Economics Research, United Nations University.

―――. 2005. *Channels and Policy Debate in the Globalization-inequality-poverty Nexus.* WIDER discussion paper, vol. 2008/08. Helsinki: World Institute for Development Economics Research, United Nations University.

Novaes, Regina, Marilena Cunha, and Christina Vital, eds. 2004. *A Memoria das Favelas.* Comunicacões do 1 SER, no. 59, vol. 23.

Overseas Security Advisory Council, U.S. Department of State. 2008. Brazil 2008 Crime & Safety Report: Rio de Janeira July 8, p. 1.

Pamuk, Ayse, and Paulo Fernando A. Cavallieri. 1998. Alleviating Urban Poverty in a Global City: New Trends in Upgrading Rio de Janeiro's Favelas. *Habitat International* 22 (4/12): 449–62.

Pandolfe, Dulce, and Mario Grynszpan, eds. 2003. *A Favela Fala.* Rio de Janeiro: Editora FGV.

Parisse, Luciano. 1969. Favelas do Rio de Janeiro: Evolução, Sentido. *Cadernos do CENPHA* 5.

Parks, Gordon. 1978. *Flavio.* Vol. 1. New York: Norton.

―――. 1961. Freedom's Fearful Foe: Poverty—Part 2 of *Life*'s Series on Latin America. *Life,* June 16.

Paugam, S. 1995. The Spiral of Precariousness: A Multidimensional Approach to the Process of Social Disqualification in France. In *Beyond the Threshold: The Measurement and Analysis of Social Exclusion,* ed. Graham Room, 49–79. Bristol, England: Policy Press.

Peattie, Lisa Redfield. 1968. *The View from the Barrio.* Ann Arbor: University of Michigan Press.

Peirce, Neal R., Curtis W. Johnson, and Farley Peters. 2008. *Century of the City: No Time to Lose.* New York: Rockefeller Foundation.

Penglase, Richard Benjamin. 2002. To Live Here You Have to Know How to Live: Violence and Everyday Life in a Brazilian Favela. Ph.D. diss., Harvard University.

Perlman, Janice. 2010. It All Depends: Buying and Selling Houses in Rio's Favelas. Report for IHC, Washington D.C., Feb. 3 (avilable at www.mega-cities.net).

Perlman, Janice E. 2004. The Metamorphosis of Marginality in Rio de Janeiro. *Latin American Research Review* 39 (1): 183.

―――. 1993. Mega-Cities: Global Urbanization and Innovation. In *Urban Management: Policies and Innovations in Developing Countries,* ed. G. Shabbir Cheema, Sandra E. Ward, United Nations University, and Program on Population (East-West Center), 19–50. Westport, CT: Praeger.

―――. 1990. A Dual Strategy for Deliberate Social Change in Cities. *Cities* 7 (1/2): 3–15.

―――. 1987. Misconceptions about the Urban Poor and the Dynamics of Housing Policy Evolution. *Journal of Planning Education and Research* 6 (3) (Spring 1987): 187–96.

―――. 1983a. New York from the Bottom Up. *Urban Affairs:* 27–34.

―――. 1983b. Voices from the Street. *Development: Journal of the Society for International Development* 2: 47–52.

―――. 1979. Grassroots Empowerment and Government Response. *Social Policy* 10 (16): 21.

———. 1978. Grassroots Participation from Neighborhood to Nation. In *Citizen Participation in America: Essays on the State of the Art*, ed. Stuart Langton, 65–80. Lexington, MA: Lexington Books.

———. 1977. *O Mito Da Marginalidade: Favelas e política no Rio de Janeiro*. Rio de Janeiro: Paz e Terra.

———. 1976a. Grassrooting the System. *Social Policy* 7 (2): 4–20.

———. 1976b. *The Myth of Marginality: Urban Poverty and Politics in Rio de Janeiro*. Berkeley: University of California Press.

———. 1975. Rio's Favelas and the Myth of Marginality. *Politics & Society* 5 (2): 131–60.

———. 1974. *Methodological Notes on Complex Survey Research Involving Life History Data*. Berkeley: Institute of Urban and Regional Development, University of California.

Perlman, Janice E., and Elwood M. Hopkins. 1997. Urban Leadership for the Twenty-first Century: Scaling Up and Reaching Out from the Neighborhood Level. www.megacitiesproject.org/publications_pdf_mcp046.pdf.

Perlman, Janice E., and Bruce Schearer. 1986. *Migration and Population Distribution Trends and Policies and the Urban Future*. International Conference in Population and the Urban Future, UNFPA. Barcelona: May 14–18.

Perlman, Janice E., and Molly O'Meara Sheehan. 2007. Fighting Poverty and Environmental Injustice in Cities. In *State of the World 2007: Our Urban Future*, ed. Worldwatch Institute, 172–90. New York: Norton.

Pero, Valéria. 2004a. Renda, Pobreza e Desigualdade no Rio de Janeiro: Balanço da Década de 90. In Relatório do Atlas de Desenvolvimento Humano do Rio de Janeiro [database online]. www.iets.inf.br.

———. 2004b. *Rio de Janeiro in Socioeconomic Perspective*. n.p.

———. 2003a. Urban Regeneration and Spatial Discrimination: The Case of Rio's Favelas. Adalberto Cardoso and Peter Elias, Proceedings of the 31st Brazilian Economics Meeting, available at www.anpec.org.br/encontro 2003/artigos/F41.pdf.

———. 2003b. Mobilidade Social no Rio de Janeiro.

———. 2002. *Tendências Da Mobilidade Social no Rio de Janeiro*. Ph. D. diss. Rio de Janeiro: Instituto de Economia da UFRJ.

Pero, Valéria, and Dmitri Szerman. 2005. *The New Generation of Social Programs in Brazil*. Rio de Janeiro: Insistuto de Economia da UFRJ.

Petesch, Patti. 2005. Evaluating Empowerment: A Framework with Cases from Latin America. In *Measuring Empowerment: Cross-disciplinary Perspectives*, ed. Deepa Narayan-Parker, 39–68. Washington, DC: World Bank.

Pieterse, Edgar. 2007. Popular Youth Cultures and the Mediation of Racial Exclusion/Inclusion in Rio de Janeiro and Cape Town. Woodrow Wilson Center [database online]. www.wilsoncenter.org/news/docs/Edgar1.pdf (accessed December 14, 2008).

Pochmann, Marcio, Andre Campos, Alexandre Barbosa, Ricardo Amorim, and Ronnie Aldrin. 2004. *Atlas Exclusão Social no Brasil: Exclusão no Mundo*. São Paulo: Terra.

Putnam, Robert D. 2000. *Bowling Alone: The Collapse and Revival of American Community*. New York: Simon and Schuster.

Putnam, Robert D., Robert Leonardi, and Raffaella Nanetti. 1993. *Making Democracy Work: Civic Traditions in Modern Italy*. Princeton, NJ: Princeton University Press.

Queiroz Ribeiro, L. C., and E. Telles. 2000. Rio de Janeiro: Emerging Dualization in a Historically Unequal City. In *Globalizing Cities: A New Spatial Order?* ed. Peter Marcuse and Ronald van Kempen, 318. Oxford: Blackwell.

Reel, Monte. 2007. In Rio's Slums, Militias Fuel Violence They Seek to Quell. *Washington Post,* March 28.

Rio de Janeiro Prefeitura. 2003. *From Removal to the Urban Cell: The Urban-social Development of Rio de Janeiro Slums.* Rio de Janeiro: Prefeitura.

Rivero, Patricia S. 2005. The Value of the Illegal Firearms Market in the City of Rio de Janeiro: Prices and Symbolism of Guns in Crime. www.vivario.org.br/publique/media/.

Roberts, Bryan R. 2004. From Marginality to Social Exclusion: From Laissez Faire to Pervasive Engagement. *Latin American Research Review* 39 (1): 195–97.

Rocha, Sonia. 2003. *Pobreza no Brasil: Afinal, De Que Se Trata?* Rio de Janeiro: FGV.

———. 2000. Poverty and Inequality in Brazil: The Depletion of the Distributive Effects of the Real Plan. http://papers.ssrn.com/sol3/papers.cfm?abstract_id=232569.

———. 1997. *Tendencia Evolutiva e Caracteristicas Da Pobreza no Rio de Janeiro.* Rio de Janeiro: IPEA.

Rohter, Larry. 2007. Drawing Lines across the Sand. *New York Times,* February 6.

———. 2004. Brazil Adopts Strict Gun Controls to Try to Curb Murders. *New York Times,* January 21.

Roy, Ananya, and Nezar AlSayyad. 2004. *Urban Informality in an Era of Liberalization: A Transnational Perspective,* ed. Ananya Roy and Nezar AlSayyad. Lanham, MD: Lexington Books.

Ryan, William. 1971. *Blaming the Victim.* New York: Pantheon Books.

Sachs, Wolfgang. 1992. *The Development Dictionary: A Guide to Knowledge as Power.* Atlantic Highlands, NJ: Zed Books.

Safa, Helen Icken. 2004. From Rural to Urban, from Men to Women, from Class Struggle to Struggles for Entitlements. *Latin American Research Review* 39 (1): 187–88.

Sanneh, Kelefa. 2009. The Wizard. *New Yorker* 84 (47) (February 2): 26.

Santos, Carlos Nelson dos. 1983. Habitação—O Que é Mesmo Que Pode Fazer Quem Sabe? In *Repensando a habitação no brasil,* ed. Licia do Prado Valladares, 79–120. Rio de Janeiro: Zahar Editores.

———. 1981. *Movimentos Urbanos no Rio de Janeiro.* Rio de Janeiro: Zahar Editores.

———. 1980. Velhas Novidades Nos Modos De urbanização brasileiros. In *Habitação em questão,* ed. Licia do Prado Valladares, 17–47. Rio de Janeiro: Zahar Editores.

———. 1971. Some Considerations about the Possibilities of Squatter Settlement Redevelopment Plans: The Case of Bras De Pina. Mimeograph.

Santos, Carlos Nelson dos, and Olga Bronstein. 1978. Meta-Urbanização—o Caso do Rio de Janeiro. *Revista De Administração Municipal* 25: 6–34.

Scheper-Hughes, Nancy. 1992. *Death without Weeping: The Violence of Everyday Life in Brazil.* Berkeley: University of California Press.

Scheve, Kenneth F., and Matthew J. Slaughter. 2007. A New Deal for Globalization. *Foreign Affairs* 86 (4) (July–August): 34.

Schiffer, Sueli Ramos. 2002. Economic Restructuring and Urban Segregation in Sao Paulo. In *Of States and Cities: The Partitioning of Urban Space,* ed. Peter Marcuse and Ronald van Kempen, 143–69. Oxford: Oxford University Press.

Sen, Amartya Kumar. 1999. *Development as Freedom*. New York: Anchor Books.

Silva, Benedita da, Medea Benjamin, and Maisa Mendonça. 1997. *Benedita Da Silva: An Afro-Brazilian Woman's Story of Politics and Love*. Oakland, CA: Institute for Food and Development Policy.

Singer, Paulo, International Institute for Labour Studies, Labour Institutions and Development Programme, and United Nations Development Programme. 1997. *Social Exclusion in Brazil*. Geneva: International Institute for Labour Studies.

Silva, Itamar. 2004. *Rio: A Democracia Vista de Baixo*. Rio de Janeiro: 1 BASE.

Soares, Fabio, and Yuri Soares. 2005. *The Socio-economic Impact of Favela-Bairro: What Do the Data Say?* Washington, DC: Inter-American Development Bank.

Soares, Luiz Eduardo, MV Bill, and Celso Athayde. 2005. *Cabeça De Porco*. Rio de Janeiro: Objetiva.

Soto, Hernando de. 2000. *The Mystery of Capital: Why Capitalism Triumphs in the West and Fails Everywhere Else*. New York: Basic Books.

Soubbotina, Tatyana P., and Katherine Sheram. 2000. *Beyond Economic Growth: Meeting the Challenges of Global Development*. Washington, DC: World Bank.

Souto de Oliveira, Jane, and Maria Hortense Marcier. 1998. A Palavra é: Favela. In *Um século de favela*, ed. Alba Zaluar and Marcos Alvito. 1st ed., 61–114. Rio de Janeiro: Fundação Getúlio Vargas.

Stokes, Charles J. 1962. A Theory of Slums. *Land Economics* 38 (3) (August): 187–97.

Telles, Edward E. 1994. Industrialization and Racial Inequality in Employment: The Brazilian Example. *American Sociological Review* 59 (1) (February): 46–63.

Telles, Edward E., and Vilma Ortiz. 2007. *Generations of Exclusion: Mexican Americans, Assimilation, and Race*. New York: Russell Sage Foundation.

Townsend, Peter. 1985. A Sociological Approach to the Measurement of Poverty—A Rejoinder to Professor Amartya Sen. *Oxford Economic Papers* 37 (4) (December): 659–68.

Trigo, Benigno. 2000. *Subjects of Crisis: Race and Gender as Disease in Latin America*. Hanover, NH: University Press of New England.

Turner, John. 1977. *Housing by People: Towards Autonomy in Building Environments*. New York: Marion Boyars.

Turner, John F. C. 1972. Housing as a Verb. In *Freedom to Build: Dweller Control of the Housing Process*, ed. John F. C. Turner and Robert Fichter, ch. 7. New York: Macmillan.

———. 1969. Uncontrolled Urban Settlement: Problems and Policies. In *The City in Newly Developing Countries: Readings on Urbanism and Urbanization*, ed. Gerald William Breese, 507–34. Englewood Cliffs, N.J.: Prentice-Hall.

———. 1968. Housing Priorities, Settlement Patterns, and Urban Development in Modernizing Countries. *Journal of the American Planning Association* 34 (6): 354–63.

Turner, John F. C., and Robert Fichter. 1972. Housing as a Verb, *Freedom to Build: Dweller Control of the Housing Process*. New York: Macmillan, chapter 7.

UN-Habitat. 2008. State of the World's Cities 2008/2009: Harmonious Cities. www.unhabitat.org/publications (accessed March 1, 2009).

United Nations. 2008. Millennium Development Goals. www.un.org/millenniumgoals (accessed March 1, 2009).

United Nations Department of Economic and Social Affairs. 2008. *World Urbanization Prospects: The 2007 Revision*. New York: United Nations.

United Nations Development Programme. 2004. *Democracy in Latin America towards a Citizens' Democracy*. New York: United Nations Development Programme.

————. 2003. *Human Development Report 2003: Millennium Development Goals: A Compact among Nations to End Human Poverty*. New York: Oxford University Press.

United Nations Human Settlements Programme. 2003. *The Challenge of Slums: Global Report on Human Settlements, 2003*. Sterling, VA: Earthscan.

United Nations Human Settlements Programme and Global Urban Observatory. 2003. *Slums of the World: The Face of Urban Poverty in the New Millennium?* Nairobi: UN-Habitat.

U.S. Army Special Operations Command. 2009. www.soc.mil/ (accessed December 9, 2008).

Valla, Victor Vincent. 1985. Educação, Participação, Urbanização: Uma Contribuição à Análise Histórica Das Propostas Institucionais Para as Favelas do Rio de Janeiro, 1941–1980. *Cadernos De Saúde Pública* 1 (3) (July–September): 282–96.

Valladares, Licia do Prado. 2003. *Sistema Urbano, Mercado De Trabalho e Violência no Brasil e no Rio de Janeiro*. Center for Migration and Development Working Paper Series. Princeton, NJ: Center for Migration and Development, Princeton University.

Valladares, Licia do Prado, Lidia Medeiros, and Filippina Chinelli. 2003. *Pensando as Favelas do Rio de Janeiro, 1906–2000: Uma Bibliografia Analítica*. Rio de Janeiro: URBANDATA.

Vargas, João H. Costa. 2006. When a Favela Dared to Become a Gated Condominium: The Politics of Race and Urban Space in Rio de Janeiro. *Latin American Perspectives* 33 (4) (July 1): 49–81.

Ventura, Zuenir. 1994. *Cidade Partida*. São Paulo: Companhia das Letras.

Vianna, Andrea. 2005. As Poiticas de Habiação no Rio de Janeiro e Seus Resultados, quoted in Fabio Soares, Yori Soares, and Loïc Wacquant. The Militarization of Urban Marginality: Lessons from the Brazilian Metropolis. *International Political Sociology* 2 (1): 56–74.

Wacquant, Loïc. 2008. The Militarization of Urban Marginality: Lessons from the Brazilian Metropolis. *International Political Sociology* 2 (1): 56–74.

————. 1999. Urban Marginality in the Coming Millennium. *Urban Studies* 36 (10) (September): 1639.

————. 1997. Three Pernicious Premises in the Study of the American Ghetto. *International Journal of Urban and Regional Research* 21 (2) (June): 341.

————. 1996. The Rise of Advanced Marginality: Notes on Its Nature and Implications. *Acta Sociologica* 39 (2): 121.

Wagner, F. E., and John O. Ward. 1980. Urbanization and Migration in Brazil. *American Journal of Economics and Sociology* 39 (3) (July): 249–59.

Ward, Peter M. 2004. From the Marginality of the 1960s to the "New Poverty" of Today: A LARR Research Forum. *Latin American Research Review* 39 (1): 183.

Warren-Scherer, Ilse. 2004. The Problem of Social Exclusion in the Construction of a Citizens' Movement in Brazil. Paper presented at the Sixth International Conference of ISTR (International Society for the Third Sector), Toronto, July 11–14.

Weber, Demétrio. 2008. Mapa Da Violência Dos Municípios Brasileiros Mostra Queda Dos Assassinatos Desde 2004. *O Globo,* 28 January.

Wheatley, Jonathan. 2009. Helping Hand Makes Homeowners of the Poor, *Financial Times,* New York, July 2.

Wilford, John Noble. 2008. Plagues of New York: How Epidemics Helped Shape the Modern Metropolis. *New York Times,* April 15.

World Bank. 2007. *World Development Indicators 2007.* Washington, DC: World Bank.

Yaqub, Shahin. 1999. *Born Poor Stay Poor? A Literature Review.* Technical Report. Brighton, UK: Institute of Development Studies, University of Sussex.

Yin, Robert. 1981. Life Histories of Innovations: How New Practices Become Routinized. *Public Administration Review* 41 (1): 21–28.

Youman, Nancy. 1991. I'd Rather Be Poor in Rio: The *New York Newsday* Interview with Janice Perlman. *New York Newsday,* October 31, Viewpoints section.

Zakaria, Fareed. 2009. A "Slumdog" in Heat. *Newsweek,* February 9.

Zaluar, Alba. 2004. *Integração* Perversa: Pobresa e Tráfico de Drogas. Rio de Janeiro: Editora FGV.

Zaluar, Alba, and Marcos Alvito. 1998. *Um Século de Favela.* Rio de Janeiro: Editora FGV.

Zaluar, Alba, Clara Lucia Inem, and Gilberta Acselrad. 1993. Drogas, Contexto Cultural e Cidadania. In *Drogas: Uma Visao Contemporanea.*

Zimbalist, Jeff, and Matt Mochary. 2005. *Favela Rising,* produced by Sidetrack Films, VOY Pictures and Genius Entertainment, Santa Monica, California.

index

Dagnino, Evelina, 208, 324
danger, physical displacement of, 173
Daniel, Sebastião, on being gente, 321
da Silva, Benedita, 209, 234–35, 322
Declaration of Human Rights, 333
de facto property tenure, 296
de França, Armando Melo, 134
dehumanization, 15, 153, 290, 323
deindustrialization, 103, 152
democracy, 136, 151, 152, 200, 273, 311
  belief-behavior disconnect, 210–13
  Brazil as incomplete, 182
  community-based mobilization and,
    195
  community groups under, 151
  community participation, 213–16
  de facto tenure under, 296
  disappointment with, 203–5
  drug lords and vote control, 206–7
  favelas under, 267, 273, 274
  patronage system and, 205–6
  political transformations, 201–2
  racial, 170
  rights and freedoms, 207–10
  upgrading and, 267
  youth, 217–18
de Souza, Lopes, 199
developing countries
  demographic shifts and, 43
  and urban population growth, 45
dignity, 22, 208, 230, 302
  being gente and, 316
  being poor and, 152
  denying, 250
  infrastructure and, 86
  quest for, 36
  suppression of, 324
discrimination
  as perceived by three generations, 155f
  and stigma, 153–55
disenfranchisement, 202
Djanira, 122–26, 142, 192
  on armed militias, 168
  children of, 138–39, 141
  describing the creation of Vila Operária,
    132–33
  family background, 137, 138, 140f
  family, as on 2008, 141–45
  finding of, 126–31

schooling, 137–38
  on Vila Ideal, 192–93
dono da boca (boca owner), 179
Dowdney, Luke, 179
drug gangs, for territorial control, 178–80,
    186–87
drug lords and vote control, 206–7
dual city, 30
Duque de Caxias. See Caxias

economic marginality, 152
ecstasy, 198
enterprise zones and empowerment zones,
    305
Environmental Benefits Program, 305
e Silva, Jailson de Sousa
  on arms in Brazil, 180
  views on globalization, 259
Estado Novo, 152
Estatuto da Cidade, 311, 312
evangelicalism, 104
Evora, Pedro, 329
exclusion, 153, 209, 216, 238, 339
  bases of, 154–55
  of people, 8
  of poor, 9
  social, 152, 155–56, 172
  territories of, 30, 37, 284
  underclass and, 201
extrajudicial violence, 167, 184

false positives, 18
family improved housed, 271f
family solidarity, 141
Favela-Bairro program, 30, 152, 278–80
  critics of, 280–81
  Phase I, 275–76
  Phase II, 276
  Phase III, 277
  as place-based approach to public policy,
    285
  room for further improvement, 281–82
favela chair, 330, 331f
Favela Chic, 332
favela-ism, 153
Favela Rising, 308
favelas, 16, 333–34 (see also individual entries)